Public Ends, Private Means

Public Ends, Private Means

Strategic Purchasing of Health Services

Edited by

Alexander S. Preker, Xingzhu Liu, Edit V. Velenyi, and **Enis Baris**

THE WORLD BANK
Washington, D.C.

©2007 The International Bank for Reconstruction and Development / The World Bank
1818 H Street, NW
Washington, DC 20433
Telephone: 202-473-1000
Internet: www.worldbank.org
E-mail: feedback@worldbank.org

1 2 3 4 10 09 08 07

This volume is a product of the staff of the International Bank for Reconstruction and Development / The World Bank. The findings, interpretations, and conclusions expressed in this volume do not necessarily reflect the views of the Executive Directors of The World Bank or the governments they represent.

The World Bank does not guarantee the accuracy of the data included in this work. The boundaries, colors, denominations, and other information shown on any map in this work do not imply any judgement on the part of The World Bank concerning the legal status of any territory or the endorsement or acceptance of such boundaries.

Rights and Permissions

ISBN-10: 0-8213-6547-9
ISBN-13: 978-0-8213-6547-2
eISBN-10: 0-8213-6548-7
eISBN-13: 978-0-8213-6548-9
DOI: 10.1596/978-0-8213-6547-2

Library of Congress Cataloging-in-Publication Data
Public ends, private means: strategic purchasing of health services / edited by
Alexander S. Preker ... [et al.].
    p. ; cm.
  Includes bibliographical references and index.
  ISBN-13: 978-0-8213-6547-2 (alk. paper)
  ISBN-10: 0-8213-6547-9 (alk. paper)
  ISBN-10: 0-8213-6548-7 (e-ISBN)
  1. Medical economics--Developing countries. 2. Medical care, Cost of--Developing countries.
3. Medical policy--Developing countries. I. Preker, Alexander S., 1951– II. World Bank.
  [DNLM: 1. Health Services--economics. 2. Developing Countries. 3. Financing,
Government--economics. 4. Organizational Policy. 5. Private Sector--economics.
W 84.1 P976 2007]
  RA410.5.P795 2007
  338.4'73621--dc22
                                                                        2006023410

Contents

ONLINE REGIONAL REVIEWS: FROM THEORY TO PRACTICE
Available at www.worldbank.org/hnp under Publications: Discussion Papers.

BOXES

FIGURES

TABLES

Foreword

Economics has been described as the "dismal science"—the science of how to use scarce resources. In this volume, the editors and authors look at how strategic purchasing of health care can achieve public ends through private means. Spending wisely means getting the best value possible from scarce money. This is imperative in low-income countries, where managing scarcity is a daily challenge.

Economics is an ideal tool for allocating scarce resources in the health sector of developing countries. Yet, in the real world, passion often trumps reason and measured spending. Misguided political pressures and ideological views often lead to a waste of money, drugs, and other precious health care resources.

The editors and authors of this volume skillfully challenge six myths of strategic allocation of scarce resources in the health sector. The myths are related to who pays, who decides, who gets, how to pay (through which payment mechanism), how much, and who benefits.

Who pays? There has been much rhetoric that a single payer—a public paymaster—is the optimal arrangement for financing health care. For a variety of reasons, this approach does not work in developing countries. Often, more than 80 percent of all health care funding comes from out-of-pocket payments by households. And increasingly, a variety of vertically funded programs offer multiple sources of parallel funding.

We may wish this situation to change and it may someday, through financing reforms and harmonization of donor funding. While waiting for this to happen, the authors suggest ways to improve funding arrangements under real-life constraints, which often lead to multiple payors.

Who decides? Health care decisions are often portrayed as too complex for individuals to make informed choices. Governments are seen as the solution. Governments clearly play an important role in allocating the budget envelope. But, as has been seen in both the former socialist states in Central and Eastern Europe and in low-income countries, encouraging individuals to participate—not just be passive recipients of care—is critical. One of the most compelling ways to empower households is to make money follow the patient, putting it directly in their hands, and to allow them to participate in decisions about their own care. Patient spending will reflect their choices.

Who gets? In low-income countries with severe resource constraints, governments often spend all the money they have to run their own network of publicly owned, managed, and staffed health care providers. Little money is left for buying health care from nongovernmental and private for-profit providers. The authors demonstrate the importance of helping low-income countries break out of this trap by offering them better ways of spending new, marginal monies—domestic or foreign—on the public or private providers that offer the best value for the money. They recommend that public and private providers compete for scarce money on a level playing field rather than just transfer money from one to another government department or public service delivery unit.

How to pay? In industrial countries, where worries about cost containment and excessive consumption of health care are a major concern, prospectively capped budgets and copayment have become popular tools in recent years. They discourage excessive supply and demand for services. The authors challenge this approach in low-income contexts, where supply is often short and demand low. They suggest that performance-based pay and parallel demand-side subsidies and insurance mechanisms can be used more aggressively in developing countries to achieve health sector objectives.

How much? Many countries deal with funding shortages by setting prices. As indicated by the authors, this often means that prices are set below cost and market values. The consequences are devastating. Health care providers faced with low fixed prices and high demand have no choice but to square the circle by scrimping on quality and volume. Worse, providers who know that the market value is higher than the amount being paid in the public sector can and do sell their services privately, in the informal economy. The poor are the biggest losers. As described by the authors, it may be better to pay more, maintain quality, and increase volume by targeting services to the poor—even if this means setting up parallel funding mechanisms for the better-off, who can and will pay.

Who benefits? In industrial countries, many people think that offering everything to everyone is the best way to reach the poor. Unfortunately, in developing countries, this approach means that no one gets anything, and the poor are most likely to be squeezed out. As in the previous example, the authors recommend that a better approach may be to target scarce public resources to the poor, so that they get the services they need, and ensure alternative channels to others, so that they still have access to needed health care.

These may be provocative ideas. But continuing business as usual will fail. What is needed in many low-income countries is a more radical paradigm shift, such as that recommended by some of the contributing authors in this book.

Eyitayo Lambo
Honorable Minister of Health
Ministry of Health
Abuja, Nigeria

January 2007

Acknowledgments

The analytical work was reviewed both internally within the World Bank Group and by senior external experts who are familiar with both the technical contents and empirical findings on resource allocation and strategic purchasing reforms.

The volume was edited by Alexander S. Preker, Xingzhu Liu (Abt Associates Inc., Bethesda, Maryland), Edit V. Velenyi (University of York, Centre for Health Economics, United Kingdom), and Enis Baris.

The volume benefited from a series of reviews. Internal peer reviewers included Alexandre Abrantes, Cristian C. Baeza, Peter Berman, Armin H. Fidler, April L. Harding, Loraine Hawkins, Toomas Palu, Fadia M. Saadah, George Schieber, Agnes Soucat. The volume also benefited from comments made by Sameh El-Saharty, Jean-Jacques Frere, Pablo Gottret, Michele Gragnolati, Anne S. Johansen, Daniel Kress, Jack Langenbrunner, Benjamin Loevinsohn, and Firas Raad.

Collaborating partners include different parts of the World Bank Group including the Hub and regions of the Health, Nutrition, and Population Network, International Finance Corporation, and Private Sector Development. External funding agencies include the Swedish International Development Cooperation Agency and the Canadian International Development Agency.

Abbreviations and Acronyms

AEP	Appropriate Evaluation Protocal
BINP	Bangladesh Integrated Nutrition Project
CT	computed tomography
DALYs	disability-adjusted life years
DEA	data envelopment analysis
DRG	diagnosis-related group
ESIS	Employee State Insurance Scheme, India
FFS	fee for service
FONASA	National Health Fund, Chile
FPS	Functional Position System, Indonesia
GP	general practitioner
HMO	health maintenance organization
IPO	independent public organization
MAP	Medical Aid Program, Republic of Korea
MIS	management information system
MRS	market rate of substitution
MRTS	marginal rate of technical substitution
NGO	nongovernmental organization
NHI	National Health Insurance, Republic of Korea
NHS	National Health Service, United Kingdom
PC	provider consortium
PRP	performance-related pay
RAP	resource allocation and purchasing
S&L	savings and loan
SID	supplier-induced demand
SOE	state-owned enterprise
UNC	unnecessary care
UPHCP	Urban Primary Health Care Project, Bangladesh
QALYs	quality-adjusted life years
QANGO	quasi-autonomous nongovernmental organization
WHO	World Health Organization

Introduction

Alexander S. Preker, Xingzhu Liu, Edit V. Velenyi, and Enis Baris

G reat progress has been made in recent years in securing better access and financial protection against the cost of illness through collective financing of health care. Promoting health and confronting disease require effective actions across a range of activities in the health system. This includes improvements in the policy making and stewardship roles of governments; better access to human resources, drugs, medical equipment, and consumables; and greater engagement of both public and private providers of services.

Managing scarce resources and health care effectively and efficiently is an important part of this story. Experience has shown that without strategic policies and focused spending mechanisms, the poor and other ordinary people are likely to be left out. The use of purchasing as a tool to enhance public sector performance is well documented in other sectors of the economy. Extension to the health sector of lessons learned from this experience is now being successfully implemented in many developing countries.

The shift from hiring staff in the public sector and producing services "in-house" from nongovernmental providers has been at the center of a lively debate on collective financing of health care during recent years. The underlying premise is that it is necessary to separate the functions of financing health services from the production process of service delivery to improve public sector accountability and performance.

This volume is part of a series of World Bank publications on ways to make public spending on health care more efficient and equitable in developing countries. How scarce money is spent in the public and private sectors has a greater impact on services available to the poor than the actual ownership of the services in question. This was the topic of three other World Bank books—*Spending Wisely: Buying Health Services for the Poor* (2005); *Innovations in Health Service Delivery: The Corporatization of Public Hospitals* (2003); and *Private Participation in Health Services* (2003). These reviews emphasize the important role that markets and nongovernmental providers play in improving value for money spent by the public sector.

Although strong public policies and government involvement are needed to secure an efficient and equitable health care system, state involvement by itself is not sufficient. This important link between health care financing and effective service delivery is emphasized in two previous reviews on health care financing—*Health Financing for Poor People: Resource Mobilization and Risk Sharing* (2004) and *Social Reinsurance: A New Approach to Sustainable Community Health Financing* (2002). To be successful, policy makers in low- and middle-income countries must become much more effective at engaging the private and nongovernmental sectors in a constructive way.

In many low- and middle-income countries, the gains that can be made through the efficient use of scarce resources have to be matched with more money. Both are needed. Neither is sustainable by itself. In *Health Financing for Poor People,* Preker and Carrin (2004) presented work from a World Bank review on the role of community financing schemes in reaching the poor in outlying rural areas and inner-city slums. In *Social Reinsurance*, Dror and Preker detailed the use of community, rather than individual, risk-rated reinsurance as a way to address some of the known weaknesses of community financing schemes.

These topics on health care financing are expanded in three forthcoming volumes. They are *Private Voluntary Health Insurance in Development: Friend or Foe?* (2007); *Affordable Health Insurance: Mandatory Government-Run Programs;* and *A Strife of Interest: Fiscal Space for Health.* In these volumes, Preker and his coeditors review the existing and potential future roles of voluntary private health insurance, mandatory government-run health insurance, and state subsidies in securing sustainable financing for the health sector in low- and middle-income countries. These books provide in-depth reviews of the role health care financing plays in providing low-income populations with better access to needed health care, protecting them from the impoverishing effects of illness, and addressing the important issues of social exclusion in government-financed programs.

Early success in improving access and financial protection through community and private voluntary health insurance has led many countries to offer subsidized insurance and make membership compulsory. Arguments in favor of this approach include the potential for achieving higher population coverage and broadening the risk pool by collecting contributions at source from formal sector workers. Although some countries have tried to "leapfrog" from no coverage to free access to government-run and -owned national health services, there are several reasons few low- and middle-income countries have succeeded in securing universal access through this approach.

First, at low income levels, weak taxation capacity limits the fiscal space available for public health care and other government programs. Second, there is a lack of trust in government-run programs where the population is asked to pay today for benefits that may or may not be available tomorrow due to shifting priorities and volatile resource flows. Finally, public subsidies often do not reach the poor when programs are designed to provide care for everyone. The resulting underfinanced and low-quality publicly financed health services leave the poor and other households without adequate care and expose them to severe financial risk at the time of illness.

The current volume provides an important bridge between these topics. Strategic purchasing of priority health services is often the missing link between effective health care financing strategies and getting results on the ground from service providers.

CONCEPTUAL FRAMEWORK FOR IMPLEMENTING STRATEGIC PURCHASING OF QUALITY HEALTH SERVICES

The success or failure of reforms that try to shift from passive subsidization of existing government-run and -owned health services to strategic purchasing of health care from both public and private providers depends on many factors. Understanding "when" purchasing works and "what and why" purchasing sometimes does not have its expected benefits is vital to getting the policy design right. Understanding "when," "how," and "how well" to execute purchasing reforms is important in implementing such reforms.

Policy makers are faced with a wide range of choices in terms of the underlying political economy and policy design framework—as well as associated organizational, institutional, and management arrangements—in purchasing health care from providers. Table I.1 provides a checklist of some of the key factors that need to be considered when designing and carrying out such reforms.

A first set of issues relates to the political economy of the reform process itself. Views on the appropriate role of the state varies greatly from one society to another, motivated significantly by a range of socioeconomic factors, including cultural background, historical context, and political and ideological views. In supporting or blocking different reform paths, views are often motivated by deeply ingrained biases about the causes and solutions to both government and market failures.

A second set of issues relates to the policy design of the three core functions in health care financing—collection of revenues, financial risk management, and spending of resources on providers. In spending scarce resources wisely, countries trying to introduce strategic purchasing need to address several issues and constraints. They include for whom to buy, what to buy, from whom to buy, how to pay, and how much to pay. The efficiency and equity by which purchasers spend money on health care providers also depends on several critical factors and constraints related to revenue collection and risk sharing in addition to the resource allocation and purchasing function itself.

A third set of issues relates to the organizational structure of purchasers at low- and middle-income levels. In countries where there are many small, community-based funds, both the scale and scope of the purchasing function and the benefits that can be bought are problematic. Although in theory many resource allocation and purchasing activities are carried out through semiautonomous agencies, they often suffer from the same rigid hierarchical incentive structures as state-owned and -run national health services. This is especially true in countries where the purchasing schemes have over time acquired extensive networks of their own providers, thereby undermining the benefits of a purchaser/provider split. In other countries, multiple employment-based insurance funds end up with fragmented risk pools and purchasing arrangements.

A fourth set of issues relates to the institutional environment of the purchasing agency. Often institutional capacity is weak, the underlying legal framework is

TABLE I.1   Implementation Arrangements for Strategic Purchasing of Health Care

Political economy	Political choice about the appropriate role of the state
	Government failure
	Market failure
	Stakeholders
Policy design	**Resource allocation and purchasing arrangement**
	For whom to buy—members, poor, sick, other?
	What to buy, in which form, and what to exclude?
	From whom to buy—public, private, nongovernmental organization?
	How much to pay—competitive market price, set prices, subsidized?
	How to pay—what payment mechanisms to use?
	Underlyling revenue collection mechanisms
	Level of prepayment (full versus partial with some copayment or cost sharing)
	Degree of progressivity (high versus flat rate)
	Earmarking (general versus targeted contributions)
	Choice (mandatory versus voluntary)
	Enrollment (unrestricted versus restrictions in eligibility, waiting periods, and switching)
	Underlying pooling of revenues and sharing risks
	Size (small versus large)
	Number (one versus many)
	Risk equalization (from rich to poor, healthy to sick, and gainfully employed to inactive)
	Coverage (primary versus supplementary, substitutive, or duplicative)
	Risk rating (group or community rating versus individual)
Organizational structure	Organizational forms (ownership, contractual relationships, and scale and scope of purchasers)
	Structural configuration (extent of horizontal and vertical linkages versus purchaser–provider split or fragmentation)
	Incentive regimes (extent of decision rights, financial responsibility, market exposure, accountability, and coverage of social functions)
Institutional environment	Legal framework
	Regulatory instruments
	Administrative procedures
	Customs and practices
Management capacity	Management levels (stewardship, governance, line management, client services)
	Management skills
	Management incentives
	Management tools (financial, human resources, health information)

	↓	↓
Possible outcome indicators	*Efficiency*	*Equity (mainly poverty impact)*
Financial protection		
Coverage		
Household consumption		
Access to health care		
Labor market effects		

Source: Modified from Preker and Langenbrunner 2005.

incomplete, regulatory instruments are ineffective or not enforced, administrative procedures are rigid, and informal customs and practices are difficult to change.

A fifth set of issues relates to the management and institutional capacity at low-income levels. Management capacity is often weak in terms of stewardship, governance, line management, and client services. Purchasers are multiplicitous agents for the government; health services and providers have to serve many masters at the same time. This leads to conflicting incentive and reward structures. Finally, the management tools needed to deliver health care through strategic purchasing are lacking in terms of effective information technology, communications, and other management support systems.

A ROAD MAP

Part I of this volume (chapters 1–5) provides a broad policy framework for understanding strategic purchasing. It reviews the associated political economy of reform, organizational incentives, institutional environment, and management attributes needed for countries to shift from passive budgetary processes to strategic purchasing of health care. Part II (chapters 6–14) reviews the underlying economics of strategic purchasing. Part III (chapter 15) provides a framework for evaluating existing resource allocation and purchasing arrangements in terms of their impact on efficiency and equity. Finally, six regional reviews of current resource allocation and purchasing arrangements in developing countries are available online at www.worldbank.org/hnp under Publications: Discussion Papers.

The volume begins with a review in chapter 1 of the "Political Economy of Strategic Purchasing." The chapter asks, "Is it possible to know which goods and services are better produced by the public sector itself and which services can be bought efficiently from nongovernmental and private providers?" It then describes both the underlying economics of public and private roles in the health sector and the associated political economy reform processes. A decision matrix is presented that allows policy makers to assess the degree of information asymmetry and measurability of different health care goods and services. Better knowledge of such factors can help policy makers decide rationally whether to "make or buy." Major public policy levers, such as information disclosure, regulations, financing, and public production, are discussed. The chapter concludes that in many low-income countries, it is not a question of deciding if the private sector can contribute to broader health objectives. It already does so in almost all low- and middle-income countries. The question is how to get from here to there.

Chapter 2, "Policy Design in Strategic Purchasing," reviews some major problems in the way resource allocation is carried out today and options for reform of the underlying policy framework for purchasing health care in the future. The chapter emphasizes the importance of addressing design flaws under each of the main health financing subfunctions—revenue collection, risk pooling, and spending of resources. A well-designed purchasing arrangement can fail if the underlying revenue collection and pooling functions are weak. The chapter turns to the underlying economics of five major design questions: for whom to buy, what to buy, from whom to buy, at what price, and using what payment mechanism. Subsidies and copayments distort the supply and demand curves. When government fee schedules and pricing differ significantly from the equilibrium price that would have been achieved in a normal competitive market, major distortions can occur that may lead patients to seek care outside the publicly mandated purchasing arrangements. The chapter concludes that suboptimal outcomes are often observed at the two extremes—an unregulated market in purchasing and that which occurs when public interventions become too heavy-handed.

Chapter 3, "The Organizational Structures of Purchasers," reviews the organizational dimensions of health care purchasers. Organizations matter in terms of their structure, function, and performance as purchasers of health care just as this is important in the case of health care providers. The chapter discusses three aspects of purchasers of health care: their organizational form (ownership arrangements), their underlying incentive regime (decision rights, market structure, residual claimant status, accountability mechanisms, and social functions), and linkages among purchasing organizations (horizontal and vertical). The first part of the chapter explores what is meant by health care purchasing organizations and why they matter. The second part explores the driving forces of organizational reform of health care purchasers. The third looks at different purchasers' interactions with each other and with other portions of the health care system. This section includes a discussion on the degree of market involvement and role of competition in purchasing. The fourth part describes several broad variations for organizing purchasing organizations. The fifth part reviews some of the main policy variables of purchasers. The sixth part presents some standard tools for policy makers trying to reform purchasing organizations. The seventh ends with a few cautionary remarks. The chapter concludes by reminding readers that organizational, institutional, and management reforms are often interdependent and take time. Reform and capacity building in each of these areas are necessary to create high-performing and strategic purchasers but are insufficient in themselves.

Chapter 4, "Institutional Environment," examines the context in which purchasers have to operate and the rules of the game. Resource allocation and purchasing is a heavily regulated function of health systems and takes place in a highly institutionalized environment involving a diversity of decision-making levels, innumerable transactions, and many different stakeholders with different interests. Various institutions provide a framework of formal and informal rules attaining major values and objectives of the entire health care system. The sources of these rules differ. They include laws enacted by parliaments, governmental regulations issued by ministries and decentralized public entities, norms and guidelines imposed by professional and trade associations, and best practices and customs. The chapter uses an understanding of institutions as "the rules of the game or, more formally, the humanly devised constraints that shape human interaction." Institutions have, in this sense, formal and informal rules and arrangements for decision making and guidance. The chapter includes discussion of both the kinds of institutions that exist and the way they work under different resource allocation and purchasing arrangements. It makes reference to four different institutional levels on which regulating takes place. These include the underlying legal framework, regulatory instruments, administrative procedures, and customs and practices.

Chapter 5, "Stewardship, Governance, and Management," discusses the challenge many purchasers face in balancing scarce resources with overwhelming demand while at the same time securing access by the population to quality health services and ensuring value for money. Ultimately it is good policy making, governance, and management that will be instrumental in improving the performance of health services in addressing the health challenges in low- and middle-income countries. Management occurs at different levels of the health system: stewardship, governance, client services, and clinical management. And there are different approaches to management—command and control, business school approaches, new public sector management approaches, and the invisible hand of markets. Each has its appropriate application. The chapter explores ways to make management of purchasing organizations more results oriented. It examines the special challenge of managing complexity and change, and reviews evidence on the degree to which "good management practices" have been applied to the health care purchasing organizations in low- and middle-income countries. The chapter concludes that purchasing organizations in many developing countries could do much better by applying to the health sector lessons learned during recent years from other service sectors of the economy.

Part II of the volume reviews the economic underpinnings for strategic purchasing. Chapter 6, "Agency Theory and Its Applications in Health Care," introduces the basic concepts of agency theory. It identifies agency problems in the health sector and suggests solutions for addressing them. Agency theory provides a theoretical base and general framework for considering many issues encountered in paying health care providers. It recognizes that the interest of those who buy goods and services through a contract (principals) and those who provide such goods or services (agents) are often different. This can lead to differences that are difficult to reconcile. The chapter suggests that optimal results are achieved when contracts in the health sector are either outcome based, if the outcome is observable, or effort based, if effort is more easily observable than outcome. Agency theory provides a framework for strategic purchasing and structuring payment systems in situations where there is asymmetry of information, uncertainty of outcome, and interdependent outputs. But even in such circumstances, it is important to monitor and evaluate proxies of the expected outcomes and outputs. The chapter recommends areas for further research on agency theory applied to the health sector. This includes more work on tracking outcomes and effort as well as on dealing with multiplicitous agency roles. The latter happens when a single purchaser (agent) has to act on behalf of several interested parties (principals)—for example, patients, government paymasters, and providers—all of whom may have quite different interests. This often puts the agent in a difficult position of conflict of interest.

Chapter 7, "Doctors' and Patients' Utility Functions," describes how the utility function of patients and doctors departs from the usual utility function of principals and agents. By examining the usual interaction between patients and doctors and reviewing the literature on patient and doctor utility functions, the chapter concludes that the relationship between these principals and agents is unusually interdependent. Furthermore, doctors almost always serve as multi-plicitous agents, which further complicates their relationship to patients. This has implications for both the design and execution of physician payment sys-tems and often leads to difficult trade-offs in simultaneously meeting the inter-ests of patients and doctors. The chapter suggests that future research on this topic should focus more on optimizing the benefits among various principals served by a single agent.

Chapter 8, "Economic Models of Doctors' Behavior," examines how the behav-ior of individual health care providers, such as medical doctors, is influenced by both the payment mechanism (how) and the level of payment (how much). The chapter first reviews several theoretical models of doctors' behavior. It then exam-ines how these models fit in a real-country context, such as the Chinese health care systems. By combining observations from these two areas of study, the chap-ter concludes that doctors' behavior in China changed significantly during the past 15 years as payment systems transformed from passive salaries to more active performances and output-based payment systems. The introduction of private practice was associated with a shift to direct out-of-pocket payments. Although this had a powerful impact on productivity, it may not always serve patients well in terms of outcomes or health policy makers in terms of productivity. Based on these observations, the chapter concludes that the design of good remuneration systems should be based on a comprehensive understanding of the doctors' behav-ior as well as other considerations about improvements in outcomes and effort. Policy makers should consider all of these and other political economy factors when they introduce new performance-based payment systems.

Chapter 9, "Economic Models of Hospital Behavior," examines how the behavior of organizations such as hospitals is influenced by payment mechanisms and other factors, including the underlying policy framework, organizational incentives, and institutional incentives and their management. The chapter suggests that for opti-mal outcomes in the hospital sector, five prerequisites must be met: (1) all internal factors (endogenous) that are significant to the function of a hospital much be con-sidered; (2) all external (exogenous) operational factors must be identifiable and measurable with reasonable validity; (3) trade-offs between competing factors must be identifiable and measurable with reasonable validity; (4) marginal utility of dif-ferent factors must be identifiable and measurable with reasonable validity; and (5) the payment systems and various other factors must have a predictable impact on the behavior of the hospital, so that the observed effects repeat themselves in dif-ferent contexts and over time. Unfortunately, a review of various models of hospi-tal behavior reveals that these requirements are not always met, which may explain why it is so hard to design and implement effective hospital payment systems.

Chapter 10, "Motivation and Performance-Related Pay," looks at the impact of alternative payment mechanisms on the behavior of providers. The mode of pay-ment often creates powerful incentives that affect the efficiency, equity, quality, and productivity of health care. The chapter suggests that an ideal payment system should meet six criteria: cost containment, quality assurance, no incentive for over-provision, no incentive for underprovision, productivity, and feasibility. Many past studies suggest that no single payment mechanism is likely to meet all of these criteria simultaneously. As a result, many countries are moving to blended or mixed payment systems, putting together different mechanisms to create the desired balance between the desired outcomes described above. The chapter concludes that whatever payment system is chosen, its validity in achieving the desired outcome should be tested through careful monitoring and evaluation of the program.

Chapter 11, "Payment Mechanisms and Provider Behavior," suggests it is unlikely that improvements in the allocation of scarce health care resources will take place unless the people responsible for delivering services are motivated to do so efficiently and effectively. In the health care sector, doctors and hospitals play a major role in the allocation of health care resources. Thus, the successes and failures in allocating and using such resources depend to a large extent on providers' decisions and the policies that influence their behavior. The chapter provides a detailed review of theories on how providers can be motivated to achieve better performance. The concepts and methods of performance-related pay are discussed. And the chapter reviews the practice of performance-related pay in both industrial and developing countries.

Chapter 12, "Supplier-Induced Demand and Unnecessary Care," describes the concern of policy makers and researchers about the adverse effects of financial incentives on provider behaviors and ways to address them. Such adverse incentives could be either overproduction or underproduction of the desired services. In the case of overproduction, providers may perform more procedures or activities than needed to treat a condition, or patients may demand more than is necessary. The former involves the concept and measurement of unnecessary care or supplier-induced demand. The latter involves the concept of moral hazard. The chapter provides a conceptual framework that helps define and clarify relevant concepts. It reviews the methods of measuring both supplier-induced demand and unnecessary care, and provides empirical evidence on its existence.

Chapter 13, "Organization of Publicly Financed Health Care Services," reviews the economic theories of health care organizations. There is widespread acknowledgment of a role for public financing of medical care and insurance, derived both from market failures (particularly in the insurance sector) and from redistribution. There is considerably less consensus, however, about how public resources should be used to attain efficiency and equity goals. Should attention focus on relatively cheap and predictable primary health care or on more-expensive and less widely used hospital care? Should publicly funded health providers be public employees? Should the ministry of health perform the administrative functions of resource allocation within the sector, or should some of these be delegated to autonomous agencies, and should they be for-profit or nonprofit? The chapter addresses these questions in a general framework in which organizational forms are characterized by alternative allocations of control and cash-flow rights. The chapter concludes by reviewing the experience of a number of countries in light of this contract theory.

Chapter 14, "Contracting for Medical Care: Providing Incentives and Controlling Costs," maintains that the question of how to purchase medical care is important because in many societies, there are multiple real and financial links between the provider of care and the final consumer. Designing a purchasing arrangement amounts to establishing the institutional relationships between various actors—including consumers, physicians, insurance pools, managers, and government ministries—as well as specifying the contingent financial flows between them. The specification of financial flows between parties is the subject of contract theory and mechanism design. The design of institutions, and the relationships between them, can be studied drawing on the theory of transaction cost and the property rights literature. The chapter describes how these tools can be used to understand the way medical care services might best be purchased.

Chapter 15, "Efficiency in Purchasing," reviews the concept of efficiency as it applies to resource allocation and purchasing. At first glance, the concept of efficiency seems straightforward, but things get complicated when considering the definition of *efficiency*. One of the problems is lack of agreement on what should be used as the unit of measure that will be related to cost. Some policy makers and researchers use outcomes, some use outputs, some use inputs, and some use other less tangible measures, such as process or user satisfaction. Different concepts of efficiency lead to very different assessments of what is efficient. This has led to a plethora of vague terms used differently by different policy makers and researchers. Examples include technical efficiency, allocative efficiency, social efficiency, organizational efficiency, macro efficiency, micro efficiency, and so on. The chapter reviews a range of definitions of *efficiency* and provides suggestions for appropriate measure.

The editors and coauthors of this book hope that the insights gained by readers will help them design and implement purchasing arrangements in low- and middle-income countries that will address the underlying shortcomings in efficiency and equity observed today. The online reviews of regional experience provide more details on what and how things are currently done in developing countries.

REFERENCES

Dror, David M., and Alexander S. Preker, eds. 2002. *Social Reinsurance: A New Approach to Sustainable Community Health Financing*. Washington, DC: World Bank and International Labour Organization.

Harding, April, and Alexander S. Preker, eds. 2003. *Private Participation in Health Services*. Washington, DC: World Bank.

Preker, Alexander S., and Guy Carrin, eds. 2004. *Health Financing for Poor People: Resource Mobilization and Risk Sharing*. Washington, DC: World Bank.

Preker, Alexander S., and April Harding, eds. 2003. *Innovations in Health Service Delivery: The Corporatization of Public Hospitals*. Washington, DC: World Bank.

Preker, Alexander S., and John C. Langenbrunner, eds. 2005. *Spending Wisely: Buying Health Services for the Poor*. Washington, DC: World Bank.

PART I

Policy Framework

CHAPTER 1

Political Economy of Strategic Purchasing

Alexander S. Preker and April Harding

In many countries today, a large, inefficient public sector produces goods and services that could be bought from nongovernmental providers. These countries could benefit from greater private sector participation in both factor markets (production of inputs) and product markets (provision of services). Moving from a public sector monopoly to a more effective balance between public and private roles is not easy. It will take time and must be accompanied by capacity building in areas such as contracting, regulation, and coordination of nongovernmental providers.

This chapter challenges the principles and nature of public intervention pursued by many governments, especially in the area of the public production of health services. Parallel to recommending that governments move away from the production of goods and services, the authors argue a strong case in favor of greater public involvement in sectoral coordination, regulation, and monitoring and evaluation.

A three-step process is proposed to move gradually from one balance in the public-private mix in service delivery and financing to another. First, when there is already a large private sector, the public sector can begin by recognizing its existence, slowly increasing the use of these resources through better coordination, contracts, and establishment of a positive regulatory environment. Once some learning has taken place in coordinating and contracting with existing providers, the positive lessons from this experience can be transferred to other priority areas where nongovernmental providers may not yet be active. Finally, in some cases where the public sector is engaged in inefficient activities, such as public production of many inputs, these can be converted through outright privatization and subsequently bought from the private sector.

The remainder of this chapter expands on the political economy aspect of implementation arrangements for strategic purchasing in the health sector as described in table I.1 of the Introduction to this volume:

Political economy	Political choice about the appropriate role of the state
	Government failure
	Market failure
	Stakeholders

A HISTORICAL SNAPSHOT

Advances in health during the past few decades are impressive. The increase in life expectancy and the decrease in fertility throughout the world have been greater in the past 40 years than during the previous 4,000 years (figure 1.1). Life expectancy is almost 25 years longer today than at similar income levels in 1900.

These gains in health are partly the result of improvements in income and education, with accompanying improvements in nutrition, access to contraceptives, hygiene, housing, water supplies, and sanitation. As described by the World Health Organization (WHO) in its 2000 World Health Report, the achievements in health during the 20th century are also a result of new knowledge about the causes, prevention, and treatment of disease, and policies that make known interventions more accessible.

International experience indicates that the underlying causes of most threats to good health are well known today, and affordable drugs, surgeries, and other interventions are often available, even in low-income countries. But, because of weakness in one or more of three core functions of health systems—*financing, generation of inputs,* and *provision of services*—potentially effective policies and programs often fail to reach the poor.

The financing function includes the collection and pooling of revenues and the use of these revenues, through purchasing or budget transfers to service providers. The resource-generation function includes the production, import, export, distribution, and retail of human resources, knowledge, pharmaceuticals, medi-

FIGURE 1.1   Unparalleled Improvements in Life Expectancy and Fertility Rates

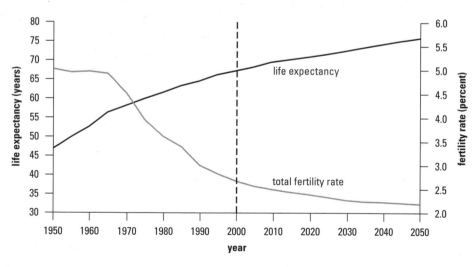

Source: Authors.

FIGURE 1.2   Core Functional Components and Performance Measures

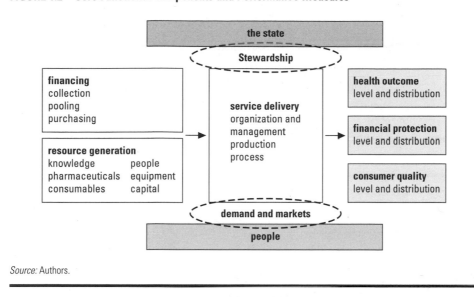

Source: Authors.

cal equipment, other consumables, and capital. The service-delivery function includes both population-base and personal clinical services provided by the public sector and private sector (nonprofit and for-profit).

These core functions are influenced by governments through their stewardship function and by the population through demand and markets. The combined effects of these five factors lead to either good or poor performance in health outcomes, financial protection, and responsiveness to consumer expectations (figure 1.2; WHO 2000).

Health systems are dysfunctional sometimes because of uneven development among the core functions and sometimes because of poor coordination and complementarity between the public and private sectors. The authors argue in favor of greater private sector participation in generating inputs and providing health services, and strong government engagement in securing equitable and sustainable financing as well as in executing the stewardship function. In too many countries, these roles are reversed, with adverse effects on equity and efficiency.

Centuries of Minimalism

Ideological views on the roles of the state and the private sector belong to a long list of false antitheses in the field of medicine and health care (Black 1984).[1] Since the beginning of written history, the pendulum has swung back and forth between minimalist and heavy-handed state involvement in the health sector. During antiquity, people used home remedies and private healers when they were ill. Yet, as early as the second millennium BCE, the papyri give fascinating evidence that Imhotep, archetypal physician, priest, and court official in ancient Egypt, introduced a system of publicly provided health care with healers who were paid by the community.[2]

This early experiment in organized health care did not survive the test of time. The *Code of Hammurabi* (1792–50 BCE) laid down a system of direct fee-for-service payment, based on the nature of services rendered and the patient's ability to pay (Chapman 1984: 4–5).[3] For the next three thousand years, the state's involvement in health care revolved mainly around enforcing the rules of compensation for personal injury and protection of the self-governing medical guild (British Medical Association 1984: 6).[4]

At best, financing, organization, and provision of health care was limited to the royal courts of kings, emperors, and other nobility who might have a physician for their personal use and for their troops at the time of battle. The masses got by with local healers, midwives, natural remedies, apothecaries, and quacks.

Minimalism to Heavy-Handed State Involvement

Unlike this early private participation in health care, during the 20th century, governments of most countries became central to health policy, often both financing and delivering a wide range of care. Today, most industrial countries have achieved universal access to health care through a mix of public and private financing arrangements and providers.[5]

Proponents of such public sector involvement in health care have argued their case on both philosophical and technical grounds. In most societies, care for the sick and disabled is considered an expression of humanitarian and philosophical aspirations. But one does not have to resort to moral principles or arguments about the welfare state to warrant collective intervention in health. The past century is rich in examples of how the private sector and market forces alone failed to secure efficiency and equity in the health sector.

Economic theory provides ample justification for such an engagement on both theoretical and practical grounds to secure the following:

- *Efficiency*—since significant market failure exists in the health sector (information asymmetries, public goods, positive and negative externalities, distorting or monopolistic market power of many providers and producers, absence of functioning markets in some areas, and frequent occurrence of high transaction costs)[6]

- *Equity*—since individuals and families often fail to protect themselves adequately against the risks of illness and disability on a voluntary basis due to short-sightedness (free-riding) and characteristic shortcomings of private health insurance (moral hazard and adverse selection).[7]

Largely inspired by Western welfare state experiences such as the British National Health Service (NHS) and the problems of market failure, during the past 50 years, many low- and middle-income countries established state-funded health care systems with services produced by a vertically integrated public bureaucracy.

Return to Neoliberalism of the 1990s

During the 1980s and 1990s, the pendulum began to swing back in the opposite direction. During the Reagan and Thatcher era,[8] the world witnessed a growing willingness to experiment with market approaches in the social sectors (health, education, and social protection). This was true even in historical bastions of the welfare state such as Australia, Great Britain, and New Zealand.

As in the ascendancy of state involvement, the recent cooling toward state involvement in health care and enthusiasm for private solutions has been motivated by both ideological and technical arguments. The political imperative that has accompanied liberalization in many former socialist states and the economic shocks in East Asia and Latin America certainly contributed to a global sense of urgency to reform inefficient and bloated bureaucracies and to establish smaller governments with greater accountability (Barr 1994; World Bank 1996: 123–32).

Yet, it would be too easy to blame ideology and economic crisis for the recent surge in attempts to reform health care systems by exposing public services to competitive market forces, downsizing the public sector, and increasing private sector participation.[9] In reality, the welfare-state approach failed to address many of the health needs of populations across the world (WHO 1996, 1999; World Bank 1993, 1997; UNICEF 1999). Hence, the dilemma of policy makers worldwide: although state involvement in the health sector is clearly needed, it is typically beset by public sector production failure.[10]

Toward a New Stewardship Role for the State

Today, governments everywhere are reassessing when, where, how, and how much to intervene or whether to leave things to the market forces of patients' demand. Consensus is growing that addressing this problem requires a better match between the roles of the state and the private sector, and their respective capabilities—getting the fundamentals right. In most countries, this means rebalancing an already complex mix of public and private roles in the health sector.[11]

To improve efficiency or equity, governments can choose from an extensive range of actions—from least to most intrusive. These include the following:

- Providing information to encourage behavioral changes needed to improve health outcomes

- Developing and enforcing policies and regulations to influence public and private sector activities

- Issuing mandates or purchasing services from public and private providers

- Providing subsidies to pay for services directly or indirectly

- Producing (in-house) preventive and curative services.

In many countries, for reasons of both ideological view and weak public capacity to deal with information asymmetry, contracting, and regulatory problems, governments often try to do too much—especially in terms of in-house service delivery—with too few resources and little capability.

Parallel to such public production, the same well-intended governments often fail to do the following:

- Develop effective policies and make available information about personal hygiene, healthy lifestyles, and appropriate use of health care

- Regulate and contract with available private sector providers

- Ensure that adequate financing arrangements are available for the whole population

- Secure access to public goods with large externalities for the whole population.

The next section presents a discussion of the most significant sources of government production failure to which market-based solutions are being applied and the market imperfections that must be addressed to optimize complementarity between the two sectors.

THE NATURE OF GOVERNMENT FAILURE

Many attempts have been made in recent years to reinvigorate the public sector through "best-practice" management techniques. Borrowed from the private sector and organizational reforms, these tools attempt to replicate the private incentive environment (Osborne and Gaebler 1993).

These reforms have included efforts to strengthen the managerial expertise of health sector personnel, both through training and recruitment policies. Frequently, attempts are also made to use business process reengineering, patient-focused care, and quality-improvement techniques. Such efforts have also included setting up clinical directorates, introducing improved information systems to facilitate effective decision making, and performance benchmarking (Saltman and Figueras 1997: 213–14).

Why has the public sector been so impervious to these types of management and organizational reforms (Donahue 1989; Wilson 1989; World Bank 1997)? A review of theories regarding governments' performance of their multiple functions is needed to shed light on the profound nature of the structural problems involved. This review complements the well-developed theories of market failure provided by health economists (Wolf 1979; Peacock 1980; Weimer and Vining

1989; Vining and Weimer 1990). Below, the authors explore the problems of poor public accountability, information asymmetry, abuse of monopoly power, failure to provide public goods, and loss in strategic policy formulation that have parallels in market failure.

Problems Relating to Public Accountability

The first set of problems relates to the difficult task of translating individuals' preferences into public policy and getting that policy implemented. Of course, all public interventions involve transfers of benefits to some people and costs to others, leaving both winners and losers.[12] Accountability means that government action accords with the will of the people it represents. Yet, since people's values are never perfectly homogeneous in any society, accountability will always be based on some imperfect rule about the aggregation of individual values or respect for minority interests.[13]

This raises several intractable procedural issues relating to accountability in the electoral process, taxation policies, content of public spending programs, and vested bureaucratic interests. Ballots are blunt instruments that cannot capture the full range of issues that may be bundled together at election time. The intensity of views on any one issue cannot be reflected. And, election promises are often not kept. So at best, public spending policies are an imprecise reflection of social values.

Majority rule in itself can be a form of tyranny if applied strictly without constraints. Most democratic societies safeguard minority interests to some extent, but even with good intentions there are limits to both practicality and desirability in this respect.

Finally, public servants may have strong conflicts between their own interests and their assigned responsibilities to execute the collective will of the society they represent. Their political overseers may also have strong vested interests that are different from those of the society that they represent.[14]

In an ideal setting, good public accountability would be secured through a large intersection (authorizing environment) between fairly homogeneous social values, a political agenda that reflects such values, and vested bureaucratic interests (figure 1.3a).[15] For example, there may be general social agreement that the population has to be protected against the financial consequences of illness through some sort of health insurance system. When the policies of the political party in power are consistent with such values and bureaucrats have the capacity to implement them, the intersection will be large.

In the health sector, a further tension exists between the authorizing environment needed for good public accountability and most individuals' desire for some sovereignty over their own health care. This leads to difficult dilemmas during the rationing of care or design of compulsory programs, based on the application of some sort of majority rule that infringes on either perceived minority group rights or individual survival.[16] Normally rational individuals

FIGURE 1.3   The Authorizing Environment Needed for Good Public Sector Accountability

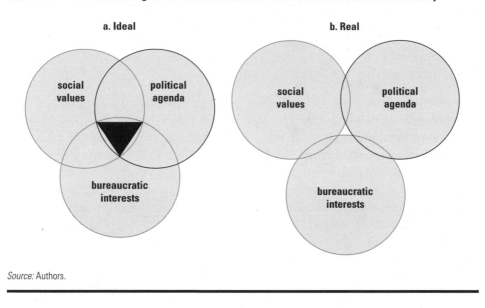

Source: Authors.

who may share social values about the need to ration health care resources often lose their commitment to such values when confronted by resource constraints in the face of serious illness or death.

Information Asymmetry in the Public Sector

Information asymmetry can occur in three major ways in the health sector—between patient (public) and health care professional; between patient and administrator or health care system; and between health care professional and administrator or health care system.

Patients know more about their symptoms than doctors do but may—unwittingly or deliberately—not articulate this clearly. Doctors know more about the causes, prognosis, and effectiveness of available treatments but may not communicate this clearly to the patient. Or, the patient may not understand the implications of what he/she is being told. For paternalistic reasons, the doctor may deliberately conceal information, based on a judgment that the patient will not be able to cope with the full knowledge of his or her ailment (e.g., terminal cancer). Through self-selection, these problems are typically worse in the public sector, which has to deal with large volumes of poorer and less educated patients.

When it comes to interactions between patients (public) and health care administrators, patients may try to avoid being excluded or paying higher health care premiums by choosing to conceal pre-existing conditions. Similarly, there is often a lack of information on and understanding of available public programs. The benefit of gathering useful data about such programs is usually undervalued compared with its cost. Some of these programs may be too complex to understand fully even if information were available. Frequently, the lack of transparency in the rationing of scarce resources is deliberate.

Finally, some serious information asymmetries exist between health care providers and the administrators for whom they work (or between administrators and owners). Health care providers—as advocates for patients—have a much better understanding of legitimate needs or demands. Administrators have a much better understanding about supply and cost of available resources but know little about a selected intervention's appropriateness or effectiveness. The doctor's information advantage over the patient is not solved by the existence of a public employer or administrator who knows even less about interactions between patients and providers.

Associated Higher Transaction Costs

Such information asymmetries add to agency costs in terms of structuring, monitoring, and bonding contracts among agents and principals with conflicting interests.[17] Private firms, concerned about profits, have a strong incentive to limit agency costs related to information asymmetry (Fama and Jensen (1983: 327–49). Public agencies that are not held to a clear "bottom line," due to unspecified social functions and many complex sources of subsidies, do not receive clear signals about the agency cost of such information asymmetry.

Not surprisingly, many public health care facilities in low- and middle-income countries do not keep detailed patient records, do not know through-put statistics, and do not know the unit costs of the procedures they are using or illnesses they treat. Hospitals are often not doing what policy makers or administrators would like, or what they think they should be doing. And, doctors working in such public hospitals maintain an information advantage that gives them a great deal of latitude to pursue their own interests. Paradoxically, since public systems often give their beneficiaries less leverage than private systems give their clients, patients may be less able to use the information they *do* possess to influence their own treatment.

Potential for Corruption

Worse than this "ignorance by default," due to information asymmetry, are the *information* problems deliberately engineered by politicians, bureaucrats, organizations, and health care providers entrusted with public accountability.

Although deliberate deception and fiscal fraud is usually sanctioned severely, it is much harder to hold the public sector accountable for petty abuses, avoidance, and obfuscation. Such deception may take the form of hidden costs, subsidies, cost shifting, or inflation. Or it may occur as an amplification of benefits, exaggeration of the consequences of alternatives, or claiming credit for activities that originate elsewhere. Given the complex nature of health care, it is not hard to imagine the considerable scope for misleading or defrauding patients and the public in the health sector.

Abuses of Public Monopoly Power

Monopoly power occurs for four reasons when the public sector gets involved in producing health services. This may be due to: (1) legal restrictions on competition; (2) access to subsidized capital and revenues, creating an uneven "playing field"; (3) below-cost distribution of goods and services to achieve equity goals; or (4) production of public goods or goods where markets are not viable. When—in addition to the accountability and information problems—the public sector enjoys monopoly power, people who work for it are given wide scope for abusing this power through the extraction of rents, internal distribution of "slack" to employees, and lowering of quality.

Public monopolies exhibit the usual negative features. First, monopoly suppliers often reduce output and quality, while raising prices. The excess in prices over and above what the market would normally bear (rents) leads to allocative inefficiency or a net deadweight welfare loss to consumers who have to forgo the consumption of other goods.

A manifestation of such rents is the informal user charges that are commonly levied on patients and their families in public health facilities. In many countries, these rents are not limited to doctors' accepting bribes or peddling influence (allowing privileged patients to circumvent the usual rules on resource allocation, to receive preferential treatment, and to cut waiting time). It also includes charges levied by other salaried workers for items ranging from toilet paper and clean linen to food, drugs, and medical supplies.

In a recent study on corruption around the world, such abuses in publicly run health services ranked number one in terms of the burden placed on households (Kaufmann and Ryterman 1998). Patients who can afford to pay formal charges in the private sector often prefer it to paying such rents in the public sector. Taxpayers charged twice for low-quality services and such abuses have little recourse but the blunt and often ineffective instrument of voting power.

Second, monopoly suppliers have strong incentives to lower expenditures through decreased output when staff members benefit from the financial residuals. Although public organizations cannot legally distribute such residuals outside the organization to shareholders, they can be internally consumed in several ways. First, executives often receive generous social benefits and travel allowances (perks). Second, time-keeping is often not enforced rigorously (doctors often work short hours in public institutions). Third, some of the residual may be used to pursue personal agendas (discretionary spending on special projects and research).

Failure of Critical Policy Formulation

The most frequently cited reason for greater government involvement in the health sector is that when left to competitive forces and prices alone, the market does not lead to welfare-enhancing production and allocation of a number of health care goods and services in the following critical areas:

- Public goods (policy making and information)

- Goods with large externalities (disease prevention)

- Goods with intractable market failure (insurance).

It is therefore surprising that governments in the health sector often neglect the exact same three areas while they are busy producing curative services that the private sector could easily provide. Furthermore, when most public funds are spent on poorly targeted public production, few or no resources are left for strategic purchasing of services for the poor from nongovernmental providers.

The next section presents a discussion of some of the key theoretical underpinnings for a new approach to optimize complementarity between the public and private sectors.

THEORETICAL UNDERPINNINGS

The current trend worldwide is to use three types of approaches to address the public sector failures in service delivery described above (Hirschman 1970; World Bank 1997). In descending order of importance, they include increased

- exit possibilities (market consumer choice),

- voice (client participation), and

- loyalty (hierarchical sense of responsibility).

When possible, one would always use the first, the exit option, unless forced to use the weaker variants, because the goods and services involved are not "marketable." The focus is mainly on this option, which relies on greater private sector participation, allowing clients and patients a choice or alternative to publicly provided services. Such exit options can be implemented in parallel with other public sector management reforms that increase voice and loyalty.

Neoclassical Economics

One of the central tenets of neoclassical economics is that in an optimally functioning market, competitive forces will lead to a more efficient allocation of resources—*Pareto-optimal* competitive equilibrium—than will nonmarket solutions.

According to the neoclassical model, when there are many firms and consumers—and prices are allowed to respond to the forces of supply and demand—competition will result in an equilibrium situation in which it is impossible to make someone better off without making someone else worse off. This will result in a welfare-maximizing situation.

The perfectly competitive *Walrasian* model, as it is sometimes called, requires a number of assumptions to be met. These include the following three:

- The goods involved behave like private goods (i.e., rivalry, excludability, and rejectability; see box 1.1).

- Rights can be perfectly delineated.

- Transaction costs are zero.

According to neoclassical theory, a breakdown occurs in both efficiency and equity when public goods or services with significant externalities are allocated through competitive markets. Likewise, as described earlier, significant problems occur in efficiency and equity when private goods are produced or provided by a public sector monopoly.

Unfortunately, most health care goods and services do not behave like perfect private or public goods. Many are not perfectly excludable but are associated with complex externalities. Rights are often difficult to delineate, leaving residual claimants. And transaction costs are often high. Therefore, though in a Pareto-optimal state, it would be impossible to make someone better off without making someone else worse off, few situations meet such criteria in the health sector.

Although many public health activities (e.g., sanitation services, control and prevention of communicable diseases, and health promotion) generate

---

BOX 1.1   PUBLIC, MIXED, AND PRIVATE GOODS

The neoclassical model classifies goods and service as *public, mixed,* and *private,* as shown in the figure. Private goods exhibit excludability (consumption by one individual prevents consumption by another—no positive or negative externalities); rivalry (there is competition among goods based on price); and rejectability (individuals can choose to forgo consumption). True public goods have significant elements of nonexcludability, nonrivalry, and nonrejectability. Mixed goods have some but not all of the characteristics of private goods.

Properties	Nature of economic good		
	Public	Mixed	Private
Excludability	−	±	+
Rivalry	−	±	+
Rejectability	−	±	+

Consumer protection	**Consumption goods**
Policy making	Medical clinics
Regulations	Hospitals
Setting standards	Medical suppliers
Quality control	Pharmaceuticals

Source: Authors.

significant externalities, they are not pure public goods. All have some element of excludability, rejectability, and rivalry. For example, a vaccine given to one patient cannot simultaneously be consumed by other patients. At will, patients can choose not to be vaccinated. And, vaccination programs can, in principle, compete with one another for market share.

Likewise, even expensive diagnostic and therapeutic care—though often provided in publicly owned inpatient facilities at highly subsidized rates—is really private goods and hence marketable. The same is true for ambulatory and community-based care. Even when governments try to fully control the market for such services, preventing their sale in the informal economy is often difficult.

Therefore, although neoclassical theory is often invoked by mainstream economists to justify public and private roles in the health sector, consumption characteristics alone almost never indicate anything about the specific production processes needed to secure technical efficiency and equity. Neoclassical theory contributes little to the understanding of optimal organizational arrangements for service production. It is essentially "institution free" (Robinson 1997: 3–24). Other theories are needed to fill this vacuum in understanding production characteristics.

The Economics of Organizations

Recently, much progress has been made in identifying the key factors causing wide variations in organizations' performance. The developments most relevant for understanding the advantages and disadvantages of different arrangements for service delivery come from *principal–agent theory, transaction cost economics, property rights theory,* and *public choice theory*. These fields are often grouped together under the title "institutional economics." Institutional economics directly addresses the issue of how best to structure organizations that consist of individuals pursuing multiple and often conflicting interests (OECD 1992: 17).

Principal Agency Theory

This framework highlights that social and political objectives may be more readily achieved through a series of explicit and transparent "contracts" for labor/services between an "agent" that undertakes to perform various tasks in an acceptable way on behalf of a "principal" in exchange for a mutually agreed award. Usually, the principal needs the agent's efforts and expertise but has only limited ability to monitor the agent's actions or evaluate whether the final outcome is satisfactory.

The agency literature surveys the range of contracts (e.g., payment and monitoring arrangements) observed in the economy as attempts to align incentives and reward cooperation between self-interested but interdependent individuals (Sappington 1991). Several studies have generalized the agency insight from the employment context to the full range of relationships that make up the firm—now conceptualized as a nexus of many contracts (Fama 1980; Jensen and

Meckling 1976). The need for incentive alignment is pervasive in the health sector: relations between patient and physician or governments and contracting agencies are classical examples of principal–agent structure.

Transaction Cost Economics

Transaction cost economics emphasizes the limitations of contracts and the need for flexible means of coordinating activities. Principals and agents are both opportunistic. Agents will seek to minimize the aggregate production and transaction costs and maximize the benefits (unless closely monitored, agents might be unreliable, engaging in behavior such as rent seeking, cheating, breach of contract, incomplete disclosure). Principals will try to maximize their benefit to the extent that the relationship could become unviable for the agent.

The extent of such opportunism varies drastically from country to country and from one cultural setting to another. In some settings, such as monopolistic national health services, opportunism may be less apparent than in other settings where providers are more accustomed to competing with each other. Although opportunism may appear to be greater in countries such as Chile, India, and the United States, there is good evidence that principal–agent relationships within national health services in places such as Costa Rica, New Zealand, Scandinavia, Sri Lanka, and the United Kingdom are also vulnerable to opportunistic behavior.

This theory sheds most light on firm boundaries and the conditions under which activities are best arranged within a hierarchy instead of through market interactions with suppliers or other contractors. More generally, vertically integrated organizations, simple "spot" contracts, franchises, or joint ventures are interpreted as discrete structural alternatives—each offering different advantages and disadvantages for effective governance (Williamson 1991). Governance arrangements are evaluated by comparing the patterns of costs generated for planning, adapting, and monitoring production and exchange.[18]

Unlike public organizations, private firms have the flexibility (indeed the requirement) to adjust their governance structure to changes in the market environment—making them fruitful sources of "better practices" for governance arrangements. Public agencies that have tried to adjust public organizations to changes in market environment (e.g., formation of NHS Trusts in the United Kingdom, establishment of the Hospital Authority in Hong Kong, and corporatization of publicly owned hospitals in New Zealand) have often run into problems with the underlying structure of incentives and its sustainability. Major policy reversals occurred recently in both the United Kingdom and New Zealand, adding weight to the argument of some critics of the original reforms that they would have been better off to privatize instead of settling for the imperfect middle ground of public sector corporatization.

For example, vertically integrated (within firm) organizations arise as a response to problems with market contracting. The firm substitutes low-powered incentives, like salaried employment, for the markets' high-powered incentives of profit and loss. Vertical integration permits the details of future relations

---

BOX 1.2   INFLUENCE ACTIVITIES

An important issue related to moral hazard and the structure of organizations is influence activities and the associated costs, known as *influence costs* (Milgrom and Roberts 1990: 57–89). Analysis has shed much light on the propensity of publicly owned service delivery organizations to capture inordinate portions of the sector budget as well as on their ability to influence sector policy to their benefit—often at the expense of the public interest.

In the health sector, provider organizations expend effort to influence decisions regarding the distribution of resources or other benefits among providers to their benefit. These *influence activities* occur in all organizations, but countervailing forces are particularly weak in public service delivery structures—and influence costs are one of the most important costs of centralized control. Evidence of influence activities is seen in public utilities where monopolies are often maintained to protect low-productivity, state-owned enterprises from competition from more efficient producers. In the health sector, the tendency to allocate resources to tertiary and curative care at the expense of primary, preventative, and public health is evidence of similar capture.

The cost of these activities includes both the losses associated with poor resource-allocation decisions as well as the loss associated with efforts to capture rents. These costs can be reduced when no decision maker has the authority to make decisions that service providers can easily influence. This condition can sometimes be brought about by creating legal or other boundaries between the policy maker, the funder, and the service provider unit. Many organizational reforms have attempted to diminish these activities. Examples include reforms separating the policy maker from the payer from the provider in public service delivery as well as privatization of utilities.

---

between suppliers (including employees), producers, and distributors to remain unspecified; differences can be adjudicated as events unfold. Vertical integration (or unified ownership) pools the risks and rewards of the organization's activities and can facilitate the sharing of information, the pursuit of innovation, and a culture of cooperation.

Despite these positive features, vertical integration suffers from characteristic weaknesses as a mechanism of governance. The two most prominent are the weakening of incentives for productivity and the proliferation of influence activities (box 1.2). The weak incentives come as individuals capture less and less of the gains of their own efforts as rewards and their losses are spread throughout the organization. Despite its focus on the contracting problems that motivate internal organization, transaction cost economics views vertical integration as the governance mechanism of last resort. Even in the many instances where policy objectives imply that spot market transactions are not desirable, contractual networks, virtual integration, franchising, or concessions will outperform unified ownership arrangements.

Property Rights Theory

Property rights theory looks at the same incentive issues from a slightly different perspective. Since private ownership appears to have strong positive incentives for efficiency, property rights theorists have attempted to find out why (box 1.3). Explanations have focused on two issues: the possession of residual decision rights and the allocation of residual returns (Milgrom and Roberts 1992: ch. 9). Residual rights of control are the rights to make any decisions regarding an asset's use not explicitly contracted by law or assigned to another by contract. The owner of an asset usually holds these rights although they may be allocated to others.[19]

The notion of ownership as residual control is relatively clear for a simple asset like a car. It gets much more complicated when applied to an organization such as a firm. Large organizations bundle together many assets, and who has which decision rights may be ambiguous. In addition to residual decision rights, an owner holds the rights to residual revenue flows from his assets. That is, the owner has

---

BOX 1.3   HIGH-POWERED INCENTIVES OF OWNERSHIP

Suppose a transaction involves several people supplying labor, physical inputs, and so on. If all but one party have contracted to receive fixed amounts, there is only one residual claimant. In that case, maximizing the value received by the residual claimant is the same as maximizing the total value received by all parties. If the residual claimant also has residual control, just by pursuing his own interests and maximizing his own returns the claimant will be led to make efficient decisions. The combination of residual control and residual claims provides strong incentives and capacity for an owner to maintain and increase an asset's value. Firms often attempt to reproduce these high-powered incentives by allocating residual claims in the form of bonuses or shares to key decision makers in their firm.

Misalignment of residual rights and returns causes serious problems. The residual claimant to the returns from a state-owned enterprise is the public purse, but the residual decision makers are effectively the enterprise manager, the workers, and the bureaucrats in the supervising ministry. None of these has any great personal stake in the value of the enterprise. The resulting low productivity is well documented. Another example of misalignment comes from the U.S. savings and loan (S&L) industry. Those who had the right to control the S&L's investment also had the right to keep any profits earned but were not obligated to make good on losses. That combination of rights and obligations created an incentive for risk taking and fraud that was not effectively countered by other devices during most of the 1980s (Milgrom and Roberts 1992: 291–92).

These fields of analysis have led to better understanding of the institutional sources of government failure. The framework has been used to design organizational reforms that seek to allocate to the holders of critical information the authority to make relevant decisions and the financial incentive to do so (in the form of residual claims on the outcome of the decision).

the right to whatever revenue remains after all funds have been collected, and all debts, expenses, and other contractual obligations have been paid out.

Public Choice Theory

Public choice theory focuses on the self-interested behavior of politicians, interest groups, and bureaucrats and studies its implications for effective government and the size of government. Individuals are viewed as rational utility maximizers. Bureaucrats, attempting to maximize their budgets, will acquire an increasing share of national income. As a result, the state will grow much bigger than necessary to deliver core functions. Powerful interest groups will capture increasing portions of resources. Institutional rigidities develop, reducing economic growth (Olson 1982). This analysis has led public choice theorists to support conservative political agendas (minimizing the role of the state).

Production Characteristics of Goods and Services

The principles of institutional economics lead to a much more refined and useful understanding of the different kinds of institutional arrangements required for efficient and effective production of goods and services. A model along these lines can be developed, based on two different and often ignored goods characteristics— *contestability* and *measurability* (Girishankar 1999).

A market can be said to be perfectly contestable if firms can enter it freely (without any resistance from existing firms) and exit without losing any of their investments, while having equal access to technology (no asset specificity) (Baumol, Panzar, and Willing 1982; Baumol 1984).[20] Contestability allows competition *for* the market to substitute for competition *in* the market.

Contestable goods are characterized by low barriers to entry and exit from the market, whereas noncontestable goods have high barriers, such as sunk cost, monopoly market power, geographic advantage, and asset specificity. Investments in specific assets represent a sunk cost since its value cannot be recovered elsewhere.[21] Two specific assets that are especially relevant in the health sector are expertise and reputation. Once incumbents have invested in activities that result in expertise or generate trust, they enjoy a significant barrier to entry for other potential suppliers, thereby lowering the degree of contestability. Opportunism, on the other hand, will lower such trust or barriers to entry. The degree of such opportunism will vary from one country to another and in different cultural settings.

Measurability in the health sector, as in other sectors, is the precision with which inputs, processes, outputs, and outcomes of a good or service can be measured. By definition, it is difficult to measure with precision the output and outcome of health services characterized by a high degree of information asymmetry. Information asymmetry is the extent to which information about the performance of an activity is available to users, beneficiaries, and contracting purchasing agencies (see discussion above under "The Nature of Government Failure").

These theoretical underpinnings are used in the following section to understand some recent reforms in the public sector.

TRENDS IN PUBLIC SECTOR REFORMS

Rarely does technical or systemic analysis alone influence the extent of public and private involvement in the health sector. In actuality, service delivery arrangements are the product of complex economic, institutional, and political factors.

Extensive reforms of public sector organizations and state-owned enterprises, implemented over the past 15 years, addressed the same problems encountered in delivering public health services. In the realization that these organizational problems were structural in nature, by using the analytical tools of organizational economics, these reforms have focused on altering the institutional arrangements for service. These developments shed light on similar problems in delivering public health services.

One way to understand organizational reforms in service delivery is to view the different incentive environments within which government's tasks can be performed (figure 1.4).[22] The civil or core public service lies at the center (usually constitutional control bodies, line ministries), and the activities of the staff are highly determined. Job tenure is also strong. Budgetary units (government departments), autonomous units, corporatized units, and privatized units are four common organizational modalities that straddle these incentive environments in the health sector (Harding and Preker 2003).[23]

The broader public sector is distinguished by the relative flexibility of the financial management regime and by managerial freedom in recruitment and

---

FIGURE 1.4   Incentive Environments

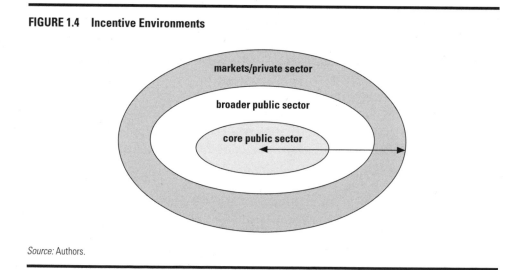

Source: Authors.

promotion. This sector may include special purpose agencies, autonomous agencies and, on the outer limits, state-owned enterprises. Beyond the public sector lies the domain of the market and civil society. Services may be delivered by for-profit, nonprofit, or community organizations. The incentives for efficient production are higher moving toward the periphery, where service delivery is often better.

Many reforms throughout the world have sought to move delivery away from the center of the circle to more arm's-length contracts with public and private organizations. However, the nature of the outputs and the existence of mechanisms for public sector management of their delivery constrains moving delivery outward.

Increased autonomy or corporatization—moving from the center of the circle to the outer limits—requires accountability mechanisms not tied to direct control. These controls (e.g., contracts) take considerable capacity to write and enforce, especially for health services where outputs and outcomes are difficult to specify.

How far countries may go in pushing activities to incentive environments in the outer circles depends on the nature of the outputs (the services involved) and their capacity to create accountability for public objectives through indirect mechanisms such as regulation and contracting.

APPLICATION TO HEALTH SECTOR

Looking at the health sector across the world, all health care goods and services can be categorized on a continuum from high-contestability and high-measurability services to low-contestability and low-measurability services, and significant information asymmetry.

Factor markets and product markets are discussed separately, since each has unique characteristics. Although the following discussion refers mainly to curative and public health services, the analysis could be extended to some of the broader intersectoral determinants of good health, such as water, sanitation, education, healthy lifestyle policies, and good nutrition.

Production Characteristics of Factor Markets

For the production of inputs, this contestability and measurability matrix would look like figure 1.5. The production of consumable items and the retail of drugs, medical supplies, and other consumables are the best example of highly contestable goods where outputs are also easy to measure (Type I). Many companies usually jostle for a share of the market, and barriers to entry are few (the initial investment capital is modest, and there are few requirements for specialized licensing or skills). Unskilled labor also belongs in this category.

FIGURE 1.5   Production Characteristics of Inputs (Factor Markets)

	High contestability	Medium contestability	Low contestability

High measurability	Type I
	• production of consumables
	• retail of
	  • drugs and equipment
	  • other consumables
	• unskilled labor
		Type II
		• production of equipment
		• wholesale
		  • drugs and equipment
		  • other consumables
		• small capital stock
			Type III
			• production of
			  • pharmaceuticals
			  • high technology
			• large capital stock

Medium measurability	Type IV	Type V
		• basic training
		  • skilled labor
			Type VI
			• research
			  • knowledge
			• higher education
			  • high-skilled labor

Low measurability	Type VII	Type VIII	Type IX

Source: Authors.

Move across the first row, and a number of factors begin to contribute to raising the barriers to entry, thereby reducing the contestability of the goods or services in question (Type I). Investment cost (sunk cost) and increasing technical specifications create moderate barriers to entry in the manufacture of specialized equipment and supplies. Wholesale trade in drugs, medical supplies, and medical equipment has some entry barriers because of the larger investment requirements and more limited supply and distribution chains. The specialization and licensing of pharmacists contribute to these entry barriers. In the case of small capital stock (e.g., clinics and diagnostic centers), entry barriers are created mainly though certification and licensing.

Finally, move across to Type III activities, and entry barriers are much higher, as in the manufacture of pharmaceuticals and high-technology medical equipment, due to large up-front investment costs that cannot be recovered later during sale of the assets (sunk costs). These production activities are also associated with costly and long lead time for research, development, and registration of new products. Other barriers to entry under this category include product differentiation (specialized medical equipment) and copyright protection (brand-name drugs). Furthermore, because of the benefits conferred through economies of scope and scale, a significant global concentration of pharmaceutical and high-technology industries has occurred over time, giving them considerable monopoly power.

For all the activities in the first row (Type I through Type III), measurability of outputs remains high. There is little information asymmetry.

Move to the second row, and measurement of the outputs and outcomes becomes more problematic. Outputs and outcomes can be measured, but it is more difficult than in the case of activities in the first row. Various barriers to entry reduce contestability. Training is almost always associated with special licensing and long lead times (Type V). The specialized labor market is usually associated with many professional barriers as well as subsequent restrictions in scope of practice and labor mobility. Contestability is even lower in the Type VI category. Most research and other knowledge-generating activities fall under this category. So does the training of highly specialized staff in universities and other higher education centers.

Move to the last row. There are no good examples of inputs for the health sector that fit into this row, with significant information asymmetry in addition to measurement problems.

Production Characteristics of Product Markets

Interventions and services can also be categorized along a similar continuum from high contestability and high measurability through to interventions and other outputs with low contestability, low measurability, and significant information asymmetry (figure 1.6). Whereas reduced contestability due to market concentration is one of the main problems encountered in factor markets (production of inputs), a key problem with interventions and other outputs (product markets) has to do with difficulties in specifying and measuring outputs and outcomes.

FIGURE 1.6   Production Characteristics of Outputs (Product Markets)

	High contestability	Medium contestability	Low contestability
High measurability	Type I	Type II	Type III

Medium measurability	Type IV
	• nonclinical activities
	   • management support
	   • laundry and catering
	• routine diagnostics
		Type V
		• clinical interventions
		• high-tech diagnostics
			Type VI

Low measurability	Type VII
	• ambulatory care
	   • medical
	   • nursing
	   • dental
		Type VIII
		• public health interventions
		• intersectoral action
		• inpatient care
			Type IX
			• policy making
			• monitoring/evaluation

Source: Authors.

Move to the second row of figure 1.6 (Type IV to Type VI), and measurement of the outputs and outcomes becomes more problematic. Although routine diagnostics such as laboratory tests may be highly contestable (many players in a competitive market with few barriers to entry), monitoring their performance in terms of effectiveness and quality of the activities undertaken is much harder (Type IV). The same is true for various nonclinical hospital activities.

Move across to the Type V category, and contestability is reduced by various barriers to entry. High-tech diagnostics usually require specialization, licensing, and large sunk costs, giving established players a marked advantage over new entrants. A further barrier to entry for these activities is government policies that control or restrict the introduction of some new technologies (CAT or NMR scanners). Clinical interventions are usually outsourced only to certified providers. In each of these cases, outputs and outcomes can be measured, but it is more difficult than in the case of activities in the first row.

In addition to difficulties in measuring output and outcomes, most clinical interventions are characterized by an additional constraint of information asymmetry. At times, information may be readily apparent to patients (e.g., the quality of "hotel services," such as courtesy of clinical staff, length of waiting periods, cleanliness of linens, palatability of food, and privacy). Without survey techniques, however, such information may not be readily available to the contracting policy makers or administrative staff. For these reasons, ambulatory clinical care falls under the Type VII category (relatively low barriers to entry other than professional qualifications and certification of staff) but high information asymmetry and difficulties measuring outputs and outcomes.

Move across the third row, and contestability diminishes due to specialization and cost, in addition to measurement problems. For these reasons, public health interventions, intersectoral action programs, and inpatient clinical care belong to Type VIII activities. This leaves a few clear-cut activities—such as policy making, monitoring, and evaluation—under the Type IX category. The contestability and measurability of these activities are extremely low. These activities are therefore usually retained as a core part of an integrated bureaucracy.

"MAKE OR BUY" DECISION GRID

In many countries "make or buy" decisions are made before policy makers and providers have gone through an explicit priority-setting process. Specified priorities should include the range of interventions to finance them through public resources (including preventive services) and should ensure that public subsidies are appropriately targeted (e.g., to the poor and other vulnerable groups) (Ham 1997: 49–66). Countries often rush into make or buy decisions before setting priorities for needed and affordable interventions. Such prioritization is complicated by the fact that the cost of treating different illnesses varies greatly and often bears little relation to the effectiveness of available interventions (Musgrove 1999). Furthermore, for a whole range of activities, information disclosure and coordination through a strong stewardship function may be sufficient.

Based on the above discussion, it is now easy to map the goods and services that can be bought, those where coordination is enough, and those that are better produced in-house by the public sector itself (figure 1.7). The size of the make in-house production triangle will depend largely on the effectiveness of policy instruments to deal with contestability and measurability problems. See "Policy Levers Available to Governments," below, for discussion.

Once make or buy options have been settled, the next questions relate to from whom to buy and how to pay or structure the purchase.

From Whom to Buy

When deciding from whom to buy, do the following:

- Consider all possible producers (public, nongovernmental, and private-for-profit; both domestic and international).

- Base purchase decision on best product at the lowest price responsive to specific needs—type of good, price, quantity, after acquisition support, timeliness, and so forth (consider international competitive bidding when possible).

FIGURE 1.7   "Make or Buy" Decision Grid

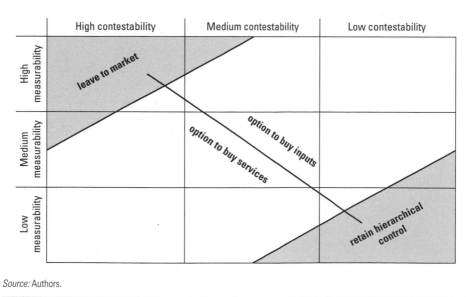

Source: Authors.

- If there is currently no market, consider stimulating demand rather than in-house production.

- If contestability is low and there is no competitive market, consider using benchmark purchasing (based on estimated reference costs) so that suppliers have to compete *for* rather than *in* the market.

- If there is a market, but it is dysfunctional, consider improving its function through appropriate incentives (strategic subsidies) or regulations (antitrust).

How to Pay

Choose the contractual arrangement most suitable for a given purchase (spot market for unpredictable items, medium-term supply contract for predictable items, franchise arrangements for standardized needs at multiple locations, and relational contract for difficult-to-monitor purchases) (Harding and Preker 2003).

Once a buying decision has been made, all potential producers must be treated alike by creating a level playing field. This includes ensuring that there are no hidden competitive advantages such as tax concessions or access to subsidized capital. And it means ensuring that no unfair competitive advantage is given to any producer through privileged access to information.

POLICY LEVERS AVAILABLE TO GOVERNMENTS

From the previous discussion, it is clear that most goods and services have some degree of market imperfection in terms of reduced contestability and measurability. Governments have at their disposal a variety of instruments that they can use to address these problems. A few of these instruments—from least to most intrusive—include requiring information disclosure, introducing regulations, contracting for services, providing subsidies or direct financing, and beginning public production. These instruments are discussed in this section as make or buy decisions.

Standard Policy Instruments

Factor Markets

For some inputs—the production of consumables, unskilled labor, and the retail of drugs, medical equipment, and consumables—there are few serious market imperfections, such as reduced contestability and low measurability (figure 1.8, upper left corner of matrix). With minimal government intervention, such as good information disclosure and some quality or safety standards, competitive markets are best at producing these inputs. Public production of these inputs usually leads to low quality, lack of innovation, and inefficient production modalities.

The other extreme—training very specialized labor and generating knowledge about rare health conditions and their treatment—is characterized by considerable market imperfections due to reduced contestability and low measurability. A mix of strong regulation and in-house production is often needed to ensure adequate generation of these inputs.

Most other inputs can be bought. However, markets often give the wrong signal about the level (surpluses and shortages), mix, and distribution of these inputs. This is especially true of human resources and the production of pharmaceuticals and medical equipment with a long development or training phase. Skilled use of regulations and contracting mechanisms is therefore needed when purchasing inputs that have moderate contestability and measurability problems.

Large producers may try to severely reduce contestability by erecting strong barriers to entry through protective policies (patents and licensing requirements), benchmarking (manufacturing standards), large sunk cost requirements, collusion, and a high degree of specialization (research and development). For these inputs, stronger policy measures may be needed, such as monopsony purchasing power and long-term contracts.

Despite this complex landscape in goods characteristics, in many areas of reduced contestability and measurability, governments could achieve most equity, efficiency, and quality objectives through regulations and contracting (Herzlinger 1997).

FIGURE 1.8   Policies to Deal with Reduced Contestability and Measurability

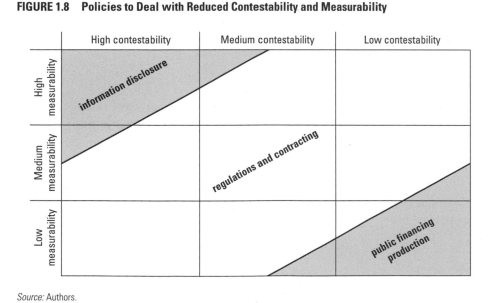

Source: Authors.

Product Markets

As in the case of inputs, the production of interventions and other outputs can be "contracted out" (purchased) and do not in principle have to be produced in-house.

In practice, decisions about which interventions to make in-house and which to contract out are complicated by a number of factors. First, for some outputs (e.g., clinical interventions) what is to be delivered is much harder to specify than the inputs. This makes it difficult to manage the resulting contracts and prevent opportunistic behavior by providers (private health insurance is especially vulnerable to opportunistic behavior). Second, contestability is often reduced for the reasons described earlier in our discussion of inputs. Finally, complex health problems often require strategic coordination among different interventions and other outputs (integrated care, continuity of care, appropriate and timely referrals, and the like).

In the case of outputs, policy makers need to examine two critical questions in addition to the degree of contestability and measurability before arriving at good make or buy decisions. Is a strategic coordinated response needed? To what degree do the goods and services benefit from ongoing innovation and adaptability?

For example, nonclinical activities such as custodial services, catering, laundry, and management do not require special strategic coordination. They can usually be unbundled and contracted-out as a standard service to firms that specialize in these activities without too much customization. In contrast, clinical and public health interventions often do need to be coordinated and tailored to the individuals and populations receiving them and the organizations providing them. Experience has shown that unbundling these activities often leads to many problems, such as cost shifting, discontinuity of care, and poor quality (Manning 1998).

Other Often Forgotten Policy Levers

The contestability and measurability of goods and services is not static but influenced by elements of the systemic environment. Government policies directly influence this environment and the "nature of the good," yielding alternative levers to take them closer to (or farther away from) the ability to use the indirect tools of contracting and regulation. These alternative levers include the following:

- *Governance*—relationship between owner (governments) and health care organizations

- *Market environment*—competition in or for goods and services markets

- *Purchasing mechanisms*—funding or payment arrangements for the goods or services.

These three factors exert a powerful influence on the nature of the goods and hence on the ability to ensure delivery through indirect mechanisms. In the next three sections, notice how these factors combine to determine the level of contestability in the market or measurability of a good. This includes a discussion of which instruments are effective in dealing with the related market and government failures.

Governance and Internal Incentive Regime

Changes made in *governance*—the relationship between government and organizations—influence the goods characteristics of the health care goods and services in question. This relationship can be modified substantially in five different dimensions: (1) the *decision rights* given managers, (2) the *residual claimant* status, (3) the degree of *market exposure*, (4) *accountability arrangements*, and (5) adequacy of *subsidies* to cover social functions.[24]

Contestability may be enhanced by the following actions:

- Unbundling large bureaucratic structures (modification in governance)

- Outsourcing other functions to specialized providers (modification in payment system)

- Leveling the playing field by exposing all the actors to the same potential benefits and losses due to market exposure (modification of payment system)

- Decreasing barriers to entry due to political interference or unwarranted trust in public production (modification in market structure)

- Explicitly separating contestable commercial functions and noncommercial social objectives (modification in governance and stewardship).

Measurability may be enhanced by the following procedures:

- Relying on quantifiable results (output or outcome measures) for accountability and performance targets rather than process (inputs and bureaucratic procedures, modification in governance and payment system)

- Shifting from difficult-to-define, long-term relationships (employment or service arrangements) to shorter term, more specific contractual arrangements (modification in payment system)

- Using quantifiable monetary incentives instead of more-difficult-to-track nonmonetary incentive payments, such as ethics, ethos, and status (modification in payment system)

- Tightening reporting, monitoring, and accountability mechanisms (modification in governance and payment system).

For example, by removing restrictive government monopolies from vaccination services (governance/market), such programs could be shifted into a Type II or even Type I position. It is easy to measure the number of children vaccinated, who contracts a given disease, and entry barriers for firms that want to provide vaccination services on behalf of the government. Similar action applied to other services could shift many away from the lower right corner of the grid toward the upper left corner (figure 1.9).

Likewise, tertiary and quaternary care provided in university hospitals could be shifted from a low-contestability/measurability grid to a medium-contestability/measurability position through better information on outcome, policies that favor clearly defined contracts, performance benchmarks, and a tightening of reporting, monitoring, and accountability mechanisms. The same would be true for public health services and activities, such as vaccination, that are often part of the responsibilities of ambulatory care providers.

Several factors may also alter the goods characteristics of pharmaceuticals, medical equipment, and consumable supplies. As recently as 10 years ago, development costs, patent protection, and a small market share may have made highly specialized medical equipment or drugs (Type III goods) very expensive. Today, they may behave like ordinary goods (Type II or Type I). Examples include the quick production of generic drugs by many companies once patent protection expires or the rapid increase in use of sigmoidoscopes and transcutaneous surgical instruments once the technology was no longer new and prices dropped.

This shift in goods characteristics is not a one-way street. The goods properties can also become less contestable and more difficult to measure. Organizational

FIGURE 1.9   The Nature of Health Care Goods Based on Organizational Economics

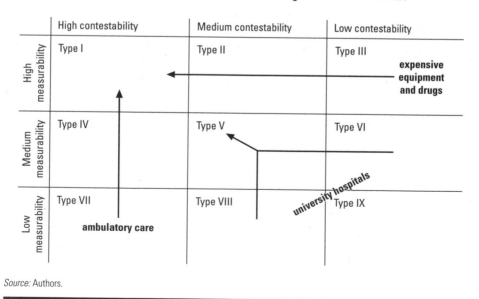

Source: Authors.

reforms do not always lead to increased decision rights, residual claimant status, market exposure, accountability arrangements, and explicit subsidies to cover social functions. In fact, during the past 50 years, many national health systems deliberately shifted goods and services in the opposite direction by nationalizing ownership and production.

And market imperfections may contribute to entry barriers instead of lowering them. Doctors, dentists, and pharmacists can and do collude to restrict entry by potential competitors. Hospitals have a natural monopoly for their services for patients living nearby and can create monopoly power through relations with other hospitals and referring doctors. Medical equipment distributors with licensing agreements for the top international companies can easily monopolize a domestic market. Pharmaceutical retailers can control their mark-up by forming professional cartels. The public and nongovernmental sectors have a competitive advantage over the private sector due to their access to subsidized or free capital from domestic and foreign donors.

Market Environment

A central argument in favor of exposing providers to market forces is that, in a functioning market, competitive forces will lead to a more efficient allocation of resources than a command economy or nonmarket solutions. The structure of the market to which organizations are exposed, therefore, has a critical influence on their behavior. It may directly determine what strategies make sense to generate more revenue.

Policies that influence the competitive environment through regulations or contracting can significantly alter the contestability of health care goods and services. Similarly, information asymmetry can be reduced by policies that increase the availability of good information on health services, enhance health care providers' institutional capacity to deal with such information, and improve patients' understanding about health problems.

Such policies not only address some of the underlying contestability and measurability problems, but they also shift both the contestability/measurability grid and the boundaries of needed government intervention to ensure favorable outcomes (figure 1.10). Conversely, in a less competitive environment, with weak policies and data to overcome information asymmetry, the grid for services that fall into the upper left corner (Type I, Type II, and Type IV) may contract, with the grid in the lower right corner (Type VI, Type VIII, and Type IX) expanding.

Market Imperfections in Service Delivery

There are two related problems in the market structure of service delivery in most segments of the health sector. First, little or no competition may emerge—reducing pressures on the provider to deliver "value for money" to maximize profits. Alternatively (or in addition), competition may emerge, but it may be dysfunctional. Both cases are discussed in this section.

FIGURE 1.10   Shifting the Contestability/Measurability Grid and Needed Public Policies

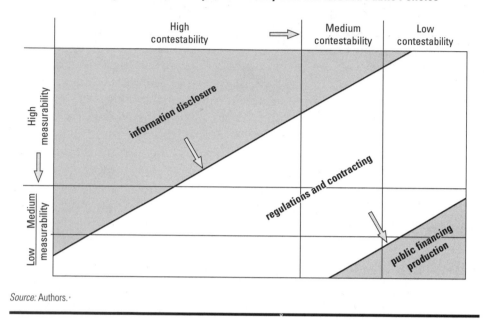

Source: Authors.

Some health services, especially tertiary and quaternary, exhibit scale econo-mies in production. This relieves incumbent hospitals from pressure from new entrants. Geographic monopoly over certain services may leave buyers very little leverage to negotiate with service providers. There are many examples of strong collusion among medical doctors that creates a virtual monopoly, thereby shift-ing the grid for ambulatory medical care toward the left—and strengthening the need for direct provision or other policy intervention. Public monopolies and policies that prevent public funds from being used to contract services from the private sector have the same negative effect on contestability.

Even for services where monopoly power is not an issue, providers may still capture market share or maximize profits through various forms of distortion-ary behavior (figure 1.11). In a competitive market, firms seek to maximize their profits—and use *any method that makes sense in that environment*. In a healthy market environment, they will try to capture market share from their competi-tors by better pleasing customers, maximize profits by reducing costs through efficiency gains, and expand their product lines through imitation or innovation. Wherever possible, however, they will seek to exploit or construct advantages. Where this is possible, the pressures for efficiency and quality generated by the market may be weak.

Such distortionary features of health service markets often enable providers to: (1) counter the bargaining power of suppliers, patients, or purchasers; (2) ward off threats posed by new entrants and imitation products; and (3) control a large share of the relevant market. Information asymmetry in the health sector

FIGURE 1.11   Market Forces that Influence Competition

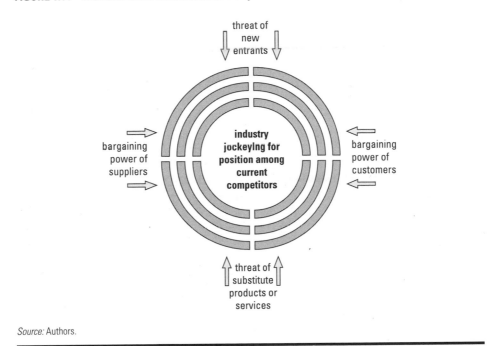

Source: Authors.

exacerbates these problems. For example, medical treatment is largely a bundled good, where the seller (doctor) guides patients' consumption decisions—which hospital to go to for surgery, which lab to use for diagnostic services, and so on. Thus, providers can parley their information advantage into control over a rigid and lucrative referral chain. Doctors may "forward integrate" into diagnostic labs or pharmacies and steer their patients toward consumption where they have a financial stake. Hospitals may "backward integrate" by creating strong links with doctors, thereby cornering part of the market where they experience little or no competitive pressure. Medical professionals are frequently able to create cartels, limiting competitive pressures that strengthen the influence of patients and purchasers.

Since patients and payers know less than providers about the true value or cost of health services, providers can cream skim, selecting patients who cost less to treat than other patients. Thus, providers can increase their profits, not by delivering better service to capture market share or cutting costs but by choosing more profitable patients.

Most of these market imperfections in service delivery can be corrected through appropriate regulations and contracting arrangements. A few examples illustrate this point. Equal access to capital and antitrust legislation—limiting the power of professional cartels—can significantly decrease the entry barriers for some segments of the health care market, especially for clinical services that fall in the middle band of the contestability/measurability grid. The same would be true for contracting practices that are open to both public and private providers and that leave open possibilities for choosing alternative providers or exercising "exit" strategies. In other instances, supplier cartels, combined with low quality-control standards, shift such activities as retail sale and distribution of pharmaceuticals and medical equipment into the lower right corner, even though such activities belong in the upper left area of high contestability and measurability.

Market Imperfections of Private Health Insurance

Even if private health insurance is contestable, due to severe information asymmetry, such services are often deliberately crowded out for strategic reasons by restrictive policies and public financing. This topic is beyond the scope of discussion in this paper but is discussed in detail elsewhere and briefly in box 1.4.

Purchasing Mechanisms

Finally, provider payment systems also influence goods properties by interacting with three of the five key elements of the internal incentive regime of health care organizations: distribution of residual claims, market exposure, and provision for social functions. Service providers, in particular, respond differently to alternative funding and payment mechanisms. For example, collective purchasing by a strategic social health insurance fund in Germany sends a different set of signals to providers than regulated competition in the United States, consumer-driven demand through out-of-pocket payments in India, medical savings accounts in Singapore, and monopsonistic purchasing in the United Kingdom.

Although reforms in governance may endow an organization with formal claims to residual revenue in different categories, the structure of the payments system will directly determine whether this claim has any real meaning or incentive effect. If, for example, services must be delivered at prices below cost, there will be no residual to claim. Thus, the relation of costs to the price-setting and capital-charging formula in the payments system is a critical determinant of the incentives of the model. The crucial factor is whether marginal cost-saving efforts by the provider can generate revenue flows that the provider can keep without deterioration in quality or effectiveness.

When reforms in organizations such as hospitals entail a shift in revenue earning by delivering services "in a market," what kind of market emerges becomes a crucial issue. Often, government is the largest or only buyer. In this case, the process and terms on which the government purchaser engages the provider may well determine the degree of pressure on the provider to "deliver the goods."

To gain maximum benefits from reforms that expose the public sector to competition with the private sector, it is crucial that adequate steps are taken to secure competitive neutrality. Two sets of policies must be built into provider payment systems to achieve competitive neutrality:

BOX 1.4   MARKET IMPERFECTIONS IN PRIVATE HEALTH INSURANCE

Private voluntary health insurance is particularly prone to market imperfections, many of them related to information asymmetries.

Insurance may succeed in protecting some people against selected risks, but it usually fails to cover everyone who wants to subscribe to insurance plans and often excludes individuals who need health insurance the most or who are at greatest risk of illness. This happens because insurers have a strong incentive to enroll only healthy or low-cost clients *(risk selection* or *cream skimming).* Private insurers also have incentives to exclude costly conditions or to minimize their financial risk by using benefit caps and exclusions. This limits protection against expensive/catastrophic illnesses.

Because of these factors, individuals who know they are at risk of illness have a strong incentive to conceal their underlying medical condition *(adverse selection).* Individuals who are—or think they are—healthy will often try to pay as low premiums as possible. This prevents insurers from raising the funds needed to cover the expenses incurred by sicker or riskier members. Worse, the healthy may even deliberately underinsure themselves in the hope that free or highly subsidized care will be available when they become ill *(free-riding).* When third-party insurers pay, both patients and providers have less incentive to be concerned about costs, and some may become careless about maintaining good health. This leads not only to more care being used (the reason for insurance), but also to less effective care, or care that would not be needed if people maintained good health *(moral hazard).*

Source: Musgrove 1996.

- Moneterization of social functions, such as explicit subsidies that cover the cost plus a reasonable margin in delivering services to nonpaying or uninsured patients

- Leveling of the playing field through standardization of the fee structure and cost of capital for both the public and private sectors.

GETTING FROM HERE TO THERE

This chapter presents a strong argument for a continued and even an enhanced role for the state in providing strong sectoral *stewardship* and securing equitable and sustainable financing for the health sector. But it challenges the principles and nature of public intervention pursued by many governments, especially in the area of the public production of health services.

Many countries today have large, inefficient public sectors producing goods and services that could be bought from nongovernmental providers. Moving from one system to another will not be easy (figure 1.12). It will take time and

FIGURE 1.12   Appropriate Role of Government

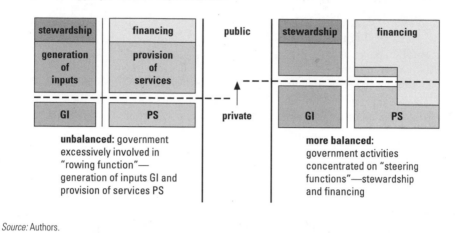

Source: Authors.

must be accompanied by capacity building in such areas as contracting, regulation, and coordination of nongovernmental providers.

A three-step process can be used to move gradually from one balance to another in the public-private mix in service delivery. First, when there is already a large private sector, the public sector can begin by recognizing its existence and slowly increase use of these resources through better coordination, contracts, and a positive regulatory environment.

Once some learning has taken place in coordinating and contracting with existing providers, the positive lessons from this experience can be transferred to other priority areas where nongovernmental providers may not yet be active. Finally, in some cases where the public sector is clearly engaged in inefficient activities, such as public production of many inputs, these can be converted through outright privatization and subsequently bought from the private sector (Harding and Preker 2003).

At the same time, the public sector may not be involved in areas of strategic importance, such as securing financial protection against the cost of illness through nongovernmental sources of financing and failing to provide critical sectoral oversight in terms of its stewardship function. Parallel to moving out of the area of production of goods and services, a strong argument can be made for a more integrated approach and greater public sector involvement in sectoral coordination, regulation, monitoring, and evaluation.

NOTES

The authors are grateful for comments provided on earlier drafts of this chapter by Navin Girishankar, Charles Griffin, Philip Musgrove, George Schieber, and Adam Wagstaff.

This chapter was previously published as a chapter in *Recent Health Policy Innovations in Social Security*, ed. A. Ron and X. Scheil-Adlung, International Social Security Series, vol. 5, London: Transaction Publishers, 2001, pp. 209–52; presented at the Senior Policy Seminar on China's Health Sector Reform and Development Strategies, Beijing, June 22–24, 2000; and presented at the British Columbia Medical Association Forum on "Medicare—Sustainability and Accountability in the 21st Century," Vancouver, BC, Canada, May 11–12, 2000.

1. Flexibility and rigidity; access and privacy; animal experiment and animal welfare; medicine and alternative medicine; science and compassion; acute and chronic sector; hospital or community; treatment or prevention; science or compassion; access and privacy.

2. Papyri are ancient Egyptian clay tablets (Mason and McCall Smith 1987:4), quoting Castiglioni (1947).

3. In this famous cuneiform legal code of the first Babylonian Dynasty, 9 of its 282 statutes relate to the services of healers. Statutes 215–17 and 221–23 deal with laws governing the fees to be received for certain services; statutes 218–20 deal with penalties to be inflicted on the healer in the case of unsatisfactory therapeutic results and death (Chapman 1984: 4–5).

4. Control of membership and secrecy, reflected in the Hippocratic Oath, was characteristic of all trades (British Medical Association 1984: 6).

5. Today, the United States, Mexico, and Turkey are three exceptions in the Organisation for Economic Co-operation and Development (OECD) where universal access has not yet been secured. For a review of the introduction of universality in the OECD, see Preker (1989).

6. For a comprehensive discussion, see Evans (1984). The classics include Bator (1958 351–79), Atkinson and Stiglitz (1980), and Musgrave and Musgrave (1984).

7. For a more comprehensive discussion, see Barer et al. (1998) and van Doorslaer, Wagstaff, and Rutten (1993). The classical reference is Arrow (1963: 940–73).

8. For a comprehensive review, see Young (1986) and Vickers and Yarrow (1992).

9. One of the first proposals for this approach was published by Enthoven (1978: 650–58 and 1988: 709–20).

10. For a review of the health care problems in the former socialist states see Preker and Feachem (1996).

11. Most health economists—even those favoring a more competitive marketplace—recognize that government needs to play a significant role in the health sector. For an excellent recent review on this topic see Rice (1998). For a more detailed discussion on the theory and empirical evidence of public and private roles in health care financing, see Musgrove (1996) and Schieber (1996).

12. Much of this discussion is not new but firmly rooted in political and moral philosophy. See Arrow (1980).

13. Although there are no technical limits, few countries like Switzerland use plebiscites, and only for major issues of national interest. Even then, it is an imperfect instrument due to low voter turnout.

14. Four interrelated causes have been identified that explain this observation (Vining and Weimer 1990: 15). First, direct democracy usually prevents the overseer from knowing the preferences of society. Second, overseers (representatives) typically pay more

attention to constituencies and sensational issues that are most likely to be influential in their reelection. Third, public officials usually have more than one overseer, often leading to conflicting and unstable political demands. Finally, since overseers themselves do not fully benefit from the effectiveness of their oversight, they often devote inadequate time and effort to this task, leaving bureaucrats with a large range of independence.

15. This conceptual framework was developed by Moore (1995).

16. This is discussed further in a later section under agency problems (Beauchamp and Childress 1983: 4; Lemmon 1962).

17. See theoretical section for a more complete discussion of the principal–agent concepts (Bennett, McPake, and Mills 1997).

18. Two useful references include Williamson (1985 and 1989).

19. For example, a person may own a house but not have the right to occupy it if he has leased it out. He may own a car but not have the right to transfer it freely if he has a loan secured by the car.

20. For a critique of this theory, see W.G. Shepherd (1995, 1984).

21. An asset is specific if it makes a much larger contribution to the production of a good than its value in alternative uses (Klein, Crawford, and Alchian 1978: 297–326).

22. Adapted from Manning (1998).

23. In other parts of the public sector, such autonomous and corporatized units are also variously referred to as public or executive agencies, independent public organizations, quasi-autonomous nongovernmental organizations, and state-owned enterprises. There is no standard functional distinction between these different organizational modalities.

24. See Harding and Preker (2003).

REFERENCES

Arrow, K. J. 1980. *Arrow's Theorem: The Paradox of Social Choice.* New Haven, CT: Yale University Press.

———. 1963. "Uncertainty and the Welfare Economics of Medical Care." *American Economic Review* 53(5): 940–73.

Atkinson, A. B., and J. E. Stiglitz. 1980. *Lectures on Public Economics.* Maidenhead, Berkshire, UK: McGraw-Hill.

Barer, M. L. Morris, T. E. Getzen, and G. L. Stoddart, eds. 1998. *Health, Health Care and Health Economics: Perspectives on Distribution.* Chichester, West Sussex, U.K.: John Wiley & Sons.

Barr, N., ed. 1994. *Labor Markets and Social Policy in Central and Eastern Europe.* Oxford, U.K.: World Bank/Oxford University Press.

Bator, F. 1958. "The Anatomy of Market Failure." *Quarterly Journal of Economics* 72(3): 351–79.

Baumol, W. J. 1984. "Toward a Theory of Public Enterprise." *Atlantic Economic Journal* 12(1): 3–20.

Baumol, W. J., J. C. Panzar, and R. D. Willing. 1982. *Contestable Markets and the Theory of Industrial Structure*. New York, NY: Harcourt Brace Jovanovich.

Beauchamp, T. L., and J. F. Childress. 1983. *Principles of Biomedical Ethics*. 2d ed. Oxford: Oxford University Press.

Bennett, S., B. McPake, and A. Mills, eds. 1997. *Private Health Providers in Developing Countries: Serving the Public Interest?* London: Zed Books.

Black, D. 1984. *An Anthology of False Antitheses*. London: Nuffield Provincial Hospital Trust.

British Medical Association (BMA). 1984. *Handbook of Medical Ethics*. London: BMA.

Castiglioni, A. 1947. *A History of Medicine*. Translated and edited by E.B. Krumbhaar, 2d ed. New York, NY: Knopf.

Chapman, Careleton B. 1984. *Physicians, Law, and Ethics*. New York, NY: New York University Press.

Donahue, J. D. 1989. *The Privatization Decision: Public Ends, Private Means*. New York, NY: Basic Books.

Enthoven, A. 1988. *Theory and Practice of Managed Competition in Health Care Finance*. New York, NY: North-Holland.

———. 1978. "Consumer Choice Health Plan." *New England Journal of Medicine* 298(12): 650–58 and 298(13): 709–20.

Evans, R. G. 1984. *Strained Mercy: The Economics of Canadian Health Care*. Toronto: Butterworth.

Fama, E. F. 1980. "Agency Problems and the Theory of the Firm." *Journal of Political Economy* 88(2): 288–307.

Fama, E. F., and M. C. Jensen. 1983. "Agency Problems and Residual Claims." *Journal of Law and Economics* 26(2): 327–49.

Girishankar, N. 1999. *Reforming Institutions for Service Delivery: A Framework for Development Assistance with an Application to the HNP Portfolio*. World Bank Policy Research Working Paper 2039. Washington, DC: World Bank.

Ham, C. 1997. "Priority Setting in Health Care: Learning From International Experience." *Health Policy* 42(1): 49–66.

Harding, A., and A. S. Preker, eds. 2003. *Private Participation Toolkit*. Washington, DC: World Bank.

Herzlinger, R. 1997. *Market Driven Health Care: Who Wins, Who Loses in the Transformation of America's Largest Service Industry*. Reading, MA: Perseus Books.

Hirschman, A. 1970. *Voice and Loyalty: Responses to Decline in Firms, Organizations, and States*. World Bank Health, Nutrition, and Population Sector Strategy. Cambridge, MA: Harvard University Press.

Jensen, M. C., and W. H. Meckling. 1976. "Theory of the Firm: Managerial Behavior, Agency Costs and Ownership Structure." *Journal of Financial Economics* 3: 305–60.

Kaufmann, D., and R. Ryterman. 1998. "Global Corruption Survey." World Bank Working Paper. Washington, DC: World Bank.

Klein, B., R. G. Crawford, and A. A. Alchian. 1978. "Vertical Integration, Appropriable Rents and the Competitive Contracting Process." *Journal of Law and Economics* 21(2): 297–326.

Lemmon, E. J. 1962. "Moral Dilemmas." *Philosophical Review* 71: 139–52.

Manning, N. 1998 "Unbundling the State: Autonomous Agencies and Service Delivery." Draft World Bank Discussion Paper. Washington, DC: World Bank.

Mason, J. K. and R. A. McCall Smith. 1987. *Law and Medical Ethics*. 2d ed. London: Butterworths,. quoting A. Castiglioni, *A History of Medicine*, translated and edited by E. B. Krunbhaar, 2d ed. 1947.

Milgrom, P., and J. Roberts. 1992. *Economics of Organization and Management*. Englewood Cliffs, NJ: Prentice-Hall.

———. 1990. "Bargaining Costs, Influence Costs, and the Organization of Economic Activity." In *Perspectives on Positive Political Economy*, ed. J. Alt and K. Shepsle, 57–89. New York, NY: Cambridge University Press.

Moore, M. 1995. *Creating Public Value*. Boston, MA: Harvard University Press.

Musgrave, R. A., and P. B. Musgrave. 1984. *Public Finance in Theory and Practice*, 4th ed. New York, NY: McGraw-Hill.

Musgrove, P. 1999. "Public Spending on Health Care: How Are Different Criteria Related?" *Health Policy* 47: 207–23.

———. 1996. *Public and Private Roles in Health: Theory and Financing Patterns*. Washington, DC: World Bank.

Olson, M. 1982. *The Rise and Decline of Nations: Economic Growth, Stagflation and Social Rigidities*. New Haven, CT: Yale University Press.

Organisation for Economic Co-operation and Development (OECD). 1992. *Regulatory Reform, Privatisation and Competition Policy*. Paris: OECD.

Osborne, D., and T. Gaebler. 1993. *Reinventing Government*. New York, NY: Plume.

Peacock, A. 1980. "On the Anatomy of Collective Failure." *Public Finance* 35(1): 33–43.

Preker, A. S. 1989. *The Introduction of Universality in Health Care*. London: International Institute of Health Studies.

Preker, A. S., and R. G. A. Feachem. 1996. *Market Mechanisms and the Health Sector in Central and Eastern Europe*. Technical Paper Series, No. 293. Washington, DC: World Bank. (Translated into Czech, Hungarian, Polish, Romanian, and Russian.)

Preker, A. S., and A. Harding, eds. 2003. *Innovations in Health Service Delivery: The Corporatization of Public Hospitals*. Health, Nutrition, and Population Series. Washington, DC: World Bank.

Rice, T. 1998. *The Economics of Health Reconsidered*. Chicago, IL: Health Administration Press.

Robinson, J. 1997. "Physician-Hospital Integration and Economic Theory of the Firm." *Medical Care Research and Review* 54(1): 3–24.

Saltman, R., and J. Figueras, eds. 1997. *European Health Care Reform: Analysis of Current Strategies*. Copenhagen: World Health Organization.

Sappington, D. E. 1991. "Incentives in Principal-Agent Relationships." *Journal of Economic Perspectives* 5(2): 45–66.

Schieber, G., ed. 1997. *Innovations in Health Care Financing*. Washington, DC: World Bank.

Shepherd, W. G. 1995. "Contestability vs. Competition—Once More." *Land Economics* 71(3): 299–309.

———. 1984. "Contestability vs. Competition." *American Economic Review* 74(4): 572–87.

United Nations Children's Fund (UNICEF). 1999. *State of the World's Children.* New York, NY: UNICEF.

van Doorslaer, E., A. Wagstaff, and F. Rutten, eds. 1993. *Equity in the Finance and Delivery of Health Care: An International Perspective.* Oxford: Oxford Medical Publications.

Vickers, J. S., and G. K. Yarrow. 1992. *Privatization: An Economic Analysis.* Cambridge, MA: MIT Press.

Vining, A. R., and D. L. Weimer. 1990. "Government Supply and Government Production Failure: A Framework Based on Contestability." *Journal of Public Policy* 10(1): 1–22.

Weimer, D. L., and A. R. Vining. 1989. *Policy Analysis: Concept and Practice.* Englewood Cliffs, NJ: Prentice Hall.

Williamson, O. 1991. "Comparative Economic Organization: The Analysis of Discrete Structural Alternatives." *Administrative Science Quarterly* 36: 69–296.

———. 1989. "Transaction Cost Economics." In *Handbook of Industrial Organization,* R. Schmalensee and R. Willig, eds., New York, NY: North-Holland.

———. 1985. *The Economic Institutions of Capitalism: Firms, Markets and Relational Contracting.* New York, NY: Free Press.

Wilson, J. Q. 1989. *Bureaucracy.* New York, NY: Basic Books.

Wolf, C. J. 1979. "A Theory of Non-Market Failure." *Journal of Law and Economics* 22(1): 107–39.

World Bank. 1997. *1997 World Development Report: The State in a Changing World.* New York, NY: Oxford University Press.

———. 1996. "Investing in People and Growth." In *1996 World Development Report: From Plan to Market.* New York, NY: Oxford University Press.

———. 1993. *1993 World Development Report: Investing in Health.* New York, NY: Oxford University Press.

World Health Organization (WHO). 2000. *The World Health Report 2000: Improving Health Systems Performance.* Geneva: WHO.

———. 1999. *World Health Report.* Geneva: WHO.

———. 1997. *Sector Strategy: Health, Nutrition, and Population.* Washington, DC: World Bank.

———. 1996. *European Health Care Reforms: Analysis of Current Strategies.* Series No. 72. Copenhagen: WHO Regional Office for Europe.

Young, P. 1986. *Privatization Around the Globe: Lessons from the Reagan Administration.* Houston: National Center for Policy Analysis.

CHAPTER 2

Policy Design in Strategic Purchasing

Alexander S. Preker, John C. Langenbrunner, and Paolo C. Belli

Some major problems in the way resource allocation is carried out today are reviewed in this chapter, together with options for reform of the underlying policy framework for purchasing health care in the future. The authors emphasize the importance of addressing design flaws under each of the main health financing subfunctions—revenue collection, risk pooling, and spending of resources (Preker and Langenbrunner 2005).

This chapter expands on the economic underpinnings of the policy design of strategic purchasing in the health sector as described in table I.1 of the Introduction to this volume:

Policy design	Resource allocation and purchasing arrangement
	For whom to buy—members, poor, sick, other?
	What to buy, in which form, and what to exclude?
	From whom to buy—public, private, nongovernmental organization?
	How much to pay—competitive market price, set prices, subsidized?
	How to pay—what payment mechanisms to use?
	Underlying revenue collection mechanisms
	Level of prepayment (full versus partial with some copayment or cost sharing)
	Degree of progressivity (high versus flat rate)
	Earmarking (general versus targeted contributions)
	Choice (mandatory versus voluntary)
	Enrollment (unrestricted versus restrictions in eligibility, waiting periods, and switching)
	Underlying pooling of revenues and sharing risks
	Size (small versus large)
	Number (one versus many)
	Risk equalization (from rich to poor, healthy to sick, and gainfully employed to inactive)
	Coverage (primary versus supplementary, substitutive, or duplicative)
	Risk rating (group or community rating versus individual)

A well-designed purchasing arrangement can fail if the underlying revenue collection and pooling functions are weak. The authors look at the underlying economics of five major design questions: for whom to buy, what to buy, from whom to buy, how much to pay, and how to pay. Subsidies and copayments distort the supply and demand curves. When government fee schedules and pricing differ significantly from the equilibrium price that would have been achieved in a normal competitive market, major distortions can occur that may lead patients to seek care outside the publicly mandated purchasing arrangements. The authors conclude that suboptimal outcomes are often observed at the two extremes—between an unregulated market in purchasing and that which occurs when public interventions become too heavy-handed.

INTRODUCTION

The potential benefits of collective financing arrangements are often not fully exploited because of a number of weaknesses in the policy design of the purchasing arrangement, flaws due to agency problems, and information asymmetry. Four specific areas are described.

Unsatisfied needs and demand with a failure to protect the poor. Purchasing arrangements often ignore the needs, expectations, and resource constraints of individuals and households. When there are subsidies and a third-party payment mechanism, demand by patients is almost always an imperfect indicator of need, and willingness or ability to pay. Copayments, informal charges, and nonmonetary costs further distort demand. Distortions in matching need and demand often lead to large inequalities across income, age, gender, ethnic groups, and geographic regions.

Supplier-induced demand, public sector monopolies, and insensitive supply. Third-party payment mechanisms and subsidy schemes lead to supplier-induced demand. If quality can be maintained, public sector monopolies often crowd out private sector production. And rationing policies may make suppliers insensitive to demand. In this context it becomes difficult for purchasing arrangements to select the best value for the money or to discipline suppliers through performance contracts.

Price fixing and conflicting incentive regimes. Often the payment mechanism and prices used to reimburse services send adverse and conflicting messages to providers about available resources, the need to target specific populations, such as the poor, and priority areas of intervention. Mixed messages make a level playing field between public and private providers impossible. Instead of supporting the policy directions set by resource constraints, poverty objectives, knowledge about the effectiveness and cost of different interventions, and the comparative strength of different providers, the payment mechanism used often establishes a policy environment that is exactly opposite the one desired.

Market context. Problems with competition, clearing of market, often mean that the market is disfunctional.

KEY POLICY DESIGN ISSUES

To spend scarce resources wisely, countries trying to introduce strategic purchasing need to address several issues and constraints in the collection of revenues, financial risk management, and spending of resources on providers (Preker and Langenbrunner 2005). They include the following:

- *For whom to buy*—lack of good data on beneficiaries (limiting ability to identify vulnerable groups)

- *What to buy*—lack of good data on cost effectiveness (limiting ability to obtain value for money spent)

- *From whom to buy*—ambulatory sector dominated by private providers and inpatient sector dominated by public hospitals (limiting the choice of providers)

- *How much to pay*—lack of good cost data (limiting transparency of prices charged by both public and private providers).

- *How to pay*—weak management and institutional capacity (limiting sophistication of performance-based payment systems that can be used)

The efficiency and equity with which purchasers spend money on health care providers also depends on several critical factors and constraints related to revenue collection and risk sharing in addition to the resource allocation and purchasing (RAP) function itself. They include the following:

- *Enrollment*—incomplete population registry (limiting the ability to identify potential members)

- *Choice*—large informal sector (limiting the segment of the population that can be forced to join under a mandatory scheme; others have to be induced to join)

- *Prepayment*—low formal sector labor participation rates (limiting the contributions that can be collected at source under a mandatory scheme from employees); lack of familiarity with insurance and risk-averse behavior (limiting willingness to pay); large share of population with low-income jobs or below the poverty level with competing demands for scarce household income (limiting ability to pay)

- *Progressivity*—lack of accurate income data (limiting information that can be used to construct progressive payment schedules).

Finally, the efficiency and equity with which purchasers spend money on health care providers also depend on several critical factors and constraints related to risk management. They include the following:

- *Size and number of risk pools*—spontaneous growth of many small funds (limiting size and increasing the number of voluntary pools); social diversity in terms of employment, domicile, and other local social factors (limiting size and increasing the number of voluntary pools); lack of trust in government or national programs (limiting size and number of mandatory pools); weak management and institutional capacity (limiting the size and number of mandatory pools)

- *Risk equalization*—small share of available fiscal space allocated to health sector (limiting public resources available for subsidizing inactive population groups); lack of national social solidarity (limiting willingness to cross-subsidize from rich to poor, from healthy to sick, and from gainfully employed to inactive)

- *Coverage*—presence of national health scheme for general public (limiting the need for universal population coverage or comprehensive benefit coverage through insurance).

OPTIONS FOR REFORMING THE POLICY DESIGN

Policy makers trying to improve the efficiency and effectiveness of health care spending face a wide range of choices that mirror the problems described above in the underlying policy framework related to demand for the services they purchase and their supply and equilibrium price. Even in highly planned health care systems, consumer demand and market forces play a large role in resource allocation and purchasing (Preker and Feachem 1996; Preker and Harding 2000; and Jakab, Preker, and Harding 2002).

Demand (For Whom to Buy?)

Core Policy Question 1: For Whom to Buy?

In a perfect principal–agent scenario, there would be an exact match between the needs, demand, and utilization of health services by individuals and households, and the demand for the same services obtained under purchasing arrangements that act as their agents. Achieving an exact match between the demand for health services through a purchaser is not the same as demand for health services by individuals without insurance or collective purchasing for several reasons:

- Simultaneous role of a purchaser as multiplicitous agents for several principals

- Individuals and households (e.g., health needs, expectations, cultural norms, revealed preferences)

- Financing (e.g., price, insurance mechanisms, willingness and ability to pay, subsidies, hidden costs)

- Health services (e.g., access, range of services, continuity of care, quality, supplier-induced demand).

In some contexts, overall demand for health services may be low due to a lack of understanding by individuals of their own health needs and the available range of effective interventions. Such information asymmetry may be compounded by cultural norms that influence personal preferences. But overall low demand for health services by individuals should not be confused with low utilization of services provided under formal purchasing arrangements when policy makers and purchasers are behaving as imperfect agents for the citizens and consumers they are supposed to represent.

When utilization patterns are low under purchasing arrangements, a look at demand for services from private providers outside these formal channels can be instructive. Often this reveals that services provided under purchasing arrangements focus on benefits with large externalities (public health interventions for which individual demand is lower) for which there is little or no individual demand while some personal health services for which demand is considerable are excluded. The demand curve may be further distorted by copayments or informal charges. And it may be altered by hidden nonmonetary costs such as waiting time, restrictions in access, narrow range of services, and poor consumer quality. Figure 2.1 illustrates shifts in the demand curve under different resource allocation and purchasing arrangements.

In other contexts overall demand may be high due to cultural norms that influence personal preferences (box 2.1). But it may also be high because price signals are removed through prepayment and subsidies or because the type of reimbursement system used—such as fee-for-service payment—encourages providers to stimulate unnecessary consumption. This may result in consumption

Figure 2.1   Shifts in the Demand Curve under Different RAP Arrangements

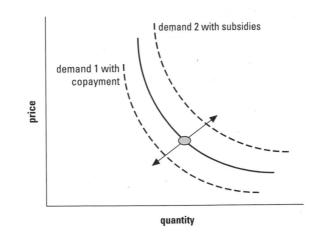

Source: Authors.

BOX 2.1   FOR WHOM TO BUY?

Demand may vary considerably across population groups and not reflect the needs of vulnerable or marginal populations. Typically, demand is lower among precisely the populations that may need health services the most such as the impoverished, women during their reproductive years, and children. If left unaddressed, such variations may undermine the equity and efficiency objectives that the collective financing arrangements were supposed to address in the first place.

Policy makers have choices when deciding which target populations benefit from the public funds channeled through collective financing mechanisms under different types of purchasing arrangements. They can design purchasing arrangements that address inequities and social exclusion, or they can ignore these issues and make them even worse.

Policy makers who undertake active and ongoing assessments of the various dimensions of needs, demand, and utilization patterns—including benefit incidence studies—are more likely to have purchasing arrangements that favor poor and vulnerable individuals, households, and populations. Those that blindly rely on historical budgets often allow large discrepancies to develop between utilization of health services in the informal sector (reflecting unmet demand) and use mediated through purchasing arrangements. Purchasing arrangements designed to actively detect and deal with such discrepancies are more likely to be effective agents for the populations they serve.

---

patterns that outstrip the resources mobilized through prepayment systems and channeled through the formal purchasing arrangement.

Supply (What and from Whom to Buy?)

Core Policy Question 2: What to Buy, in Which Form, and What to Exclude?

In a perfect market with complete information and competition, the supply of services would reflect willingness and ability to pay as expressed through consumer demand. When financing is mediated through purchasing arrangements, the extent to which the supply of services reflects such an equilibrium will depend on a variety of factors that shift supply in different directions (box 2.2). The supply of health services under purchasing arrangements may likewise vary depending on a number of factors besides demand:

- Input markets (labor, supplies, capital)

- Product markets (hospitals, ambulatory care, diagnostic services, allied services)

- Entry barriers (specialization)

- Threat of imitation and substitution.

BOX 2.2   WHAT TO BUY, IN WHICH FORM, AND WHAT TO EXCLUDE?

What to buy using public funds? Musgrove (1996, 1999) provides a decision tree for rational use of public financing in the health sector. It starts with the over-arching issue of allocative efficiency by asking if the proposed expenditure is for public goods, generally population-based services. If the answer is "yes," the next step is to rank such expenditures in terms of cost-effectiveness—or even better, benefit-cost analysis—to decide which will be funded. If proposed expenditures do not meet public goods criteria, the tree asks whether signifi-cant externalities are involved, whether risk of catastrophic costs is involved, and whether the proposed beneficiaries are poor. Thus, allocative efficiency, risk, equity, and cost-effectiveness interact to determine public financing deci-sions in health. Economic principles govern each decision point, but many other factors are often weighed, so the outcomes will vary considerably from country to country. The overriding principle is to maximize the potential impact on people, especially the poor.

In which form? Purchasing arrangements may allocate resources or spread purchases across a complex continuum. At the lower end of complexity, resources may be spent on suppliers of inputs such as pharmaceuticals, equip-ment, materials, or labor. Moving up the ladder, they may be spent on suppli-ers of specific interventions such as vaccinations or diagnostic services. At a higher level of complexity, they may be spent on suppliers that offer multiple services such as integrated ambulatory and inpatient care. At the highest level of complexity, resources may be spent on suppliers that try to maximize out-comes such as a reduction in morbidity or mortality. Purchasing arrangements that designate specialized suppliers of the specific items and services desired are more likely to get good value for money than those that blindly follow histori-cal patterns of resource allocation.

If the unit desired is periodic blood pressure checks—a low-complexity intervention—providers do not have to coordinate. Individual doctors, nurses, medical aids, and others are all able providers. If the unit of purchase is reduc-tion in morbidity due to cardiovascular disease, however, the range of providers able to deliver that service would change dramatically. Integrated provision of such care often requires a much greater range of services and complex coordi-nation of networks of doctors, ambulatory care centers, lab and imaging facili-ties, and hospitals as well as public health services that can handle outreach and health promotion activities. The purchasing arrangement would no longer want to identify individual doctors or nurses as eligible providers but rather complex networks of provider organizations already operating in coordination. Although integrated population interventions would be the most effective way to provide health services, this means is extremely demanding organizationally and institutionally for both purchasers and providers.

(continued)

BOX 2.2   *(continued)*

Although improving overall health status would be the most desirable unit to focus on, most purchasing arrangements do not have direct control over the nonhealth sector determinants such as education, income, and housing that affect such outcomes. Output proxies are therefore usually used instead.

What to exclude? In most countries, purchasing arrangements exclude certain services from the benefits package. This often occurs through: *low-end truncation* by introducing copayments or excluding high-frequency low-cost interventions from the publicly financed package such as dental care, drugs, eye glasses, hearing aids, allied health services; *high-end truncation* by excluding low-frequency high-cost interventions such as high-technological diagnostic services; *elimination of ineffective care* such as alternate therapies and unproven interventions; and *random quality deterioration* by not making any explicit decision but allowing the quality to slowly erode over time.

As in the case of demand, the supply curve may shift due to factors related to the purchasing arrangement used (figure 2.2). Under third-party payment mechanisms and subsidies, providers often stimulate demand and production. Conversely, public production and rationing policies may crowd out and reduce supply. This may occur as a result of deliberate attempts to control input markets by, for example, putting caps on the number of doctors and nurses being trained, limiting formularies for pharmaceuticals, and restricting the introduction of new technology. Or it may result from restrictions on the number of beds or doctors working in urban areas, both enforced through certification requirements. In both cases, service providers become insensitive to demand and prices as signals of consumer preferences.

In other contexts, deliberate attempts may be made to reduce the price and increase the supply of services with large externalities such as vaccinations or maternal and child services or services that benefit the poor, in the hope of stimulating consumption. Following this logic many governments have built up a large capital stock of public clinics and hospitals in an attempt to reach rural and vulnerable urban populations. The success of such strategies is limited unless accompanied by parallel social marketing strategies to increase demand for these services whose benefits consumers do not feel directly and immediately.

When public policy and purchasing arrangements try to restrict supply for which there is an underlying demand, such services often become available in the informal sector in response to individual preferences and household demand. Bypassing collective purchasing arrangements in this way exposes patients to prices at whatever the market will bear and financial risk at the time of catastrophic illness.

Figure 2.2   Shifts in the Supply Curve under Different RAP Arrangements

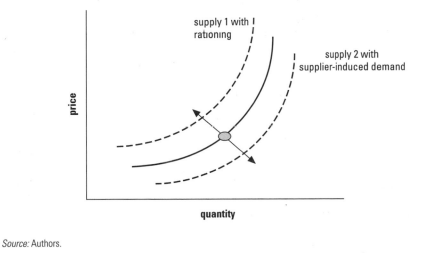

Source: Authors.

Price and Incentive Regime (How Much to Pay?)

Core Policy Question 3: What Price to Charge and How to Pay?

In a perfect market, where patients express their willingness and ability to pay through consumer demand and where suppliers compete in a full market, prices are the equilibrium point between the expressed demand and supply (figure 2.3).

The health sector is not a perfect market, and when financing is mediated through purchasing arrangements, the equilibrium point may be further altered by subsidies, copayments, and informal charges in the case of demand and by restrictions on production and monopolies on the supply side. The net effect of these distortions on market prices also depends on the reimbursement mechanism used. Two major reimbursement policy options under purchasing arrangement are

- direct payment to providers by the patient with full or partial reimbursement later through the purchasing mechanism, and

- indirect reimbursement of the provider by the purchasing mechanism with the patient facing only a limited copayment or informal charge.

When the equilibrium point is significantly different, however, for the price of services used for reimbursement purposes by purchasing arrangements, quality and utilization of services will be affected. It also provides a powerful stimulus for a parallel market to develop in the informal sector.

The advantage of direct payment by the patient is that it sends the consumer a clearer signal about the price of the service used. The major disadvantage is that poor patients or patients receiving expensive care for major illnesses may not have the disposable income to pay for it.

Figure 2.3   Shifts in Prices under Different RAP Arrangements

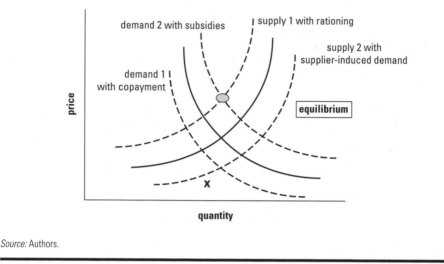

Source: Authors.

Reimbursing providers indirectly through purchasing arrangements instead of directly by patients opens a further dimension, the actual payment mechanism used (in addition to price and demand), which creates the incentive environment for service suppliers. The payment mechanism can be analyzed along two different axes: the unit of payment and the level of payment (box 2.3).

Lack of capacity and baseline information may force payers to merge these two elements and allocate resources on a historical basis or on the basis of gross input categories. More sophisticated purchasers will try to link payment with performance, outputs, and ultimately, outcomes (although the latter is still not employed much). These purchasers may also couple these mechanisms with demand-side mechanisms such as copayments or deductibles.

More sophisticated payment systems generally produce more and better information on costs and quality, a public good. However, these payment systems may raise transaction costs and heighten the need for increasingly sophisticated information and management systems. This is true for both purchasers and providers as the unit of payment increases and risk necessarily shifts relative to providers. Appropriate management information systems cannot always be designed and implemented quickly. Robinson (1997) notes that managed care organizations and private purchasers in the United States use fee-for-service payment for primary care and do not use diagnosis-related groups (DRGs) to reimburse hospitals—relying instead on bed-days. For them, the benefit of using DRGs in terms of transferring full and appropriate risk bearing onto providers is not worth the administrative cost associated with this system.

BOX 2.3   TRENDS IN PAYMENT MECHANISMS: HOW TO PAY?

Many countries have moved away from line-item budgets. Initially, simple units of payment were introduced (e.g., per service) on a retrospective basis. This payment mechanism is typically referred to as fee for service (FFS) for outpatient care and per diem (per day) for inpatient care (e.g., India, Malaysia, Sri Lanka, parts of the Russian Federation). Initially, the change can encourage provider participation and improve productivity (as measured by volume) and performance. Experience in member countries of the Organisation for Economic Co-operation and Development (OECD), and increasingly in non-OECD countries, is that FFS correlates with a pronounced increase in health expenditure and the purchasing arrangement generally bears most of the financial risk (e.g., Taiwan, China; Czech Republic). One short-term response to expenditure growth under FFS is to cap overall spending on the supply side and to encourage some patient cost-sharing to minimize moral hazard (e.g., Philippines, parts of Canada).

During the past two decades, new and more sophisticated payment systems have evolved, with the "unit" of payment encompassing a broader bundle of services (e.g., admission or episode versus procedure only) and payments set prospectively. Many purchasers have adopted a fixed-price payment for definable products that mimic entire clinical episodes such as an outpatient surgery (e.g., Lebanon) and more often, for inpatient stays (e.g., Brazil, Hungary, Kyrgyz Republic, Portugal). Hospital global budgets fix price as well as volume for inpatient services (the Republic of Korea; Taiwan, China; parts of Russia) and global budgets can be used for outpatient services (China, parts of Russia). Some countries also use capitation payments set at a fixed amount per patient for all covered services, regardless of service type or delivery setting. Examples of this include Indonesia and Thailand as well as many of the managed care schemes in the United States and in Argentina and other South American countries (Bitran and Yip 1998; Langenbrunner and Wiley 2002). In all cases, part of the financial risk is transferred from the purchasing arrangement back to the provider and patient.

Provider response to new payment incentives has been analyzed through both principal–agent models and monopolistic competitive models. The relative advantage of principal–agent theory is that it recognizes and models explicitly the potential conflicts of interest between different actors, emphasizing asymmetry of information as the critical problem in the discipline of providers. The relative advantage of monopolistic competitive models is that, unlike principal-agent models, these explicitly consider the effects of competition among a plurality of health providers. Using these models from the perspective of the tensions outlined above, the literature suggests that retrospective payment systems address issues of access, acceptable levels of provider risk, adequate revenues, patient selection, and quality enhancement. Prospective payments do better on optimal levels of services, efficiency, and cost containment.

(continued)

BOX 2.3   *(continued)*

An optimal payment system for providers should induce providers to perform high-quality, effective treatments, while at the same time promoting a rational allocation of resources to and within the health sector. In reality, international experience and the literature reflect tensions across these multiple objectives. Several objectives may be equally desirable, but mutually irreconcilable, in the sense that payment systems that can achieve each objective are not the same and may conflict with each other. Among the tensions illustrated by the literature on provider payments are the following:

• Supply and demand issues (Ellis and McGuire 1993)

• Risk-selection and production efficiency (Newhouse 1998)

• Pro-poor orientation of payment systems (Belli 2005).

Recently, purchasing arrangements have been striving to find equilibrium among these conflicting objectives. The European Union countries provide an interesting example of convergence toward a mix of mechanisms, with most using fee for service for "priority services" such as preventive care and selected primary care services, while using prospective payments to set rates and cap expenditure for inpatient care services (Langenbrunner and Wiley 2002).

Because of information asymmetry, neither consumers nor producers have full information about preferences, prices, or the market in which they operate. The level, mix, and quality of care for consumers can be ascertained only ex post, and good health depends on factors other than the health services consumed. Although physicians act as agents for their patients (Arrow 1963), even they often do not know the full impact of the interventions they recommend. The behavior of both consumers and providers is therefore important. Pricing and payment mechanisms provide an opportunity to shape their behavior through incentives as do improved knowledge about clinical outcomes, cultural factors, and the professional ethics of providers. Table 2.1 summarizes possible impacts on health system performance under different types of payment arrangements.

Finally, there are important choices and trade-offs: (1) can government departments engage in effective purchasing or will they always suffer from bureaucratic capture; and (2) what degree of decision rights must purchasing agencies have to execute their functions effectively as strategic purchasers?

CONCLUSIONS

This chapter reviewed some of the economic underpinnings of strategic purchasing of health care. Even in highly planned health care systems, the economics of supply and demand and market equilibrium exert pressures on purchasers and

TABLE 2.1   Impact of Selected Payment Incentives

| Payment characteristics | | Possible impact on health system performance | | | | |
Payment type	Risk shouldered by	Health outcomes	Financial protection	Consumer quality	Level of spending by purchasing	Distribution of spending
Line-item budget	Provider[a]	?	?	+/−	+++	+/−
Global budget	Provider[a]	?	?	+/−	++	+/−
Fee for service	Purchaser	?	?	+/−	−	++
Capitation	Provider[a]	ı/	?	+/−	++	+/−
Case mix	Purchaser and provider[a]	?	+/−	+	+	

Source: Authors.

a. Assuming hard budgets and full compliance with services to be provided. In case of soft budgets, the purchaser ends up retroactively absorbing the risk, thereby creating a moral hazard for providers. In the case of noncompliance of necessary services by the provider, the patient bears the risk of incomplete care.

providers of health care as well as consumers themselves. Issues related to industrial organization, institutional arrangements, and management are discussed in the next three chapters.

REFERENCES

Arrow, K. J. 1963. "Uncertainty and the Welfare Economics of Medical Care," *American Economic Review* 53(5): 940–73.

Belli, P.C. 2005. "The Equity Dimensions of Purchasing." In *Spending Wisely: Buying Health Services for the Poor,* ed. A. S. Preker and J. C. Langenbrunner. Washington, DC: World Bank.

Bitran, R., and W. C. Yip. 1998. *A Review of Health Care Provider Payment Reform in Selected Countries in Asia and Latin America.* Working Paper 1, Partnerships for Health Reform Project. Abt Associates Inc., Bethesda, MD.

Ellis, R. P., and T. G. McGuire. 1993. "Supply-Side and Demand-Side Cost Sharing in Health Care." *Journal of Economic Perspective* 7(4): 135–51.

Jakab, M., A. S. Preker, and A. Harding. 2002. *The Introduction of Market Forces in the Public Hospital Sector: From New Public Sector Management to Organizational Reform.* HNP Discussion Paper. A.S. Preker, Series Editor. Washington, DC: World Bank.

Langenbrunner, J. C., and M. Wiley. 2002. "Hospital Payment Systems: Theory and Practice in Transition Economies." In *Hospitals in a Changing Europe,* M. McKee and J. Healy, eds. Buckingham, United Kingdom, and Philadelphia, PA: Open University Press.

Musgrove, P. 1999. "Public Spending on Health Care: How Are Different Criteria Related?" *Health Policy* 47: 207–23.

———. 1996. *Public and Private Roles in Health: Theory and Financing Patterns.* Washington, DC: World Bank.

Newhouse, J. 1998. "Risk Adjustment: Where Are We Now?" *Inquiry.* Summer 35(2): 122–31.

Preker, A. S., and R. G. A. Feachem. 1996. *Market Mechanisms and the Health Sector in Central and Eastern Europe.* Technical Paper Series, No. 293. Washington, DC: World Bank. (Translated into Czech, Hungarian, Polish, Romanian, and Russian.)

Preker, A. S., and A. Harding. 2000. *The Economics of Public and Private Roles in Health Care: Insights from Institutional Economics and Organizational Theory.* HNP Discussion Paper. A.S. Preker, Series Editor. Washington, DC: World Bank.

Preker, A. S., and J. C. Langenbrunner, eds. 2005. *Spending Wisely: Buying Health Services for the Poor.* Washington, DC: World Bank.

Robinson, J. 1997. "Physician-Hospital Integration and Economic Theory of the Firm." *Medical Care Research and Review* 54(1): 3–24.

CHAPTER 3

The Organizational Structure of Purchasers

*Alexander S. Preker, Edit V. Velenyi, Cristian C. Baeza,
and Melitta Jakab*

Finding ways to manage the increasing resource scarcity in the health sector and improve health system performance has been occupying policy makers and technical experts across the globe for the past decade. Buying the best services for the money to achieve the maximum health gains for the people requires dynamic system adjustment. The switch from passive payer to strategic purchaser takes a lot of coordination and sensible sequencing of the reform components in resource allocation and purchasing.

This chapter explores the role and potential of one dimension of purchasing reforms—the way purchasers are organized and their underlying incentive regimes. The authors present an anatomy of the organizational structure of purchasers. The analysis is presented through the lens of industrial organizations. The central question is, "How does the organizational structure of purchasers make a difference in system efficiency and equity?"

INTRODUCTION

As described in the Introduction and chapter 1, throughout the world in recent years, there has been a shift from hiring staff in the public sector and producing services "in-house" to better engagement of nongovernmental and private providers through contractual relationships (Donahue 1989: 116). Chapter 2 described some of the key design questions that policy makers need to ask themselves as they orient their health systems from producing to purchasing services.

This chapter describes the organizations and organizational reforms needed to shift from passive supply-side subsidization of public providers to active strategic purchasing of health care from competing public, nonprofit, and private providers. The chapter explains why organizations are important in resource allocation and purchasing of health care. It describes their structure and function. It summarizes some of the main problems with organizational arrangements. And it reviews key policy options for reform.

ORGANIZATIONS MATTER

Organizations are the way people join together to fulfill specific functions (box 3.1). According to Arrow (1970) "the use of organizations to accomplish his ends" is among man's "greatest and earliest" innovations. In purchasing, a multiplicity of organizations exist side by side to carry out this role. Williamson (1985) elaborated on this concept, developing a complex theory of industrial organization that has applicability to the health sector. Organizations matter in terms of achieving both maximum health gains for those in need and value for money spent on health care (Savedoff 1998).

Before the 20th century, knowledge about the origins of poor health and effective interventions was limited. Most people approached health care as they did the consumption of other goods and services in the economy. There was no expensive technology, and most serious conditions led to death. Loss of employment and burial costs were the most expensive part of illness.

Industrialization and the scientific revolution changed all this. As understanding about the causes, prevention, and treatment of illness deepened, interventions become more complex and expensive. Health care was no longer the exclusive domain of traditional healers. Other actors become involved. This included policy makers, specialized institutions involved in regulation and finance, complex organizations specialized in delivery of services (hospitals, clinics, diagnostics), and a range of specialized providers (doctors, nurses, pharmacists, dentists, allied health workers). Through this process, the health system slowly became differentiated beyond the simple patient-healer relationship (figures 3.1 and 3.2).

This still does not, however, explain why individuals need help in purchasing health services from providers. Is the "middle man" really necessary? Can an individual not just buy health services in the same way he or she would go to the local market to buy bread, milk, or fruit? The answer is both yes and no. Much of the time, consuming health care is no different from consuming other goods and services. Patients have to inform themselves about their health problems and learn about which part of the health care system can help them. In doing this, they may ask for help when the problem is complex, just as the average consumer needs help when the TV, computer, or car break down. Modern technology forces people to become increasingly interdependent. Health care is not unique in this respect.

But in other respects, health care is very different. The fear of pain, disability, and death is different from the fear of living without a TV or computer for a few days. Asymmetry in information is often great between patients and their health care provider about both the causes and likely effectiveness of treatment. Often a third party—the government or an insurer—pays the bill. This can make individuals and households make irrational decisions they would not make when consuming other goods and services. They usually need help from both a health care provider who can advise them what to do and from organizations that handle the dual complexities of financing and delivering high-level care.

BOX 3.1   THE UNHOLY TRIAD OF INFORMATION ASYMMETRY IN HEALTH CARE

Information asymmetry can occur in three major ways—between patient (public) and health care professional; between patient and policy maker or administrator of the health care system; and between health care professional and the policy maker or administrator of the health care system. The importance of these information flaws and interactions within this client–policy maker–provider triad is now well recognized in both the health sector (Preker and Harding 2003) and public service delivery in general (World Bank 1995).

Patients know more about their symptoms than doctors but may—unwittingly or deliberately—not explain them clearly. Doctors know more about the causes, prognosis, and effectiveness of available treatments but may not communicate this clearly to the patient. Or, the patient may not understand the implications of what he/she is being told. When it comes to interactions between patients (public) and health care administrators or policy makers, patients may deliberately conceal pre-existing conditions for fear of embarrassment, having to pay higher health care premiums, or a variety of other reasons. Likewise, health care administrators or policy makers frequently conceal the rationale behind rationing of scarce resources to avoid a public backlash.

Finally, some serious information asymmetries exist between health care providers and the administrators for whom they work (or between administrators and owners). Health care providers—as advocates for patients—have a much better understanding of legitimate needs or demands. Administrators have a much better understanding of supply and cost of available resources but know little about a selected intervention's appropriateness or effectiveness. The doctor's well-known information advantage over the patient is not solved by the existence of a public employer or administrator who knows even less about interactions between patients and providers.

Such information asymmetries add to agency costs in terms of structuring, monitoring, and bonding contracts among agents and principals with conflicting interests. Private firms, concerned about profits, have a strong incentive to limit agency costs related to information asymmetry (Fama and Jensen 1983). Public agencies that are not held to a clear "bottom line" due to unspecified social functions and many complex sources of subsidies do not receive clear signals about the agency cost of such information asymmetry.

This "ignorance by default," due to information asymmetry, may even lead to deliberate misinformation engineered by politicians, bureaucrats, organizations, and health care providers entrusted with public accountability. Although deliberate deception and fiscal fraud is usually sanctioned severely, it is much harder to hold the public sector accountable for petty abuses, avoidance, and obfuscation. Such deception may take the form of hidden costs, subsidies, cost shifting, or inflation.

The purchaser, as a multiplicitous agent, becomes the "arbitrator" or "honest broker" by trying to minimize such information asymmetry.

Source: Authors.

Figure 3.1   The Patient–Healer Relationship

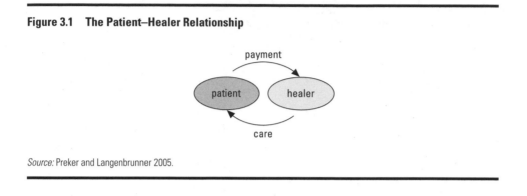

Source: Preker and Langenbrunner 2005.

Figure 3.2   Functional Differentiation

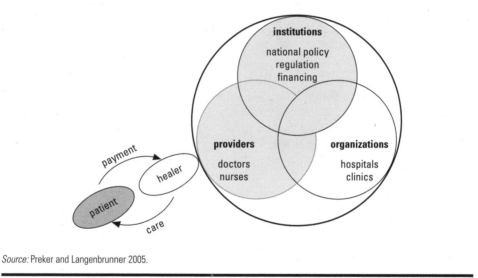

Source: Preker and Langenbrunner 2005.

By controlling the "purse strings," such health care providers and the organizations involved in resource allocation and purchasing are in a powerful position to create the needed incentives for providers to behave in ways that would secure not only the highest quality of care but also be responsive to the needs of the patients that they serve. So why does this so often not happen?

Agency theory provides valuable insights into this question, highlighting both the strengths and weaknesses of health care resource allocation and purchasing organizations (Stiglitz 1989). According to this theory, a principal (the hirer) contracts with an agent (the hired) to perform certain duties. The contract must be attractive to both principal and agent. From the agent's point of view, the contract must be at least as attractive as alternative available contracts *(participation constraint)* (Arrow 1986). From the principal's point of view, the contract must be structured in such a way and have incentives to ensure that the agent will act in the principal's best interest *(incentive compatibility constraint)* (MacDonald 1984).

In Theory

As described in chapter 1, agency theory has been used extensively to examine purchasing and contracting by firms (Eisenhardt 1988; Bergen, Dutta, and Walker 1992). Principal–agent relationships work best when several preexisting conditions are met:

- Both the principal and the agent must try to maximize their utility independently.

- Agents must try to maximize income but minimize effort.

- Pay must be correlated with outcomes and with effort by the agent.

- The principal must have perfect information about the agent's activities.

- The principal and the agent must enter voluntarily into a contract.

When the above conditions hold, the principal cannot exploit the agent because the contract is voluntary. And the agent cannot shirk or cheat if his pay is related to effort and outcomes. A well-designed contract maximizes the utility of this relationship for both the principal and the agent.

In Practice

In practice, several constraints are notable (Fama and Jensen 1983): uncertainty of outcomes, information asymmetry, moral hazard, and adverse selection. Most outcomes depend on factors other than a single agent's actions. The effectiveness of any agent is often codependent on the action of others (Holmstrom 1982). Success in terms of outcomes cannot be fully attributed to any single agent. In fact, outcomes often depend on the aggregate effort of a team, making it equally difficult to blame any one agent for failure.

Because successful outcomes are difficult to attribute to any given action and sometimes difficult to observe, agents are often paid according to inputs (effort or time spent) or output (units of production) rather than true outcomes or results in terms of better health or financial protection against illness. However, in most instances, outcomes are not perfectly correlated with inputs or outputs, but instead result from both effort and some other unobservable variables (Stiglitz 1989). Due to information asymmetry (one party knowing more about a given situation than the other party), principals often do not have full knowledge about the action that agents should or did take on their behalf (Arrow 1986).

For instance, when individuals use insurance to pay for risk-related events, special incentives are needed to ensure that the purchasing agents address (1) adverse selection problems by charging high-risk individuals higher subscription rates than low-risk individuals (Rothschild and Stiglitz 1976), and (2) moral hazard problems, in which an individual, once insured, increases risky behavior (Pauly 1968). In both cases, the purchaser who is paid on the basis of input or output volumes rather than outcomes, has little incentive to execute policies that limit unnecessary utilization of services. Since the principal cannot observe an agent's every action, it is easy for the agent to use this information asymmetry to his advantage (Holmstrom 1979). Designing payment systems that share such risk in a balanced way between the principal and agent is, therefore, crucial to the success of contracting arrangements (Stiglitz 1974; Shavell 1980).

APPLICATION TO HEALTH CARE PURCHASING

The most frequently described agency relationship in the health sector is the interaction between the patient and his or her doctor. Patient advocacy and ethical confidentiality dimensions are the most frequent focus of this type of agency relationship. Special agency issues arise when patients are not fully competent to make decisions about their own health care as is the case of children, the mentally ill, or the physically impaired (Beauchamp and Childress 1983; Zweifel and Struwe 1998; Cuffel et al. 1996). Related issues arise when dealing with poor or disenfranchised population groups that financial or social constraints may prevent from exercising full autonomy.

In addition to the doctor-patient relationship, agency and contract theory have been extensively applied to the purchasing and contracting of health services (Evans 1983a, 1983b; Dranove and White 1985; McGuire, Henderson, and Mooney 1988; Ryan 1992; Mooney and Ryan 1993; Ovretveit 1995a; Propper 1995a, 1995b; Levaggi 1996; Rice 1998). As agents, purchasers of health care confront many of the same problems of adverse selection, moral hazard, and information asymmetry that plague the insurance industry in general (Outreville 1998; Dionne 2000) and health insurance more specifically (Enthoven 1978a, 1978b, 1988; Newhouse 1993; Cutler and Zeckhauser 2000; van de Ven and Ellis 2000). Similar observations have been made in low-income countries (Musgrove 1996; Schieber 1997; Preker et al. 2001; Dror and Preker 2002).

One Servant, Many Masters

But under whose instructions should the people and organizations act in an agency role? How do they behave in reality? Do they really follow the orders they are given? When do they merely execute decisions made elsewhere and when do they exercise decision rights of their own? And when they exercise such decision rights, in whose interest do they act—for the individual patient, the population at large, politicians, health care professionals, or bureaucrats with their own vested interests? Answers to these questions provide insights into the role that resource allocation and purchasing agencies play as agents of public policy, health care providers, and consumers of health care and into the policies that must be put in place to make resource allocation and purchasing agencies responsive to the needs of poor and ordinary people who need health care and protection against the cost of illness.

At a deeper level lies a more basic question: Who should decide on what to spend resources when there are not enough for everyone and on what basis should such decisions be made? Patients, households, health care workers, health insurance agencies, civil society, and governments all have legitimate—but often conflicting—claims. The interest of the principal(s) involved and the extent of decision rights given to the resource allocation and purchasing agency can have a profound impact on the way priorities are set and executed, who benefits from collective purchasing arrangements, which providers are used, the payment mechanism, and the price paid for the resulting services. The impact on the health and human welfare of people affected by such decisions can be dramatic. These decisions often determine who lives or who dies.

The Multiplicitous Agent

In the health sector, resource allocation and purchasing agencies usually serve as multiplicitous agents for several powerful principals other than individual patients. Three important agency relationships are predominant. They encompass the relationship between resource allocation and purchasing arrangements and individual health care providers (doctors, nurses, allied health care workers), the relationship between resource allocation and purchasing agencies and various institutional actors (policy makers, regulators, insurers, and other funding agencies), and the relationship between resource allocation and purchasing agencies and health care organizations (hospitals, clinics, ambulatory services). In reality, there are more than three agency relationships because the stakeholders under each of these three major categories all exert some influence over the resource allocation and purchasing agents. Policy makers, regulators, and funding agencies often have very different interests. Hospitals, clinics, and ambulatory services expect different services from resource allocation and purchasing agencies. While private (self-employed) doctors often have direct contact with resource allocation and purchasing agencies, nurses and other health care professionals do not. Their expectations will be different.

The greater the overlap in interest among the various powerful stakeholders, the more likely it is that the resource allocation and purchasing agencies will have a coherent authorizing environment that will coincide with the interest of the patients that they should also serve (Moore 1995) and achieve optimal social welfare outcomes in resource allocation and purchasing (Mirrlees 1974). When the overlap is small, there is a risk of poor performance by the agent and dissatisfaction on the part of the principals.

The objectives of the three organizational principals described above are often very different. Institutional-level actors are often closely aligned with the current political agenda, while health care organizations are more likely to be aligned with the bureaucratic interests of civil servants and the staff running them. Individual health care providers are usually aligned with the underlying social values of the society in which they work and professional concerns. This difference in perspective causes serious problems for the principal who does not have the undivided attention of a loyal agent (Ross 1973), for the agent who has to serve several masters (Cuffel et al. 1996), and for the patient who is often left out of the discussion (figure 3.3).

Tensions often arise between health care providers who act on behalf of individual patients and policy makers and institutions that focus more on national and population-level issues. The purchaser is often pressured by individual health care providers to finance the most recent and best quality of care for his or her patient. At the same time, the institutional actors in the ministry of health (MOH) are often concerned about aggregate health outcomes and those in the ministry of finance (MOF) are concerned about the overall fiscal affordability of such care. This leads to an irreconcilable situation for the purchaser who has to act as an agent on behalf of two or more principals, each with a very different agenda.

Figure 3.3   The Multiplicitous Agency Relationships

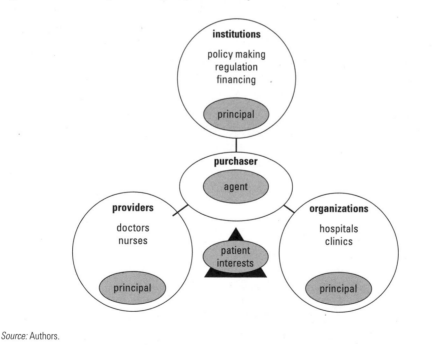

Source: Authors.

A concrete example of this is the treatment of HIV/AIDS in Sub-Saharan Africa. Individual health care providers often pressure resource allocation and purchasing agencies to provide funding for antiretroviral treatment in the hope it will extend their patients' life expectancy, if only marginally. Policy makers, however, often apply pressure on their resource allocation and purchasing agencies to ration expenditure on such care so that scarce resources are available for more effective and lower-cost treatments for childhood illnesses and other common conditions. And those in the ministries of finance may impose strict budget constraints that prevent the resource allocation and purchasing agencies from satisfying either of the above needs. During the East Asian economic crisis, a different situation arose in Indonesia, Malaysia, and Thailand. At the height of the crisis, many ministries had to dramatically reduce overall funding to resource allocation and purchasing agencies. These reductions meant that the resource allocation and purchasing agencies could no longer act as an effective agent in securing sustainable financing for the health care organizations. As a result, many hospitals and clinics started charging patients direct fees, thereby bypassing what they viewed as ineffective collective financing arrangements.

In such cases, the final outcome depends on complex trade-offs between political power, market share/concentration, and related bargaining power of the various stakeholders. There is seldom a single right or wrong way to do things. Some will gain. Others will lose. The winners will be happy; the losers, unhappy.

Several characteristics influence how effectively health care resource allocation and purchasing organizations can behave as multiplicitous agents. In the following sections, three dimensions—organizational forms, structural configuration, and incentive regimes—are discussed and expand on the organizational structure described in table I.1 of the Introduction to this volume:

Organizational structure	Organizational forms (ownership, contractual relationships, and scale and scope of purchasers)
	Structural configuration (extent of horizontal and vertical linkages versus purchaser–provider split or fragmentation)
	Incentive regimes (extent of decision rights, financial responsibility, market exposure, accountability, and coverage of social functions)

ORGANIZATIONAL FORMS

Organizational form is formally defined as ownership. In an effort to better understand the complex array of ownership arrangements in resource allocation and purchasing of health care, this section looks at several related issues that affect ownership arrangements. This includes ownership, contractual relations between purchasers and providers, and the scale and scope of purchasers.

Ownership

The ownership arrangements of health care purchasers varies greatly from country to country and is often a complex mix of public and private engagement (OECD 1992; van de Ven, Schut, and Rutten 1994; Chernichovsky 1995, 2002; World Health Organization 2000; Kutzin 2001). There are four stereotypes: (1) a traditional British or Beveridge-style national health service (resources are allocated by a government department to an integrated network of public providers); (2) a German or Bismarck-style social insurance system (services are purchased by multiple social health insurance funds from a loose network of public and private providers); (3) a U.S. or free market-style health system (patients as well as public and private insurance programs purchase services largely from independent public and private providers); and (4) laissez-faire direct spot-market transactions between patients and providers. In reality, most countries rely on a mixture of these models. For example, there are private purchasers in the United Kingdom. The United States has two large public purchasing programs—Medicare and Medicaid. Large social health insurance systems often use a budget process rather than active purchasing. And households in most countries buy some services directly from providers even when they also have access to more formal purchasing arrangements. Ownership arrangements can trigger different behavioral responses from providers that may affect their performance and, ultimately, outcomes.

Contractual Relationship between Purchasers and Providers

The contractual relationship between purchasers and providers may take one of three different forms—hierarchical bureaucratic relationships, long-term contracts among different entities, or short-term spot-market transactions among different entities (figure 3.4).

One way to illustrate the differences between these three classifications of resource allocation and purchasing (RAP) arrangements is to think of a continuum from an integrated hierarchical bureaucracy to spot-market transactions in an open market place. Using the Philippines as an example, the core public services lie at the center of this circle (hierarchical budget allocations made by the Ministry of Health (MOH) to primary care providers and specialized institutions under its direct responsibility). Some of the private health maintenance organizations (HMOs) that have integrated the financing and service delivery function under a single organizational form would belong to the same category. Public or private is therefore not the key issue but rather the extent of the separation between the financing and the service delivery functions and the way in which relations between the two separate functions are structured. The Philippines also has a National Health Insurance Program (NHIP) which has been given the

Figure 3.4   Organizational Forms

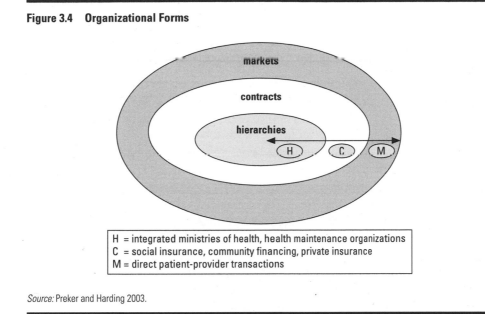

H = integrated ministries of health, health maintenance organizations
C = social insurance, community financing, private insurance
M = direct patient-provider transactions

Source: Preker and Harding 2003.

mandate of purchasing hospital-based care for its subscribers (mainly workers in the formally employed sector). The NHIP "buys" services from its providers on a long-term basis (often using an implicit relational rather than explicit written contract). To a lesser extent, some of the community financing schemes and private health insurance funds also use long-term relational contracts with selected providers. Finally, there is the domain of direct interactions between the population and providers that bypasses formal purchasing arrangements. They rely mostly on one-off spot-market transactions on a fee-for-service basis. Some community financing and private health insurance funds also behave in this way through ex post reimbursement of direct out-of-pocket spot-market transactions between patients and providers.

Both hierarchical and fragmented purchasing arrangements have serious shortcomings. Dissatisfaction with these extremes has been one of the reasons for recent trends toward long-term contracts, which try to combine control over strategic objectives and financial protection with some choice and flexibility (World Health Organization 2000).

Scale and Scope

Purchasing arrangements, like health service providers, may be structured either as dispersed or concentrated organizational entities.

Limited Scale and Scope of Dispersed Purchasing Arrangements

Some activities such as first level ambulatory care, pharmacies, dental offices, field-based implementation of public health programs, counseling, social work, and community- and home-based care do not benefit from economies of scale. Such services usually involve a limited range of activities of varying degrees of complexity such as the management of common clinical and nonclinical activities by individuals or small teams of people. Many of the activities carried out by these dispersed service delivery configurations also fall into the low-cost, high-frequency category, which makes them largely uninsurable risks. Although they may benefit from prepayment and subsidies for low-income groups, they often do not benefit to the same degree as lower-frequency and higher-cost catastrophic care from insurance-based revenue-pooling and risk-sharing arrangements.

Purchasing arrangements (e.g., community financing schemes for rural and informal sector populations) mirror these service delivery configurations in that they often have a small membership, offer a limited range of uninsurable benefits, and are furnished by many small providers. Given the dispersed nature of such community financing schemes, close supervision is often difficult, if not impossible. When these dispersed activities are integrated into larger national health insurance programs, they often run into problems with contribution compliance in the case of the rural and informal sector populations covered, moral hazard, adverse selection, and difficulties establishing effective accountability structures. When their benefit coverage is expanded to cover lower-frequency and higher-cost events, they often become insolvent within three to five years. Establishing effective purchasing arrangements that cover rural and informal population groups remains a major developmental challenge in many low-income countries that have large rural populations and informal labor markets.

Economies of Scale and Scope of Concentrated Purchasing Arrangements

In countries with large urban populations and high formal labor market participation rates, RAP arrangements that offer both scale and scope, such as large social insurance organizations, avoid the fragmentation characteristic of multiple small schemes. However, even in these countries, special programs are often needed to reach marginal population groups and to maintain adequate supervision over the programs that deal with dispersed ambulatory providers.

Many of these activities carried out by large and complex purchasing arrangements are highly specialized and expensive and require large teams of people with a wide range of skills. As with other large systems, these require continuous monitoring to avoid fraud and abuse. Accountability can usually be enforced through direct hierarchical controls over inputs and outputs within these organizations. Most of the personnel employed by such organizations can be hired as regular or part-time staff rather than under the relational contracts often used for more dispersed organizational forms. There are important trade-offs between different contractual arrangements (box 3.2).

BOX 3.2   TRADE-OFFS BETWEEN DIFFERENT CONTRACTUAL ARRANGEMENTS

Debate is ongoing about the relative advantages of the first and second of these organizational forms—health maintenance organizations (HMOs) versus provider–purchaser splits. Clear trade-offs between strategic control over all aspects of the production process conferred under a hierarchically integrated HMO arrangement outweigh the greater efficiency and flexibility that can be achieved through a purchaser–provider split arrangement. Hierarchical bureaucracies also have some serious shortcomings that have become apparent in recent years in the provision of health services. They are vulnerable to capture by the vested interests of bureaucracies and providers working within them. They are often less effective in downsizing or reorienting priorities than they are in expanding capacity. And they are often associated with many of the same shortcomings as private markets in terms of abuse of monopoly power (e.g., collection of rents in the form of informal charges) and information asymmetry. Over time, many hierarchical service delivery systems have become bloated bureaucracies, with inefficient production processes and low-quality care.

There are also trade-offs between the advantages of strategic purchasing and resource allocation that can be achieved under either hierarchies or long-term contracts, and spot-market arrangements can achieve greater consumer responsiveness. Long-term contracts rely on resource allocation and purchasing (RAP) arrangements that are good agents for the populations they represent, but they often are not—especially when the RAP arrangements give way to political and bureaucratic pressures instead of being accountable to the patients they are supposed to serve.

Each of these ways of organizing RAP arrangements therefore has strengths and weakness in different contexts and when applied to different types of clinical and population-based health services. When innovation and responsiveness to individual demand are needed, for instance to develop new drugs and equipment, spot markets may be better.

However, direct market interactions between patients and health care providers have the major disadvantage of exposing individuals to the financial risks of illness. In countries like India, where 80 percent of health care expenditure is out of pocket (often on over-the-counter drugs and low-quality care in nursing homes), patients are deprived of advantages they could have had if these resources had been pooled and channeled through a financing function. These trade-offs are explored in greater detail in subsequent chapters.

Source: Authors.

Hybrid Purchasing Arrangements

Recently some countries have experimented with "bundling" and "unbundling" some purchasing activities that do not fit comfortably under one or the other of these configurations. An example of bundling includes inclusions of coverage of higher-cost catastrophic care under community financing through reinsurance mechanisms. Examples of unbundling include the separation of uninsurable risks or "first $1 coverage" from larger purchasing arrangements by establishing separate medical savings accounts to cover some high-frequency but lower-cost events that are predictable across the life cycle and may require differentiated benefits standards such as long-term care. Supplementary insurance for "above" standard care is another example.

In the real world, these differences in scale and scope have been translated into distinctly different purchasing arrangements:

- Spending under an MOH/NHS–type system exhibits the greatest concentration of purchasing power. Although concentrated monopolies have greater collection efficiency, better cost control, and equity,[1] efficiency may be undermined by the lack of competition, innovation, and internal incentives.[2]

- Spending under social health insurance systems typically occupies the middle ground in terms of concentration, depending on the number of schemes and their respective market shares.

- Spending under micro-insurance is much more fragmented and confers less purchasing power.

- Spending by individual households confers the most dispersed and least concentrated configuration, with associated weak purchasing power.

Table 3.1 highlights how ownership arrangements, contractual relationships, and economies of scale and scope combine under the different dominant health care systems across the world and ultimately affect the degree of market competition.

This framework captures the recent trend of moving away from the inefficiencies of "core public sector" bureaucracies toward a new and more flexible "broader public sector" (table 3.1, column 2). The new organizational context is expected to provide an enabling environment that will take advantage of the energy and dynamics of competition in the private sector—achieving public ends using private means. It follows a global attempt to improve efficiency through

TABLE 3.1   Overview Matrix for the Analysis of Organizational Forms of Purchasing Arrangements

Dominant health system	Ownership	Contractual relationship	Economies of scale	Competitive model
NHS	Core public sector	Hierarchical bureaucratic relationship	Highly concentrated	Monopoly model
Insurance	Broader public sector	Long-term contracts	Concentrated increasing dispersion	Single/multiple payers
Laissez-faire	Market/private sector	Short-term (spot) market transactions	Highly dispersed	Mixed/fragmented model

Source: Constructed from World Health Organization 2000.

market mechanisms by splitting the insurance/third-party-payer function from the provision and management of services, thereby making providers compete for contracts through "internal" (Enthoven 1994) or "quasi-markets."

STRUCTURAL CONFIGURATION OF PURCHASERS

The ownership arrangement, contractual relations between purchasers and providers, and their scale and scope allow a better understanding of the structural configuration of current purchasers throughout the world. Although in principle each one of the following stereotypical health systems could have similar resource allocation and purchasing arrangements, in reality there is considerable diversity often associated with the underlying model of the health system in general.

- *Ministries of health* usually rely on progressive general taxation collected by the ministries of finance to support a broad range of provider organizations that are often organized as a hierarchically integrated national health service. Providers are paid directly. Participation is compulsory.

- *Health maintenance organizations*, though privately owned and usually relying on flat-rate or risk-rated premiums from their members, have a striking similarity to MOHs and social insurance organizations in that they often contract or manage a broad range of provider organizations structured as hierarchically integrated networks. Payment is made in advance, but a copayment may be required at the time of service utilization. Membership is usually voluntary although participation may be required by the employer that carries the scheme.

- *Social health insurance organizations* usually rely on progressive payroll-tax contributions and often own at least part of their provider networks although many are beginning to contract with independent and private providers. Providers are usually reimbursed indirectly, not directly by patients. Membership is usually compulsory.

- *Private health insurance funds* usually rely on flat-rate or risk-rated premiums to reimburse patients directly for services bought by patients on a spot-market, fee-for-service basis. Membership is usually voluntary.

- *Community financing organizations* usually rely on flat-rate contributions from individuals and communities that have banded together to protect themselves against the cost of illness. Services may be bought on a spot-market, fee-for-service basis or obtained from panel providers that the scheme reimburses indirectly. Membership is usually voluntary.

- *Individual patients* purchase services for themselves from providers in an open spot market at whatever price the market will bear. Pooling is limited to household and family savings. Some providers offer regular and frequent users discount packages. Purchases are usually voluntary.

The chapter next explores some of the implications of these organizational forms on the structural arrangements of purchasers in terms of systems differentiation, fragmentation, and vertical and horizontal linkages.

Systems Differentiation

An inherent positive aspect of purchasing reforms is the structural and functional differentiation that has occurred during recent years. When such reforms are implemented effectively, they often lead to improved efficiency and equity in service delivery. The following reforms are typically designed to differentiate the resource allocation or purchasing function from other parts of the health care system:

- Decentralization and/or agency formation where central responsibility and accountability is transferred to either a lower level of government or semi-autonomous agency

- Purchaser–provider split with separation of the purchasing function from ownership of the delivery system

- Increased consumer choice and participation.

Decentralization and agency formation essentially unbundles the ownership and governance of the purchaser from direct authority by the central government (figure 3.5).

Examples of such reforms include (1) decentralization of the budget process (e.g., regional health authorities in Poland, Sri Lanka, and the United Kingdom); (2) establishment of semiautonomous health financing agency structures (e.g., Croatia, Estonia, and Hungary); and (3) corporatization of the purchasing arrangements under a parastatal health insurance company that is subject to private company law and market pressures (e.g., Australian Health Insurance Commission, Czech Republic).

Reforms that introduce decentralization or agency formation often split the purchasing function into one of three distinct levels of purchasing: *macro*, *meso*, and *micro* (Figueras, Robinson, and Jakubowski 2005a). The size of the country and the degree of decentralization affect both the number and behavior of each of these levels of purchasing. A few examples are provided below.

Macro-level purchasing is prevalent in Central and Eastern European countries. Examples include (1) central health funds (e.g., Hungary's National Health Insurance Fund, a single purchaser nonprofit organization supervised by Ministries of Health); (2) single state insurance scheme with branches but strong central control and decision-making power (e.g., Lithuania); and (3) central insurance funds largely independent of the Ministries of Health (e.g., in Estonia, following a series of decentralization and recentralization efforts).

Meso-level purchasing is widespread under both the social health insurance and regional government-based models. Examples include (1) national health systems with general taxation raised by central governments with fund transfers to

Figure 3.5   Decentralization /Agency Creation and Purchaser–Provider Split

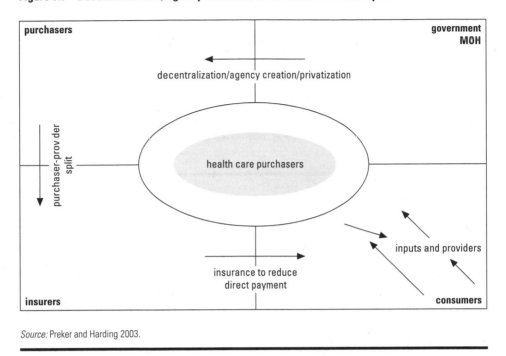

Source: Preker and Harding 2003.

regions with purchasing responsibilities (Southern Europe); (2) statutory health funds (nonprofit, corporatists) and private health insurance companies (Western Europe); and (3) national funds that are company based or organized around professional groups; public nonprofit organizations that receive funds from the government but have a degree of autonomy from it; and pluralistic territorial-based funds (transition economies in the European Union).

Micro-level purchasing through local governments (Nordic countries) and primary care–based purchasers (England) takes place to a lesser extent, but it has been increasingly attracting attention from policy makers. These arrangements are characterized by a high degree of local autonomy. Purchasing budgets are devolved to local organizations: local government and primary care–based purchasing (Nordic countries).

During the past decade or two, there has been an important move from the macro to meso level of purchasing in the health sector, parallel to reforms that promote decentralization, with agency formation in both the service delivery and health insurance systems. At the same time, a move has occurred away from individual spot-market transactions toward micro-level purchasing under small micro-insurance schemes.

Purchaser–provider splits separate the governance and ownership of health care facilities from purchasers. It often accompanies reforms that establish semi-autonomous health care providers such as hospitals. Three types of purchaser–provider splits predominate: total split (the purchaser does not own or manage any services or employ any staff who provide such services); partial split (the purchaser retains some ownership and continues to employ some staff but is allowed to outsource and purchase some services); and noncompetitive split (Ovretveit 1995b).

In the 1990s, the formerly unified British National Health Service (NHS) was split into purchasers and providers, with the NHS District Health Authorities becoming purchasers, and the NHS hospitals becoming providers (Jost et al. 1995). During the same time period, the U.S. health care system, driven by market forces rather than government fiat, moved toward greater functional integration of financing and service delivery under HMOs. Many countries have followed the U.K. trend toward purchaser–provider splits in both Europe (Hermans and Nooren 1998) and developing countries (Preker and Harding 2003).

Although much has been written about the added transaction costs of such splits (Hutchison, Hardee, and Barns 1997), at least some of the criticism has been tactical and ideological rather than based on real evaluation of their successes and failures (Paton 1995). Reviews of such experiences highlight that there are both advantages and disadvantages to reforms that introduce purchaser–provider splits.

- Advantages include a shift in the balance of power away from providers toward purchasers; greater focus by purchasers on policy objectives rather than managing services; the need to make running costs and investments more explicit; and the possibility of increased patient choice if a large number of providers are allowed to contract with the purchasers.

- Disadvantages include some loss of control over providers; complication of planning and coordination; increased transaction costs; need to learn new skills to manage and monitor contracts; and possibility of decreased patient choice if the range of providers who can contract with the purchaser is restricted to only a few.

Increased consumer choice and participation also leads to a differentiation of the purchasing function when individuals and households use at least part of their own money to purchase health care rather than go through a collective purchasing arrangement. Although such reforms can have a negative impact on equity and affordability, some countries such as Singapore and the United States have recently begun experimenting with medical savings accounts as a way to buffer against the immediate impact of out-of-pocket expenditures. Targeted subsidies can be used to ensure that the poor are not excluded under such schemes. Often cited by critics of this approach is the United States, where around 15 percent of the population does not carry insurance coverage. The importance of this example is, however, exaggerated in comparison with most developing countries where up to 80 percent have no access to collective financing mechanisms and where fragmentation in purchasing arrangements is the rule rather than the exception.

Fragmentation

Fragmentation is a potentially negative part of purchasing reform. Such health services fragmentation may deprive individual organizational units of choice from among the full range of interventions. This limitation will curtail allocative efficiency as they try to perform certain functions they were not designed to perform or as they attempt to shift costs. For example, small cottage-type hospitals or "nursing homes"—with 10 to 20 beds are common in South Asia (e.g., in Bangladesh, India, and Sri Lanka) because of poor integration between the large ambulatory private sector and basic community hospitals. The bed occupancy rate for these hospitals is typically low, and the doctors working in them often do not see enough patients to keep up their clinical skills to treat rare conditions. Nonclinical health facilities designed to provide population-based services in Hungary and Poland often engage in secondary prevention and a wide range of basic care when they are not adequately linked to ambulatory care networks. The recently autonomous university hospitals in Malaysia provide a wide range of inpatient and outpatient care for conditions that could be treated effectively at lower levels in a community setting. The newly autonomous general practitioners in the Czech Republic have been quick to buy a wide range of expensive equipment that is rarely used.

Fragmentation can also have negative equity consequences. When the whole health financing system is composed of multiple community financing or sickness fund schemes with their associated RAP arrangements, the differences between the benefits that can be provided by the poorer and richer schemes are usually significant. This is true even in rich countries like Germany where the differences between the financing and benefits provided by the various funds are often significant. Likewise, when small autonomous provider units (districts, hospitals, clinics, or public health facilities) are given global prospective budgets, the risk pool is often fractured, thereby eroding the financial protection that should be afforded though prepayment and collective purchasing arrangements. Frequently cross-transfers are not available, and the pool is too small to bear the risk of expenditure variations that may occur in any given population group.

The solution to fragmentation is not necessarily a return to bureaucratic integration through hierarchical structures. Some countries seem to have fallen into this trap without improving their situation (e.g., Armenia, Hungary, New Zealand, and the United Kingdom). Before proceeding too far down this path, some of the shortcomings of this approach might usefully be recalled. Under centralized systems, national political interests often drive the stewardship function, bureaucratic interests capture the budget processes, local politicians control the governance arrangements, and hierarchical compartmentalization can still create severe functional fragmentation between different parts of the resulting bureaucratically integrated system. This was observed in Costa Rica, the Former Soviet Union (FSU), Sri Lanka, Sweden, and the United Kingdom prior to splitting purchasers off from providers. Similarly, integrating revenue collection with the purchasing function may exacerbate contribution compliance instead of improving it.

As an alternative to a return to hierarchical structures under a centrally integrated system, many countries are introducing more dynamic vertical and horizontal links under their new strategic purchasing arrangements.

Vertical Linkages

Vertical linkages that have been tried include both linkages between different parts of the health system such as revenue collector(s), the organizations in charge of pooling (if separate), and spending on providers and between different levels of purchasers themselves (figure 3.6). Sometimes these linkages are achieved through the bureaucratic structures of ministries of health. The former U.K. NHS (prior to the reforms that introduced a purchaser–provider split), Hong-Kong's Hospital Authority, and the U.S. staff-model HMOs are good illustrations. Increasingly, hierarchical integration between funding, production, and distribution units is being viewed as a coordination mechanism of last resort, used mainly when contractual alternatives are not available.

Figure 3.7 demonstrates how even in the three major health financing functions—revenue collection, insuring, and purchasing—there are both important linkages and divisions among the various subcomponents of the system.

These vertical dimensions of purchasing are shaped largely by the institutional environment and management arrangement in the country. The distribution of labor and level of responsibility under each level is typically defined under the constitution. Reforms often shift responsibility among these levels—for example, in Pakistan, the government has been experimenting with devolving service delivery to municipalities (Tehsil Municipal Administrations) (Asian Development Bank/World Bank 2004).[3]

Figure 3.6   Vertical and Horizontal Fragmentation in RAP Arrangements

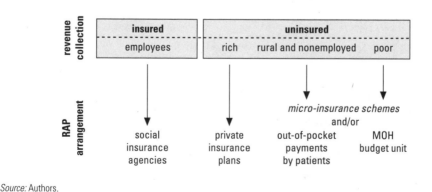

Source: Authors.

Figure 3.7   Institutional Characteristics of Health Financing Subfunctions

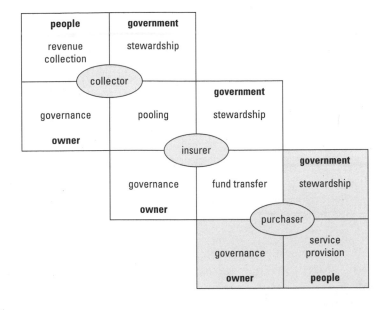

Source: Authors.

Horizontal Linkages

The horizontal dimension captures the number of purchasers, their market share, and the level of competition. This dimension examines the nature of market structure within which purchasers operate, based on the level of concentration and the level of competition and contestability. The study by the European Observatory concludes that it is "striking from the empirical overview how little competition seems to exist, despite the rhetoric of market-based reform sweeping through policy debates" (Figueras, Robinson, and Jakubowski 2005b; Robinson, Jakubowski, and Figueras 2005). The presence of spatial monopoly constitutes a major barrier to demand-side competition at both the meso and micro levels.

Based on the degree of market pressures, noncompetitive purchasers and competitive purchasers can be distinguished (figure 3.8). These can be characterized as follows:

1. Noncompetitive purchasers

- Macro purchasers are in a monopsonistic position. There is no scope of competition. The private sector is underdeveloped, leaving little scope for increasing competition.

Figure 3.8   Topology of Purchasing Arrangements Based on Market Concentration and Competition

concentration	market type	purchaser type		
high	monopoly	macro		
medium	managed competition		meso	
low	open competition			micro

Source: Constructed by authors based on Figueras, Robinson, and Jakubowski (2005a).

- At the meso level, although the national market is less concentrated and more heterogeneous than above, and interregional rivalry may stimulate competition, within the region the model still translates into a quasi-monopoly (*spatial monopoly*). Limited competition may exist as a result of more pronounced private sector operation.

- Micro-level purchasing is identified with demand-side competition, that is, with competition between purchasers for enrollees.

2. Competitive purchasers

- Despite the general absence of competition, elements of it have been introduced. Arguments for introducing market-type mechanisms and the associated growth of new public management approaches to managing organizations have been influential in Germany and the Netherlands (Chernichovsky and van de Ven 2003; van de Ven, Schut, and Rutten 1994).

- This requires legislation that enables increased competition, by phasing in free choice of funds, introducing restrictions in the rate of growth of premiums between insurers, and by encouraging cost consciousness through copayments.

- Pro-competition policies lead health insurers to operate in an environment that more closely resembles the private sector. Competition translates mostly to price-competition where the range of services is set by law and their quality is regulated. However, the risk-adjustment formulas and redistribution between funds has led to convergence of premiums, which in turn, decreases competitive pressure.

These concepts of vertical and horizontal linkages are also associated with the principles of vertical and horizontal equity (Wagstaff and van Doorslaer

2000) in that they affect the way the purchaser addresses different needs and people with different financial means.

Virtual Integration

Sometimes linkages are achieved through the bureaucratic structures of ministries of health. The former socialist countries of Central and Eastern Europe and the FSU, the U.K. NHS (prior to the reforms that introduced a purchaser–provider split), and the U.S. staff-model HMOs are good illustrations (table 3.2). Increasingly, however, hierarchical integration between funding, production, and distribution units is being viewed as a coordination mechanism of last resort, used mainly when contractual alternatives are not available (Robinson 1999) (box 3.3).

Instead, many countries try to achieve a type of virtual integration among autonomous and semiautonomous units as a way of dealing with the problems of horizontal fragmentation among splintered purchaser arrangements. In the case of community financing schemes and sickness funds, virtual integration can be achieved through equalization transfers, subsidies to cover noncontributing population groups, and reinsurance to enlarge the virtual risk pool. For example, Chile and, to a lesser extent, Colombia, subsidize the poor or elderly out of general revenues, which adds to employee contributions. Networking among flexible units that are more responsive to local needs may be a better organizational arrangement than the leakage that occurs under large hierarchical bureaucracies, even if the marginal transaction cost of such configurations is higher.

Robinson's study of U.S. health care market evolution provides instructive lessons on the move from vertical to virtual integration (Robinson 1999). The accelerating shift from staff HMO models to network HMO models highlights the disadvantages of vertical integration, the exclusive linkage between a single health plan and provider organization, and the advantages of nonexclusive contractual or more virtual linkages among multiple plans and providers. This contradicts the

TABLE 3.2   Organizational Form of Purchasers, Markets, Competition, and Linkages

Contractual relationship	Hierarchy			Long-term contract		Market
Organizational form	MOH MOF	Staff-model HMOs	Network HMOs	Social security organizations	Community schemes	Private insurance
Linkages	Vertical	Vertical	Virtual	Virtual	Horizontal	Horizontal
Competition	Low	Low	Low to moderate	Low to moderate	Moderate	High
Concentration	High	High	Medium	Medium	Low	Low

Source: Authors.

BOX 3.3   ECONOMICS OF VERTICAL INTEGRATION

Starting with the assumption that in the beginning there were markets,
progressively more ramified forms of internal organizations
have successively evolved.   —Williamson (1985)

The literature on industrial economics describes internal organization and market exchange as substitutes (Williamson 1975). Mainly the incentive for vertical integration is explained by the cost of writing and enforcing inter-organizational contracts that are avoidable by resorting to internal organizations. But internal organizations, mainly for bureaucratic reasons, are also costly. Vertical integration, by itself, has no immediate effect on market concentration at any stage. It may, however, be a means of mobilizing latent monopoly power.

Stigler's explication, as it applies to vertical integration, of Adam Smith's theorem that "the division of labor is limited by the extent of the market" leads to his deduction of the following life cycle implication: Vertical integration will be extensive in organizations in young industries; disintegration will be observed as an industry grows; and reintegration will occur as an industry passes into decline (Stigler 1951). The basic argument is that organizations will spin off production stages subject to increasing returns to scale in response to market growth. Stigler's hypothesis is confirmed when entry into markets is free and firms compete. However, when entry into the intermediate goods market is restricted, or intermediate goods producers collude, vertical integration increases with market size (Elberfeld 2002).

These life cycles are illustrated by distinct cost functions. Though having a specialized supplier service for the whole industry would permit economies of scale to be more fully exploited, vertical integration is rational only if the declining cost advantage exceeds the set-up cost of specialized suppliers (Stigler 1951). Long-term contracts are principally impeded by bounded rationality. While spot market (short-term) contracting is an obvious alternative, this is hazardous, as the buyer incurs the risk that the supplied service will, at some time, be provided under monopolistic terms (Williamson 1985).

While vertical integration economizes on transactions by harmonizing interests and permitting a wide variety of sensitive incentive and control processes to be activated, three key qualifications need to be considered. (1) Markets often work better than a legalistic analysis would suggest because of institutional adaptations. (2) There are anticompetitive aspects of vertical integration, such as price discrimination, barriers to entry, and circumventing regulation, which may have adverse welfare consequences.(3) Internal organizations are subject to limitations such as firm size and complexity, and organizational form.

---

previous hypothesis of managed competition, which maintains that full integration of physician, hospital, and insurance functions produces the most efficient health care organizations and will survive in a competitive medical marketplace.

The success of network HMO models stems from three interrelated factors: (1) economies of scale, (2) physician performance incentives, and (3) rapid diffusion of innovations. The separation of marketing and insurance functions from those of organizing and delivering care permits health plans and medical groups to achieve economies of scale in their respective sectors without formal or structural integration. While vertical integration increases the overall size of the firm by combining insurance with delivery functions, it typically leads to a narrower clinical network than the insurance unit needs and to a smaller patient volume than the delivery unit needs. This tension stems from the fact that the optimal geographic scope of a health insurance plan often exceeds the geographical scope of a medical group.

Robinson concludes that the early prominence of the staff-model HMO was due not to any inherent efficiency of vertical integration but to the special features of a fledgling industry that changed as it matured. Path-breaking firms in new industries frequently are forced to develop their own supply and distribution networks because independent firms are not present in the market (Williamson 1985; Robinson 1999). As consumer demand grows, however, independent suppliers and distributors emerge and focus on particular segments of the industry, thereby reaping economies of scale. Formerly integrated firms find it profitable to divest their internal units and contract with independent suppliers and distributors. As the managed care industry matured there was less need for HMOs, which had developed skills in capitation contracting and delegation, to create delivery units, and less need for medical groups, which had developed skills in managing utilization under capitation, to create health plans. Loss of economies of scale, performance incentives, and access to innovation experienced by the staff-model HMO parallels experiences elsewhere in the economy.

In virtual integration, the relationships between the revenue collection mechanisms and provider networks are more committed than arms-length spot contracting but more flexible than unified ownership and vertical integration (Robinson 1999). Virtual integration is one way of preserving the virtues of autonomy for providers without fragmentation. While spot contracting through indemnity insurance froze the solo practice, and vertical integration through the staff-model HMO froze salaried employment, virtual integration permits, even requires, innovation on forms of physician organization. This enables nonexclusive contracting with HMOs, and growth through capitation and delegation of clinical responsibilities. Virtual integration means using modern communication systems to share information quickly and without cumbersome controls. This form serves progressive health insurers, which offer multiple provider networks, rather than those that remain wedded to a single design, in order to accommodate heterogeneity among consumers in what they are willing to buy and among physicians in what they are willing to sell.

Although this example has focused mainly on the U.S. context, it is easy to translate its relevance to a developing-country setting (table 3.2). The trend today in many low- and middle-income countries is toward virtual integration between revenue-collection mechanisms and provider networks. Linkage through purchasing arrangements such as social health insurance agencies, private health insurance funds, and community financing schemes provides such virtual integration by allowing greater flexibility and less opportunity for bureaucratic capture. Similarly, the U.K. reforms of the past decade made strategic purchasers of the former district health authorities (DHAs). The DHAs used to function as part of the core public bureaucracy with limited decision rights and financial responsibility. Accompanying the purchaser–provider split, DHAs' autonomy was increased, and they were subjected to greater market pressure and held more closely responsible for their financial and technical performance.

There is, however, a flip side to this coin. Semiautonomous purchasing agencies that manage the resource-allocation process can also contribute to a fragmentation of the financing function if the policies for the revenue-collection processes are not coordinated adequately with those of the purchaser and if the purchaser function provides incomplete benefit coverage. For example, if a purchasing arrangement has a mandate to cover the whole population but receives revenues only to cover part of the population, a dysfunctional structural deficit results. The most common origin of this problem is incomplete pooling arrangements to cover the inactive part of the population such as the elderly or children. Many social health insurance programs have provisions to cover rich-poor and healthy-sick transfers, but not intertemporal transfers. An example of this is the National Health Insurance Fund in Hungary, which has to cover benefits for the elderly as an unfunded mandate. Purchasing arrangements may also contribute to vertical fragmentation when there are benefit gaps such as lack of coverage of pharmaceutical benefits and ambulatory care, as under the National Health Insurance Plan in the Philippines.

INCENTIVE REGIME

A large body of literature and empirical experience now indicates that three sets of systemic factors jointly determine the incentive regime and hence the behavior of both service providers and purchasers. These factors include:

- Alterations in the relationship between health care providers and governments (governance)

- The market environment to which such organizations are exposed

- The incentives embedded in the funding or payment mechanisms (provider-payment systems).

Structural changes in governance, the relationship between the government and the organization, may lead to significant differences in the amount of autonomy given to the managers, the mechanisms used to generate new incentives, and accountability.

Five Internal Incentives

Each purchaser reform can be characterized by the magnitude of control shifted from the hierarchy, or supervising agency, to the hospital. Critical decision rights transferred to management may include control over inputs, labor, scope of activities, financial management, clinical and nonclinical administration, strategic management (formulation of institutional objectives), market strategy, and sales:

Decision rights

Vertical hierarchy ————— Management autonomy

Giving managers and staff the material incentive to economize is the structural complement to delegating decision-making control to them. As James Q. Wilson queries, "Why scrimp and save if you cannot keep the results of your frugality?" (Wilson 1989: 116). Therefore, a critical distinguishing feature of the reforms that shifts decision rights from central governments to semi-autonomous purchasers is the degree to which the public purse ceases to be the "residual claimant" on revenue flows. Aligning the revenue flows and decision rights is crucial to get those in the right place to make the right decisions:

Residual claimant

Public purse ————— Private individual

The third key element of the high-powered incentives sought in these reforms is the degree to which revenue relies on market forces rather than hierarchical allocation of a budget:

Market exposure

Direct budget ————— Nonbudget income

The question is, to what extent does the purchaser earn or sell services to earn its revenue? The first two factors imply that managers will focus more on financial viability. Thus, the issue of which strategies will best generate revenue becomes critical. If purchasing quality services for patients is the best way of generating revenue, that strategy will be pursued. If political lobbying or extracting monopoly rents is the best way to get revenue, these strategies will be pursued.

Purchasing reforms can also be characterized by the degree to which accountability for achieving objectives is based on hierarchical supervision of the organization versus regulation or contracting:

Accountability

Hierarchical control ————— Rules/regulations/contracts

As decision rights are delegated to a semi-autonomous purchasing organization, the government's ability to assert direct accountability (through the hierarchy) is diminished. Partially, accountability is intended to come from market pressures, because the market is seen as generating a nonpolitical, nonarbitrary evaluation of organizational performance, at least in its economic performance.

Accountability pressures under such an arrangement will come via a contracting and monitoring process rather than from direct line command and control levers.

Finally, in the health sector, markets are far from capable of delivering the full range of sectoral objectives—both due to market failures and due to social values. Thus, rules and regulations regarding the operation of these organizations constitute an alternative form of accountability mechanism. Strengthening these mechanisms constitutes a fourth critical element of organizational reforms of purchasers that reduce the use of traditional, hierarchical accountability mechanisms.

The final critical factor characterizing organizational reform of purchasers is the extent to which "social functions" delivered by the hospital shift from being implicit and unfunded to specified and directly funded:

Social functions
Unspecified mandates ————— Specified/funded/regulated

If the purchaser is motivated to focus more on financial viability, due to the changes discussed above, management may move to decrease output of services that do not cover their costs. Thus, the financial bottom line could undermine the ability to cross-subsidize certain services internally. Thus, purchasing reforms must create alternative mechanisms to ensure that previously cross-subsidized services continue to be delivered (i.e., explicit funding, demand-side subsidies, insurance regulation).

These elements combine to create new incentives for the allocation of resources through purchasing rather than hierarchical budgetary transfers. Two external elements strongly influence the new incentive regime: the funding or payments arrangements, and the structure of the market to which the organization is exposed. The influence of these factors on the five components of the incentive regime is discussed below and summarized in figure 3.9.

Reform Modalities

The incentives faced by the reformed purchaser are characterized according to five critical elements. In this final section, each organizational reform modality is described according to these features, and how they fit together is explained.

Budgetary Organizations

For the sake of comparison, let us start our discussion with the case of a budgetary unit, such as a purchaser run as a government department. The manager of such a purchaser is essentially an administrator. The government's hierarchy of officials and rules controls all strategic issues and determines most day-to-day decisions related to production and delivery of the purchasing function, for

Figure 3.9   Incentive Regimes of Purchasers

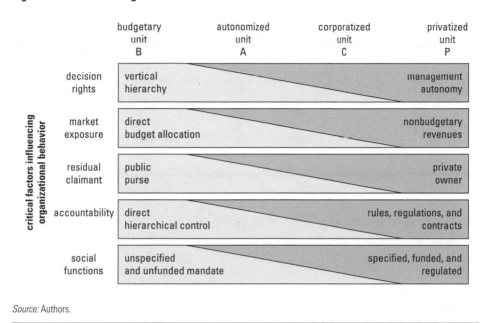

Source: Authors.

example, staff mix and staff levels, services offered, technology used, accounting and financial management methods, salaries, and so on. In general, the government determines the revenue of the purchaser and all related activities. Any "excess revenues" generated along the way belong to the public sector—and must either be returned to a superior agency or spent as directed. Any "excess losses" also are covered by the public purse.

Autonomized Organizations

Dissatisfaction with the weak performance of such budgetary organizations has led to various approaches to reform described earlier, such as agency creation, decentralization, and a purchaser–provider split. The roots of many of the most serious efficiency and quality problems have been discovered in management's pervasive lack of control over resources (especially labor) and production. Autonomization of such organizations is a reform that focuses on "making managers manage"— by shifting much of the day-to-day decision-making control from the hierarchy to management. These changes are often accompanied by increases in the scope for generating revenue tied to service delivery. This may be achieved by moving toward funding via performance-related contracts, by allowing paying patients to be served, or by allowing copayments to be charged. Additional revenue opportunities motivate only if revenue can be retained. A comprehensive review of performance contracts throughout the world in other sectors has, however, found that they had a weak, and sometimes negative, influence on performance (World Bank 1995). For these reasons, in the case of commercial companies and infrastructure, the preferred organizational reforms have been corporatization and privatization (Girishankar 1999).

Corporatized Organizations

The corporatization of a purchaser is based on efforts to mimic the structure and efficiency of private corporations while assuring that social objectives are still emphasized through public ownership. Under corporatization, provisions for managerial autonomy are stronger than under autonomization, giving managers virtually complete control over all inputs and issues related to production of services. The organization is legally established as an independent entity and hence the transfer of control is more durable than under autonomization. The independent status includes a hard budget constraint or financial "bottom line"—which makes the organization fully accountable for its financial performance—with liquidation, at least theoretically, the final solution in case of insolvency. The greater latitude of management is complemented by market pressures as an important source of incentives, crucially including some element of competition or contestability.

These market incentives come from the combination of an increased portion of revenue coming from sales (rather than budget allocation) and increased possibilities for keeping and using extra revenue, as well as a hard budget constraint. The corporatized purchaser is thus much more a residual claimant than is the autonomized one—in that it can retain excess revenues, but is also responsible for losses. Accountability is generated on three fronts: direct hierarchical control (or ownership accountability), funding/payment, and regulatory accountability. Ownership accountability is usually narrowed to cover a limited range of economic targets—as part of the effort to mimic the effective governance structures associated with private corporations. However, this emphasis on economic performance necessitates alternative arrangements for ensuring social functions (services previously cross-subsidized) are still delivered. Under corporatization, these are usually pursued through purchasing, insurance regulation, demand-side financing, or mandates that apply to all organizations, rather than simply to public facilities.

Privatized Organizations

Finally, the most extreme version of "marketizing" organizational reforms in purchasing is privatization. This reform entails transforming the public purchaser into a private entity, either as a for-profit or nonprofit organization. Nonprofit privatization is conceptually quite distinct from for-profit privatization (Torres and Mathur, 1996). Privatization naturally removes the purchaser from all direct control of the hierarchy of government officials or public sector rules. The organization is thus fully independent of the hierarchy, although the management is likely quite constrained by the new owners. All incentives come from opportunities to earn revenue, and the incentives are relatively strong, because private owners or shareholders are now the residual claimants on extra revenues, now called "profits." It is the combination of these two forces that drives the high-incentive features of this model—complete exposure to a market to earn revenue under owners who are strongly motivated to capture the revenues and monitor the management.

CONCLUSIONS

Organizations matter in making strategic purchasing of health care work. They are an essential part of supporting the political economy of reform and implementing the desired underlying policy framework. But even a well-designed policy framework and highly performing organizational structures are not enough. In order for strategic purchasing to have a maximum impact on both efficiency and equity, the underlying policy framework and organizational structures need to be surrounded by a strong institutional environment and capable governance and management arrangements. These latter factors are discussed in the next two chapters.

What the optimal organizational structure will be depends on the objective function defined and system capacity. The objective function is derived from prioritizing the shortcomings of system performance that can be tackled through the resource allocation and purchasing agency (i.e., need assessment) and the relative political/economic power of the players in the system.

These translate into questions such as:

- What does the system need most to improve its performance? That is, what is expected to bring about the greatest marginal gain—focusing on some efficiency dimension (e.g., innovation, cost), responsiveness aspects as perceived by the consumer (quality, choice), or on equity?

- What is required in terms of organizational reconfiguration to attain them?

- Who dominates the shaping of organizational structures?

- To what extent is the reform process provider-, patient-, steward-driven?

These clearly involve trade-offs and will have profound impact on how the system evolves, and whether changes in purchaser organizations create the desired effect and add value over the long term.

As shown, equity considerations often turn out to be secondary. This is not just a limitation of looking through the lens of the economist; evidence suggests that often policy makers only insert the equity bullet as a last-minute item in the list of reform objectives. Of course, how equity weighs in can vary depending on the (1) degree of inequity, (2) consumer/citizen dissatisfaction, (3) voice/power of the inequitably treated groups, (4) the government's responsiveness to social pressures (degree of accountability and stewardship), and (5) the leverage and extent of external pressure to improve on equity (donor conditionality and international policy objectives).

NOTES

1. Potential advantages of highly concentrated arrangements, in principle: collection efficiency, cost control, and equity; single pool with lower threat of adverse selection; increased negotiation power, which may result in better prices; and, greater sense of solidarity through national redistribution of resources. Observed challenges: limitation where taxation capacity is low; monopsony suffers from lack of competition, which compromises efficiency; monopsony leads to price controls, which trigger underprovision; challenged cost containment, given the "insurer of last resort" function, and the need for filling deficits (especially problematic if there is no gatekeeper at primary provider level); typically overextended central role at the expense of decentralized governance and management; and, transparency and accountability problems.

2. Accountability is enforced through hierarchical control over inputs and outputs. There is little economic incentive. Most personnel are employed as staff, protected by civil service laws.

3. See South Asian regional review on CD supplement to this volume.

REFERENCES

Arrow, K. J. 1986. "Agency and Markets." In *Handbook of Mathematical Economics,* ed. K. J. Arrow and M. D. Intriligator, Vol. 3. Amsterdam: Elsevier.

———. 1970. *The Organization of Economic Activity: Issue Pertinent to the Choice of Market versus Nonmarket Allocations.* Chicago: Markham Publishing Company.

Asian Development Bank/World Bank. 2004. *Devolution in Pakistan.* Manila: Asian Development Bank

Beauchamp, T.L., and J.F. Childress. 1983. *Principles of Biomedical Ethics.* 2d ed. Oxford: Oxford University Press.

Bergen, M., S. Dutta, and O.C. Walker. 1992. "Agency Relationships in Marketing: A Review of the Implications and Applications of Agency and Related Theories." *Journal of Marketing* 56(3): 1–24.

Chernichovsky, D. 1995. "Health System Reforms in Industrialized Democracies: An Emerging Paradigm." *Milbank Quarterly* 73(3): 339–72.

———. 2002. "Pluralism, Public Choice, and the State in the Emerging Paradigm in Health Systems." *Milbank Quarterly* 80(1): 5–39.

Chernichovsky, D., and W.P.M.M. van de Ven. 2003. "Risk Adjustment in Europe." *Health Policy* 65(Special Issue): 1–3.

Cuffel, B.J., L. Snowden, M. Masland, and G. Piccagli. 1996, "Managed Care in the Public Mental Health System." *Community Mental Health Journal* 32(2): 109–24.

Cutler, D. M., and R. J. Zeckhauser. 2000. "The Anatomy of Health Insurance." In *Handbook of Health Economics,* ed. A. J. Culyer and J. P. Newhouse. Amsterdam: Elsevier.

Dionne, G. 2000. *Handbook of Insurance.* Boston, MA: Kluwer.

Donahue, J.D. 1989. *The Privatization Decision: Public Ends, Private Means.* New York, NY: Basic Books.

Dranove, D., and W.D. White. 1985. "Agency Theory: New Insight into the Health Care Industry." *Journal of Medical Practice Management* 4(3): 165–69.

Dror, D., and A.S. Preker, eds. 2002. *Social Re-Insurance: A New Approach to Sustainable Community Health Financing.* Washington, DC: World Bank/International Labour Organization.

Eisenhardt, K.M. 1988. "Control: Organization and Economic Approaches." *Management Science* 31: 134–49.

Elberfeld, W. 2002. "Market Size and Vertical Integration: Stigler's Hypothesis Reconsidered." *Journal of Industrial Economics* 50(1): 23–42.

Enthoven, A. 1994. "On the Ideal Market Structure for Third-Party Purchasing of Health Care." *Social Science and Medicine* 39(10): 1413–24.

———. 1988. *Theory and Practice of Managed Competition in Health Care Finance.* New York, NY: North-Holland.

———. 1978a. "Consumer Choice Health Plan." *New England Journal of Medicine* 298(12): 650–58.

———. 1978b. "Consumer Choice Health Plan." *New England Journal of Medicine* 298(13): 709–20.

Evans, R.G. 1983a. "Incomplete Vertical Integration in the Health Care Industry: Pseudomarkets and Pseudopolicies." *Annals of the American Academy of Political and Social Science* 468(Health Care Policy in America—July): 60–87.

———. 1983b. "The Welfare Economics of Public Health Insurance: Theory and Canadian Practice." In *Social Insurance,* ed. L. Soderstrom, 71–104. Amsterdam: North-Holland.

Fama, E.F., and M.C. Jensen. 1983. "Agency Problems and Residual Claims." *Journal of Law and Economics* 26(2): 327–49.

Figueras, J., R. Robinson, and E. Jakubowski. 2005a. *Purchasing to Improve Health System Performance.* Buckingham, United Kingdom: Open University Press.

———. 2005b. "Purchasing to Improve Health Systems Performance: Drawing the Lessons." In *Purchasing to Improve Health System Performance,* ed. J. Figueras, R. Robinson and E. Jakubowski. Buckingham, UK: Open University Press.

Girishankar, N. 1999. *Reforming Institutions for Service Delivery: A Framework for Development Assistance with an Application to the HNP Portfolio.* World Bank Policy Research Working Paper 2039. Washington, DC: World Bank.

Hermans, H., and J. Nooren. 1998. "Contracting and the Purchaser-Provider Split in Western Europe: A Legal-Organizational Analysis. *Medicine and Law* 17(2): 167–88.

Holmstrom, B. 1982. "Moral Hazard in Teams." *Bell Journal of Economics* 13(2): 324–40.

———. 1979 "Moral Hazard and Observability." *Bell Journal of Economics* 10(1): 74–91.

Hutchison, J., P. Hardee, and C. Barns. 1997. "Bureaucracy of Purchaser-Provider Split Delays Treatment." *British Medical Journal* 314(7089): 1275.

Jost, T.S., D. Hughes, J. McHale, and L. Griffiths. 1995. "The British Health Care Reforms, the American Health Care Revolution, and Purchaser/Provider Contracts." *Journal of Health Politics, Policy, and Law* 20(4): 885–908.

Kutzin, J. 2001. "A Descriptive Framework for Country-Level Analysis of Health Care Financing Arrangements." *Health Policy and Planning* 56: 171–204.

Levaggi, R. 1996. "NHS Contracts: An Agency Approach." *Health Economics* 5: 341–52.

MacDonald, G.M. 1984. "New Directions in the Economic Theory of Agency." *Canadian Journal of Economics* 17(3): 415–40.

McGuire, A., J. Henderson, and G.H. Mooney. 1988. *The Economics of Health Care: An Introductory Text*. London: Routledge & Kegan Paul.

Mirrlees, J. 1974. "Notes on Welfare Economics, Information, and Uncertainty." In *Contribution to Economic Analysis,* ed. M.S. Balch, D. McFadden, and Sy Wu. Amsterdam: North-Holland.

Mooney, G., and M. Ryan. 1993. "Agency in Health Care: Getting Beyond First Principals." *Journal of Health Economics* 12: 125–35.

Moore, M. 1995. *Creating Public Value*. Cambridge, MA: Harvard University Press.

Musgrove, P. 1996. *Public and Private Roles in Health: Theory and Financing Patterns*. Washington, DC: World Bank.

Newhouse, J.P. 1993. *Free for All? Lessons from the RAND Health Insurance Experiment*. Cambridge, MA: Harvard University Press.

Organisation for Economic Co-operation and Development (OECD). 1992. *The Reform of Health Care: A Comparative Analysis of Seven OECD Countries*. Paris: OECD.

Outreville, J.F. 1998. *Theory and Practice of Insurance*. Boston, MA: Kluwer.

Ovretveit, J. 1995a. "Purchasing Agency Organization." In *Purchasing for Health: A Multidisciplinary Introduction to the Theory and Practice of Health Purchasing*. Buckingham, United Kingdom: Open University Press.

———. 1995b. "Purchasing for Health." In *Purchasing for Health: A Multidisciplinary Introduction to the Theory and Practice of Health Purchasing*. Buckingham, United Kingdom: Open University Press.

Paton, C. 1995. "Present Dangers and Future Threats: Some Perverse Incentives in the NHS Reforms." *British Medical Journal* 310(6989): 1245–48.

Pauly, M.V. 2000. "Insurance Reimbursement." In *Handbook of Health Economics*, ed. A.J. Culyer and J.P. Newhouse. Amsterdam: Elsevier.

———. 1968. "The Economics of Moral Hazard," Comment. *American Economic Review* 58: 531–37.

Preker A.S., G. Carrrin, D. Dror, M. Jakab, W.S. Hsiao and D. Arhin-Tenkorang. 2001. *Role of Communities in Resource Mobilization and Risk Sharing: A Synthesis Report.* HNP Discussion Paper. Washington, DC: World Bank.

Preker, A.S., and A. Harding, eds. 2003. *Innovations in Health Service Delivery: The Corporatization of Public Hospitals.* Health, Nutrition, and Population Series. Washington, DC: World Bank.

Propper, C. 1995a. "Agency and Incentive in the NHS Internal Market." *Social Science and Medicine* 40(12): 1683–90.

———. 1995b. "Regulatory Reform of the NHS Internal Market." *Health Economics* 4: 77–83.

Rice, T. 1998. *The Economics of Health Reconsidered.* Chicago, IL: Health Administration Press.

Robinson, J.C. 1999. T*he Corporate Practice of Medicine: Competition and Innovation in Health Care.* Berkeley: University of California Press.

Robinson, R., E. Jakubowski, and J. Figueras, 2005. "Organization of Purchasing in Europe." In *Purchasing to Improve Health System Performance*, ed. J. Figueras, R. Robinson, and E. Jakubowski. Buckingham, United Kingdom: Open University Press.

Ross, S. 1973. "The Economic Theory of Agency: The Principal's Problem." *American Economic Review* 63(2): 134–39.

Rothschild, M., and J. Stiglitz. 1976. "Equilibrium in Competitive Insurance Markets." *Quarterly Journal of Economics* 90(4): 630–9

Ryan, M. 1992. "The Economic Theory of Agency in Health Care: Lessons from Non-economists for Economists." Discussion Paper No. 03192. Aberdeen, United Kingdom: University of Aberdeen, Health Economic Research Unit.

Savedoff, W.D. 1998. *Organization Matters: Agency Problems in Health and Education in Latin America.* Washington: Inter-American Development Bank.

Schieber, G., ed. 1997. *Innovations in Health Care Financing.* Washington, DC: World Bank.

Shavell, S. 1980. "Damage Measures for Breach of Contract." *Bell Journal of Economics* 11(2): 466–490.

Stigler, G.J. 1951. "The Division of Labor Is Limited by the Extent of the Market." *Journal of Political Economy* 59(June): 185–93.

Stiglitz, J.E. 1989. "Principal and Agent." In *Allocation, Information and Markets,* ed. J. Eatwell. London: Macillan.

———. 1974. "Incentives and Risk Sharing in Sharecropping." *Review of Economic Studies* 41(2): 219–55.

Torres, G., and S. Mathur. 1996. *The Third Wave of Privatization: Privatization of Social Sectors in Developing Countries.* Washington, DC: World Bank.

van de Ven, W.P.M.M., K. Beck, F. Buchner, and D. Chernichovsky 2003. "Risk Adjustment and Risk Selection on the Sickness Fund Insurance Market in Five European Countries." *Health Policy* 65: 75–98.

van de Ven, W.P.M.M., and R.R.P. Ellis. 2000. "Risk Adjustment in Competitive Health Plan Markets." In *Handbook of Health Economics*, ed. A.J. Culyer and J.P. Newhouse. Amsterdam: Elsevier.

van de Ven, W.P.M.M., F.T. Schut, and F.F. Rutten. 1994. "Forming and Reforming the Market for Third-Party Purchasing of Health Care." *Social Science and Medicine* 39(10): 1405–12.

Wagstaff, A., and E. van Doorslaer. 2000. "Equity in Health Care Finance and Delivery." In *Handbook of Health Economics,* ed. A.J. Culyer and J.P. Newhouse. Amsterdam: Elsevier.

Williamson, O. 1985. *The Economic Institutions of Capitalism: Firms, Markets and Relational Contracting.* New York, NY: Free Press.

Wilson, J.Q. 1989. *Bureaucracy.* New York, NY: Basic Books.

World Bank. 1995. *Bureaucrats in Business: The Economics and Politics of Government Ownership.* Washington, DC: World Bank.

World Health Organization (WHO). 2000. *Health Systems: Measuring Performance.* Geneva: WHO.

Zweifel, P., and W. Struwe. 1998. "Long-Term Care Insurance in a Two-Generation Model." *Journal of Risk and Insurance* 65 (1): 13–32.

CHAPTER 4

Institutional Environment

Hernán L. Fuenzalida-Puelma, Reinhard R. Haslinger,
and Alexander S. Preker

Resource allocation and purchasing is a heavily regulated health system function. It takes place in a highly institutionalized environment involving a diversity of decision-making levels, innumerable transactions, and many different stakeholders with different interests. Various institutions provide a framework of formal and informal rules to attain major values and objectives of the entire health care system.

Regulation takes place at four different institutional levels. These include the underlying legal framework, regulatory instruments, administrative procedures, and customs and practices. These rules come from different sources and include laws enacted by parliaments; governmental regulations issued by ministries and decentralized public entities; norms and guidelines imposed by professional and trade associations, and best practices and customs.

This chapter expands on the political economy of strategic purchasing in the health sector as described in table I.1 of the Introduction to this volume:

Institutional environment	Legal framework
	Regulatory instruments
	Administrative procedures
	Customs and practices

INTRODUCTION

The authors use an understanding of institutions as the "*rules of the game . . .* or, more formally . . . the humanly devised constraints that shape human interactions" (North 1990). Institutions are, in this sense, formal and informal rules and arrangements for decision making and guidance. In this chapter, both the kinds of institutions that exist and the way they work are discussed under different resource allocation and purchasing arrangements, As used in this chapter, "institution" is not a synonym for "organization."

For a broader understanding, the authors also adopt an argument presented by Ogus (1994). Ogus defines *regulations* as a system of control over behavior founded in the goal of ensuring interests. Exploring the sense of institutions, the authors expand Ogus's concept to an understanding of institutions not only controlling behavior but influencing behavior with a range of factors (Afifi, Busse, and Harding 2003). This leads us to define *institutions* as "the rules of the game" that control behavior but, at the same time, change behavior through incentives.

By issuing, interpreting, and enforcing rules, norms, or orders, institutions regulate and guide. They subject certain actions to governing principles and procedures by allowing, prohibiting, directing, or controlling them. Institutions can also be understood in the broader sense of encompassing (1) all normative regulations including laws for economic and administrative regulations, and (2) cultural and informal modes of behavior including the interpretation of norms, laws, and regulations. In this sense, institutions paradoxically regulate behavior with rules and procedures. At the same time, they are themselves regulations (regulated behavior).

Institutions secure major values and objectives of the health system. They play an important role in determining the availability, cost, and equity in access, insurance, and quality of health care services. High quality is a goal that most countries pursue and ensure through licensing, accreditation permits, and inspections. Institutions are also important for setting up accountability mechanisms and for the protection of patient rights, which most countries have come to regulate through, for example, patient bills of rights and malpractice procedures. All these issues dramatically affect health care purchasing.

In exploring the institutional framework of health care purchasing, this chapter first creates a basic understanding of institutions and answers such questions as: What interests create the demand for institutions? and What is the purpose of institutions and how do they regulate health care purchasing? It then briefly examines the scope of institutions to determine what they regulate and to see the power of institutions. For this purpose, two theoretical models are applied to mark the range in which institutions can vary from highly interventionist to barely interventionist. The chapter also discusses different forms of institutions and makes two distinctions: (1) between formal regulations, for example, formal legal control mechanisms, and informal relationships and structures of regulations; and (2) between external and internal institutions. Finally, four different institutional levels on which regulation takes place are discussed; these include the legal framework, regulatory instruments, administrative procedures, and customs and practices.

RATIONALE FOR INSTITUTIONS

Why are institutions created? What interests create a demand for institutions? Why do institutions actually make sense? Exploring the latter question, one is confronted with two kinds of interests. Social and economic interests provide the rationale for institutions to regulate and guide the purchasing and financing of health care goods and services (Ogus 1994).

The consideration of health as a basic human need is the main social interest. In many countries, securing good health for the entire population is regarded as an essential public interest, as essential as education. This is why the state or government, as a country's major political and social institution, is considered (at least partly) responsible for providing health care. To achieve this goal, social health insurance and other comprehensive financing schemes have been established, based on employment and on individual or family income.

More specifically, social interests create a demand for institutions to regulate issues like protection and safety, access to health care, quality of services, and the like. Institutions tackle market failures such as *asymmetric information,* which leaves individual persons or buyers of health care with much less information about needs and quality of services than the providers or sellers possess. Lack of information causes externalities that discriminate against sufficiently informed purchasing decisions by individuals and buyers of health care. For instance, the doctor or provider of health care is better informed than individuals who do not know the symptoms of and the best way to treat a stomach ulcer, and they may find it difficult to assess their own health status.

Informed consent regulations are being gradually incorporated into the regulatory systems in most countries, forcing providers to disclose information in clear and intelligible language. Labeling requirements and warnings on pharmaceuticals are also put forward to protect the public. As a result, this is not a one-way street. Purchasers insist on compliance with requirements, and suppliers have to comply to become eligible for purchasing contracts.

Economic interests lead to a demand for institutions that primarily target markets with monopolistic tendencies. Lack of market regulation through competition might lead to a limited supply of health services due to low prices, low-quality services, or inefficiency. Economic interests lead to substitutes for market-force regulation. A monopolist's interest in maximizing profits can be limited by price regulation and by the selection of providers (public only or also private health care providers). Purchasers obtaining a monopoly right can be forced to compete or can be limited in their operations through regulations that designate, for example, certain rates of contribution to social insurance or the size of the benefits package.

Governments regulate the health care market by deciding on the qualifications that health care purchasers and providers must have to conduct their respective buying and selling activities. This activity recognizes that regulations control behavior not only to protect interests but also to make competing and conflicting interests compatible and to restrict behaviors that are against the public interest.

In addition, governments address market failures and, in many circumstances, they establish prerequisites such as the provision of adequate information. They avoid or minimize externalities that may discriminate against individual purchasers and providers. Rules for proper disclosure of specifications and requirements in bidding and tender procedures, public announcements, and disclosure of bids and tender results serve to protect economic interests. Purchasing tenders and bidding with inadequate or incomplete information may work against purchasers. Another example is contracting, an extremely complex process that is regulated in such details as contract types, qualified parties, purpose of contracts, compulsory specifications, conditions for the delivery of the goods and services, quality, prices, unit costs, payment mechanisms, medical and administrative data, accounting and reporting, monitoring and auditing, and contract enforcement.

Purchasers act as economic institutions. They are not just confronted with governmental regulations, but also impose their own rules and institutions for the purchasing and delivery processes within the margins of freedom of contracting. Typical cases are, for example, negotiated fees and performance incentives that managed care organizations include in contracts. Medical professionals in the United States have protested these regulations, arguing that the economic power of these organizations leads to an erosion of their incomes. For that reason, some well-reputed physicians refuse to take insurance or managed care payments for private consultations and require an up-front fee-for-service payment.

PURCHASING ISSUES REQUIRING INSTITUTIONAL REFORM

Three major issues relating to health care purchasing that require institutional reform in many countries are briefly reviewed: the roles of consumers and markets, insurance markets, and the factor and product markets.

Role of Consumers and Markets

Performance-based purchasing requires action at two levels, each of which is necessary but not sufficient in itself. First, individual patients must be empowered to influence collective purchasing decisions so that they are responsive to the needs and concerns of ordinary citizens, not just those of policy makers, health care facility managers, and health professionals. Second, the strategic policy objectives of purchasing agencies must be made explicit so that they reflect more accountably the interests of various stakeholders.

Under traditional resource allocation arrangements with government economic departments or purchasers, the interest of the patient is often left out. Popular dissatisfaction with this aspect of collective funding of health care is pervasive throughout the world, irrespective of the system. Dissatisfaction extends to countries such as Denmark, Sweden, and the United Kingdom, which traditionally use an integrated funding model; France, Germany, and the Netherlands, which use a contracting model; and Canada, Switzerland, and the United States, where ex post reimbursement is more prevalent.

In the United States, dissatisfaction is particularly high in relation to securing access to common curative services such as emergency room care, low consumer quality in the management of services, and waiting lists. Typically such dissatisfaction leads higher-income groups to opt out. Often patients are more satisfied when they have a private doctor dealing with their care. Such lack of choice by patients is a major issue, and there are clear trade-offs between increased choice and out-of-pocket payments.

In other countries there are similar issues, such as lack of out-of-hours care and bed blocking in the United Kingdom. Some improvements in patient satisfaction have been observed under a mixed fee-for-service and capitation system in Denmark. Likewise, New Zealand has tried using purchasing reforms to pare down long waiting lists and other problems associated with clinical care.

The current trend worldwide is to use three types of approaches to address the public sector failures in service delivery described above in descending order of importance. They include the following (Hirschman 1970):

- Increased exit possibilities (market consumer choice)

- Voice (client participation)

- Loyalty (hierarchical sense of responsibility).

When possible, "exit" would be the preferred escape route, unless forced to use the weaker variants because the goods and services involved are not "marketable." This approach relies on greater private sector participation, allowing clients and patients a choice or alternative to publicly provided services. Such exit options can be implemented in parallel with other public sector management reforms that strengthen voice and loyalty. Patients can have their role as consumers enhanced in several ways that will strengthen their role as principals vis-à-vis the purchasing agency.

A common approach is to separate financing from provision (purchaser–provider split in Eastern Europe and Central Asia), to separate governance from stewardship (decentralization and agency formation in the Latin America and East Asia and Pacific Regions), and to allow the introduction of some direct user charges by individual health care providers and organizations (user fees in the Africa Region). A second approach is to subdivide the financing function into several semi-autonomous or fully autonomous entities, each representing a specific interest group.

All such reforms require complex institutional reforms and have important transaction costs that need to be taken into consideration before addressing agency problems with consumer sovereignty and choice.

Role of Insurance Markets

As described above, under many purchasing arrangements, the collection of revenues, pooling of funds, and allocation of resources and purchasing subfunctions of health care financing are combined under a single organizational configuration. Sometimes these consolidated functions are also merged with the stewardship, governance, and provider system functions. Such blurring of functional boundaries may not be an optimal arrangement for both equity and efficiency reasons:

- When social health insurance contributions are collected at the source by employers, big economies can be gained by merging that collection process with the collection of other social insurance contributions, and even taxes. Countries that use the Treasury to collect all three have much lower administrative costs and often higher contribution compliance than countries where the organizations responsible for purchasing set up a parallel taxation structure.

- The economies of scale and scope are different for revenue collection, pooling of funds, and purchasing activities. In revenue collection, there may be considerable benefits in terms of contribution compliance and evasion prevention by unifying this function at the national level and by using a single personal identification database. In the case of pooling, larger is often better because it spreads risks over a bigger population. In contrast, purchasing activities may be more responsive to consumers and better able to monitor provider activities if parts of their functions are decentralized.

For these reasons, although there may be benefits from a clear demarcation between the stewardship, governance, and insurance functions related to purchasing, in recent years there has been a move toward reintegration of the revenue collection and insurance subfunctions with the tax collection system in many countries.

Such a separation of the revenue collection and insurance subfunctions from purchasing is not without risks. Many countries have purchasing arrangements that have a built-in structural deficit because the premiums collected and subsidies available for some inactive population groups do not cover the purchaser's expenditure obligations (e.g., Croatia). For example, if the purchaser is required to cover expenditures incurred for the elderly and the unemployed but receives no contributions or subsidies for these two population groups, the only way to balance the budget is by cross-subsidizing those expenses from funds received from the active population and by enforcing expenditure controls to the point where the quality and scope of benefits received is below what the contributing population expects. When this occurs, contribution compliance may deteriorate, and patients may choose to circumvent the formal insurance arrangements to get services they expect from private providers and paying fees for those services. Such an exodus undermines the financial protection that the formal schemes should confer.

Roles of Factor and Product Markets

A perfectly competitive market would present no entry barriers to either consumers or suppliers, and each would have all the information needed to make rational choices. When purchasing arrangements are created as agents for consumers at the health system level, one or more of four dominant market configurations usually emerge, depending on whether there is a single provider or multiple providers and a single purchaser or multiple purchasers. First, the number of purchasers or budget agencies may be restricted. Second, the formal purchasing arrangements may have a mandate to deal with only one set of providers such as the public sector. Third, the number of suppliers may be restricted and even limited to a single public sector entity. Fourth, only rarely does a truly competitive market emerge with multiple purchasing arrangements and suppliers competing with each other. A characteristic feature of the health sector is therefore incomplete markets. Table 4.1 shows these four market modalities.

In reality, however, the health sector is considerably more complex than suggested by this simple matrix due to segmentation of both the factor market and product markets. The markets for inputs (factor markets) include several noncompeting segments such as knowledge, pharmaceuticals, medical equipment, consumables, labor, and capital. Each of these markets has its own characteristics and does not really compete with the others, although there has been a recent trend for some pharmaceutical companies to also produce a limited range of medical equipment and consumables. Likewise, the various segments of the product market (programs and services) often to do not compete with each other. Public health programs, ambulatory diagnostic facilities, primary care, and the various levels of hospital services are often independent entities, linked through referral systems and complex networks of providers that "cooperate" (collude) instead of competing with each other. The move toward managed care networks in many countries has reduced the number of independent providers but, unlike passive public sector providers, has also increased competition in the product market. Whether competition will continue remains to be seen.

Since most health care markets are incomplete, purchasing arrangements often have to use other techniques than competition among multiple providers to create performance pressures. This can be done through mechanisms such as contestability, yardstick competition, and benchmarking.

Many countries have been experimenting with reforms of the purchaser–provider interface. The common feature of these reforms is greater reliance on provider performance information in purchasing decisions. Purchasers increasingly look at clinical quality, efficiency, consumer satisfaction, financial risk, and other aspects of provider performance. The distinguishing feature of these

TABLE 4.1   Market Structure Modalities between Purchasers and Providers

Purchaser provider	Single	Multiple
Single	Bilateral monopoly (e.g., rural Hungary)	Competitive purchasing with monopolistic provision (e.g., rural Chile)
Multiple	Monopsonistic purchasing with competitive provision (e.g., Brazil, Kyrgyz Republic, urban Hungary)	Competitive purchasing and provision (e.g., urban Chile, Lebanon)

Source: Authors.

reformers is how radical they are in their use of provider performance information. The more radical reformers use provider performance data to contract selectively with chosen providers. This is equivalent to creating a market that rewards good performers and penalizes poor performers.

The health care market is fraught with market imperfections related to information asymmetry, barriers to entry, and principal–agent problems. Table 4.2 summarizes key market imperfections in health services purchasing.

- *Information failures.* Purchasing is a transaction that involves serious information and measurability failures due to the nature of health services. Although collective purchasers are in a better position to address information and measurability failures than individual consumers, this information asymmetry impedes efficient functioning of markets. In particular, information and measurability failures lead to high transaction costs and principal–agent problems. These can be addressed through incentive alignment, monitoring, measurement, and accountability instruments.

- *Barriers to entry and exit.* Significant natural and constructed barriers to entry limit the play of competitive forces.

- *Principal–agent problems.* Both purchasers and providers behave as imperfect agents for the patients that they are supposed to represent, frequently demonstrating conflicting interests. Purchasers may try to contain costs by limiting the benefits package even when the need and demand for services are obvious. And, depending on the payment mechanism, providers may try to artificially stimulate demand in order to maximize income under fee-for-service payment systems or limit demand in order to reduce costs under budget caps or prospective payment systems.

The following section discusses the types of institutional arrangements that can be used to address these problems.

TABLE 4.2   Market Imperfections in Purchasing Health Services

Functional market	Purchaser–provider market	Patient–provider market
Perfect information	Medium asymmetry	High asymmetry
Many sellers (no barriers to entry and exit)	Monopoly or small number of sellers (high barriers)	Monopoly or small number of sellers (high barriers)
Many buyers (no barriers to entry and exit)	Monopsony or small number of buyers (high barriers)	Many buyers but catastrophic care unaffordable (high barrier)

Source: Authors.

SCOPE OF INSTITUTIONS

Institutions regulate certain areas such as volume, price, competition, and quality in a range from low to highly interventionist. Here, the scope and dimension of their influence are explored.

What Do Institutions Regulate?

Regulations can be used to address the problems described above to enforce limits on certain behaviors and encourage desired behaviors. Incentives can be either in the form of a reward (positive) or fines (negative) (Ogus 1994). Overall purchasing institutions aim to regulate the following:

- Market entry and exit

- Market size and competition

- Remuneration and price

- Volume and size of health care goods and services

- Quality of care and safety standards.

Institutional regulation of market entry and exit for public health care purchasers is usually found in the constituent laws and regulations of ministries of health and social health insurance funds and in social assistance regulations. Providers of health care services—such as physicians, hospitals, laboratories, and pharmacies—and vendors of health care goods—such as drugs, equipment, or general supplies—must comply with specific regulations on corporate norms and fulfill the corresponding permitting, licensing, and accreditation requirements to do business. In countries such as Bolivia, Guatemala, Mexico, or Peru, where both Western and traditional medicine are practiced, the regulation of market entry and exit is more complex than in other countries. Traditional healers are part of the local community and accepted throughout the population; their practice is hard to monitor and regulate.

Market size and competition are a function of the financing and the delivery of health care. In the United States, indemnity through health insurance is declining, and managed care, the main form of employer-based health insurance, is becoming more and more attractive as a tool for financing and delivering health care. Managed care has had a remarkable impact on the size of the market and on the subjugated competition that is controlled by managed care. Whereas traditional health insurance plans do not restrict providers or patients in their treatment choices, managed care intervenes in the care decisions of patients and doctors. Health maintenance organizations, the first contact point for patients, deliver all primary health care through one designated primary care physician. Treatments and providers are limited, as managed care requires advance approval and review of proposed treatments. Further treatment is delivered by a specified group of providers, preferred provider organizations, and a network of separate contracted health care providers providing health care services at discounted rates.

Social health insurance systems are learning from experience with competition in the private sector. If regulations call for fair play and no hidden policy gives preference to public health care establishments, the option of purchasing from both public and private providers forces the public providers to become more efficient and competitive. In such settings, health insurance funds can become selective purchasers. These concepts of market, competition, efficiency, and pricing are becoming more popular and permeate the institutional levels in almost all countries. In Chile, for instance, the social health insurance fund FONASA is a major purchaser from both public and private providers, obeying fairly competitive pricing rules and procedures. Legislation, institutions, and new commercial and contractual practices are gradually making inroads toward interplay of the public and private in health care purchasing.

Still, in many countries market competition plays a minor role. In India, for instance, the Employee State Insurance Scheme runs its own health care facilities, employs its own health care professionals, and maintains its own pricing and remuneration regime. Only a limited amount of health care goods and services is contracted out on a fee-for-service basis. Single-payer systems have more room to impose prices in terms of capitation based on daily rates for hospitals or on Diagnosis-Related Group–based systems whereas multiple-payers allow more space for price competition within the regulatory limits.

Without realistic and properly designed regulations on the scope and content of health service packages, health care financing can become a futile exercise. For that reason, rationing health care services has become common. The volume and size of benefits packages are widely regulated to stretch limited financial resources. Basic benefits packages determine the type, volume, and extent of services. Still, basic benefits packages are a limited way of providing sufficient health care services by obtaining financial control over health care costs. Both financial resources and service volume are limited, leading to both coverage and financial problems. In India, for instance, health insurance offered by the state-owned insurance companies has so many exclusions and limitations that it covers only around 1 percent of the population. Regarding financial constraints, the example of a patient admitted into a hospital for a condition included in the basic package illustrates the limitations of basic benefits packages as a cost controller. Once admitted, if the patient develops an additional condition not included in the package, he or she will receive services exceeding the package coverage.

Quality of care and safety standards often depend on institutional quality, compliance with the regulations, and, especially, on the authorities that impose and enforce the regulations. Double standards, for example in accreditation procedures, are common in the public sector. Public regulators and inspectors are generally tough with the private sector, but in most former Soviet Union countries and in nearly all developing countries, a substantial number of public health care establishments would not pass minimum accreditation inspections. For instance in 2003, accreditation standards broke down in Mongolia when the government ordered all public health care institutions to be accredited automatically in order to qualify for funding from the Health Insurance Fund. Also, under the pretext of encouraging the private sector in health care delivery, more than 200 small (5 to 10 beds) private hospitals have been licensed and accredited (few if any would meet the minimum standards). All of them now receive funding through the Health Insurance Fund.

Low- and High-Interventionist Models

The social interest turns an individual's health condition, normally a private good, into a public good. This is why the state determines the conditions for providing and financing health care in many countries. In this sense, states combine several interventionist methods by setting up "rules of the game" for financing, purchasing, providing, and controlling health care within the regulated boundaries of contracting. Health care purchasing is a classic example of regulated contracting.

Ogus (1994) and Allsop and Mulcahy (1996) discuss two conceptual models to try to explain the scope of intervention performed in a country. In the first model, a minimalist state performs little intervention and relies on the market to organize and guide the collective interest, in our case, the provision of health care services. In the second model, an interventionist state proactively establishes a range of institutions to protect interests and to discipline various actors such as purchasers and providers of health care services. Both models are ideal-typical assumptions based on theoretical concepts. Reality encompasses varying mixtures of both models. Still, the two ideal-typical models serve as two landmarks to see the extent to which formal institutions intervene.

The minimalist state relies on the market and supports individuals by ensuring free market conditions with minimal regulations. There is little attempt to influence the behavior of the various players. Unencumbered by heavy regulations, purchasers are fairly free to pursue their own goals. Formal institutions are imposed mainly to ensure smooth agreements between private players by giving private players an enforcement tool. In that sense, regulations are based on private interests and private rights. Therefore, private laws are highly decentralized, and it is up to individuals to enforce their rights. The minimalist state plays a limited role in these functions.

The interventionist state puts greater emphasis on state action in the pursuit of the collective interest. The state aims to achieve the collective goal by proactively influencing the behavior of the various players on the assumption that the goal would not be reached without its intervention. The state imposes a broad range of formal rules to control and direct the system and enforce obligations. In this system, regulation is centralized and comes from above. Players engaged in a prohibited activity, violating an imposed standard, or failing to carry out the required procedures imposed by law can expect sanctions. It is assumed that the threat of these regulations (also known as command-and-control regulations) will bring about the desired behavior.

In practice, the minimalist state does not exist. Even the United States, a well-known example of the "free market" system, is heavily regulated, particularly in health care. Licenses, accreditation, and permits are required at federal, state, and local levels. Purchasing is always an active endeavor that follows formal rules; it is highly regulated, usually by contracts. Even freedom of contracting is regulated by civil and commercial codes defining what can and cannot be contracted.

FORMS OF INSTITUTIONS

Institutions come in many different shapes. Bosk (1979) identifies four parameters along which institutions can be categorized: formal, informal, internal, and external. As in any simplification, individual categories and distinctions overlap. Table 4.3 gives some examples of institutional types.

The following sections describe both the formal and informal institutions that are involved in strategic purchasing and the internal and external institutions as discussed, with modifications, by Allsop and Mulcahy (1996).

Formal and Informal Institutions

Institutions encompass not only formal rules but also the broader "rules of the game," including informal ways of regulation. Institutions generate expectations about rights and obligations and therefore reduce uncertainty by giving everyday life a structure. This happens through formal regulations and rules, unwritten codes, and interactions over time. Formal regulations might change overnight as a result of a political decision, but informal constraints embodied in customs and practices are much more resistant to change. It takes much longer to change society's informal "rules of the game" (North 1990).

TABLE 4.3   Some Institutional Types

Type	External	Internal
Formal	Legal framework and other regulatory instruments	Administrative procedures (e.g., guidelines)
Informal	Customs and practices	Customs and practices

Source: Authors.

Formal institutions include every kind of written prescriptive or statutory rule and rules determined and executed by virtue of a formal position such as ownership or authority. They include explicit incentives, contractual terms, and firm boundaries.

Informal rules are defined as rules based on implicit understandings. They are socially derived to a large extent and therefore not accessible through written documents or necessarily sanctioned through a formal position. They include social norms and routines and develop in the course of day-to-day interactions (Zenger, Lazzarini, and Poppo 2001). To be accepted, however, informal rules and customs need to be widely practiced and socially tolerated. For instance in India and Mongolia, traditional medicine is widely practiced and socially tolerated, and in both cases public financing is available for purchasing traditional medical services.

In Ukraine and other former Soviet republics, the collapse of the socialist system provoked a breakdown of the economic, social, legal, institutional, and political systems and led to a large informal economy. This is also true for the health sector, where physicians and hospitals started to sell goods and services informally, a practice that is still very much alive. The dividing lines between the formal and the informal sectors have become less apparent. Formal enterprises in the private sector use "informal practices." Health care providers often have formal employment but also work in the informal sector. Informal undertakings produce or "procure" (smuggle) goods and services for the formal sector; public and private hospitals obtain supplies and services such as cleaning, food, and waste disposal free of any regulations. Identifying and eliminating the causes of informality in the purchase and delivery of health care goods and services and establishing a clear formal regulatory framework are major health policy challenges in these countries. Solving them will entail a commitment by both the public and private sectors to abide by the rules.

Internal and External Institutions

The second distinction (besides formal and informal) is between internal and external institutions. Internal institutions are established within the individual organization whereas external rules are imposed from outside. This includes external regulations put in place by the government, parliament, or judicial system as well as internal regulations such as formal guidelines.

Governments impose a variety of external rules regulating the provision of health care (box 4.1). Among these regulations are instruments such as fiscal policies, licensing, accreditation, and permit systems, quality and risk standards, imposition of fines and penalties and, the size of state budget allocations. These external control-based regulations are passed into law by the legislative branch of the state; through administrative decrees, orders, rules, and regulations by the executive

---

BOX 4.1   PURCHASING POLICY FOR THE NHS

The Purchasing and Supply Agency for the National Health Service (NHS) in the United Kingdom is an example of a formal institution imposed by an agency. The agency, set up in 2000 as an Executive Agency of the Department of Health, was created to bring a national focus to health service procurement. Its role is to act as a center of expertise and knowledge in purchasing and supply matters for the NHS. Besides its advisory and coordination function, the agency contracts on a national basis for products and services that are strategically critical to the NHS and publishes guidelines regarding terms and conditions for that purpose.

As an integral part of the Department of Health, the NHS Purchasing and Supply Agency is in a key position to advise on policy and the strategic directions for procurement and its impact on developing health care across the NHS. One of its mandates is to develop and implement a policy to improve and modernize purchasing and supply in the NHS.

Policies covering key areas of purchasing and supply activity have been developed in consultation with a range of stakeholders. The policies set out the legal and policy framework within which all NHS procurement should be undertaken and define the basic policy in each area such as pharmaceuticals or medical work. They also set out a national standards framework and such key drivers as risk management or contract management that need to be considered in managing NHS expenditures on goods and services.

The agency has published a number of policies on its website. These include, for example, policies on e-commerce, best practice, quality management, environmental purchasing, quality management, process standardization, and undertaking internal audits on procurement activities.

Source: NHS Purchasing and Supply Agency 2003.

---

branch of the state and decentralized regulatory entities such as a Health Superintendency or Health Authority; or by means of judicial decisions in cases before the courts by the judicial branch of the state. Each of these regulatory forms has different sources, formats, and scope of enforcement (Afifi, Busse, and Harding 2003).

For example, governments have established a broad range of external control mechanisms such as licensing and accreditation of health care professionals and hospitals, financial incentives, and sanctions and guidelines, not only to ensure the quality of health care services but also to ensure efficiency in the allocation of resources. The Netherlands and Sweden did not implement similar mechanisms such as external audit or accreditation procedures, most probably because health care providers developed their own quality measures. Both countries have established internal regulation mechanisms that attempt to encourage good behavior by providing stronger principles than sanctioning bad behavior (Or 2002). If delegated internal regulations fail to accomplish their goals, governments can always retrieve their external regulatory functions.

The role of governments in setting regulations is crucial but the scope and form of its involvement differs from country to country. For instance, it can have an extensive control function by defining "intolerable" medical practices and declaring them illegal. Also, it can encourage good practices by providing positive values and principles. Whichever way the government chooses, one of its most important functions is to ensure public accountability in health service provision by ensuring that the allocation of resources is in line with the public interest and the health care delivered meets quality standards.

Another major role of governments is to implement quality measures within government health programs. In the United States, where the government is the largest purchaser of health care (accounting for more than 43 percent of local health care spending), the interest of ensuring quality is justified partly because the government is a medical service purchaser and provider, but also because it has a general responsibility to help make the health care market work as effectively as possible for all its citizens (Eisenberg 1998). The Norwegian health care system, for instance, makes efficient provision of high-quality services a priority in an approach established through several national policies in the early 1990s. The Norwegian authorities recognized that one of the major challenges was to start focusing on the entire health system rather than on isolated areas. In Norway primary health care services are decentralized. Authority is transferred to largely independent local governments. There is no direct command-and-control line from the central authorities down to municipalities. In the attempt to serve the public interest, quality requirements for health services are specified through legislation (Norwegian Board of Health 2002).

Internal institutions originate from within the organization and can also be defined as self-regulation mechanisms. Self-regulation occurs in several ways such as administrative procedures and customs and practices. Administrative procedures are formally established through written guidelines, whereas customs and practices are informal and develop through social interaction and individual experiences. Depending on the goals of the government, self-regulation can be limited through, for example, statutory rules, periodic government oversight, or rules passed by ministers. Substantial benefits can be achieved if the participants or the regulatory regime are given sufficient incentives to achieve the desired outputs. This may help reduce the cost of external regulations such as high monitoring and enforcement costs (Koenig, Taylor, and Ballance 2003).

LEVELS OF INSTITUTIONS

Institutions can be laws passed by parliament, decrees or directives issued by a ministry, guidelines passed by administrative authorities or purchasing agencies, as well as informal best practices or customs. The different forms of institutions (formal-informal, internal-external) and the levels on which they are established are described in this section.

Legal Framework

Among the main sources of formal institutions are rules established through legislation. Ideally, law normatively translates a defined policy on the scope and content of health care into a formal written document with definitions and procedures. Health law is largely statutory rather than common law and is therefore found in acts of parliament or delegated legislation made under those acts. In democratic states, the legislature is the primary rule-making authority, holding the power to enact laws. Legislation cannot cover all issues, and therefore, the same laws often delegate the regulatory, monitoring, and enforcement authority. This is a recognition of the complex processes involved, affecting a broad range of actors and creating the need for control and monitoring mechanisms. In Australia, for example, local governments traditionally exercise a strong role in monitoring and in implementing legislation. In the Republic of Korea, the state's involvement in health care provision is minimal, limited mainly to a safety net role (box 4.2). Regulation through government may vary between jurisdictions and involves many regulatory instruments (e.g., regulations, instructions, decrees, and so on) (National Public Health Partnership 2002).

Regulatory Instruments

Usually laws delegate legislative authority to governmental authorities (ministries and autonomous public entities) with a mandate to expand and detail the law through general and specific regulatory powers. The idea is to have institutions issued by administrative authorities while they are carried out according to the intent of the law by consulting stakeholders and getting their technical assistance. The law can delegate regulatory functions to ministries and other public entities but also to private entities. Professional associations, for instance, are often given the legal power to issue licenses and to conduct, and require attendance in, continuous education programs as a condition for relicensing.

Based on the idea that laws should provide the broad framework for health care provision, regulatory instruments are much less comprehensive. They are a tool that enables a quick response to economic and social needs by not having to go through parliamentary procedures for the enactment and amendment of laws. For example, in Mexico, state governments issue regulations for purchasing health care services. In Chile, the Ministry of Health issues norms for purchasing health care supplies and equipment, and in Colombia technical regulations controlling the purchase of syringes are issued by the Ministry of Health. In the United States, in Minnesota, the state Department of Human Services has issued model contracts for the purchase of health care services.

Increasingly, regulatory agencies are granted full regulatory powers for issuing regulations. For example, the Superintendency of Previsional Health (private health care financing and delivery system) in Chile has full regulatory powers.

BOX 4.2   GOVERNMENTAL REGULATION IN THE REPUBLIC OF KOREA

The main responsibilities of the government of the Republic of Korea in the health systems are regulation, policy making, and insurance; its involvement in the provision of health care services is minimal and limited to a safety net role. The government established an overall legal framework for the steward-ship of health care; its main elements include the National Health Insurance Act, the Health Insurance Finance Stabilization Special Act, the Medical Service Act, and the Pharmaceutical Affairs Act.

Korea's entire population is covered for the risk of medical illness, either through the National Health Insurance (NHI), a social health insurance scheme financed by mandatory contributions, or through the Medical Aid Program (MAP), a social assistance scheme for the very poor, financed through general taxation. The NHI, as a single-payer, functions like a quasi-autonomous, largely centralized public organization and pays providers for the health care goods and services they deliver; local branches carry out administrative functions of collecting contributions. Besides the coverage through the insurance scheme, all patients except for some MAP beneficiaries also have to make substantial payments toward their treatment.

Under the national health insurance scheme, all health care providers are automatically eligible and obliged to treat patients for services covered under the NHI scheme. Provider payments are based on a fee schedule that is negoti-ated annually between providers and the NHI Corporation. Fees used to be set unilaterally between the Ministry of Health and Welfare, but the new process involves a committee consisting of representatives of the government, medical professions, and other stakeholders.

The government historically has combined both a laissez-faire and an authoritarian attitude in its regulatory approach. It retains strong control over medical fees, benefits, and system changes, for example. On the supply side, it is minimally involved with providers and stays out of health care markets, leav-ing much space for private initiatives. For example, to open a hospital the only requirement is to have a minimal number of beds and departments. Meeting these requirements suffices to obtain licensing for a new hospital. In addition, hospitals can decide independently on their capacities, medical technology, and human resources.

Source: Colombo and Hurst 2002.

The National Health Fund in Chile, for instance, has its own regulations. The purchase of health care services from private providers is based on contracts; purchase from public providers is based on management agreements. However, most former Soviet Union countries are reluctant to grant regulatory powers to decentralized entities. Their regulations are issued and promulgated by the gov-ernment, usually the Ministry of Health or the Cabinet of Ministers.

Administrative Procedures

Purchasers such as social health insurance funds, ministries of health, local health authorities, private insurance companies, and managed care organizations issue administrative procedures to acquire health care goods and services. Administrative regulation through guidelines, instructions, and letters of interpretation is becoming increasingly common. It is important for health care purchasers and providers that want to follow the prescribed regulations and procedures so that resources are used in efficiently and effectively.

Administrative procedures need a formal foundation. For example, social health insurance funds issue internal regulations and procedures in the constituent laws. Private insurance companies also issue and include internal procedures in the terms and conditions of health insurance polices. Within the framework of what is permissible under insurance laws and regulations, hospitals issue internal regulations and guidelines.

BOX 4.3   PURCHASING UNDER THE NEW NATIONAL HEALTH INSURANCE SCHEME IN GHANA

Expenditures on health care in Ghana are among the lowest in the world. Still, Ghanaians have demonstrated both an ability and a willingness to pay for additional health care. Health care is bought through a system of direct "cash-and-carry" payments to providers, exposing patients to prices set at whatever the market can bear and the impoverishing effects of expensive illness. The government of Ghana is firmly committed to a social policy of helping the poor and in achieving the United Nations Millennium Development Goals. This has led to recent reforms that abolished user charges, expanded access to health services for the poor, and increased spending on health care programs. The introduction of a National Health Insurance System in Ghana should be seen in the context of this transformation in both the Ghanaian society and health sector. It is a natural evolution in the maturing health sector.

The primary *legislative framework* for the National Health Insurance Scheme is set out in the Ghanaian National Health Insurance Act, which was enacted in September 2003. Three types of health insurance schemes were established under the National Health Insurance Act:

- District mutual health insurance schemes (social health insurance scheme)

- Private commercial health insurance schemes

- Private mutual health insurance schemes.

With these schemes, the act provides for the establishment of a National Health Insurance Council. The council exercised a stewardship and governance

(continued)

In many countries, the legal system enables the medical profession to take the lead in developing clinical protocols. In New Zealand, for example, they are developed by a range of professional groups such as specialist societies (or associations) and hospitals. Still, in most countries the focus has been on the development of guidelines rather than on their implementation (see box 4.3 for an example of this from Ghana). Direct involvement of medical professionals—not just in the development but also in the implementation of appropriate health care standards—increases the chances that guidelines will be put into practice (Or 2002).

Customs and Practices

Informality (customs and practices) plays a significant role in purchasing health care goods and services. As mentioned earlier, customs are based on unspoken understandings. They are courses of action repeated under like circumstances

---

BOX 4.3   *(continued)*

role in the implementation of a national health insurance policy that ensures comprehensive access to health care. Among its responsibilities are

- providing policy advice to the Ministry of Health;

- licensing and registering insurance schemes;

- regulating, supervising, and ensuring quality of insurance schemes;

- accrediting and registering health care facilities and providers; and

- managing the National Health Insurance Fund.

The National Health Insurance Act enables the Minister of Health to make certain regulations and prescriptions by legislative instrument on the advice of the council. These *regulatory instruments* include, for example, prescriptions regarding minimum health care benefits under all insurance schemes or the setting of fees and tariffs.

Some *customs and practices* may ease the local introduction of the National Health Insurance Scheme. People working in the formal sector are already used to making mandatory contributions to the Social Security and Pensions Fund Scheme. In addition, in past years the development of voluntary mutual health insurance organizations has been supported by various donors and Ghanaian organizations and led to 47 fully established mutual insurance organizations. These factors will contribute to the implementation of the comprehensive insurance scheme.

Source: Preker 2004.

and socially derived to a large extent. They consist of established patterns of objectively verifiable behavior within a particular social setting that have been memorized, assimilated, and passed down from generation to generation. Customs and practices do not function through written documents; their great regulatory power comes through ingrained routines, norms, or social contracts.

Under-the-table or informal payments to health care providers are a classic example of informal practices. They are rooted in medieval customs of gratuities for healers and are current in Africa and among Indian populations in Latin America. In former Soviet Union countries, this practice was one way of accessing health care services, medicines, and other materials in short supply. Informal payments are hard to eradicate. The obligation to pay, reciprocated by the obligation to provide satisfactory services, is a form of social contract between the patient (purchaser) and the doctor (seller or provider).

CONCLUSIONS

Institutions are needed to regulate resource allocation and purchasing to protect social and economic interests in health care. By regulating volume, competition, quality, and prices, institutions can serve the overall goal of securing the public right to health. Institutions can be formal or informal, can be exposed externally or internally, and can be established on different levels. Without realistic and well-designed regulation of the scope and content, financing health care becomes a difficult exercise.

Whether established institutions are capable of managing efficiently to reach the goal of comprehensive financing of health care products and services is still to be determined. Many countries face serious problems regulating health care providers. India, for instance, has a myriad of providers. They range from world-class physicians and hospitals to providers of dubious capacity and quality (most individuals, clinics, and hospitals). Moreover, in India and elsewhere, modern medicine coexists with different versions of traditional medicine, regulated by customs and traditions with practically no control by the state. This issue is also becoming important in Western countries. Millions of dollars are being spent over the counter on alternative and complementary medicines such as homeopathic and natural-based self-treatments despite the lack of scientific proof of their effectiveness or safety.

Nearly every country has institutions similar to the U.S. Food and Drug Administration to deal with drug and pharmaceutical safety, but unlabeled, expired, and smuggled pharmaceuticals and antibiotics are still commonly sold over the counter. In the United States, traveling to Canada and Mexico to buy pharmaceuticals at better prices is becoming more and more popular. Developing and transition countries suffer from the "donor initiative syndrome," where second-hand equipment is sent to them without any instruction manuals or maintenance and safety records. Regulations covering second-hand equipment are rare, and any that have been put in place are neither consistently applied nor enforced.

Institutions are not just a fact. They are an imperfect, insufficient, but highly relevant intervention, a basic necessity for balancing social and economic interests. Their scope and the way they are implemented reflect not only current social systems and values, but also the challenges of tomorrow. As long as informal institutions such as under-the-table payments are a common way for the population to gain access to health care services, goods, and drugs, the balance of interests needs to be regulated. Institutions are the tools with which to do so.

NOTE

Invaluable insights from thematic reviews and country case studies were provided by Francesca Colombo and Gergana Haralampieva.

REFERENCES

Afifi, N., R. Busse, and A. Harding. 2003. *Regulation of Health Services*. Washington, DC: World Bank.

Allsop, J., and L. Mulcahy. 1996. *Regulating Medical Work: Formal and Informal Controls*. Buckingham, United Kingdom: Open University Press.

Bosk, C. L. 1979. *Forgive and Remember*. Chicago, IL: University of Chicago Press.

Colombo, F., and J. Hurst. 2002. *Review of the Korean Health Care System*. Paris : Organisation for Economic Co-operation and Development.

Eisenberg, J. 1998. *Testimony before the House Committee on Ways and Means, Subcommittee on Health, Hearing on Assessing Health Care Quality*. Washington, DC: Hearings from the 105th Congress, Feb. 28.

Hirschman, A. 1970. *Exit, Voice, and Loyalty: Responses to Decline in Firms, Organizations, and States*. Cambridge, MA: Harvard University Press.

Koenig, A., A. Taylor, and T. Ballance. 2003. *Infrastructure Regulation: An Introduction to Fundamental Concepts and Key Issues*. Germany: Deutsche Gesellschaft für technische Zusammenarbeit (GTZ) GmbH.

National Health Service Purchasing and Supply Agency. 2003. *Overarching Purchasing Policy for the NHS. Purchasing and Supply Policies*. Reading, United Kingdom: D. Brassington.

National Public Health Partnership. 2002. *The Role of Local Government in Public Health Regulation*. Melbourne, Australia: National Public Health Partnership.

North, D.C. 1990. *Institutions, Institutional Change and Economic Performance*. Cambridge, United Kingdom: Cambridge University Press.

Norwegian Board of Health. 2002. *Quality in Health Care—The Role of Government in Supervision and Monitoring in Norway*. Norwegian Board of Health Report Series, Report 8/2002. Oslo.

Ogus, A.I. 1994. *Regulation: Legal Form and Economic Theory*. New York, NY: Oxford University Press.

Or, Z. 2002. *Improving the Performance of Health Care Systems: From Measures to Action (A Review of Experiences in Four OECD Countries)*. Labour Market and Social Policy Occasional Papers No. 57. Paris: Organisation for Economic Co-operation and Development.

Preker, A. 2004. *Strategic Purchasing of Priority Health Services under the New National Health Insurance Scheme in Ghana*. Washington, DC: World Bank.

Simidjiyski, J. 1999. *Legal Support to Health Reforms in Central Asian Republics 1994–1999*. Submitted by the Zdrav Reform Program to USAID/CAR. Almaty, Kazakhstan.

Zatkin, S. 1997. "A Health Plan's View of Government Regulation." *Health Affairs* 16 (6): 33–35.

Zenger, T., S. Lazzarini, and L. Poppo. 2001. *Informal and Formal Organization in New Institutional Economics*. St. Louis, MO: John M. Olin School of Business, Washington University.

CHAPTER 5

Stewardship, Governance, and Management

Alexander S. Preker, Reinhard R. Haslinger, Reinhard Busse,
and Magda Rosenmöller

The challenge many purchasers face in balancing scarce resources with over-whelming demand while at the same time securing access by the population to quality health services—and ensuring value for money is reviewed in this chapter. Ultimately, it is good policy making, governance, and management that will be instrumental in improving the performance of health services in address-ing the health challenges confronting low- and middle-income countries. Man-agement occurs at different levels of the health system: stewardship, governance, client services, and clinical management. And, there are different approaches to management—command and control, business school approaches, new public sector–management approaches and the invisible hand of markets. Each has its appropriate application. In this chapter, the authors explore ways to make man-agement of purchasing organizations more results oriented. They examine the special challenge of managing complexity and change and review evidence on the extent to which "good management practices" have been applied to the health care purchasing organizations in low- and middle-income countries. They conclude that purchasing organizations in many developing countries could do much better by applying to the health sector lessons learned from other service sectors of the economy in recent years.

INTRODUCTION

Governance and management are an important aspect in the economics of resource allocation and purchasing (RAP). The various purchasing arrangements regarding the organizational structure, the different numbers of purchasing institutions, and their purchasing power are discussed in the previous chapter. This one takes a closer look at the management of purchasing and discusses it in a framework based on the model in Preker et al. (2004). In this model, four managerial levels are identi-fied; the specific roles and responsibilities assigned to each level are discussed in this chapter and summarized in figure 5.1.

The four management levels include stewardship, organizational governance, operational management, and case management (figure 5.2). Stewardship is performed on the macro level and includes the development and oversight of strategic purchasing policies at the national/provincial/state or regional level.

Figure 5.1   Management Types and Objectives

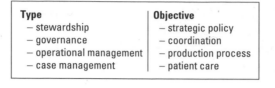

Type	Objective
– stewardship	– strategic policy
– governance	– coordination
– operational management	– production process
– case management	– patient care

Source: Modified from Preker et al. 2004.

It means that the national or regional government steers and coordinates the purchasing function.

Below the stewardship level, the management of the individual purchaser is performed on three organizational levels: governance, operational management, and case management. Governance, the meso-level of management, regards the executive management and work of the board of the purchasing institution. Operational management reflects the micro- or process level of management and includes supervision and day-to-day operations. Case management is performed at the household or individual level and involves the management of client services in the insurance fund's various business units (Preker et al. 2004).

Figure 5.2   Type and Target Level of Management

Type of management	Level			
	Macro	Meso/ organizational	Micro/ operational	Household/ individual
Stewardship	★	☆		
Governance	☆	★	☆	
Operational management		☆	★	☆
Case management			☆	★

Source: Modified from Preker et al. 2004.

MANAGEMENT AT DIFFERENT LEVELS

Stewardship

Stewardship is defined as a "function of a government responsible for the welfare of the population, and concerned about the trust and legitimacy with which its activities are viewed by the citizenry" (World Health Report 2000: 119). Stewardship is the responsibility of government—usually through the health ministry—and means "steering" and "guiding" the entire health system by strategic planning, regulating, monitoring, and evaluating (Travis et al. 2002). It guides the system along policies and coordinates the various stakeholders and players within an established framework.

Why Stewardship?

In modern health systems, governments do not take care of all levels and components of the entire system. Health systems are gradually but steadily moving away from the integrated model to a contractual model and represent complex mixes of different public, quasi-public, nonprofit, and for-profit actors. In these systems, a stewardship function is assigned to the government in order to ensure efficiency, quality, and universal access to health care. Governments are still involved in the provision of several health care services (public hospitals, maternal health clinics, and the like) but their stewardship role does not mean involvement in day-to-day business. It means overall coordination of the health system, the provision of an appropriate institutional framework, and the development of a comprehensive health policy.

Regarding the purchasing function of a health system, governmental involvement is essential to balance the various actors' different interests and ensure well-coordinated delivery of services to a country's population. Depending on the strength and power of the individual government relative to the purchasers, and more important, depending on the numbers of purchasers, tension can arise between the government and individual purchasers. Both players have different roles and are accountable to different client groups. Whereas sickness funds are accountable only to the clients whose benefits are covered, governments are accountable to the general public and, as stewards, they oversee the entire social system. In pre-reform Argentina, for instance, the health insurance system consisted of many separate insurance funds that were administered by unions and had monopolistic rights over their specific sectors. Most of the funds were too small to deliver services, so they contracted them out to providers such as private hospitals or clinics. This purchaser–provider split was unusual in Latin America but did not lead to more efficiency based on competition. Since there was no steward overseeing this, the purchaser–provider split led to a chaotic situation with unaccountable contractors and subcontractors (Barrientos and Lloyd-Sherlock 2000).

In many East European countries, system changes after 1989 and the implementation of comprehensive social health insurance systems led to serious problems. The decision-making and financing structures changed from a state-owned and centrally planned communist system to a market-based liberal system. A liberal market economy replaced the monopoly of funding and providing health services and seemingly led to a reduced importance in the role of the state. In an attempt to improve incentives for efficiency, in Slovakia, for example, reform agendas included a wide range of initiatives such as the privatization of purchasers, decentralization, and change in reimbursement mechanisms. Payments to hospitals oscillated between per diem payments and prospective budgets, switching several times. In addition, responsibilities moved from the government to local municipalities (Colombo and Tapay 2003b). These new circumstances created the need for governments to assume a different, proactive leadership and stewardship role.

Overall, reforms in the 1990s seemed to have lacked a systematic approach guided by stewardship. The Czech Republic, for instance, liberalized its economy in the early 1990s and replaced the Soviet health system with one allowing private institutions to purchase health care. In the new system, the government pulled back from its overall dominant role but had not put a broad regulatory structure in place (see annex to this chapter). In this situation, several private purchasers went bankrupt, resources were wasted, and people were left without proper health insurance. As a consequence, the Ministry of Health (MOH) established a now active and leading role in monitoring a comprehensive regulatory system, including institutionalized protection against coverage failures (Brundtland 2002).

Accordingly, governments ensure the establishment and maintenance of a policy and regulatory framework, steer the system in a constantly changing environment, guiding and coordinating all the stakeholders (local governments, health insurance agencies, purchasing institutions, private insurance companies, public and private health care providers).The ultimate responsibility for the performance of their country's health system thus rests with the government.

Who Controls Decisions?

When purchasing arrangements are made "intelligently," tensions can and do arise between the government's roles as purchaser and steward. The balance between these two loci of decision making depends on a number of factors, two of which appear to be particularly prominent: (1) the policy-making capacity and accountability of the government, and (2) pressures exerted directly on the purchaser by patients' demand for services. When the government's stewardship capacity is weak, purchasers may try to maximize their own objectives instead of implementing the officially sanctioned sectoral policies. Significant divergence in providers' and patients' demand patterns from the mandated agency role also sets the stage for tension between the purchasing and stewardship functions. Typically, countries deal with this dilemma through some sort of decision sharing between the government's stewardship function and the purchasing arrangement (figure 5.3).

Figure 5.3   Sharing Decision Rights between Stewardship Function and Purchasing Arrangement

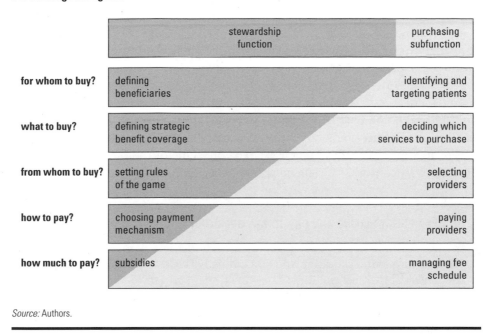

	stewardship function	purchasing subfunction
for whom to buy?	defining beneficiaries	identifying and targeting patients
what to buy?	defining strategic benefit coverage	deciding which services to purchase
from whom to buy?	setting rules of the game	selecting providers
how to pay?	choosing payment mechanism	paying providers
how much to pay?	subsidies	managing fee schedule

Source: Authors.

In some countries, the various roles are bundled in one hand, and governments act as funding agents, regulators, providers, and purchasers of health care—all at the same time. Some of these roles might be better performed by other stakeholders, such as those in the private sector or nonprofit organizations, and can actually be provided through contracting or purchasing. This does not, however, result in disengagement of the government. The global and steering stewardship role remains with the government: taking an overall view of the health system is one job of the steward. In that capacity, the government provides a clear sense of vision and strategic direction concerning how the health system should look and develop. It monitors the system, adjusts policies and goals, and makes required changes. Within this framework, the government identifies key stakeholders and assigns each player clear roles and responsibilities that need to be coordinated. Among matters needing definition are the scope of government involvement; the roles of the public, private, and voluntary sectors in terms of financing health care and pooling funds; resource generation and allocation; and the delivery of services.

Irrespective of the purchasing arrangement for transferring funds from the collection and pooling subfunctions to providers, governments have a stewardship responsibility to ensure that the broad policy objectives of maximizing health, financial protection, and consumer satisfaction are achieved at any given level of available resources. This stewardship function is the essence of good government. It includes activities such as exerting influence over the behavior of financing mechanisms, providers, and patients through regulation and advocacy; securing appropriate coordination among often disparate activities in the health sector; and collecting, monitoring, and disseminating information.

A critical policy option that countries must continually confront is the extent of restrictions on the executive powers of the purchasing arrangement—whether it will be a passive executor of policies determined elsewhere or whether it will play an "intelligent" or strategic decision-making role. Passive purchasing arrangements act as "cashiers" for providers. They focus on paying providers without evaluating their performance in terms of meeting health, financial protection, or responsiveness objectives. Most of the time, passive resource allocation and purchasing arrangements rely on a historical pattern of resource allocation. In contrast, "[s]trategic purchasing involves a continuous search for

---

BOX 5.1   POLICY MAKING AND DAY-TO-DAY OPERATIONAL BUSINESS

In most countries, the policy-making phase and the day-to-day operational business of resource allocation and purchasing is a clear cleavage point between the stewardship responsibilities of the government and the operational responsibilities of the purchasing arrangement.

Policy making. Policy making is usually—but not always—under the stewardship responsibility of the government. This includes deciding (1) who will benefit from the program, (2) the range of services to be included, and (3) the mechanism to be used to pay providers. The first two are rarely left to the discretion of the purchasing arrangement, but the purchasing arrangement sometimes has some control over the payment mechanism. Although tough rationing decisions are often left under the government's stewardship responsibility, this may not be an optimal solution since the purchasing arrangement and service providers may be in a better position to respond appropriately to need and demand; they are closer to the people who have to bear the risk and consequences of such decisions.

Policy making often includes critical decisions about the organizational design of the purchasing arrangement such as: (1) the organizational form in terms of contractual arrangements and economies of scale and scope, (2) the desired initial incentive regime (decision right, market exposure, and so on), and (3) linkages in terms of the degree of integration or fragmentation. The first decision is rarely left to the discretion of the purchasing arrangement; the last two often evolve over time in response to local contexts that are difficult to anticipate by policy makers. Finally, deciding on the rules of revenue transfer and governance (ownership) is usually under the stewardship responsibility of the government, not the purchasing arrangement.

Day-to-day operational business. Clear operational decisions have to be made under almost each of the above categories. For example, deciding who should benefit from a purchasing arrangement still leaves a wide range of strategic decisions about how best to reach those populations through various targeting

(continued)

the best ways to maximize health system performance by deciding which interventions should be purchased, how, and from whom" (WHO 2000: 97).

Typically, the purchasing arrangements of countries that have retained hierarchical structures (e.g., the regional health authorities in the United Kingdom) tend to be "passive" implementation agencies for decisions made elsewhere. In countries that have created one or more semiautonomous health insurance funds (e.g., the Health Insurance Commission in Australia) the purchasing arrangements have a greater "intelligent" policy-making function. Finally, in countries that rely more heavily on private health maintenance organizations or indemnity insurance (e.g., the Czech Republic or the United States) the "intelligent" policy-making function is almost entirely transferred to the purchasing arrangements, and the government retains only a very high-level policy oversight (box 5.1).

BOX 5.1   *(continued)*

techniques (by eligibility, income, vulnerable socioeconomic group, age or gender, disease risk) and about the services most frequently used by the targeted group in question. Once the range of interventions or services has been decided, considerable scope remains for decisions about input, process, and output questions.

A strong argument can be made in favor of moving toward a system focused on outcomes instead of inputs, process, and outputs. In an ideal situation, the purchasing arrangement would buy outcomes for population groups, leaving it to the providers to identify the most effective and least costly interventions, as well as ensure efficient organizational and institutional arrangement. Theoretical arguments support this hypothesis and empirical evidence:

- It is easier for providers than purchasers to know better which services are more likely to result in greater health gains and to arrange for continuous necessary care through referral and coordination arrangements with other providers.

- It is impossible to foresee every possible contingency (imperfect contract arguments of bounded rationality and opportunism).

- Integrated organizations can optimize the cost and effectiveness (health) of care (allocative efficiency argument); individual organizations have no incentive to do so.

In reality, however, there are also some disadvantages. Providers, like public agencies, are vulnerable to bureaucratic capture by vested interests who may distort priorities, seeking personal gain or the gain of a particular community at the expense of the broader population. And prospective budgets may fracture the revenue pool, thereby passing the risk back.

Source: Authors.

Balance of Power—Implementing Regulations

Stewards set and enforce rules with a mix of incentives and sanctions to influence the behavior of different stakeholders including purchasers. The government as the steward is responsible for the implementation of policies that are designed to achieve the goals of a comprehensive health system. This role requires the ability and power to influence the behavior of the different actors. The stewardship role assigns this power, distributes roles, and sees to the implementation of fair rules and regulations that include a realistic incentive regime, as well as sanctions for misbehavior (Travis et al. 2002).

Mismatches of responsibility at any level of the system are not uncommon, especially in arrangements where the funding goes directly from the ministry of the treasury to the local authorities or purchasers. This setting implies a weak stewardship role for the MOH. Because the MOH does not have the necessary power to back its decisions and guidance, the agencies and other stakeholders tend to operate on their own. To guarantee a strong stewardship role for the MOH, a law that gives the local authorities responsibility for all local health services but not any control over the funding of these services may be passed (Travis et al. 2002). A transparent regulatory framework provides the basis for cooperation and coordination.

The Australian health care system, for instance, involves several public and private players, a complex system that requires a strong stewardship function. Responsibilities are split between the Commonwealth of Australia (the national government) and state and territory governments. The Commonwealth runs two benefit schemes with universal coverage: Medicare, which is Australia's universal social insurance system, and the Pharmaceutical Benefit Scheme. Public hospitals are jointly funded, and both the Commonwealth and the states are responsible for their administration. Medicare is financed through taxation; the funds, negotiated every five years, are transferred from the Commonwealth government to the states. Policies rely on the trust for financial and fiscal incentives and market mechanisms such as competition among providers, free choice of provider by individuals (even private providers), and private financing and delivery. In addition, several regulations are put in place to meet market failures and equity goals (Colombo and Tapay 2003a).

In Estonia, the Ministry of Social Affairs holds the stewardship role, guiding the entire health system under a well-coordinated strategy. In practice, however, the government's stewardship role is somewhat weak because of short-term political considerations (box 5.2).

Information

With the "big picture" in mind, stewards do not base their decisions on short-term goals or short-term political interests. Their actions are defined by an overall policy and strategy. This requires high-quality information and essential knowledge from a range of formal and informal sources such as routine information, research,

BOX 5.2   GOVERNANCE OF PURCHASING UNDER SOCIAL HEALTH INSURANCE IN ESTONIA

After the collapse of the communist system and Estonia's independence, the Soviet *Semashko* system was replaced by a comprehensive social health insurance system with a number of small sickness funds serving a population of around 1.3 million. Over the years, the number of sickness funds was reduced because these small funds lacked sufficient administrative capacity and central coordination and also were experiencing financial problems. In 2002 the remaining sickness funds were merged into seven regional branches of the newly established Health Insurance Fund, a single-payer system financed through payroll taxes. The Health Insurance Fund is established as a legal person in public law and an autonomous organization that operates independently from the government. The local branches, recently reduced to four, do the health care purchasing and contract with about a thousand health care providers.

The Health Insurance Fund is overseen by a Supervisory Board of 15 members, 5 from each of the three stakeholder groups—government, industry, and civil society. The government is represented by the Minister of Social Affairs (who is also in charge of health care matters), the Minister of Finance, and the chairman of the Social Affairs Committee of the Parliament. The Social Affairs Committee nominates one member of Parliament to serve on the board. In addition, the Minister of Social Affairs designates one ministry official as a member. Five board members are designated from both the civil society, representing the interests of insured persons, and employers' organizations.

The Management Board manages the Health Insurance Fund. The board consists of three to seven members, (one of them the chairman, designated by the Supervisory Board). Board members serve terms of up to five years. The Management Board, reporting to the Supervisory Board, performs the functions imposed on it by the Health Insurance Act, the Statutes of the Health Insurance Fund, and the decisions of the Supervisory Board. On the basis of the national health care policy, the Management Board prepares the development plan and the budget of the Health Insurance Fund and submits them to the Supervisory Board for approval.

The Estonian government, specifically the Ministry of Social Affairs, holds the stewardship role, guiding the entire health system under a well-coordinated strategy. Its responsibilities include health policy formulation, analysis of the population's health status, general organization and surveillance of health care, and the development and enactment of standards and licenses for health care providers. The Minister of Social Affairs officially leads the State Health Council, an advisory body to the Estonian government in health care issues. The government is also strongly represented on the Health Insurance Fund's board; the Minister of Social Affairs functions as the board's chairman and retains a veto right. The design of the Estonian health insurance system delineates clear levels of power, but, in practice, the government's stewardship role is somewhat weak due to short-term political considerations.

Source: Authors.

media, polls and surveys, and case studies. Reliable information is needed reflecting current and future trends and inequalities in such areas as budgetary health expenditures, human resource expenditures, coverage, provider performance, and resource allocation. In a fast-changing political, economic, and institutional environment, the roles of different players change as do consumer behavior and user preferences. Stewards gather relevant and reliable information to get the current picture as well as changes in the setting. Good information is an essential tool to guide the system successfully and to adapt policy options (Travis et al. 2002).

Information and communication are not a one-way street. To build partnerships and to develop support for policies and strategies, effective communication with the public is essential. The National Health Service, Britain's health maintenance organization, has successfully integrated public involvement and stays in touch with patient-lobby groups. Patient surveys are being conducted, in addition to research on patient concerns by the Commission for Health Improvement. This independent supervisory function is crucial to detect system failures and to achieve and maintain high-quality services by identifying bottlenecks in the system (Berland 2002).

Organizational Governance

What Is Governance?

Governance is a closely related but distinct institutional characteristic from stewardship. *Governance* is defined as the relationship between the owner of an organization and its management.

Whereas the steward steers the entire health system, organizational governance refers to the individual purchaser within this system. Governance is an organizational function reflecting the function of corporate governance. Organizational governance basically talks about the relationship between the owners and the management of each purchasing organization. Governance structures are usually carried out by a board of representatives representing the institutional stakeholders and their collective and indivisible objectives and interests in the organization. The representatives oversee the institution and determine its key goals. The board is basically the owners' agent, whereas the management is the board's agent (Pointer and Orlikoff 1999). The board addresses the challenge of allowing management adequate freedom while at the same time enforcing appropriate guidance and oversight mechanisms (Pointer and Orlikoff 1999). The board has a supervisory role and ensures that the organization functions efficiently and in line with the purpose it was originally founded for (public mandate).

Why Governance?

According to Pointer and Orlikoff organizational governance structures estab-lished through boards must answer the following four questions (Pointer and Orlikoff 1999):

- Why do we exist?
- Whom do we represent?
- What should we be doing?
- How should we go about doing it?

The answers to these questions are crucial for leading and governing the orga-nization because they are the foundation for management structures and account-ability mechanisms. The answers add up to a corporate mission statement—"why to do it"—and a corporate strategy statement—"what and how to do it." The board does not perform every step involved in this planning process but bears the principal responsibility for strategic planning (Orlikoff and Totten 2001).

A board's function is to govern the institution, not to manage it. Governance structures direct and oversee professional management and provide guidance and help. The board is chiefly responsible for monitoring the organization's perfor-mance and approving its operational risk-management framework including all the major aspects of the institution's operational risks. It approves and oversees strategic planning and implementation. In addition, the board has the authority to select, compensate, and monitor senior management to ensure high performance, which will determine the organization's success (Pointer and Orlikoff 1999).

What Does Organizational Governance Look Like?

Governance structures depend on corporate structures but do not necessarily mirror them (Pointer and Orlikoff 1999) because their size depends on their roles and responsibilities. Various commentators suggest about 20 people as the upper size limit for effective and efficient group decision making. Larger boards are harder to coordinate and prone to communication problems. To ensure a smooth and transparent flow of information between the board and senior man-agement, the board should have only one person responsible for reporting, the chief executive officer, who conveys to the board information on risk profiles and operational practices (Orlikoff and Totten 2001).

Good governance is said to exist when managers closely pursue the owner's objectives and when "principal–agent" problems are minimized. Governance is usually not a problem in small businesses or organizations where owners can directly observe and evaluate managerial staff performance. The key ingredients of good governance in these contexts include the following:

- *Objectives.* Clear, nonconflicting objectives of owners, translated into narrow, clear, and measurable criteria for evaluating management performance. Managers in a private corporation can be monitored relatively easily because owners have two objectives: to maximize profits and to maximize share price, both observable and measurable.

- *Supervisory structure.* Responsibility for supervising management is vested in an effective, professional body (board of directors) whose individual members have clear responsibilities and accountability.

- *Competitive environment.* Competition in the product, labor, supply, and capital markets promotes managerial efficiency by forcing the adoption of the most efficient production arrangements in order to stay competitive and capture market share. Competition in the product market allows the owner to compare performance of its company (and management) with the performance of other companies and diminishes monopoly rents, which management might misallocate to hide weak performance. Ability to monitor performance, combined with a competitive managerial labor market, allows owners to compare performance of company managers and to motivate them through rewards and job security. Well-functioning market institutions such as stock markets and accounting standards drastically reduce the cost of monitoring management. Under such standards, corporate profits can be easily compared, and share prices can be easily observed.

Many of the problems seen in purchasing arrangements relate to bad governance. First, the objectives of resource allocation and purchasing are often not made explicit. This is especially true when purchasing arrangements are part of the core function of the MOH and when historical global budgets are used to pay providers. The budget allocation process is often mechanical, and key strategic questions about patient needs and demand, supplier behavior, and changes in the market environment and prices are not regularly reviewed. As a result, inequities and inefficiency often creep into the system, remaining unobserved for years and leading to a waste of public resources and loss of the financial protection that collective financing was designed to address.

Second, the agency role and accountability mechanisms of such purchasing arrangements are often unclear. Frequently, there are no effective mechanisms for monitoring managerial performance. As a result, politicians and bureaucrats involved in supervision have wide latitude to pursue their own agendas (unrelated to health and including employment generation and sinecures for loyal supporters), which leads to conflicts among the different functions of the government (stewardship, governance, financing, and service provision). Patients—to whom the purchasing arrangement should ultimately be accountable—are often not involved in discussions of governance and accountability. Even when managerial performance criteria exist, lack of competition or other external pressures hamper performance. Frustrated by their lack of responsiveness, even poor patients eschew formal purchasing arrangements and continue seeking care directly from private providers who provide more responsive care, shorter waiting lines, and so on.

These problems in governance of purchasers are part of the core public bureaucracies and have led many countries to try to unbundle the health financing function, paralleling the institutional changes that have accompanied organizational reforms of provider systems (autonomization, corporatization, and privatization). Two institutional reform modalities have a profound impact on the governance structure of purchasers. The first is a separation of ownership and governance of the purchaser from the government's stewardship function through decentralization of ownership and creation of semiautonomous agencies (health insurance funds). The second is a separation of the revenue collection and insurance subfunction of health care financing from the purchasing subfunction (figure 5.4).

- *Decentralization and agency creation (semiautonomous or corporatized social health insurance funds).* Many countries have tried to split off the financing function from the core MOH through four different types of reforms: (1) decentralization of the budget process (e.g., regional health authorities in Poland, Sri Lanka, and the United Kingdom); (2) establishment of semiautonomous health financing agency structures (e.g., Croatia, Estonia, and Hungary); (3) corporatization

Figure 5.4   Decentralization/Agency Creation and Insurance/Purchaser Split

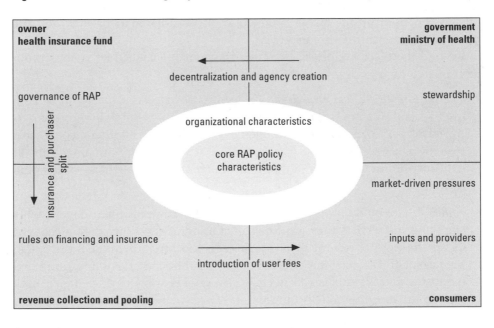

Source: Authors.
Note: RAP = resource allocation and purchasing.

of the purchasing arrangement under parastatal companies that are subject to private company law and market pressures (e.g., Australian Health Insurance Commission, Czech Republic); and (4) privatization of the financing function (e.g., Chile).

- *Insurance and purchaser split.* Another reform of purchasing arrangements in recent years has been a split in the revenue collection and insurance subfunctions of health care financing. In some countries the resulting revenue collection and insurance subfunctions have been reintegrated into the tax collection system. In other countries, it has been privatized.

These institutional reforms were intended to address governance problems by narrowing the range of objectives for which managers of purchasing arrangements are accountable and by establishing measurable performance criteria. Often the new objectives focus on economic efficiency, which is easier to monitor than the previously unspecified objectives. The reforms often include the creation of a professional organization (agency or board), vested with responsibility for monitoring performance targets, and management employment and salaries are tied to the achievement of these targets. The more successful reforms have also tried to depoliticize management (although the new purchasing arrangements are often vulnerable to a different type of capture by vested interest groups such as organized labor). Capital funds may be allocated on a competitive basis to encourage accountability in financing improvements and repayment of debt. The more sophisticated reforms (e.g., Chile and Colombia) have tried to introduce competition in the factor, product, and insurance markets to which the purchasing arrangements are exposed.

Despite these achievements, these reforms remain plagued by serious problems related to:

- *Continued politicization of decision making and opaqueness of intervention.* Failure to establish an oversight structure that ensures accountability for the narrowed range of goals; failure to develop or ensure the use of other mechanisms to achieve key sector goals (e.g., related to access and equity) usually results in continuation of old habits of informal intervention by "owners" in hospital operations.

- *Failure to hive off or ring-fence "social" goods.* Governments often have trouble clarifying the services they want delivered and targeting subsidies effectively. Often, these objectives end up relying on cross-subsidization inside the hospital. Management then may make reference to the ad hoc interventions, unfunded mandates, and the associated costs to excuse poor economic performance. Lack of clear instructions for delivering social services reduces the owner's ability to hold the manager accountable for economic or other performance targets.

There are many reasons for these failures. Defining narrow objectives is hard in health care because multiple interests within government may disagree on what the key objectives are or should be. Government owners may have many health objectives and not know what their key objectives are or their priorities (weights). Specifying objectives and priorities can make explicit what is not a priority and what the state will not deliver or fund. This is often politically costly. Creating alternative mechanisms to pursue other sector objectives (besides organizational efficiency) is hard because it requires governments to engage in more complex activities (contracting, purchasing, regulation). Under an integrated public system (budgetary organizations) governments can functionally pursue sector objectives through implicit understandings that they will transfer x-amount of resources and that the hospitals will provide services in some form to the population that walks through the door. Under an organizationally reformed system, the government would have to identify which services would be delivered to the poor (for example) and purchase (or sometimes mandate) their delivery. Finally, even when alternative accountability mechanisms exist, politicians and bureaucrats usually prefer ad hoc direct interventions with fewer constraints on their relations to the new purchasing arrangements. Lack of constraints on these interventions creates many problems.

Governments that are trying to improve governance by emulating the "corporate model" need to enhance their capacity to develop and implement sectoral policy through indirect mechanisms such as contracting and regulation. They must create structures for administering the new accountability arrangements—and for restraining ad hoc intervention by politicians and bureaucrats (box 5.3).

The governance of a RAP arrangement by its owners is often poorly defined and confused by the government's stewardship function and public monopoly in the factor, product, and insurance markets. In many countries, where RAP arrangements are an integral part of the government's core bureaucracy (e.g., the economic department of an MOH or other government department), the ownership of the stewardship function, health financing function, and providers are merged into one. Differences in objectives, decision rights, and accountability arrangements, and market pressures among the various functions and subfunctions, are often not made explicit. Some key governance lessons from other sectors that are applicable to RAP arrangements are reviewed below.

The Operational Level: Operational Management and Case Management

Two levels in the organization of health care purchasers are directly involved in day-to-day operations: operational management and case management.

What Happens at the Operational Management Level?

Operational management is a "systematic and integrated approach to assurance and review of clinical responsibility and accountability that improves quality and safety resulting in optimal patient outcomes" (Department of Health, Government of Western Australia 2002: 3). Operational management has parallels

---

BOX 5.3   ORGANIZATIONAL GOVERNANCE STRUCTURES IN SENEGAL'S SOCIAL SECURITY FUND

Senegal introduced sickness protection for employees in the 1950s in its occupational social security framework, consisting of: the Social Security Fund, which provides insurance for occupational accidents; the Social Insurance Institute for Old-Age Pensions, which provides a pension scheme for all employees; and the Sickness Insurance Institutions, which protect employees against sickness. Each of these organizations was based on fairly autonomous management structures and had its own statutes and rules that could be amended by its members.

Senegal's Social Security Fund is a self-regulating system in which all stakeholders are represented. The social partners (employers and workers) are represented on three decision-making bodies: the College of Representatives, the Board of Directors, and the Bureau. The government is represented in a double role: it is both a full member of the organization as an employer and also has trustee powers granted by the Minister of Labor (technical trusteeship) and the Minister of Finance (financial trusteeship).

The College of Representatives discusses and comments on reports by the Board of Directors on activities and financial management. The Board of Directors, elected for two years, carries out decisions of the College; prepares the Annual Report, the Annual Work Plan; investments; decides on salaries and employee benefits; and nominates the director-general. Management was given a fair degree of autonomy because the government was not running the system within an overall social security strategy. The state did not apply a consistent provision policy nor had it established efficient procedures for controlling payments and monitoring contributions. It actually used institutional funds for unrelated policy objectives.

Autonomous management allowed for the improvement of the quality of services and a stabilized financial situation. This method of representation helped to create a harmonious relationship between the public authorities and the insurance fund and between the fund and its senior management. These arrangements afford the basis for efficient allocation of resources.

Source: Diop 2003.

---

to organizational governance. It is the main instrument for making a purchaser accountable and responsive to its clients. Whereas organizational governance talks about the relationship between the owner/stakeholder and the purchaser, operational management operates one level below that.

Senior management is responsible for running the institution and overseeing its daily operations, and especially for making sound business and financial decisions and maintaining high service quality and client responsiveness. Operational management includes activities that promote, review, measure, and monitor the quality of purchasers' various business units. It exercises a supervisory function over its case management level to ensure good performance and reputation of the entire institution. Managers at this level need a good understanding of the clinical and business processes in the units that work closely with clients and provide services (Preker et al. 2004).

What Happens at the Case Management Level?

The function of *case management* is to provide insurance services, work with clients, and purchase responsive health care services. In addition, it includes responsibilities such as the development of work plans, work schedules, revision of procedures and workloads as well as recommendations regarding organizational structures, methods, and processes. Furthermore, the clinical management level performs a supervisory personnel function including selecting employees, training of staff, and changing employees' duty stations (United States Office of Personnel Management 2002).

QUALITY PERFORMANCE

A working definition of *quality* that facilitates measurement is an important and crucial thing to be developed (Orlikoff and Totten 2001) because quality goals need to be measurable, meaningful, and part of the organization's corporate strategy.

What Are Quality Goals?

The organization's quality goals are based on the objectives of its leadership. Each level of management is responsible for ensuring the appropriateness and effectiveness of the institution's policies, procedures, and processes. Operational management ensures the translation of the quality and risk-management framework set by the board into practical policies, processes, and procedures. Operational management needs to take care of communicating the goals throughout the organization and creating preconditions for quality management as a permanent element of the organization's everyday business. Management at case level is responsible for translating quality goals into everyday procedures in client management and service delivery. Quality management is not really a goal by itself but rather a method for meeting objectives, goals, and demands (Ministry of Social Affairs and Health [Finland] 1999). Effective monitoring processes are crucial for managing and ensuring quality. Regular monitoring will help to quickly detect and correct deficiencies in both policies and operational procedures. For that reason, regular reports to senior management will help identify problematic areas for corrective actions.

How Is Quality Control Being Performed?

A common method of providing a continuous supervisory function on the purchaser is by establishing a quality control system through clinical audits. Clinical audits include a regular process for reviewing performance, refining practices, and measuring the outcomes against agreed standards (Department of Health, Government of Western Australia 2002). Measuring aspects of purchasing health care services and providing services allows both internal comparison to set benchmarks and external comparison with other institutions operating in the same market. In addition, this function gives feedback on performance, efficiency, and other goals defined by senior management and approved at the organizational governance level. Measures must, however, be relevant and appropriate and lead to evaluations that will help improve quality and performance of the organization. Monitoring, measurement, and evaluation provide the relevant information, documentation, statistics, and data necessary for quality management. Information gathered from these monitoring processes is a leadership tool of crucial importance for an organization's decision making. For that reason, information should be collected and managed with suitable information technology that has the capacity to edit the data according to specific needs. Outcomes of quality activities need to be documented suitably for governance purposes (box 5.4).

CONCLUSIONS

Purchasers might have different views about service quality and methods for achieving it. To ensure delivery of high-quality services, a key issue is the promotion of intense collaboration and discussion between steward, purchaser, and provider.

The levels of management concept provides a clear framework, including crucial elements for effective management by establishing clear lines of responsibility, clear segregation of duties, and a strong internal control culture. The framework includes every level on which management is required and is implemented throughout the entire organization. The organizational governance level, in conjunction with the operational management, provides clear strategies and oversight for the entire institution and its quality and performance goals. It is responsible for implementing the necessary framework for quality control and operational risk management and oversees the day-to-day client services performed at the case management level.

BOX 5.4 GOVERNING HEALTH INSURANCE IN CHILE

Chile, with a population of around 15 million people, has a mandatory and comprehensive health insurance system, financed mainly through a combination of payroll taxes and general taxation. Workers in the formal sector have the option of choosing between two insurance providers, the national health fund (FONASA) or private health insurance organizations (ISAPREs), purchased mainly by upper-income groups. FONASA covers around 70 percent of the Chilean population. Chilean social health insurance also provides health insurance for informal workers, the poor, and the indigent. It is open for enrollment regardless of income and risk; contributions are based on salary (7 percent of earnings). Insurance for the poor and the indigent, about 40 percent of all FONASA-covered clients is free of charge, fully subsidized, and paid for by the state. The FONASA system has been quite successful in channeling government contributions to the poor and providing them with sufficient health care.

The stewardship role of the Ministry of Health has grown significantly over the past years. A recently passed law (Sanitary Authority Law) gave the ministry more power over the entire health sector, including the private insurers and health service providers. The stewardship function is separated under four entities. The general planning and surveillance system is directly under the Ministry of Health. Both insurance and health services are now regulated by the newly created Superintendency of Health; environmental regulation is under a specialized autonomous agency; and the regulation of pharmaceuticals and medical devices is under an autonomous agency equivalent to the U.S. Food and Drug Administration. The Ministry of Health oversees all of these autonomous agencies. The main objective of the Chileans was to separate the policy function from the actual enforcement of the regulatory framework to ensure independence from day-to-day political affairs.

The new organization, the Superintendency of Health, was established as an autonomous agency. All functions had previously been integrated in one organization, a structure that jeopardized the independence and effectiveness of the regulatory function. This split-up greatly contributes to solving this problem. Starting in 2005, the superintendency acquired regulatory power over FONASA.

FONASA was established as a highly autonomous government agency. As part of its stewardship role, the Ministry of Health oversees the national insurance fund's operations. FONASA is regulated by the Superintendency of Health as part of its control function of overseeing the entire health sector. FONASA's director is appointed by the president of Chile and enjoys a significant degree of independence and autonomy. This autonomy allows for setting up internal organizational arrangements including the appointment of the management team.

Source: Authors.

ANNEX: MANAGERIAL CHALLENGES

Collection Function as a Financial Basis for Purchasing Health Care

In low- and middle-income countries, the ability to collect contributions as the basis for purchasing is limited, because only a small number of people earn enough to make contributions. In addition, the tax base for financing health care purchases is also limited by the extent of the informal sector in both rural and urban areas, the high degree of income inequality, and governments' limited tax administration capacity. The very fact that income taxes are not a reliable source of revenue has led many governments to introduce purchasing institutions that are separate from government. This is based on at least two different thoughts: first, a smaller community of insured feels a higher responsibility to contribute; second, it may be easier for such a community to develop rules on how to contribute in the absence of formal income. Still, in developing countries this collection function is difficult to manage.

The Republic of Korea, for example, had problems collecting contributions when introducing its compulsory health insurance system in 1976 because the true size of individuals' incomes was hard to determine. Here, cross-subsidizing through taxes on sales or other indirect taxes was common but made the public health insurance system more expensive. Moreover, indirect taxes are regressive, meaning that the poor made a higher contribution to health insurance than the better-off because they spent a higher proportion of their income on basic goods and services.

Impact of Different Purchasing Arrangements

As discussed in chapter 3, different purchasing arrangements can be found worldwide. The various organizational arrangements have a major impact on managerial issues such as the collection of contributions, cost control, corruption, or purchasing power. In many health insurance–based systems, several institutions are financial intermediaries between providers and users of health services. They collect revenue from employees, employers, and the government, and reimburse providers for services delivered. Depending on the strength and power of the government's role relative to the sickness funds and, more important, on the number of purchasing institutions, tension can arise between these actors. Both sides—the government and the purchaser—have different roles and have to respond to different client groups. Whereas the government is accountable to the public and takes care of the entire social system, purchasers are accountable only to their beneficiaries.

The various purchasing arrangements show advantages and disadvantages. Multiple-payer systems have an advantage in managing the collection of contributions, because the resource pool can be broadened. The contribution collection function is assumed by a number of institutions and does not depend solely on the tax base through the government (Hussey and Anderson 2003), which increases flexibility in collection. As a consequence, this might lead to higher revenues and therefore might be a more applicable system for low-and middle-income countries.

Cost Control, Political Influence, and Corruption

A single-payer system usually has an advantage over the multiple-payer system in managing the overall costs of health care by having better control over expenditures. Cost control is much harder to perform in multiple-payer systems because the various purchasers may use different monitoring, payment, and information systems. The problematic fact of single-payer systems is their vulnerability to political influence. Strong political control over health care spending and monopsony power in purchasing health services makes the provision of health care dependent on the political environment. In the British National Health Service as a result of various reforms, public bodies with government-appointed boards were put in place and made responsible for service delivery, but it would still be the government to decide on issues such as hospital mergers or contracting with private providers (Berland 2002). When, in a single-payer system, the funding comes directly from the treasury, the purchaser's position vis-à-vis the ministry of health is powerful and can influence the government. If the entire system ran out of money, the one-and-only purchaser could just ask the government for more. Political influence can disarm cost controls or even create a favorable climate for corruption.

Corruption, in fact, is often the underbelly of political influence. "Illicit appropriation of public resources for private uses" endangers the entire system. It is a major problem in developing countries, but more sophisticated and better-hidden forms of corruption can be found in health systems anywhere, for instance, in illicit charges in public facilities. Eliminating or curtailing its outreach demands huge efforts of managers. Corruption impairs service quality, undermines social funding and financing instruments such as social insurance systems, interferes with efficient allocation of public resources, and thus narrows access to public facilities (Green and Collins 2003).

Purchasing Power

The whole point of managing resource allocation and the relationship between buyers and sellers of health services is the ultimate goal of getting value for money in health service purchases. This means finding the best balance between effective incentives and acceptable risks for providers (Hussey and Anderson 2003). In single-payer systems with multiple providers, the purchaser is in a much stronger position than in multi-payer systems. In systems with only one purchaser, the purchaser holds monopsony power, which therefore creates incentives for providers to supply cheaper care.

The danger, however, is that monopsony power might create pressure to drop certain services if the price goes too low. In such a situation, alternative sources of services typically emerge, such as private consultation of doctors or out-of-pocket payments for services. Parallel markets like this might lead to disadvantages for public patients because doctors might be tempted to concentrate on private patients, thus undermining the public system. This is an issue in low- and middle-income countries where out-of-pocket payments represent a much larger share of total health spending than in most industrial countries. However, within single-payer systems, control can be used to selectively encourage the provision of cost-effective treatments and discourage noncost-effective care.

Managing multi-payer systems is more complex because individual purchasers do not have the same degree of purchasing power. Ideally, diversity and competition stimulate innovation and encourage the provision of diverse types of health care (Hussey and Anderson 2003). Reality, however, often follows a different scenario.

The Czech Republic has transformed its single-payer system into a multiple-payer system, including governmental coverage of special population groups. Under the old, communist system, contributions were collected through general taxation. After the reform, 10 insurers provided services previously offered by only one. But the purchasing power of Czech insurers is still limited. The national regulation put in place by the government prescribes the operations of insurers, the benefits packages, as well as the rates for insurance contributions. It therefore eliminates the advantages of competition and marketability in a multiple-payer system.

NOTE

Invaluable insights were provided by Cristian Baeza, Hernan Fuenzalida, Pablo Gottret, Toomas Palu, Alain Enthoven, Dov Chernikovsky, Veronica Hancock, and Philip Davies.

REFERENCES

Barrientos, A., and P. Lloyd-Sherlock. 2000. "Reforming Health Insurance in Argentina and Chile." *Health Policy and Planning* 15: 417–23.

Berland, A. 2002. "Insights from Overseas: A Canadian Health Care Consultant Shares His Observations after a Year Working in Britain's National Health Service." *Canadian Health Care Manager* 9(6): 17–18.

Brundtland, G.H. 2002. *Seminar on Stewardship of Health Systems at the Board of Health.* (Speech in Oslo). Geneva: World Health Organization.

Colombo, F., and N. Tapay. 2003a. *Private Health Insurance in Australia. A Case Study.* OECD Health Working Papers. Paris: Organisation for Economic Co-operation and Development.

————. 2003b. *The Slovak Health Insurance System and the Potential Role for Private Health Insurance: Policy Challenges.* OECD Health Working Papers. Paris: Organisation for Economic Co-operation and Development.

Department of Health, Government of Western Australia. 2002. *Introduction to Clinical Governance.* Government of Western Australia, Department of Health.

Diop, Y.A. 2003. "Governance of Social Security Regimes: Trends in Senegal." *International Social Security Review* 56(3–4): 17–23.

Green, A., and C. Collings. 2003. "Health Systems in Developing Countries: Public Sector Managers and the Management of Contradictions and Change." *International Journal of Health Planning and Management* 18: 67–78.

Hussey, P., and G.F. Anderson. 2003. "A Comparison of Single- and Multi-Payer Health Insurance Systems and Options for Reform." *Health Policy* 66: 215–28.

Ministry of Social Affairs and Health (Finland), National Research and Development Centre for Welfare and Health (STAKES), Association of Finnish Local and Regional Authorities. 1999. *Quality Management in Social Welfare and Health Care for the 21st Century. National Recommendation.* Sarrijärvi, Finland: Gummerus.

Orlikoff, J.E., and M. Totten. 2001. *The Trustee Handbook for Health Care Governance.* San Francisco, CA: Jossey-Bass.

Pointer, D., and J.E. Orlikoff. 1999. *Board Work. Governing Health Care Organizations.* San Francisco, CA: Jossey-Bass.

Preker, A., M. McKee, A. Mitchell, and S. Wilbulpolprasert. 2004. *Managing Scarcity, Complexity and Change. A Call for Leadership in the Health Sector.* Health, Nutrition and Population Discussion Paper. Washington, DC: World Bank.

Travis, P., D. Egger, P. Davies, and A. Mechbal. 2002. *Towards Better Stewardship: Concepts and Critical Issues.* Geneva: WHO.

United States Office of Personnel Management. 2002. "Position Classification Standard for Social Insurance Administration Series." *General Schedule Position Classification Standards.* Washington, DC: OPM.

WHO (World Health Organization). 2000. *The World Health Report 2000—Health Systems: Improving Performance.* Geneva: WHO.

PART II

Economic Underpinnings

CHAPTER 6

Agency Theory and Its Applications in Health Care

Xingzhu Liu and Anne Mills

In this chapter, the authors introduce the basic concepts of standard agency theory, identify agency problems and their origins, and suggest solutions. In addition, they propose a framework for reimbursing the agent, review how the agent is paid in practice, and provide a full discussion of the application of agency theory in health care.

Agency theory provides a theoretical base and general framework for considering issues connected with paying health care providers. The theory recognizes that the utility functions of the principal and agent are divergent, and sometimes conflictual, and that, for the agent to behave in the interests of the principal, the principal has to work out a compatible remuneration contract and force the agent to serve the principal's utility function. Agency theory stresses that an effective remuneration contract should be either effort-based, if the effort can be observed or estimated, or outcome-based, if the outcome is observable. The theory provides a framework for designing the remuneration system in situations where there are information asymmetry, outcome uncertainty, and dependent output. Monitoring the effort, the outcome, or both is regarded as an irrevocable element of the remuneration contract. This suggests that, when implementing the designed health care, the payment system should be monitored and the monitoring information should be incorporated into the provider's payment process.

The authors recommend future research topics that include the utility functions of patients and providers and interactions between them; double agency in health care and its applications; the dual role of a provider acting as agent for two parties that may come into conflict; and the best estimation of efforts and outcomes on which providers are paid.

BASIC CONCEPTS

The concepts of agency theory are based on Ross (1973). Other early contributions to this literature include Mirrlees (1974) and Stiglitz (1974).

To understand agency theory, first consider an example in which the owner of an orchard plans to hire several people to pick apples. The orchard owner knows how to pick apples, but it is too much work to do by himself, and he has to hire people to pick apples for him. He wants his hired hands to work hard and honestly and would like to pay them the minimum necessary to get the job done. But he fears his apple pickers may want more money and not put in an honest day's work. Thus, he thinks long and hard about how much and how to pay his apple pickers. If he pays less than the people expect, he may not be able to hire enough apple pickers. If he pays more than they expect, he will feel that he is suffering a loss. If their pay is based on the quantity (weight) of apples picked, they may just gather fallen apples from the ground, pick only the large apples from the trees and leave the smaller ones behind, or pick only low-hanging apples. If the workers are paid by the day, they might not work as hard, but the likelihood of their gathering only easy-to-pick apples will be reduced. The orchard owner has been pondering these issues for three days without making a decision.

This story illustrates a principal–agent relationship in which the principal (the hirer) contracts with the agent (the hired) to perform some actions (to pick apples) on the principal's behalf. To activate this relationship, the principal and the agent must agree on what the agent is paid. This agreement is called the *compensation contract* or the *remuneration contract*, which specifies how much is to be paid and under what conditions.

The remuneration contract must be attractive to the agent, or the agent will take a different contract. The agent's acceptance of the contract terms is determined by the expected utility implicit in the contract offered by the principal. The expected utility of this contract must be at least equal to that achieved by alternative contracts with other principals. Stated formally, the benefit of this contract must not be less than the opportunity cost to persuade the agent to enter into this contract. This is referred to as the *participation constraint* (Arrow 1986).

The principal is not foolish. He will try his best to design a contract that not only is attractive to the agent but also provides incentive for the agent to act or behave in the best interests of the principal. Stated in economic terms, the contract must be able to maximize the utility of both the principal and the agent, and the maximization of the principal's utility must be compatible with the attainment of the minimally acceptable level of expected utility for the agent. This is called the *incentive compatibility constraint* (MacDonald 1984). Stated more formally, an incentive compatible contract requires solution of the following maximization problem (Scott 1996):

Max U[x − w(x)]

S.t. V[w(x), e] ≥ V₀

where $U(.)$ is the utility function of the principal; $V(.)$ is the utility function of the agent; x is the outcome of the agent's action (expressed in monetary term); $w(x)$ is the fee schedule facing the agent (dependent on x); e is the effort made by the agent; and V_0 is the participation constraint. The utility function of the principal is therefore a function of the outcome minus the outcome-related payment to the agent. The outcome is a random variable dependent on e. The utility function of the agent is a function of his share of outcome and of the action taken. For the contract to be acceptable to the agent, the utility it offers, $V(.)$, must be greater than or at least equal to that available in other alternatives, V_0.

The critical issue underpinning agency theory is to design the remuneration contract or to work out the fee schedule that is incentive compatible (Ryan 1992a). The payment (that the orchard owner is worrying about) can be based on either of the two factors, namely, efforts or inputs and outcomes or outputs (Stiglitz 1989). If the payment to the agent is to be based on efforts, the efforts must be observable and susceptible to monitoring, as in the case of picking apples where the orchard owner can watch or direct the hired hands' activities if they are paid according to the number of days worked. Unfortunately, not all efforts are observable. For example, one cannot know the difference in degree of efforts by two scholars who sit at a desk, reading and writing for the same length of time, and who are hired to design new products for a factory. Clearly, if an individual's actions and efforts are not observable, compensation cannot be based on those actions (Stiglitz 1989). Another alternative is to pay on outcome, as in the case of an owner who pays hired hands according to the weight of apples picked. In some cases, as Stiglitz put it, even if an individual's actions are not directly observable, his actions may be inferred if outcome is a function only of effort $[x = f(e)]$. The perfect outcome-based payment requires an observable outcome that is perfectly correlated with efforts.

Agency relationships are ubiquitous both within and among firms. The theory, as the economic theory of control, is now being used in many areas (Eisenhardt 1989; Bergen, Dutta, and Walker 1992; Eisenhardt 1988), including the health care sector (Pontes 1995; Ryan 1992b; Zweifel 1994; Propper 1995; Levaggi 1996; Mooney and Ryan 1993; Clark and Olsen 1994; Scott and Shiell 1997a).

STANDARD AGENCY THEORY

The standard agency theory has many important assumptions that were not mentioned systematically in several publications (Pontes 1995; Stiglitz 1989; Mooney and Ryan 1993; Scott 1996). The present authors summarize below the five major relevant assumptions described in the literature.

1. Both the principal and the agent are utility maximizers, and the utility functions of principal and agent are mutually independent. This means there is no common argument in their utility functions.

2. Income and effort are two major arguments in the utility function of the agent. Income will provide utility to the agent, but efforts will provide disutility. Thus, the agent will always attempt to maximize income and minimize efforts. Facing this utility conflict, which means that the utility of one argument is the disutility of another, the agent will not act in the interest of the principal unless he is motivated by the remuneration contract to do so.

3. The principal knows perfectly what actions should be taken by the agent, but the information about the agent's actual actions is available only to the agent himself. Because the agent's effort is observable or unobservable, but information about it can be collected, the principle can monitor the agent's actions by direct observation or indirect information collection to obtain knowledge about the agent's effort.

4. The information about outcome is directly available to the principal, and the outcome is perfectly correlated with the agent's efforts.

5. The principal and the agent enter into the contract voluntarily.

With these assumptions, it is possible to design an incentive-compatible remuneration contract that can motivate the agent to behave in the principal's best interest, and meanwhile the expected utility of the agent can be satisfied. Although the agent has a tendency to shirk or cheat, he cannot do so for fear of reduced payment. This is because the principal can detect the agent's shirking and cheating, which will result in less effort-related payment, or because the shirking and cheating can reduce outcome if that is the basis for payment. The principal cannot exploit the agent because the entry into the contract is voluntary. Low fee schedules will not attract the agent.

A number of other factors may influence the remuneration contract and its contractual efficiency in terms of the principal. First, in the single-agent model, the existence and degree of monitoring influence the mode of payment and the degree of incentive offered in the payment. Because information about the agent's action is available only to the agent, as assumed by the standard theory, the principal must seek information about the agent's actions to incorporate the agent's efforts into the remuneration contract. Absence of monitoring means absence of information about the agent's efforts. Effort-related payment is not appropriate in this case. If the agent's actions are monitored and the monitoring is not perfect, as is usually the case (Holsmstrom 1979), the effort-related payment can be based on the estimation of efforts. To avoid distortion of payment, more than one explanatory factor is usually included in this estimation, which may lead to complex payment systems. Examples include rewarding a salesperson by reference to the number of miles of travel as well as sales volume, and paying a professional according to the number of hours worked as well as having a set fee (Mooney and Ryan 1993).

Second, a dynamic agency relationship leads to more efficient outcomes than are achieved under the single-period model. Rubenstein and Yaari (1983) argue that, when the agency model is extended to allow for repeated contracts, the role of rewards and penalties in devising the optimal contract is reduced, as emphasized by Holmstrom (1979) and Shavell (1979). Because the principal and the agent will interact more than once, the principal will tend to offer a favorable contract to those who act in the interest of the principal, and the agent will behave more favorably to the principal in expecting more compensation by renewal of the contract. For example, by recognizing multi-period interaction, the insurance company would like to offer discounts to the insured with the best claim history, and an employee tends to work harder when approaching the end of the first work contract and expecting the next contract.

Third, the supply of and demand for agents will have significant effects on the pattern of the remuneration contract. Because the ratio of marginal benefits to marginal costs of the agent is a function of the market structure (defined as the number of principals relative to agents), greater competition among principals for agents would make agents less likely to accept a given contract since many alternative contracts are available. To realize the demand for agents, principals have to offer agents more favorable contracts, hence attracting more agents into the market. In a situation where the supply of agents exceeds demand for them, competition among agents exists. Agents would be more likely to accept a given contract since fewer alternatives are available. In this case, the level of payment to agents will be reduced.

AGENCY PROBLEMS AND THEIR ORIGINS

Thus, things are not as ideal as originally assumed. Interactions between principal and agent will be less efficient than anticipated if the assumptions of the standard agency theory cannot be met. It is difficult to design a remuneration contract that may motivate the agent to behave in the best interests of the principal, when information asymmetry, outcome uncertainty, dependent outcome, and aggregated outcome exist.

The Reasons for Agency Problems

Agency problem arise for multiple reasons, explored below.

Information Asymmetry

Information asymmetry refers to a situation in which the principal does not have knowledge about what actions the agent should take and what actions the agent has taken. Arrow (1986) identifies two forms of information asymmetry. The first form is *hidden action,* which means that the principal cannot observe the actions or efforts of the agent, only the outcome of those actions. The second form is *hidden information,* which means that the agent has information or knowledge about the actions that the principal does not have. In this case, although the actions or efforts may be observable, the principal does not know whether they are appropriate. In the case of information asymmetry, remuneration of the agent cannot be based perfectly on efforts or actions. The behavior-based remuneration contract will lead to distorted remuneration, which has little controlling effect on the agent's deviant behavior. Put another way, under information asymmetry, the behavior-based remuneration contract will not be an incentive-compatible remuneration contract.

Outcome Uncertainty

The existence of information asymmetry requires that payment be based only on outcome, because outcome information is available to the principal. But the incentive-compatible, outcome-based remuneration contract requires perfect correlation of the outcome with efforts. In many cases, however, outcome has an uncertainty character. Besides the efforts of the agent, the outcome may be affected by some other factors that are beyond the agent's control. Stated formally, the outcome is a function of efforts and some unobservable random variables (Stiglitz 1989), that is, $x = f(e, r)$, where x is the outcome, e is the agent's efforts, and r is a vector of random variables. In this situation, the outcome-based remuneration contract cannot reflect the real effort of the agent, and the optimal remuneration system will depend in part on whether the agent is risk neutral or risk averse (Ryan 1992a). If the agent is risk neutral, the resulting payment would be simply outcome (in monetary terms) minus the principal's share, as in the case of a landlord's renting land to a farmer in which the landlord charges a fixed rent independent of the output and the agent bears all the risk due to outcome uncertainty. Such a remuneration contract, as commented on by Shavell (1979), can provide the right incentive to the agent. If the agent is risk averse, however, such a contract is not optimal because the agent no longer wants to take on board all the risk. The optimal fee schedule with a risk-averse principal and agent will be a function of outcome, where both parties share the risk. But the benefit of risk sharing will come at the cost of reducing the strength of the agent's incentive to accept the contract and to behave in the interest of the principal.

Dependent Outcomes

The outcome-related remuneration contract to individuals requires that the individuals' outcomes are mutually independent. In other words, an individual's outcome is a function of only that individual's effort, not a function of other individuals. In some cases, however, one individual's outcome may reflect the effort of others. In the extreme case, if agents' outputs are completely dependent, in that the output of individual i reveals information about the state of nature facing individual j, then payment cannot be directly related to the individual agent. The first-best solution will be achieved by using relative performance indicators derived from performance evaluations. Payment can be made on the *rank-order tournament* (taking no account of their real outputs) to promote efficiency (Holmstrom 1982). However, as Holmstrom points out, such a system will be efficient only if the agent's outcomes are dependent and the individual outcome is observable. If the outputs are independent and the individual outcome is observable, the optimal fee schedule is one where individual i's payment depends on his or her output alone.

Aggregated Outcome

The rank-order tournament, based on relative performance indicators, is suitable in a situation in which individual outcomes are dependent and observable. In some cases, however, the outcome reflects individuals' joint efforts, and the individual outcomes cannot be separated from one another. What can be observed is only the total outcome of the individuals' joint efforts. In this case, payment can be based neither on the individual outcome nor on the equally shared outcome among agents, because the former is impossible and the latter will lead to inefficient outcome due to free-riding (Holmstrom 1982). Alchian and Demetzs (1972) suggest that, in such a situation, efficiency will be improved if a principal is brought in to monitor agents' actions. Payment will be based on the estimation of their efforts and contributions to the aggregated outcome. Holmstrom suggests the imposition of group incentives, that is, penalty or bonus schemes to improve the efficiency of the remuneration. Payment based on monitored information on effort plus an equal share of outcome-based payment might be an alternative for the multi-agent and aggregated outcome situation.

Agency Problems

Agency problems refer to the possibility of opportunistic behavior by the agent that works against the welfare of the principal. Such behavior will occur when there is information asymmetry between the agent and the principal. The existence of outcome uncertainty, dependent outcome, and aggregated outcome make the problem more difficult to solve through the proper design of the remuneration contract. The divergent and independent utility functions of the principal and the agent, and information asymmetry between them, are recognized as the major sources of agency problems. Because the principal lacks knowledge about how the agent should behave and what actions have already been taken, the agent may misbehave for his or her own interest and away from the welfare of the principal. The outcome-based remuneration contract may provide a solution to this problem. However, if outcomes are uncertain, individuals' outcomes are dependent upon each other, or individuals' outcomes are aggregated as a total. An incentive-compatible remuneration contract is difficult to design.

Arrow (1986) notes two major kinds of agency problems: moral hazard and adverse selection, both of which are related to information asymmetry between principal and agent.

Moral Hazard

Moral hazard arises because the principal has imperfect information about the agent's actions (Holmstrom 1979), namely, what actions should be taken and what actions have been taken. Moral hazard involves a situation in which many of the agent's actions are either hidden from the principal or are costly to observe. Driven by self-interest, the agent may take advantage of the principal, pursuing his own interests to the detriment of the principal.

Adverse Selection

Adverse selection arises because the agent possesses information that is unobservable or costly to obtain by the principal. For lack of information, the principal cannot judge the agent's competence before the two parties enter into the contract (Akerloff 1970). The agent may be tempted to exaggerate competence, ability, or willingness to provide the effort required by the principal in order to obtain a contract or a contract with more favorable terms. Thus, the principal may unwittingly enter into a contract with an agent with limited ability or with limited intentions to exert the contractually required efforts (Pontes 1995). In this case, the principal may select an agent who acts against his or her expectations.

Solutions to Agency Problems

To prevent adverse selection and moral hazard and to protect the principal's interests, attempts must be made to reduce the possibility that agents will misbehave. At the most general level, the method of protection depends on the design of the remuneration contract. To be specific, principals and agents resolve agency problems through monitoring and bonding.

Monitoring

Monitoring involves observing the behavior or the performance of agents, or both. Because agency problems can arise, principals will find trying to monitor agents in their self-interest (Eisenhardt 1985). Principals can try to monitor agents by collecting complete information about an agent's actions or behavior. If the principal knows how the agent should behave, monitoring will be effective, and payment can be totally based on the monitoring information. If some information is hidden, the principal may employ peers to monitor the agent's behavior. In this situation, however, monitoring rarely generates perfect information about the agent's behavior, and the monitoring cost is high. Perfect information is especially unlikely if the agent engages in complex and highly unstructured tasks. This does not mean, however, that behavior monitoring does not or should not take place. The information, though not perfect, will help to control the agent's behavior by relating the information to rewards and penalties, but there will be a trade-off between the principal's monitoring costs and the benefits gained through monitoring. If hidden actions exist, namely the behavior of the agent is not observable, monitoring will have no role in evaluating the agent's efforts. As an alternative or supplement to monitoring the agent's behavior, the principal can also monitor the consequences of the agent's behavior. Thus, instead of monitoring actions, the principal may monitor the performance implications of those actions. As assumed by standard agency theory, most outcomes are observable. In general, monitoring performance (or output) is more efficient when tasks are not highly programmable (Eisenhardt 1985). Output measurement is not, however, without problems. This measurement becomes more problematic when it involves team production and dependent and aggregate outcomes.

Bonding

Bonding refers to the arrangement that penalizes agents for acting in ways that violate the interests of principals or reward them for achieving the principal's goals. While the principal has an incentive to monitor the agent, the agent also has an incentive to assure the principal that he/she is behaving in ways consistent with the principal's interests, particularly in the situation of agent competition. In general, the agent can use bonding mechanisms to reassure the principal (Barney and Hesterly 1996). Bonding mechanisms frequently take the form of incentives that the agent creates for himself, incentives that make the agent behave in the agent's self-interest and in ways consistent with the principal's interests. Perhaps the most common form of incentive bonding focuses on the agent's compensation package. If the agent's compensation is tied to behaving and performing in ways consistent with the principal's interests, the agent will be likely to behave appropriately. An agent's willingness to accept this form of compensation can be understood as a bond that reassures the principal that the agent's behavior will respect the principal's interests. For example, a lawyer receives an immigration case and allows the applicant to pay half of the charge as a down payment and the balance upon success. Ideally, the principal would prefer an incentive scheme that fully penalizes the agent for shirking and opportunism. This, however, is extremely difficult to achieve without exposing the agent to risks he or she will find unacceptably high. Thus, although principals prefer schemes that emphasize incentives, they must design compensation between pure incentive and fixed compensation plans.

Besides monitoring and bonding, trust is important; contracts are developed on a basis of trust between the principal and agent and their recognition of mutual dependence. Also, professional bodies set standards of practice, and the government regulates licensing. These help strengthen the trust between the principal and agent and promote the development of contracts.

ALTERNATIVE PAYMENT SYSTEMS

How to pay the agent lies at the heart of the remuneration contract between principal and agent. Research in agency theory has examined a variety of compensation plans, including bonuses and stock sharing (Murphy 1986), salary versus commissions (Eisenhardt 1985), effects of incentive payment on turnover (Zenger 1992), and choices between piece rates and time rates (Lazear 1986). The following is an introduction to different ways of payment related to the agency theory.

A Framework for Payment Systems

Figure 6.1 shows the flow chart of alternative incentive payment methods under different bases and conditions. The chart is created according to the above-mentioned literature related to agency theory. In general, incentive payment methods can be divided into effort-based payment and outcome-based payment (Pontes 1995). *Effort-based payment* links payment to the agent's effort, about which the principal either has perfect information or has an estimation, based on information gathered by monitoring. *Outcome-based payment* is defined as payment that is related either to the outcome, if the outcome is separable and perfectly related to the individual's effort, or to the estimated outcome, if individual outcomes are dependent or characterized by uncertainty.

In designing incentive payments, whether the agent's effort is observable should be the first consideration. If actions are hidden, payment cannot be based on effort but on outcome. If no actions are hidden, the next consideration should be whether there is hidden information. If there is no hidden information, payment should be based on the effort. If information is hidden, payment methods will depend on whether or not information collection is costly. If collecting information for estimating the effort is too costly, payment has to be based on outcome; otherwise payment can be based on the estimated effort. If that is impossible, payment must be based on outcome. If there is no outcome uncertainty, whether dependent outcome involving many agents exists should be considered. If the outcome is certain and independent, payment can be directly based on outcome. If the outcome is certain and dependent, payment will depend on whether the outcome is aggregated. If not aggregated, payment

Figure 6.1   Alternative Incentive Payment Methods under Different Bases and Conditions

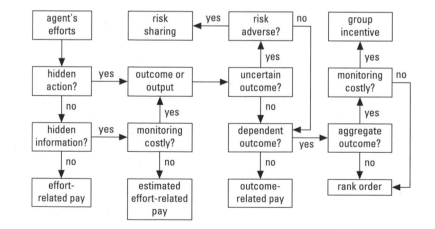

Source: Authors, based on Murphy 1986, Eisenhardt 1985, Zenger 1992, and Lazear 1986.

should be based on the rank-order tournament (based on the relative outcome indicators, as described previously). If it is aggregated, and the individual's contributions to the aggregated outcome can be monitored costlessly, payment can also be based on the relative rank-order; otherwise the group incentive payment will be used. If the outcome is uncertain, payment will depend on whether the agent is risk averse. If he is risk neutral, payment can be directly based on the outcome. If the agent is risk averse, the payment will be related to some kind of risk-sharing payment schemes based on the uncertain outcome.

Payment Mechanisms in Practice

Different types of payment systems of practical use are now introduced within the framework of figure 6.1. The introduction to the payment systems is based on Ehrenberg and Smith (1991), Mangum (1964), Marriott (1968), and Armstrong (1995). These references are not repeated in this section.

Salary

Salary (also called "time rates" or "flat rates") is an arrangement under which agents (employees or workers) are paid a predetermined rate per month, week, day, or hour for the time worked. The pay is set in accordance with the work intensity of the job and the skill required. The pay varies only with time specified, never with the output, performance, or any additional skills the workers acquire. Time is the most straightforward estimation of the effort. Usually, the more time spent, the more effort will be contributed. In some situations, however, the principal offers high time rates to some agent(s) that do not reflect effort. The purpose is to attract or retain highly qualified agents. In this case, the salary includes a consolidated bonus element and is probably greater than the local labor market rate. Wage and salary are similar concepts except that wages are generally paid over shorter time periods, for example, per hour.

Salary is often used when operating an incentive scheme relating payment directly to effort or the outcome is believed undesirable or impossible. Salary is also suitable if outcome-based payment proves unsatisfactory because it creates *wage drift* (a situation in which an increase in wages exceeds the increase in output), is costly to run, creates conflict, or does not provide value for money in the shape of increased productivity. Salary may also be chosen when the focus is on total quality.

The advantages of salary payment to the principal are that the cost of salary is predictable, the salary system is less likely to cause conflict between principals and agents, and the administrative cost of the salary system is relatively low. The disadvantages are that the salary system does not provide the motivation of a direct financial incentive that ties pay to performance. Without close supervision, disciplinary measures, and other nonfinancial forms of incentive, the salary system alone may not work well. Salary is neither effort-based nor outcome-based payment. It can be categorized as a risk-sharing payment scheme in which the principal takes the risk for outcome and the agent is accountable for the defined tasks. A real-world overview shows that salary payment is probably the most commonly used payment method. It is complemented by nonfinancial incentives that persuade workers to identify with the organization's objectives.

Piece Rate

Piece rate (also known as "piece work," "individual piece work," or "straight piece work") is a payment mechanism in which a uniform price is paid per unit of production. Agents are therefore rewarded according to the number of pieces they produce or provide. By means of a time study, the average amount of time an operator, working at a normal pace, needs to perform a certain job is determined. This time standard is converted into a set price or piece rate to be paid for each unit of production. The agent's earnings consist of the number of units produced multiplied by the piece rate, ordinarily with some fall-back rate or minimum hourly guarantee. The fall-back rate might be a specified percentage of the average earnings per unit of time, below which the agent will be paid the fall-back rate and above which the agent will get marginal earnings equaling the piece rate. The piece rate payment system is applicable when the individual's contribution to production is separable, measurable, and standardized. It is suitable for small-scale, low-technology production.

The advantages of the piece rate are that the system is easy to operate and simple to understand and provides the agent with strong incentives to work productively. The disadvantages are that production quality may suffer without close quality control and that production may exceed demand if not well planned and regulated.

Because payment is directly proportionate to results, the piece rate is outcome-based in most cases. For example, payment according to the number of lathed machine parts is an outcome-based payment. In this case, the principal usually need not monitor the agent's action. The principal needs only to evaluate the quality of the machine parts and pay for the agent's work. If the result is ambiguous and not the outcome that the principal expected, the piece rate can be regarded as effort-based payment rather than outcome-based payment. For example, the number of visits to a medical doctor is the estimation of the doctor's effort. The outcome of visits should be mainly the patient's health status improvement, not the visits per se. Thus, payment according to the number of visits to the doctor's office is an effort-based payment, not an outcome-based payment.

Standard Hour Plans

Standard hour plans are payment mechanisms in which agents are paid according to the amount of work that will be performed within an hour by an average competent worker. In practice, tasks will be standardized and analyzed in terms of standard time needed to perform the task, and each task will be allocated the number of standard hours. The total payment will be the total number of units of production times the standard hours allocated to this unit of production times the money rate of the standard hour. The major difference between piece rate and standard hour plans is that, in the latter, the standards are expressed in terms of time per unit of production rather than, as in the former, in terms of money.

The application of standard hour plans is similar to the piece rate and offers the same advantages and disadvantages. It also offers an additional advantage: time-rates are not affected when wages are raised, unlike piece rates, which have to be changed throughout the range. It is less understandable, however, than the piece rate, which directly links effort or output to money, not standard hours. Standard hour plans can be thought of as effort-based payment because jobs and tasks are measured by the standard hour, a measurement of efforts.

Work-Measured Schemes

Work-measured schemes are payment mechanisms in which agents are paid according to the time saving over the time standard for performing a task. The amount of incentive pay received depends on the difference between the actual time taken to perform the task and the standard time allowed. If a task is done in less than the standard time, a reward is paid for the time saving. In a work-measured scheme, the job or its component tasks, is timed, and the incentive payment is related to performance superior to the standard time allowed for the job. Work measurement involves working out standard time for the task components and then calculating the standard time for the job.

Payment in relation to time saving can be either proportional or regressive. Setting a ceiling for the amount of incentive pay that can be earned is usually advisable to avoid excessive amounts or wage drift. This is sometimes called "capping."

In work-measured schemes, more time saving means more effort by the agent, and less time spent completing a task means more intense effort in a given time period. Thus, it can be categorized as an effort-based payment. However, if the output is measurable and the ultimate objective of the effort, payment can be based on the extra output. In this situation, the work-measured scheme would be an outcome-based payment.

Measured Day Work

In *measured day work,* the agents' payment is fixed on the understanding that they will maintain a specified performance level, but the pay does not fluctuate in the short term with their performance. The fundamental principles of measured day work are that there is an incentive level of performance and that the incentive payment is guaranteed in advance, thereby obligating the agents to perform at the requisite effort level. In contrast, a conventional work-measured incentive scheme allows employees discretion on their effort level but relates their pay directly to the effort made or the results achieved.

Measured day work seeks to produce an effort-reward bargain in which enhanced and stable earnings are exchanged for an incentive level of performance. Its disadvantages are that the set performance target can become an easily attainable norm and may be difficult to change and that the agent may need close monitoring.

Measured day work is different from salary in that it is short-term based (usually per day) and has a clearly stated working target. Salary usually entails a long-term contract, and the working target is less specific than for measured day work. Measured day work is an effort-based payment mechanism.

Group Incentive Schemes

Group or team incentive or bonus schemes provide for the payment of a supplement either equally or proportionately to individuals within a group or team. The bonus is related to group output in relation to the defined targets or the time saved on jobs—the difference between the allowed time and the actual time.

The advantage of the group incentive scheme is that it develops team work, breaks down demarcation, and encourages the group to monitor its own performance and discipline itself to achieve the targets. In addition, job satisfaction may be enhanced by associating the team more closely with the complete operation. The potential disadvantage is that the group can decide what earnings are to be achieved and can restrict output. Thus, the scheme may fail to provide an incentive to agents.

This incentive scheme is suited for the situation in which individual output is dependent on or aggregated into total output, as previously described. Group incentive schemes are appropriate where people have to work together, and teamwork has to be encouraged. They are most effective if based on a measured work system in which the targets and standards are agreed upon by the team, which is provided with the information it needs to monitor its own performance. Group incentive schemes can be considered either an outcome-based payment if the incentive pay is based on the output standard or an effort-based payment if the incentive pay is based on the time saved from the time standard.

Gainsharing

Gainsharing is a formula-based organization-wide bonus plan that allows employees to share in financial gains resulting from increases in the organization's measured productivity. Gainsharing may be either an effort-based payment if the share of the gain is based on the improvement in productivity indicators or an outcome-based payment if the share of the gain is based on the monetary value added to the organization.

Profit Sharing

Profit sharing is a payment mechanism in which an organization's employees are eligible to share in its profits within predetermined criteria. Profit sharing, unlike gainsharing, is based on more than improved productivity. Factors outside the individual employee's control may affect profits. Gainsharing payouts are related more closely to productivity and performance improvements within employees' control. The disadvantage of profit sharing is its weak incentives, because the link between individual effort and reward is so remote for most employees. The advantages are that it is easy to operate and that it can be a useful tool to increase the employees' identification with the organization by sharing the organization's success and failure. This scheme can be thought of as an outcome-based payment in which the agents and the principal share risk, as indicated in figure 6.1.

Profit-Related Pay

Profit-related pay is a government-sponsored and regulated scheme in the United Kingdom for linking pay to profits in accordance with a predetermined formula. The scheme offers significant tax advantages over traditional profit sharing schemes but is governed by exacting statutory criteria. Profit-related pay is an outcome-based payment system in which agents and principal share the risk.

Skill-Based Pay

Skill-based pay is linked to the number, kind, and depth of skill developed and used by the individual. It involves paying for the horizontal development of skills required at one level of work or the vertical development of skills required at a higher level of work. Individuals are paid according to the number and level of skills achieved rather than how well they use their skill at work. This payment method motivates the agents to acquire more and better skills that may improve their performance and result in productivity improvement. Its disadvantage is that it is not performance related, and the skill improvement may not necessarily improve performance. Because skill is a rough estimation of intensity of effort, skill-based pay can be classified as an effort-based payment mechanism.

Competence-Based Pay

Competence-based pay relates pay progression to the achievement of a defined level of competence measured on several dimensions. Competence-based pay is usually operated through a pay-curve system in which pay increases as competence increases. Competence is an estimation of effort given an assigned job and working time. Thus, competence-based payment can be considered an effort-based payment mechanism.

Performance-Related Pay

Performance-related pay bases additional financial rewards on performance ratings and individual contribution. The ratings are derived from performance reviews, assessments of overall contribution, achievement of objectives, and individual competence. Performance-related pay is primarily applied to individuals, but increasing attention is being paid to developing good teamwork through some form of group bonus scheme.

The rewards may take the following three forms:

- Pay increases that move individuals through a pay range by job grade at rates that vary with performance

- Lump-sum achievement bonuses paid when an individual performs particularly well and beyond the normal line of duty in delivering the results or completing a project

- Bonuses paid to individuals at the top of their pay range but still performing outstandingly well. This avoids the demotivating impact of reaching the end of the road as far as financial rewards are concerned.

The advantages of performance-related pay are that rewarding people according to their contribution is thought to be equitable, that it provides a tangible means of recognizing achievement, and that it gives people a strong incentive to understand the principal's imperatives and perform well. Its major disadvantages are that it is difficult to measure the performance objectively, that it may lead to short-term behavior detrimental to the principal's long-term objectives, and that it is administratively costly.

The major principles for measuring performance are: the measures should relate to results, not effort; the results must be within the job holder's control; measures should be objective and observable; data must be available for measuring performance; and the existing measures should be used or adapted wherever possible. In general, performance-related pay is outcome-based, with rank order minor, although some effort-based indicator, such as individual competence may be used in assessing performance.

Executive Bonus

Bonus or incentive schemes for directors and senior executives provide additional, often substantial, sums on top of base salary. These payments generally reward the attainment of growth and profitability targets. Executive bonus often incorporates an element of risk money in the remuneration package, which specifies penalties and rewards and their conditions. The executive bonus allows for large awards that are not necessarily justified by the executive's individual contribution. This bonus is used to attract key management people and to emphasize the importance of management. The bonus system can be regarded as an outcome-based payment, because the bonus is linked to the general performance of the organization in which the executive takes a leadership role.

Summary

The payment alternatives are summarized from the labor economics and reward management literature. In practice, some of these mechanisms are usually used in combination with others according to the conditions of agents and principals, output characteristics, and the objectives of the contract between principals and agents. Except for salary, other alternatives belong to incentive payments, which provide the agents with a financial incentive to behave in the interest of the principals. Each alternative can be related to either an effort-based payment or an outcome-based payment, as described in the conceptual framework shown in figure 6.1. The introduction to the available payment systems in the economy would provide a basis for considering the alternatives of the medical payment systems, described in chapter 11, and relating them to the payment alternatives introduced in this chapter.

AGENCY IN HEALTH CARE

The economic theory of agency, developed in the early 1970s, has been applied to the health care sector since the mid-1980s (McGuire, Henderson, and Mooney 1988; Clark and Olsen 1994; Ryan 1992a; McLean 1989; Dranove and White 1985; Propper 1995; Levaggi 1996; Scott and Shiell 1997b; Mooney and Ryan 1993; Wolff 1989; Pontes 1995; Zweifel 1994). The theory is used mainly for designing incentive-compatible contracts between health care providers and third-party payers of health insurance schemes, namely, payers' systems for paying health care providers. Although efforts have been made, the ideal solution based on this theory is not in sight. This section first identifies the agency relationships in the health care sector. Second, the concepts of perfect agency and the reasonable payment system are introduced. Third, the distinguishing features of health care that create challenges to the application of the agency theory to health care payment systems are described. Last, the application and future research are discussed.

Figure 6.2 shows the principal–agent relationship in the health sector. This relationship exists between government and health funds; private owners and health funds (the private insurance company); private owners and private hospitals; government and public hospitals; health funds and hospitals; health funds and general practitioners; hospitals and hospital-based doctors; patients and health funds; patients and hospitals; patients and general practitioners; and patients and hospital-based doctors. Several of these pairs related to the payment system are discussed.

The typical principal–agent relationship is between a private doctor and a patient who pays out of pocket. This relationship is common in developing countries where health insurance schemes are underdeveloped. When the patient perceives the need for health care, he may visit a medical doctor. The patient asks the doctor to make medical decisions on his behalf because the patient lacks professional information to do so, the cost of searching for the needed information is prohibitively high, or the patient cannot make decisions due to mental impairment (McGuire, Henderson, and Mooney 1988). In turn, the patient pays the doctor for his decisions. To motivate the doctor to behave in the interests of the patient, the remuneration contract must be incentive compatible. Because

Figure 6.2   The Principal–Agent Relationship in the Health Care Sector

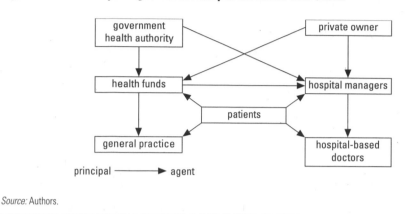

Source: Authors.

most research attention is paid to the payment system between third-party payers and health care providers, few studies deal with the ideal remuneration contract between private patients and private doctors.

The second principal–agent relationship is between health funds (health insurance schemes) and general practitioners. Health funds have to design the reimbursement system carefully to induce general practitioners to behave in the interests of the health funds. Literature on the application of agency theory to health care focuses mainly on the design of a remuneration system through which general practitioners are reimbursed by third-party payers (Pontes 1995).

The third is the principal–agent relationship between health funds and hospitals, in which hospitals provide medical services to patients covered by health funds, and health funds pay the hospitals for services rendered. Although the hospital payment is as important as the doctors' payment, the authors found few papers on the application of agency theory to hospital payment. One reason may be that hospitals' objective function and behavior models are less clear than those of doctors.

The fourth principal–agent relationship is between hospital managers and hospital-based medical doctors. This employee-employer relationship is identified as a typical principal–agent relationship (Stigliz 1989). The hospital manager hires and pays doctors to work in a way that is consistent with the hospital's objectives. The amounts and ways in which hospital-based doctors are paid will have impacts on hospital performance and patient welfare. Although performance-related pay as a mechanism for hospital managers to remunerate hospital staff is gaining attention (Boyce and Morris 1992; Kline 1993), agency theory has not yet received much attention.

The fifth principal–agent relationship is between hospital owner (government or private owner) and hospital managers (Levaggi 1996). The hospital owner delegates management authority to the hospital managers and may provide incentives for managers or executives to work in the interests of the owner. In an era of separating management from ownership and contracting out for management, agency theory may provide a theoretical basis for studies and practices. The authors found little literature on its application in this area.

The sixth principal–agent relationship, the most interesting one, is between patients and hospital-based doctors. In their relationship, the patients delegate medical decisions to medical doctors, but the hospitals pay the doctors with money received either directly from patients (if patients are uninsured) or from health funds (if patients are insured). This principal–agent relationship follows a unique pattern in which the ideal remuneration should satisfy all parties (patients, doctors, hospitals, and third-party payers) in the relation network. This issue has never been explored in the literature.

The seventh principal–agent relationship is between health fund owner (government or private owner) and health funds (Levaggi 1996). The government allocates funds and delegates to the health funds discretion in their use. The private owner provides investment to set up the private health funds and delegates management authority to fund managers. Although the relationship between health funds owners and health funds seems less relevant to the health care payment system, the volume of funds raised and their allocation pattern will influence other pairs of relationships.

The eighth principal–agent relationship is between patients and health funds. Patients pay premiums to the health funds and delegate to them the tasks of risk pooling and risk coverage and contracting with health care providers. Unlike traditional agency theory, however, this relationship is a one-agent and multi-principal relationship that is not mentioned in the literature.

The ninth principal–agent relationship is between patients and hospitals in which patients pay the hospital for the hospital's medical decisions on their behalf and the services rendered.

In summary, as depicted in figure 6.2, different parties in the health sector constitute several agency relationships that can be constructed as a *relation network*. The change in one pair of relationships will affect others. This may be a unique characteristic of health care that makes the development of the incentive-compatible remuneration system difficult.

Perfect Agency Relationship and Reasonable Payment System

In the *perfect agency relationship,* the agent behaves completely in the interests of the principal and tries to maximize the utility of the principal. In health care, the perfect agency relationship can be achieved as long as the doctor behaves like an altruist under the tutelage of Hippocrates, the "father" of Western medicine. In addition, the doctor should behave so as to maximize the utility of patients rather than only information or patient health (Evans 1984). A near-utopia can be imagined in which the medical doctor is an economically rational individual, acting as a perfect agent. Because even the doctor tends to work in the interests of the patients, the perfect agency relationship will be limited by the lack of knowledge about the patient's utility function. As Williams (1988) states, the perfect agency relationship appears only when the doctor gives the patient all the information he/she needs, and the patient then makes the decision. Thus, the assumption here is that the patient's utility is maximized by the provision of information.

Because the perfect agency relationship is impossible, the perfect payment system, which ensures the perfect agency relationship through financial incentives, is even more impossible. As Scott (1996) indicates, the prerequisites of the perfect fee schedule for health care should be that the physician or third-party payer knows the content of the patient's utility function; the content of the patient's utility function is measurable; the remuneration contract specifies every possible contingency or outcome; and the patient's welfare is influenced only by the physician's actions and not by the quality of housing and other environmental factors at the health care institution. As can be seen, such prerequisites are impossible to meet. The perfect payment system will therefore never be possible.

Because the perfect payment system is impossible, the principals or the third-party payers have to do their best to design the best payment system to motivate health care providers. A payment system representing the best design effort and delivering the best possible outcome most efficiently can be called a *reasonable payment system*. A reasonable payment system should allow providers to earn a reasonable income to ensure a steady supply of quality personnel; motivate them to provide a sufficient volume of necessary, good-quality services; and prevent waste and unnecessary provision (Normand and Weber 1994).

Distinguishing Features of Health Care

Besides the networked agency relationship in the health care sector, the distinguishing characteristics of health care challenge the application of agency theory in health care.

Information Asymmetry

The patient-principal's lack of knowledge to make medical decisions is the most important characteristic of health care (Ryan 1992a). The patient does not know what action should be taken (hidden information), but the patient can usually observe the actions of the doctor-agent (in most cases there are no hidden actions). Yet, although the patient can observe the doctor's actions, lack of knowledge prevents the patient from judging whether they are appropriate. The key problem here is how can patients monitor the agent's behavior? One alternative is for the patient to search for the information needed for monitoring; another alternative is to contract with another doctor to monitor the behavior of the first (Fama 1980). Unfortunately, both alternatives are costly, and the patient is not inclined to do either. Thus, information asymmetry and the difficulty of correcting this asymmetry hinder the use of the effort-based remuneration system. Monitoring by the agent has been used by third parties, however, as a way of controlling costly behavior by health care providers, for example, through peer review and second-opinion programs in the United States (Leape 1989). The information collected can be combined in the remuneration contract, but the major objective of this activity is to control medical costs rather than to apply this information to the fee schedule.

Outcome Uncertainty

The outcome of medical care is improvement in health, not the financial outcome assumed by standard agency theory. But the nonfinancial outcome does not necessarily prohibit the use of an outcome-based payment system. The real problem is that health status (the outcome) is not a perfect function of health care (the doctor's effort) because of the uncertainty surrounding health outcomes. Besides health care, many other factors can affect patients' health (McGuire, Henderson, and Mooney 1988). These factors include the consumption of other commodities (such as food), environmental goods (good housing conditions in a hospital) that may accompany health care services, and the patients' own character. In addition, the effect of health care on health improvement is difficult to measure. As Weisbrod (1978) points out, the human body is endowed with its own ability to recover. An improvement in health after using a service may be unrelated to the service. If the patient's condition worsens after receiving health care, that does not add up to no effect or a negative effect, because the patient might become sicker without the care. That is why the effect of health care on health status is difficult to measure and payment cannot be perfectly based on the outcome of doctors' efforts.

Some doctors may charge patients according to their improvement in health. As the ancient Chinese traditional doctors stated, "No cure, no charge." This is a special case in which payment is based on health outcome, and the doctor is willing to assume the risk of outcome uncertainty. In most situations, particularly in modern medicine, health care providers are risk averse, and they want patients or third-party payers to take the risk. This means that payment is based on the volume of services, regardless of the health outcome (Scott 1996).

Dependent Utility Functions

Standard agency theory assumes that the utility functions of principal and agent are independent and somewhat conflictual, but in health care the utility functions exist in some degree of dependence. Some arguments are included in both the patient's and doctor's utility functions (Ryan 1992a; Mooney and Ryan 1993). For example, in traditional theory the agent's efforts provide utility to the principal, but disutility to the agents. In health care, however, the efforts might be positively related to the doctor's utility (Woodward and Warren-Boulton 1984) or the effort might be positively related to the doctor's utility, but the marginal utility of effort diminishes and eventually becomes negative. The characteristic of the dependent utility function, however, might not necessarily be bad in terms of the payment system design: if, at the extreme, the patient's utility function coincides with the doctor's utility function, the perfect agency relationship will automatically come into existence. Details on the utility functions are discussed in chapter 7.

Health Care Provider as Double Agent

As shown in the lower part of figure 6.2, the health care provider serves as agent for both patients and another party. If an insured patient visits an independent general practitioner, the doctor will be the agent of both patient and health fund. If a patient visits a hospital-based doctor, the doctor will be the agent of both patient and hospital. If an insured patient is hospitalized, the hospital will be the agent for both patient and health fund. The double-agent nature of health care, which may have not been reported in the literature, may have significant implications for payment system design. Under the situation of the double agent, the patient as principal delegates medical decision making to the provider, but money is paid to a third party for whom the provider is an agent. The agent receives payment from the third party. In this case, an incentive-compatible remuneration contract should be designed by taking into consideration the utility functions of the three interrelated parties. If the providers are under-paid, they may either exploit the patient by exerting less effort or develop "black market contracts" by which the provider receives supplementary money such as patient's gifts and under-the-table money from pharmaceutical industries.

The Dual Roles of the Provider

The medical doctor in countries such as China and Japan not only serves as the patient's agent in prescribing medical products but also serves as the seller of the products, pharmaceuticals, and medical materials. The utility gains of the doctor come from two sources, service fees and profits from product sales. The payment is agreed based on the medical service (decision making), but the doctor can gain extra income from selling products under his control. This dual role of the provider makes it difficult to design the ideal payment system, which should take both sources of income into consideration.

Other Features

Other features of health care that originated in the standard principal–agent relationship are that medical care prices are not usually set by the patient-principal but by the agent or the third-party payer; that the patient-principal and the doctor-agent may not enter into the contract voluntarily if the patient is assigned to a specific provider by the third party; and that the doctor's behavior is influenced not only by the remuneration contract but also by nonfinancial constraints such as regulations and ethical codes (Ryan 1992a; Mooney and Ryan 1993). These features may make the remuneration contract somewhat different from that under the standard agency theory.

Application and Future Research

Agency theory provides a theoretical base and general framework for considering issues of paying health care providers. First, the overarching objective of this theory is to try to maximize the utility of the principal that is in line with the objective of health care, namely, to satisfy health care consumers and protect or promote the health of the population. Second, it recognizes that the utility functions of the principal and agent are divergent and may sometimes conflict. The principal has to work out a compatible remuneration contract and force the agent to serve the principal's utility function so that the agent will behave in the interests of the principal. This is somewhat the case in health care: the health care provider is designated an income maximizer, and the patient's main concern is health status improvement. Without a compatible payment system, the health care provider's behavior to earn extra income may diverge from the patient's utility. Third, the theory stresses that an effective remuneration contract should be either effort based, if the effort can be observed or estimated, or outcome based, if the outcome is observable. This point provides guidance for designing an effective payment system for health care providers. Fourth, the theory provides a framework for designing a remuneration system in a situation in which information asymmetry, outcome uncertainty, and dependent output are present. Because these situations exist only in health care, the remuneration framework should be appropriate to health care. Fifth, monitoring effort, outcome, or both are regarded as indispensable parts of the remuneration contract. This suggests that during the implementation of the designed health care payment system, the provider should be monitored, and the monitoring information should be incorporated in the payment to the provider. In addition, because of the trade-off between the benefit and cost of monitoring, the economic efficiency of alternative payment methods should be considered when selecting the payment method.

Several recent papers discuss the application of agency theory in health care. Pontes (1995) argues that a salary contract for physician services is superior to fee for service and capitation, because it incurs less agency cost for monitoring. It also avoids the financial incentive of restricting necessary care in capitation and providing unnecessary care in fee for service. It is suggested that "large third-party payers might be better off if they directly hire physicians and pay them salary." He also suggests that the absence of direct incentive to lower costs can be overcome by profit sharing and physician ownership of the third party and that service quality can be ensured by incorporating patient satisfaction in the physician's salary payment and involving the physician in administration.

Zweifel (1994) conducts an economic analysis of the agency relationship in psychotherapy to explore the scope and limitations of the agency relationship in that treatment. He points out that, while the agency relationship cannot be counted upon to provide a panacea for the remuneration of somatic medical care, which is characterized by outcome uncertainty and negative externality of illness, the agency relationship encounters even greater challenges in mental and psychic health care in which the patient is likely to express inconsistent preferences. He concludes that, in the case of psychic care, general practitioners can be relatively good agents of the patient, provided that the patient carries a sufficiently high "price tag," which shows he is able and willing to pay for the care (say, covered by insurance). Zweifel (1994: 621) states that "the economic analysis of the agency relationship in psychotherapy and psychiatry suggests a different policy for the future, pointing to an increased price tag carried by the individual patient. In this way, the agent's incentive to perform in the best interests of his or her patient could be strengthened. This suggestion, of course, runs against the attempts to curtail overdoctoring in somatic medicine by replacing fee-for-service remuneration by capitation payment."

Clark and Olsen (1994) discuss how a doctor as a perfect agent will behave with an endogenous budget constraint. They show that to be a perfect agent when the budget is endogenous, the doctor must take into account not only patient preferences but also the wider preferences of the society. Thus, the doctor will generally not provide the patient-preferred combination of effective health care and non-health-enhancing services. This argument may have implications for the design of remuneration systems in health care. The ideal payment systems may vary in the eyes of different system designers (patients, third-party payers, and governments) because the preference of different parties and the concept of perfect agent may be different.

Levaggi (1996) applies agency theory to the theoretical evaluation of the health care reform of provider–purchaser separation. She highlights some difficulties caused by the creation of the internal market for health care. She states that uncertainty and information asymmetry create important failures and do not allow first-best allocation of resources; that in the light of information asymmetry, a block contract may be attractive to the purchaser, but it is advantageous for the purchaser only if the provider wants to share the risk; and that, in the long run, the use of this contract could have perverse effects, because of outcome uncertainty; and that competition among providers could reduce their opportunities for cheating.

Propper (1995) identifies the agency relationship and analyzes the incentives in the internal market reform of British health care. He argues that the presence of the internal market creates two sets of principal–agent relationships, government–purchasers and government–hospital managers; that government should force purchasers to compete by introducing a bidding system that allows the successful purchaser to expand and forces unsuccessful purchasers to shrink or exit the market; that hospital management trusts should be made more competitive and responsible for their performance by defining clearly hospital property rights; and that the performance of the purchaser and provider should be monitored and the information generated should be related to rewards and penalties.

Judging from several of the most recent publications on the potential use of agency theory, it is not yet being applied to optimal fee schedules or payment systems. Mooney and Ryan (1993: 125) conclude that "although research in the past twenty years resulted in an increasingly sophisticated literature on the theory of agency, the application of this literature to the doctor-patient relationship remains somewhat limited," and that "more thought needs to go into methods of remuneration of doctors. The theory of agency suggests that complicated fee schedules will prevail in the markets characterized by asymmetry of information. Health economists can be criticized here for a lack of detailed consideration of optimal remuneration systems. Indeed, it is still possible to find health economists arguing against the fee-for-service medicine as a system rather than considering the details of the fee schedule."

The application of agency theory is just beginning and far from a sound and final conclusion. Several topics need scrutiny. The first topic is the utility functions of patient and doctor and interactions between them (Mooney and Ryan 1993). To design a remuneration system that maximizes the patient's utility function, the nature of that function, which extends beyond just health status, should be made clear. Studying the doctor's utility function is equally important. Only establishing the nature of the doctor's utility function will show how to make the remuneration contract most attractive within the constraint of the patient's utility function and in what direction to move regarding optimal remuneration methods. In addition, the interactions between the two utility functions need to be tapped, because the dependent character of the two functions will result in a different remuneration system from the one that would result from consideration of either of them separately.

The second topic concerns the double-agent nature of health care. As indicated previously, the doctor can serve as agent for both the patient and the third party (if the patient is insured) or for the hospital (if the doctor is hospital based). The ideal payment system under the trilateral agency relationship should be different from the standard bilateral agency relationship. Study should be directed to how to define the optimal payment system in the case of dual agency and how the objective functions of the three interrelated parties interact.

The third topic concerns the dual role of the providers, which presents difficulties in controlling provider behavior. The two research-related questions are: Does the dual role make a difference in the provider's behavior and what is the optimal remuneration contract in this situation?

The fourth topic concerns variations stemming from the design of remuneration contracts by different parties to the contract and their impact on the remuneration system. In standard theory, the remuneration contract is designed by the principal, whereas, in health care the payment schedule is usually set by the agent, the third-party payer, and the government. Hypothetically, the designer of the remuneration system may first consider its owner's interests, and different payment designers may come up with different payment systems. This hypothesis needs to be tested, and, in addition, the ideal payment system needs to be defined in terms of differences in points of view.

The fifth topic concerns the effectiveness of nonfinancial incentives and constraints and the ways in which nonfinancial incentives are incorporated into financial incentives. This is important not only to the design of remuneration contracts with nonfinancial incentives and constraints, but also to the education of medical professionals and the regulation of health care providers.

The sixth topic suggested concerns the best estimation of efforts and outcomes. Because of information asymmetry and outcome uncertainty in health care, payment cannot be based directly on effort and outcome. Because the optimal method of remuneration should be, at least in part, a function of effort or outcome (Ryan 1992a; Pontes 1995), payment for medical care should also be based in part on estimated effort and outcome. Methods for estimating effort and outcome should be investigated.

The research areas suggested above are not exhaustive but could be priorities in the quest for reasonable remuneration systems in health care. The application of agency theory requires focusing study of the remuneration system not only on the evaluation of current payment systems, but also on the development of new systems.

NOTE

This chapter is based on a review of the literature by the authors when Xingzhu Liu was pursuing his PhD under the supervision of Professor Anne Mills at the London School of Hygiene and Tropical Medicine. The initial work was funded by the United Nations Development Programme/World Bank/World Health Organization Special Programme for Research and Training in Tropical Diseases and the Overseas Research Students Awards Scheme in the United Kingdom. The authors are also grateful for the follow-up support provided by the World Bank and Abt Associates Inc., Bethesda, Maryland.

REFERENCES

Akerloff, G. 1970. "The Market for Lemons: Quality and the Market Mechanism." *Quarterly Journal of Economics* 84: 488–500.

Alchian, A., and H. Demetzs. 1972. "Production, Information Costs and Economic Organizations." *American Economic Review* 62: 777–95.

Armstrong, M. 1995. *A Handbook of Personnel Management Practice.* London: Kogan Page.

Arrow, K.J. 1986. "Agency and the Market." In *Handbook of Mathematical Economics*, ed. K.J. Arrow and M.D. Intriligator, vol. 3. Amsterdam: North-Holland.

Barney, J.B., and W. Hesterly. 1996. "Organizational Economics: Understanding the Relationship Between Organizations and Economic Analysis." In *Handbook of Organization Studies,* ed. S. Cleff. London: Sage.

Bergen, M., S. Dutta, and O.C. Walker. 1992. "Agency Relationship in Marketing: A Review of the Implications and Applications of Agency and Related Theories." *Journal of Marketing* 56(3): 1–24.

Boyce, J., and T. Morris. 1992. "Performance-Related Pay for Hospital Doctors." *British Medical Journal* 305(6846): 131–32.

Clark, D., and A. Olsen. 1994. "Agency in Health Care with an Endogenous Budget Constraint." *Journal of Health Economics* 13: 231–51.

Dranove, D., and W.D. White. 1985. "Agency Theory: New Insight into the Health Care Industry." *Journal of Medical Practice Management* 4(3): 165–9.

Ehrenberg, R.G., and R.S. Smith. 1991. *Modern Labor Economics: Theory and Public Application.* New York, NY: Harper Collins.

Eisenhardt, K.M. 1989. "Agency Theory: An Assessment and Review." *Academy Management Review* 14(2): 57–74.

———. 1988. "Agency- and Institutional-Theory Explanations: The Case of Retail Sales Compensation." *Academy of Management Journal* 31(3): 488–511.

———. 1985. "Control: Organization and Economic Approaches." *Management Science* 31: 134–49.

Evans, R.G. 1984. *Strained Mercy: The Economics of Canadian Health Care.* Toronto: Butterworths.

Fama, E.F. 1980. "Agency Problems and the Theory of the Firm." *Journal of Political Economy* 88(2): 288–307.

Holmstrom, B. 1982. "Moral Hazard in Teams." *Bell Journal of Economics* 13(2): 324–40.

———. 1979. "Moral Hazard and Observability." *Bell Journal of Economics* 10(1): 74–91.

Kline, R. 1993. "Measuring Sown: PRP Pitfalls." *Health Visit* 66(6): 222.

Lazear, E.P. 1986. "Salaries and Piece Rates." *Journal of Business* 59: 405–31.

Leape, L. 1989. "Unnecessary Surgery." *Health Service Research* 24(3): 351–407.

Levaggi, R. 1996. "NHS Contracts: An Agency Approach." *Health Economics* 5: 341–52.

MacDonald, G.M. 1984. "New Directions in the Economic Theory of Agency." *Canadian Journal of Economics* 17(3): 415–40.

Mangum, G. 1964. *Wage Incentive Systems.* Berkeley: University of California, Institute of Industrial Relations.

Marriott, R. 1968. *Incentive Payment Systems: A Review of Research and Opinion.* London: Staples Press.

McGuire, A., J. Henderson, and G. Mooney. 1988. *The Economics of Health Care: An Introductory Text.* London and New York, NY: Routledge Kegan Paul.

McLean, R.A. 1989. "Agency Costs Complex Contracts in Health Care Organisations." *Health Care Management Review* 14(1): 65–71.

Mirrlees, J. 1974. "Notes on Welfare Economics, Information, and Uncertainty." In *Contribution to Economic Analysis,* ed., M.S. Balch et al. Amsterdam: North–Holland.

Mooney, G., and M. Ryan. 1993. "Agency in Health Care: Getting Beyond First Principals." *Journal of Health Economics* (12): 125–35.

Murphy, K.J. 1986. "Incentives, Learning, and Compensation: A Theoretical and Empirical Investigation of Managerial Labor Contracts." *Rand Journal of Economics* 17: 59–76.

Normand, C., and A. Weber. 1994. *Social Health Insurance: A Guidebook for Planning.* Geneva: World Health Organization.

Pontes, M.C. 1995. "Agency Theory: A Framework for Analyzing Physician Services." *Health Care Management Review* 20(4): 57–67.

Propper, C. 1995. "Agency and Incentive in the NHS Internal Market." *Social Science and Medicine* 40(12): 1683–90.

Ross, S. 1973. "The Economic Theory of Agency: The Principal's Problem." *American Economic Review* 63(2): 134–39.

Rubenstein, A., and M. Yaari. 1983. "Repeated Insurance Contracts and Moral Hazard." *Journal of Economic Theory* 30: 74–97.

Ryan, M. 1992a. "The Economic Theory of Agency in Health Care: Lessons from Non-economists for Economists." Discussion Paper No 03/92. Aberdeen, UK: University of Aberdeen, Health Economic Research Unit.

———. 1992b. "The Agency Relationship in Health Care: Identifying Areas for Future Research." Discussion Paper No 02/92. Aberdeen, UK: University of Aberdeen, Health Economic Research Unit.

Scott, A. 1996. "Agency, Incentive and the Behavior of General Practioners: The Relevance of Principal-Agent Theory in Designing Incentives for GPs in the UK." Discussion Paper No. 3. Aberdeen, UK: University of Aberdeen, Health Economic Research Unit.

Scott, A., and A. Shiell. 1997a. "Do Fee Descriptors Influence Choices in General Practice? A Multilevel Discrete Choice Model." *Journal of Health Economics* 16(3): 323–42.

———. 1997b. "Analysing the Effect of Competition on General Practitioners' Behavior Using a Multilevel Modelling Framework." *Journal of Health Economics* 6(6):577–88.

Shavell S. 1979. "Risk Sharing and Incentives in the Principal and Agent Relationship." *Bell Journal of Economics* 10: 5–73.

Stiglitz, J.E. 1989. "Principal and Agent." In *Allocation, Information and Markets,* ed. J. Eatwell. London: Macmillan.

———. 1974. "Incentives and Risk Sharing in Sharecropping." *Review of Economic Studies* 41 (2): 219–55.

Weisbrod, B.A. 1978. "Comment on M. V. Pauly." In *Competition in the Health Care Sector,* ed. W. Greenberg. Proceedings of a conference sponsored by the Bureau of Economics, U.S. Federal Trade Commission. Germantown, MD: Aspen Systems.

Williams, A. 1988. "Priority Setting in Public and Private Health Care: A Guide Through the Methodological Jungle." *Journal of Health Economics* 7: 173–83.

Wolff, N. 1989. "Professional Uncertainty and Physician Medical Decision-Making in a Multiple Treatment Framework." *Social Science and Medicine* 28(2): 99–107.

Woodward, R.S., and F. Warren-Boulton. 1984. "Considering the Effects of Financial Incentives and Professional Ethics on 'Appropriate' Medical Care." *Journal of Health Economics* 3(3): 223–37.

Zenger, T.R. 1992. "Why Do Employers Only Reward Extreme Performance? Examining the Relationships Among Performance, Pay, and Turnover." *Administrative Science Quarterly* 37: 198–219.

Zweifel, P. 1994. "Agency Relationship in Psychotherapy: An Economic Analysis." *Social Science and Medicine* 39(5): 621–28.

CHAPTER 7

Doctors' and Patients' Utility Functions

Xingzhu Liu and Anne Mills

The dependent utility function of patients and doctors is a departure from the assumption of standard agency theory and makes remuneration contracts for doctors different from those under the independent utility function. In this chapter, the authors scrutinize doctors' and patients' utility functions and their implications for the design of doctor remuneration systems. The authors develop an economic framework of interactions between patients who pay out-of-pocket for services and doctors with independent practices and review the literature on both patients' and doctors' utility functions. The degree of dependence between doctors' and patients' utility functions and the implications for remuneration system design for doctors are discussed. Some common arguments are identified in both doctors' and patients' utility functions. The authors conclude that manipulating the common arguments through the design of the financial incentive systems seems to be unnecessary and that instead payment system designers should pay attention to the independent arguments. The authors suggest that future research should be directed to empirical study to test the model provided here and to theoretical study of the nature of the utility functions of other types of patients (e.g., patients with insurance coverage) and doctors (e.g., hospital-based doctors).

INTRODUCTION

Standard agency theory assumes that the utility functions of the principal and the agent are independent and somewhat conflictual, while in health care, the utility functions exist in some degree of dependence. In traditional theory, the agent's efforts provide utility to the principal, but disutility to the agents. In health care, however, efforts might be positively related to the doctor's utility.

The dependence of the patient's and doctor's functions is a departure from the assumption of standard agency theory. If it holds true, remuneration contracts for doctors will be different from those under an independent utility function. Thus, scrutinizing the doctor's and patient's utility functions is of significance for the design of doctors' remuneration systems. Mooney and Ryan (1993) identify three research questions regarding utility functions in health care: What is the nature of the patient's utility function; what is the nature of the doctor's utility function; and what are the interactions between the doctor's and patient's utility functions? The present literature review follows the general guidelines framed by these three questions.

In this chapter, first an economic framework is developed for interactions between patients and doctors. The second section is a review of the literature on the nature of the patient's utility function. In the third section, the utility function of the doctor is discussed. The last section provides a discussion of the degree of dependence between the doctor's and patient's utility functions and the implications for the design of the remuneration system for doctors.

A FRAMEWORK OF INTERACTIONS BETWEEN PATIENTS AND DOCTORS

The interaction between patients and doctors is an extremely complicated procedure. Doctors in different settings (e.g., hospital-based, employed by health funds, and independent practice) and different competitive pressures may interact differently with patients. Patients subject to different conditions (e.g., covered by insurance, with free choice of doctors) may vary in their service-seeking behavior. Thus, the nature of the doctor's and patient's functions may vary with these situations. To simplify and narrow the analysis, a model is developed for independent medical doctors with the following assumptions: the patient has free choice of doctors; the patient is not covered by any insurance scheme and pays out of pocket for services and drugs; the doctor engages in independent, individual private practice; and the medical market is competitive, meaning that the patient can choose from a large pool of medical doctors.

Based on these assumptions, figure 7.1, describing the process of a patient's visit to a doctor, is constructed. When the patient needs health services, he or she will enter the medical market to search for a doctor and to obtain care.

At first contact, both the doctor and the patient will make decisions. The doctor will first decide whether or not he or she can diagnose and treat the presenting condition. If he thinks he cannot do so, he may refer the patient to other doctors. The doctor has to decide what prescriptions (diagnosis versus treatment) are needed if he thinks he is able to accept the patient. If the doctor can make a definite diagnosis, he will prescribe the treatment. If no definite diagnosis is made at the first contact, the doctor has to decide the diagnostic prescription. If dissatisfied for any reason after the first contact, the patient may decide to go to a different doctor.

If the patient decides to comply with the doctor's prescription, he may either have his treatment prescription dispensed or have his diagnostic procedures conducted. In either case, if dissatisfied after the test and drug dispensary, the patient may decide to leave the doctor for another.

Normally, the patient revisits the doctor after the diagnostic tests. If the doctor can make a diagnosis, he decides the treatment prescription. If he cannot make a diagnosis at that time, the doctor decides on a further diagnostic prescription.

Figure 7.1   A Patient's Visit to a Doctor: An Economic Conceptual Model of Interactions between Patients and Medical Doctors

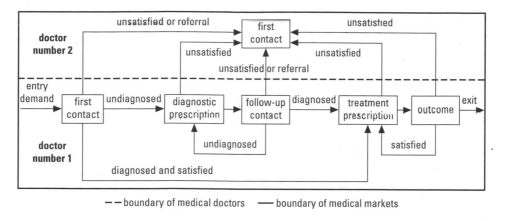

Source: Authors.

The patient may leave the doctor for another either due to the patient's dissatisfaction or the doctor's referral for the undiagnosed condition.

If the patient continues with the doctor, and the doctor makes a diagnosis after further tests, he will prescribe a treatment. At this point, if the patient is satisfied, he may have his prescription filled and take the drug expecting a positive outcome from the treatment. There is also a possibility that the patient may leave the doctor for another immediately after the drugs are dispensed.

While taking the medicine and expecting an outcome, the patient may feel the need, or be advised by the doctor, to return for further treatment or diagnostic prescriptions. The patient may also be dissatisfied with the outcome and decide to leave this doctor for another. If the patient's condition clears up or, for any other reason, the patient has no further medical demand, he will leave the medical market.

This complicated process involves both doctor's and patient's objectives, utility and disutility, and behaviors or actions. It also involves interactions between the doctor's and patient's behaviors, and the relationship between the doctor's and patient's utility functions.

THE PATIENT'S UTILITY FUNCTION

The nature of the patient's utility function can be understood by investigating the patient's objectives for the visit, his expectation in the process of interacting with the doctor, and the arguments that may enter into the patient's utility function.

The Objectives of the Patient's Visit

The utility of the patient's visit to the doctor depends upon the objective of the visit. Clarifying the possible objectives furthers an understanding of the patient's expectations and the content of the utility function. The objectives of patients' visits to doctors vary, and they are identified as follows. Although the objectives listed here may not be exhaustive, the major ones are captured.

The first and most common objective is the diagnosis and treatment of illness. The illness can be divided into two groups: somatic conditions and psychic conditions. For somatic conditions, the patient has a clear-cut objective, namely having the illness accurately diagnosed and appropriately treated. For psychic conditions, the patient usually expresses inconsistent preferences (Zweifel 1994). In this case, the patient's family members and relatives may serve as his or her perfect agent to make a choice, and the objective of the visit is similar to the former.

The second possible objective is to check their health status. A patient may visit the doctor without a perceived condition, and the only objective is to make sure he is in good health and, if not, identify the problem. If a health problem is identified, the patient may visit the doctor for the first objective.

The third possible objective is to confirm a diagnosis (Ryan 1992). In this case, a disease has already been diagnosed in the patient, and this visit is to test the consistency of diagnosis by different doctors to head off incorrect treatment stemming from an inaccurate diagnosis.

The fourth possible objective is to obtain an official certificate of diagnosis for use in a lawsuit, as security payment for an occupational disease, and justification for paid sick leave. In this case, the patient may know the diagnosis, and the purpose of the visit is to have his diagnosis legitimized (Ryan 1992).

The fifth possible objective is to obtain a treatment prescription. In this case, the patient is clear about his own problem, and the purpose of the visit is to get the drug prescription that the patient prefers according to his experience in past visits.

The last possible objective is the "placebo visit," in which the patient and his family members know that the disease is incurable, and the visit is intended for the psychological benefit of the patient, his family members, or both. This often happens in some Asian countries when the patient's child brings a very ill parent to a doctor and spends some money on him or her to show respect for his father or mother.

The Patient's Expectations

The patient's expectations are closely related to the objectives of the visits. The expectation of a visit should vary with different objectives. For the purpose of generalization and to avoid clutter and repetition, instead of discussing the expectations of the patients with different objectives one by one, the patient's expectations are examined by following the process of interaction between doctor and patient.

A good outcome is the ultimate expectation of the whole process, but two points must be made clear. One is that the outcome is not necessarily improvement in health status, because the outcome should be defined according to the patient's objective. For example, the ideal outcomes for the second through the fourth objectives are accurate clinical conclusions; the outcome for the fifth objective is the doctor's treatment prescription required by the patient; and the outcome for the last objective is smooth completion of the whole process. Another point is that, apart from the ideal outcome, the patient's satisfaction is involved at every step of the process; satisfaction will provide utility to the patient, and dissatisfaction will provide disutility.

When the patient enters the medical market, he intends to search for a doctor with reasonable perceived quality, no matter what objective he has for his visit. The contact should be conducted in a friendly way, with the doctor gently questioning the patient and providing information the patient wants. Diagnostic and treatment prescriptions should be made considering the patient's preferences, and the doctor should involve the patient in the decision-making process. The diagnosis-and-rediagnosis cycle, as indicated in figure 7.1, should not be repeated too many times, because it is a signal of delayed diagnosis to the patient. In general, the patient expects not only good outcomes, but also good perceived behavior.

The patient's expectations should also include another important component, the expectation of the least cost for obtaining given amounts of effort by the doctor and a good outcome. *Cost* here is broadly defined. It includes all charges in the medical encounter process, opportunity cost (such as waiting time and the time of delayed diagnosis), and intangible cost (such as pain and suffering due to diagnostic and treatment procedures). It is obvious that the cost will provide disutility to the patient.

The Possible Arguments in the Patient's Utility Function

What should enter into the patient's utility function is controversial. Some people argue that it is only health status (Culyer 1989). Others argue that the arguments should include nonhealth outcomes and that process factors may provide utility to the patient (Ryan 1992; Scott 1996).

Mandy Ryan, in her Ph.D. dissertation (1995) and her discussion paper (1992), thoroughly reviews the points of view of noneconomists and provides excellent information for discussion. She states that

> [a] review of literature shows that economists have ignored such factors as the importance of nonmedical reasons for visiting the doctor, as well as factors important in the process of treatment; the need of patients to have trust in the doctor, and the implications of this for patients wanting both information and involvement in the decision making process. . . . [I]ndeed, economists have emphasized the importance of health in the patient's utility function, to the exclusion of many other potentially important arguments. . . . [O]nly recently have economists begun to question this assumption, and asked what is important to patients in the provision

of health care. A small group of economists are now arguing that when doctors consider the preference of patients, it is not just the health status that is important to patients, but also the process of treatment or process utility. It is argued that factors such as the provision of information and the patient's involvement in the decision process may also be important to some patients.

Ryan (1992) goes on to say that "economists have assumed for many years that the only factor important to patients in the provision of health care is the outcome of that treatment. The implicit assumption here is that health is the only relevant argument in the patient's utility function. A review of the noneconomics literature suggests that this is not the case." The following is a summary of Ryan's literature review of the noneconomic literature.

Cartwright (1967) argues that many patients' visits to doctors are to have their illnesses legitimized and to obtain a doctor's certificate. Thus, the argument in the patient's utility function here may not be health, but income.

Tuchett (1979) states that one reason for the patient to visit a doctor might be to obtain a diagnosis for an illness, hoping to rule out other potentially more dangerous illnesses. In other words, an important argument in the patient's utility function may be the reassurance of a diagnosis.

Turner (1987) notes that within the medical consultation, the process of giving the patient information and legitimizing illness is important, thus suggesting that these are important arguments in the patient's utility function.

Hall and Dornan (1988) identify a number of aspects of care that are important to patients. These include satisfaction with access (convenience, hours, distance, perceived availability, ease of getting appointments); satisfaction with cost; satisfaction with humaneness (warmth, respect, kindness, willingness to listen, appropriate nonverbal behavior, interpersonal skill); satisfaction with competence (technical performance and competence as defined by traditional medical terms); satisfaction with the amount of information supplied by the provider (explanation of treatment, procedures, and diagnosis); satisfaction with bureaucratic arrangements (e.g., waiting times); satisfaction with physical facilities (esthetic and functional aspects, parking, adequacy of equipment, laboratories); satisfaction with the provider's attention to psychosocial problems of the patient; satisfaction with continuity of care; and satisfaction with the outcome of care.

Beecher (1955) argues that as much as one-third of the success of any medical treatment may be due to the fact that patients believe that something is being done for them. As Lupton (1990) stated "the patient may receive considerable relief simply from being in medical surroundings where they feel protected, or from being treated as a sick person needing attention and therefore having their illness legitimized, without having received any medical treatment as such. Even the process of the doctor sharing information with the patient and labeling their symptoms as a disease can be an important therapy." These suggest the placebo effect may be an argument of the patient's utility function.

Haug and Lavin (1981) note that 95 percent of the respondents in their study feel that they have a right to medical information. Waitzkin (1984) argues that with regard to the question of how much information to give patients, patients almost always want as much information as possible. Studies show that the patient desires information on the nature and cause of their illness, its seriousness, treatment plans, results of tests, process and aftereffect of tests, and whether their illness is terminal (Mathews 1983). While patients appear to want information, they place the responsibility for medical decision making on the doctor. As Beisecker and Beisecker (1990) note, this suggests that patients "want to be knowledgeable about their medical care without necessarily becoming responsible for medical care decisions." Ryan (1992) argues that this conclusion is important when looking at the nature of the patient's utility function. It suggests that information and involvement in the decision-making process are not synonymous.

Regarding the patient's utility, Ryan (1992) concludes that "when visiting the doctors, factors other than an improvement in health status are important to patients. In looking at the nature of the patient's utility function, important factors include both those that motivate patients to visit their doctor as well as those that are important in the process of treatment."

To provide a more general conclusion about the patient's utility function, divide the doctor's effort by two dimensions, (1) positive effort versus negative effort and (2) perceived effort versus nonperceived effort. *Positive effort* is defined as the actions of the doctor that can yield utility to the patient through the process of contact or through the outcome the patient expects, or both. *Negative effort* is the actions of the doctor that can yield disutility to the patient through the process of contact, and/or through the outcome the patient expects, and/or unnecessary cost without the detriment of the outcome. *Perceived effort* (positive or negative) refers to actions the patient can observe in the process of contact. *Nonperceived effort* (positive or negative) refers to actions the patient cannot perceive. The perceived positive effort can provide utility to the patient, while the perceived negative effort can provide disutility to the patient. The nonperceived effort (positive or negative) cannot provide utility or disutility to the patient in the contact process. In the outcome, all kinds of efforts will be finally reflected, at least partially.

In summary, the factors that are important to the patient can be divided into three categories. The first category is the outcome of the contact, which may include health status improvement, reassurance of diagnosis (the assurance of existence or absence of disease, and the definite diagnosis of a disease), and the positive externalities that the contact may bring about to the patient's family members. The second category is the patient's perception of the doctor's efforts. It includes all actions that provide satisfaction (utility) or dissatisfaction (disutility) to the patient. The third category is the cost of contact, which includes the direct cost (medical charges, cash payment for travel), the indirect cost (opportunity cost of time), and the intangible cost (inconvenience, suffering during treatment and diagnosis). The authors note that all of the factors in the previous discussion can be put into one of these three categories.

In conclusion, the patient's utility function can be formally described by the following nested function:

$$U_p = f(O(o_1, o_2,..., o_n), E(e_1, e_2,..., e_m), C(c_1, c_2,..., c_k)),$$

in which U_p refers to the utility of the patient; o_1 through o_n are the possible outcomes of the medical contact; e_1 through e_m are the items of the perceived effort of the doctor; c_1 through c_k are the items of the costs of the contact; and O, E, and C are the aggregated outcome, the perceived effort, and the cost of medical contact.

THE DOCTOR'S UTILITY FUNCTION

The nature of the doctor's utility function can be understood through investigation into the doctor's objectives in medical contact with the patient, the expectation of the doctor in the process of interaction with the patient, and the arguments that may enter into the doctor's utility function.

The Objectives of the Doctor

The doctor is an economic individual. The income-seeking motive is one impetus for his or her work. There are two possibilities for increasing the doctor's income from work. One is to increase the money income per unit of time, and the other is to increase the number of hours of work. But the doctor's work is limited by the total number of hours available per day and by the trade-off between work and other activities such as leisure. If the doctor spends more time working for more income, time for other activities must be sacrificed. If the doctor wants to have more leisure or other activities, he will have less time to work for income. Labor economics recognizes that increases in income have both income effect and substitution effect. The *income effect* means that, as the wage increases, income will increase and the marginal utility of income will decrease; and that, when the marginal utility of wage income becomes less than the marginal utility of leisure or other activities, the individual will reduce the number of hours of work. The *substitution effect* means that, as the wage increases, the opportunity cost of leisure or other activities will increase, and the individual will substitute leisure or other activities for work; and that, as the wage decreases, the individual will substitute work for leisure. Thus, the increase in income will lead to an increase in the number of hours of work or a decrease in the number of hours of work, depending on which effect is dominant. The dominance will depend on the valuation of the marginal utility of the money income (wage) and the marginal utility of leisure or other activities. The economic theory of labor implicitly means that income is important, but it is not the only thing that provides utility to the medical doctor. This can also explain why the doctor's work morale will be reduced by a very high workload (Scott 1996).

The doctor is a social individual. Apart from income, achieving and maintaining ideal status may be one of the important objectives of the doctor's medical practice. Here, *status* can be defined as the respect or esteem of medical peers and patients, manifested by recognition, attention, deference, and appreciation (Maslow 1954).

The doctor is an active learner. Because clinical medicine is somewhat a science of experiences, the doctor's medical practice is a constant learning cycle (Kolb, Rubin, and McIntyre 1974). The learning cycle consists of four stages: (1) *concrete experience*, which can be planned or accidental; (2) *reflective observation*, which involves actively thinking about the experience and its significance; (3) *abstract conceptualization*, which entails generalizing from experience in order to develop concepts and ideas that can be applied when similar situations are encountered; and (4) a*ctive experimentation*, which involves testing the concepts or ideas in new situations. This gives rise to a new concrete experience and the cycle begins again. The desire to learn stems from the need for *self-fulfillment*, which is the need to develop potentialities and skills and to become a person perceived to be capable (Maslow 1954). Here, learning theory tells us that gaining new knowledge and skills in the process of medical practice is another important objective of the medical doctor.

The Doctor's Expectations

In light of the above possible objectives of a doctor's medical practice, the more important things are what the doctor is expected to do to achieve these objectives.

One of the most possible ways of expanding income is to increase service volume, which can be done in several ways. First, the doctor is expected to try to please the patient by providing the perceived positive effort, because otherwise the patient may leave the doctor for another due to dissatisfaction according to the assumed model in figure 7.1. Second, the doctor has to do his best to produce a good outcome for the patient to win long-term attractiveness to patients. Third, the doctor may reduce the prices of services to compete with other doctors for patients. Fourth, the patient may be induced to come for follow-up visits (some may be necessary and some may not). Last, the doctor may provide more and costlier diagnostic and treatment prescriptions if his income is linked to these prescriptions through the ownership and other income-sharing mechanisms. The first three possibilities are good for the patient. The first increases process utility, the second increases outcome utility, and the third decreases cost disutility for the patient. The last two behaviors (the nonperceived negative effort) will yield disutility to the patient through a reduction in outcome, increase in costs, or both for the patient. The doctor may want to raise charges for units of services and medical products, but may be constrained by the risk of a reduction in volume. Only if demand for the individual doctor is high enough, can the doctor earn extra income by raising fees (participation constraint) because, even if the total demand for the medical service is inelastic and the increase in price will always generate more profit, demand for an individual doctor will be elastic. This means that the doctor's price increase will result in a significant reduction in service volume in the assumed competitive medical market.

To gain a high status and good reputation, the doctor has to be of good competence, provide as much as possible the perceived positive effort that leads to the patient's process satisfaction, provide as much as possible the technical effort that leads to good outcome, act in accordance with regulations and ethnics, and avoid negative behavior (effort). In addition, the doctor will pay close attention to nonmonetary rewards and penalties and try to gain these rewards and avoid these penalties. In short, for high status, the doctor not only has to be competent, but also to act (or be perceived to act) altruistically in the best interests of the patient.

To gain new knowledge and skill, the doctor may put emphasis on effective care, while neglecting the cost the patient may suffer; emphasize technical effort (usually nonperceived), while neglecting the nontechnical effort (usually perceived); seek accurate diagnosis and right treatment and pursue better outcome, while neglecting the patient's preference in the diagnosis and treatment.

These hypothetical expectations of the doctor are under each of the three dependent objectives. In fact, the three possible objectives are pursued simultaneously by the doctor. In this case, the doctor's possible behaviors may become complicated.

The Possible Arguments in the Doctor's Utility Function

Scott and Shiell (1997) and Ryan (1992) thoroughly review the possible arguments of the doctor's utility function. That income from the doctor's medical practice is an argument of the doctor's utility function seems to be uncontroversial. But contrary to standard agency theory, Scott, Shiell, and Ryan show that other factors are important to the doctor's utility. The two most important such factors are the doctor's effort and the outcome of medical contact.

In standard agency theory, it is assumed that the agent's effort will have disutility to the agent, but, in health care, as Scott argues, this is not the case. He gives an example in which Woodward and Warren-Boulton (1984) assume that the doctor's production of medical care per patient is positively related to the doctor's utility, and Woodward and Warren-Boulton justify this by the statement that "artists, scientists, professional people, and businessmen often regard their work not merely as a mean of earning income but as an important and interesting part of their lives." Scott (1996), however, notes that a heavy workload may cause low morale and recruitment difficulties in the general practice. He concludes that by combining those two assertions, it may be that the effort is positively related to the utility of the doctor, but that the marginal utility from the effort diminishes and eventually becomes negative.

Ryan (1992) argues that, as an element of the doctor's effort, his provision of information is related to both the doctor's and patient's characteristics. She states that the doctor is more likely to provide information for middle-class patients than for their working-class counterparts and that doctors tend to provide more information for people who request more information.

Scott (1996) discusses the possibility that nonmonetary rewards and penalties enter into the doctor's utility function. He argues that "It is not difficult to imagine how a doctor's reputation amongst peers and patients can act as a reward or penalty. The existence of nonmonetary rewards and penalties points to the existence of other arguments in the doctor's utility function, such as the status amongst peers. These arguments will undoubtedly influence the doctor's behavior and, in turn, could themselves be influenced by nonmonetary incentives."

Although the literature can provide an unprecedented understanding of the doctor's utility function, the present authors are not clear about the conditions under which the doctor's utility is assessed. To fit in with the model assumed in figure 7.1 and the previous discussions, the following explanations and summary are provided. First, the doctor's income and the patient's outcome from the medical contact yield two arguments that can enter into the doctor's utility function, because the doctor always expects more income and good outcomes for all of the three objectives mentioned above. Even with a negative effort (behavior), the doctor does not want a bad outcome, which provides the doctor with disutility. Second, the perceived positive effort is positively related to the doctor's utility function, but subject to some constraints such as the time available and the patient's ability to understand the information. The authors would argue that, even though the doctor acts in the best interests of the patients, the degree of information provision, and the degree of patient involvement, may be different because the intensity of these efforts depends on how the doctor perceives the patient's valuation of these efforts. For example, if the patient cannot understand the doctor's explanation, the patient will put less value on the doctor's effort to provide information, thus leading the doctor to shift his effort to the technical part, which may result in more patient satisfaction. Third, the negative effort, which may be positively related to the doctor's utility function, is driven by income motives. In the situation specified in figure 7.1, the doctor is more likely to take advantage of outcome uncertainty to behave in his own interests and at the expense of the patient. But this negative effort is constrained by the possibility of reduced income due to decreased demand for the individual doctor's services.

To sum up, the doctor's utility should be a function of the income from the medical practice; the patient's outcome from the medical contact; and the doctor's positive effort (perceived and nonperceived). The income is a function of medical service prices and service volume due to both positive and negative efforts. The doctor's utility function is expressed in the following equation:

$$U_d = f(Y(P, V_p, V_n), O(o_1, o_2,..., o_n), PE(e_1, e_2,..., e_i)),$$

where U_d refers to the utility of the doctor; P is the prices of medical services and products; V_p is the volume of services and medical products in the interests of patients; V_n is the volume of services and products in the economic interests of the doctor; o_1 through o_n are the possible outcomes of the medical contact; e_1 through e_i are the elements of the doctor's positive effort; O, PE, and Y are the aggregated outcome, aggregated positive effort, and the doctor's income due to the medical contact.

This utility function model is based strictly on the encounter between private patients and private doctors and on its underlying assumptions posited at the beginning of this chapter. Although this model might be suitable in the specified situation, it may not apply to other types of doctors without modification. In addition, the utility function here is hypothetical. It is based on discussions in the literature and on the idea developed by the authors based on medical practice experience. It cannot be used directly in designing remuneration contracts without substantiating empirical proof.

THE INTERACTION BETWEEN THE DOCTOR'S AND PATIENT'S UTILITY FUNCTIONS AND ITS IMPLICATION FOR THE REMUNERATION SYSTEM

To make the patient's utility function and the doctor's utility function meaningful, they have to be compared to see which arguments are common, which arguments are independent between doctor and patient, and what the implications of these characteristics are for designing doctors' remuneration systems.

The Common Arguments

The outcomes of medical encounters are a common argument in the patient's and doctor's utility functions. It is clear that good outcomes will provide utility to patients, no matter what types of outcomes the patients expect. Similarly, good outcomes can also provide utility to doctors, because good outcomes help doctors gain high status among both patients and peers. In addition, doctors expect good outcomes to contribute to their own knowledge and experience, attract return visits and new patients, and increase their service revenue. No doctor would want to sabotage the patient's outcomes, if for no other reason, because a poor outcome would provide disutility instead of utility to the doctor. Malpractice, because of penalties of various kinds, hurts doctors as well as patients. For extra income, some doctors may provide unnecessary services and drugs, which may produce negative effect on the outcome, but they have to swallow their own bitter medicine, in the form of impaired outcomes they themselves have brought about.

The perceived positive effort may be a common argument between patients and doctors. Without a doubt, the perception of the doctor's positive effort will provide process utility as well as outcome utility to the patient. But these positive efforts can only be reflected through the ultimate outcomes. In his own interests, the doctor would try to satisfy patients by providing perceived positive effort, because it would provide him with obvious utility through gains in status, knowledge, and income. A specific positive effort may not, however, meet the wants of the patient, because of constraints on the doctor's effort in terms of time and the trade-off of utility gains between different kinds of positive effort.

The perceived negative effort is almost a common argument. The perceived negative effort will provide disutility to the patient. The doctor would try to avoid it because it will cost him patients and loss of status, although it may generate extra revenue for him. The doctor has to balance the utility gain from the extra income generated by misbehaving against the utility loss due to the loss of patients' trust. The cost of perceived negative effort may outweigh the utility gain for the doctor, thus discouraging misbehavior.

The nonperceived positive effort can generate utility for both patients and doctors, and it is a common argument. The utility gain of the patient does not come through the process of the nonperceived effort, simply because the patient cannot perceive it, but through the improvement in outcome. The positive effort of the doctor, perceived or nonperceived, will generate utility to the doctor.

The nonperceived negative effort can be divided into two groups. One is what can bring about both the cost and the bad outcome for the patient. Another is what can bring about only cost for the patient without doing significant harm (but never good) to the outcome. Logically, the doctor should be reluctant to harm the patient's interests, because the psychological cost is too high for a prestigious medical doctor; in addition, disutility results from the loss of patients in the form of reduced outcome.

The Independent Arguments

The part of the nonperceived negative effort that can lead only to extra financial cost to the patient without significant harm to the outcome may be an independent argument. This kind of effort is driven by two forces. One is the force of the doctor's income motive, and another is the force of learning. The doctor's income motive makes him behave negatively in his own interests (income generation) at the expense of the patient. The constraint on the doctor's misbehavior is limited because this kind of effort is unobservable to the patient and does no harm to the outcome of the medical encounter. The doctor may also be driven by the desire to learn from some experimental diagnoses and treatments at the patient's expense. Because this activity might not lead to a reduction in outcome, the doctor should stand a good chance of benefiting. The possible constraint on this kind of action is the patient's ability to pay.

The second independent argument concerns the doctor's income, usually the cost of his services. The patient always wants to pay less, and the doctor always wants to earn more. This argument is the same as under the assumptions of standard agency theory.

The third independent argument concerns the cost for the patient. Apart from service charges, the patient has other costs such as time and intangible costs. Although these patient costs are not gains for the doctor, they should be recognized as an independent argument of the patient because the doctor may show little concern about these costs.

The Implication for the Doctor's Remuneration

Identifying the arguments in the doctor's and patient's utility functions and differentiating dependent from independent arguments are important to the design of the system for remunerating medical doctors. In the design process, the designer need not to worry about the arguments common to both the doctor's and the patient's utility functions, because maximizing the contribution by the common argument to the doctor's utility will automatically maximize the patient's utility. There is no need to manipulate the common argument in designing the financial incentive system. What the designer should do is pay attention to the independent arguments.

In the case assumed here, if the hypothetical common arguments are true, the designer should not be concerned about the outcome of the medical encounter, the effort that is perceivable by the patient, the perceived positive effort, and the perceived negative effort that may yield a bad outcome. The factors that should be considered are the patient's costs, the doctor's income, and the nonperceived negative effort that is not detrimental to outcome but at the cost of the patient. By analyzing the three factors, things become straightforward. The key concern in the design of the remuneration system is how to remove the doctor's incentive to provide the nonperceived negative efforts that can raise his income through the patient's financial cost. This interesting conclusion can explain why fee schedules in health care are relatively simple compared to those suggested by standard agency theory, which are predictably complex (Arrow 1986).

The meaning of this conclusion is limited by the fact that, in the real world of health care, agency relationships are much more complicated than assumed. The number of patients paying out of pocket for health care and the number of doctors receiving individual private fees for service are small, particularly in the developed countries. In addition, various types of patients (principals) and doctors (agents) can be combined into many kinds of principal–agent relationships. Patients can be grouped into patients paying out of pocket, patients covered by social health insurance financed from tax revenue, and patients covered by health insurance schemes financed by premiums. Insured patients can be further subdivided into those with copayments and those without. Medical doctors can be categorized as doctors employed and remunerated by hospitals; doctors employed and remunerated by health funds; doctors contracted by health funds; doctors with both office-based and hospital-based practices (as in the United States); doctors working as a team and referring patients to each other; and doctors engaged in individual private practice, as is assumed in our case. In designing a remuneration system, variations in the utility functions for different pairs of principal and agent have to be considered.

This chapter may provide a base and a framework for expanding the model to other types of doctors and patients. Although the common arguments and independent arguments of the utility functions of various types of doctors and patients might be different from those in the assumed case, the utility functions can be revised according to the different types of patients and doctors. For example, if the patient is covered by a social health insurance scheme and is not charged at point of service, the charges as costs for the patient should be removed from the patient's utility function. In addition, the patient's ability to pay is no longer a constraint for the doctor to provide the nonperceived negative effort. This chapter may provide a guideline for investigation into the double-agent relationship between doctors and other parties, as indicated in chapter 6. The doctors' ideal remuneration should consider the common and independent arguments of the utility functions of the doctors and of their two principals.

The authors suggest that future research should be directed to empirical study to test the model provided here and to theoretical study of the nature of the utility functions of other types of patients and doctors. Because the doctor usually serves as a double agent, only after the nature of the utility functions of the three parties in the trilateral agency relationship is made clear can the remuneration system for medical doctors be built on a sound scientific base.

NOTE

This chapter is based on a review of the literature by the authors when Xingzhu Liu was pursuing his PhD under the supervision of Professor Anne Mills at the London School of Hygiene and Tropical Medicine. The initial work was funded by the United Nations Development Programme/World Bank/World Health Organization Special Programme for Research and Training in Tropical Diseases and the Overseas Research Students Awards Scheme in the United Kingdom. The authors are also grateful for the follow-up support provided by the World Bank and Abt Associates Inc., Bethesda, Maryland.

REFERENCES

Arrow, K.J. 1986. "Agency and the Market." In *Handbook of Mathematical Economics*, ed. K.J. Arrow and M.D. Intriligator, vol. 3. Amsterdam: North-Holland.

Beecher, H. 1955. "The Power of Placebo." *Journal of the American Medical Association* 159: 602–6.

Beisecker, A.E., and T.D. Beisecker. 1990. "Patient Information-Seeking Behavior When Communicating With Doctors." *Medical Care* 28: 19–28.

Cartwright, A. 1967. *Patients and Their Doctors.* London: Routledge and Keegan Paul.

Culyer, A.J. 1989. "The Normative Economics of Health Care Finance and Provision." *Oxford Review of Economics and Policy* 5: 34–58.

Hall, J., and M. Dornan. 1988. "What Patients Like about Their Medical Care and How Often They Are Asked: A Meta-Analysis of the Satisfaction Literature." *Social Science and Medicine* 27: 935–9.

Haug, M., and B. Lavin. 1981. "Practitioner or Patient—Who's in Charge?" *Journal of Health and Social Behavior* 22: 212–29.

Kolb, D.A., I.M. Rubin, and J.M. McIntyre. 1974. *Organizational Psychology: An Experimental Approach.* Englewood Cliffs, NJ: Prentice-Hall.

Lupton, D. 1990. "Consumer Sovereignty or Blissful Ignorance? Consumerism in Health Care." Dissertation for the Degree of Master of Public Health, University of Sydney, Australia.

Maslow, A. 1954. *Motivation and Personality.* New York, NY: Harper and Row.

Mathews, J. 1983. "The Communication Process in Clinical Settings." *Social Science and Medicine* 17: 1371–8.

Mooney, G., and M. Ryan. 1993. "Agency in Health Care: Getting beyond First Principles." *Journal of Health Economics* 12(2): 125–35.

Ryan, M. 1995. "Economics and the Patient's Utility Function: An Application to Assisted Reproductive Techniques." Ph.D. Dissertation. Aberdeen, UK: University of Aberdeen, Department of Economics.

———. 1992. "The Economic Theory of Agency in Health Care: Lessons from Non-Economists for Economists." Discussion Paper No. 03/92. Aberdeen, UK: University of Aberdeen, Health Economic Research Unit.

Scott, A. 1996. "Agency, Incentive and the Behavior of General Practitioners: The Relevance of Principal-Agent Theory in Designing Incentives for GPs in the UK." Discussion Paper No. 3. University of Aberdeen, Health Economic Research Unit.

Scott, A., and A. Shiell. 1997. "Do Fee Descriptors Influence Choices in General Practice? A Multilevel Discrete Choice Model." *Journal of Health Economics* 16(3): 323–42.

Tuchett, D. 1979. "Doctors and Patients." *An Introduction to Medical Sociology.* London: Tavistock.

Turner, B. 1987. *Medical Power and Social Knowledge.* London: Sage.

Waitzkin, H. 1984. "Doctor-Patient Communication of Information about Illness." *Advances in Psychosomatic Medicine* 8: 180–215.

Woodward, R.S., and F. Warren-Boulton. 1984. "Considering the Effects of Financial Incentives and Professional Ethics on Appropriate Medical Care." *Journal of Health Economics* 3: 223–307.

Zweifel, P. 1994. "Agency Relationship in Psychotherapy: An Economic Analysis." *Social Science and Medicine* 39(5): 621–28.

CHAPTER 8

Economic Models of Doctors' Behavior

Xingzhu Liu and Anne Mills

How and how much doctors are reimbursed influences their decision-making behavior. The design of the remuneration system for medical doctors is therefore of key importance to the allocable efficiency of health care resources. Understanding doctors' behavior is the prerequisite for good design. In this chapter, the authors review the theoretical models of doctors' behavior and examine how the models fit in with real situations in the context of Chinese health care systems. They find that transforming Chinese salary-based payment systems into systems with strong economic incentives may have induced doctors to behave contrary to their patients' best interests.

INTRODUCTION

In the health care sector, most consumers are unable to assess their own needs for services and therefore rely heavily on medical doctors for advice about the appropriateness of alternative diagnostic and treatment strategies. As a result, doctors have a great deal of influence not only on the supply of health care services but also on demand for such services. Medical doctors' decisions about health care services can thus have a big impact on the quantity, quality, and distribution of a society's health care resources.

Because how and how much doctors are reimbursed influences their decision-making behavior, the design of the system for remunerating them is of key importance to the allocation efficiency of health care resources. However, designing a good remuneration system is not easy and must be based on a comprehensive understanding of doctors' behavior. This understanding is the prerequisite for good design.

In this chapter, first the theoretical models of doctors' behavior are reviewed. Then, how the models fit in with real situations is examined in the context of Chinese health care systems. The second section introduces various types of suggested objective functions of medical doctors. The third section describes doctor's supply behavior and its implications for remuneration policy. In the fourth section, doctors' pricing models are reviewed. In the last section, the behaviors of various types of doctors in China are discussed.

THE DOCTOR'S OBJECTIVE FUNCTIONS

The literature on doctors' behavior has been characterized by three approaches: utility maximization models, income maximization models, and target income models.

Utility Maximization

The advocates of utility maximization models (Feldstein 1970; Eastaugh 1981; Eastaugh 1992) argue that the doctor's utility function includes some of the following elements: profit (net income), leisure time, professional status, internal ethics, complexity of case mix, study time to keep up to date, number of support staff under the physician's supervision, and so on. Sometimes the utility function is stated in negative terms, for example, the disutility to the physician of working more and the disutility of coercing doctor-induced patient visits. They believe that income is important, but it is not the whole story, because doctors' behaviors are too complicated to be explained only by income. The supporters of the utility maximization models view the classical maxims concerning simple income maximization as totally unrealistic. For simplicity, instead of working with all the elements of the doctor's utility function, many economists opt for standard competitive analysis of a two-element utility function (income and leisure or slack) as the first-best approximation of physicians' behavior (Pauly and Redisch 1973).

The utility maximization hypothesis predicts that doctors would behave to make the effort (including inputs such as time, working intensity, and monetary inputs) up to the point where the marginal utility of each unit of effort is equal for the different elements of the utility function. The implication of this hypothesis is that the doctor's behavior cannot be directed only by pecuniary incentive. Regulations or policies that focus on other elements of the utility function may work equally well. This theory means that the doctor's behavior should be managed or controlled by using multiple countermeasures. Using the financial incentive to the exclusion of other elements may result in failure to fully motivate the doctor's positive behavior.

Income Maximization

The income maximization models assume that income (or profit) is a dominant element that affects the doctor's behavior, that the doctor's behavior is driven by income. These models are supported by several health economists (Sloan 1976; Baumol 1988). The advocates of this hypothesis argue that income for doctors, as for any other businessperson, is the most important element that can capture a dominant part of what can influence doctors' behavior; that the simple model explains doctors' behavior almost equally well; and that the utility maximization models complicate empirical implementation and are unnecessarily fuzzy and complex. This income maximization hypothesis predicts that the doctor will behave in a way that maximizes his or her income, and that proper design of remuneration methods and financial incentive schemes can direct a doctor's behavior.

Target Income

The target income hypothesis (Newhouse 1970) is accepted by many health economists (Rice 1983). This hypothesis recognizes that the doctor has an expected level of income in relation to other equivalent doctors in the medical market. It implicitly assumes that, below the income target, the doctor's behavior will be predominantly driven by income. After reaching the income target, the doctor will consider other factors (as indicated in the utility maximization models) that may become more important to his satisfaction.

The target income hypothesis predicts that, if the doctor is paid less than he expects, he will behave like an income maximizer and do what he can (e.g., inducing patient demand) to maximize his income. If paid the target income or more, the doctor will be more likely to behave in a way that satisfies other wants and needs. Put in economic terms, before reaching the target income, the doctor will value the marginal utility of income per unit of input more than those of other gains; after reaching the target income, the doctor will value the marginal utility of other gains (such as status) per unit of input more than income. The target income hypothesis is a hybrid of the income maximization and the utility maximization models.

The target income hypothesis has several policy implications. First, for the medical doctor to behave in the interests of the patient, he should be paid no less than the expected target income. Otherwise, he may behave in a way that adds income toward his income target to the detriment of the patient. This is what happens in developing countries where doctors are poorly paid, and the gap between target and actual income becomes a driving force for misbehavior by doctors. For example, patients in a township hospital in China complain that medical doctors are reluctant to discharge patients; one reason may be that they are paid less than their income targets and keep patients in the hospital longer than necessary to earn more income. Second, if doctors are paid less than their target income, a properly designed incentive payment system may be more effective in controlling their behavior, because they will value the utility of the incentive more highly than the extra income from needlessly long hospital stays. Third, if doctors are paid the target income or more, the financial incentive may exert less effect on their behavior, and interventions affecting other factors that provide utility to the doctor should be paid more attention.

THE DOCTOR'S SUPPLY BEHAVIOR

Analysis of the doctor's supply behavior examines changes in the supply of doctors in relation to changes in their income (wage). This framework is a simplified form of the doctor's utility function in which the utility is assumed to be derived from either work or leisure. As described in chapter 7, the income effect predicts a decrease in the number of hours worked as wages increase, while the substitution effect predicts an increase in the number of hours worked as wages increase. Whether a physician works more or less as a result of an increase or decrease in his wages is an empirical question that cannot be predicted by current labor economic theory.

The predictable change in the number of hours worked in response to changes in the doctor's wage is an important subject for doctors' remuneration policy (Eastaugh 1992). The ultimate objective of remuneration-system design is to provide financial incentive to motivate the doctor's effort. If the behavior of the doctor's labor supply shows a dominant income effect, more financial incentive means less effort. Thus, raising the payment to encourage the doctor to work harder and more hours must be a policy mistake. This model reflects only the trade-off between work and leisure within the total number of discretionary hours available; it does not reflect change in intensity of effort while at work. Thus, while the income effect means fewer hours of work as wages increase, it does not mean that financial incentive schemes cannot improve intensity of effort and overall performance within the given number of working hours. Another important point to remember is that, even if the supply curve for a specific doctor is backward-bending ("individual labor supply" in figure 8.1), the doctors' aggregate labor supply curve may instead be uniformly upward-sloping ("aggregate labor supply" in figure 8.1). This is usually the case in most labor markets (Eastaugh 1992), because the wage increase will lead to increases in the number of medical doctors in the medical market.

The results of empirical studies on doctor labor supply behavior are mixed. Some commentators find support for the backward-bending supply curve (Feldstein 1970; Brown and Lapan 1979; Reinhardt 1975), while others find no support for the hypothesis (Sloan 1976; Hu and Yang 1988). Although empirical examinations of the backward-bending supply curve are not conclusive, the supply curve of individual labor seems inelastic, and the increase in the doctor's wage (or fee schedule) does not result in a significant increase in the doctor's number of hours worked. The policy implications of this conclusion are that increasing doctors' wages should not be expected to increase their hours worked; that any shortage of medical doctors may not be solved by trying to lengthen their work week by raising the regulated fees; and that a surplus of doctors may not be reduced by trying to shorten their work week by lowering the regulated fees.

DOCTORS' PRICING MODELS

Monopoly Equilibrium Model

The monopoly equilibrium model, reported first by Kessel (1958), assumes that medical demand cannot be shifted by doctors (either because patients have enough

Figure 8.1   The Doctor Labor Supply Curve: Individual Labor Supply versus Aggregate Labor Supply

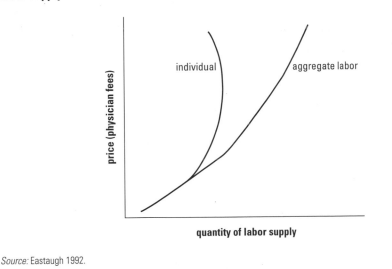

Source: Eastaugh 1992.

information or because doctors are reluctant to induce demand); that doctors are price setters who can set prices at the most profitable levels; and that the market can "clear" (namely, that interaction between demand and supply will bring about equilibrium). This model recognizes that the medical doctor is a monopolistic profit maximizer who cannot only set charges at the most profitable levels but also charge each patient at a rate that the patient can and will pay. The objective of price discrimination is not to give charity to the poor, but to maximize monopolistic profit by capturing the entire area under the demand curve.

This model is suitable for traditional individualized medicine in which the doctor engages in individual private practice, the patient pays out of pocket, and doctors are in short supply. It is not suitable for modern medicine in which health insurance does not allow price discrimination, the fee schedule is regulated by the government or health insurance funds, and organized medicine (such as the hospital) is unlikely to negotiate charges with individual patients.

Monopolistic Demand Shift Model

The monopolistic demand shift model assumes that the doctor is in a monopolistic position and can price his medical services irrespective of what other doctors are doing; that the doctor can manipulate the patient's wants and inflate his demand; and that the market can clear. According to this model, the doctor cannot only set the price at the most profitable level (though not necessarily discriminatory prices) but, for extra profit, he can also induce demand from the patient. The model puts the medical doctor at the apex of power.

The model is supported by Evans (1974) who, based on empirical evidence from Canada, argues that the doctor has the power to induce patient demand because of the information asymmetry between doctors and patients. Evans also argues that, because the patient has imperfect information on health care quality, the patient is often led to believe that higher price means higher quality. Thus, the patient may demand more of the higher-priced services. As Eastaugh (1992) points out, solid evidence of consumers' searching for higher-priced providers would be a revolutionary attack against economic normalcy in the medical market. However, this model is difficult to test, because true demand, the basis for estimating shifts in demand, cannot be estimated. This model has been rejected by Fuchs (1986), Pauly (1980), and Feldman and Sloan (1988).

Excess Demand Disequilibrium Model

The excess demand disequilibrium model assumes that the doctor is a price setter and can set prices irrespective of the market; that the doctor cannot manipulate consumer demand and demand cannot be shifted; and that the health care market is a market with chronic excess demand. Because excess demand is assumed, the doctor is in a position to choose the most profitable or interesting cases. According to this model, it is not necessary for the doctor to induce demand, because the supply of doctors' services cannot meet consumer demand; the increase in demand as supply increases does not mean demand inducement, but that more demand is being met by the increased supply. Feldstein (1970), rejecting the monopolistic model and the monopolistic demand shift model, suggests that physician services are in a state of permanent excess demand and indicates that doctors can benefit from this kind of market by increasing supply as much as they like to increase earnings. This model is untestable because neither a demand curve nor a supply curve can be estimated.

Competitive Equilibrium Model

The competitive equilibrium model assumes that there are many competitive doctors and doctors have to be price takers (who accept whatever price is offered); that patient demand cannot be shifted; and that the market can clear through interaction between demand and supply. This model is a classic competition equilibrium model.

According to Eastaugh's review (1992), this model has been tested by Feldstein (1970), Newhouse (1970), Fuchs and Kramer (1972), Newhouse and Phalps (1974), and Dychman (1978). These studies suggest that the positive association between the price and physician supply ratios is inconsistent with the competitive model and that the observed low price elasticity is also not consistent with competition theories.

Although many health economists reject competition in the medical market, some subgroups of physicians or surgeons may actually exhibit competitive pricing behavior. Steinwald and Sloan (1974) and Sloan (1976) reported mostly negative association between general practitioner (GP) density and fees. Holahan et al. (1978) also found the same relationships for GPs. Most health economists reject the hypothesis that the market for GPs is perfectly competitive, but high net price elasticity indicates a considerable degree of competition in the medical market. Eastaugh (1992) summarized that the competitive equilibrium model appears to have validity in the case of GPs and possibly general surgeons as early as the 1970s.

Oligopolistic Target Income Model

The oligopolistic target income model assumes that the doctor is a price taker; that as input costs inflate and demand declines, the doctor can manipulate and shift the patient demand to meet his target income; and that the market can clear.

This model received some support from Feldstein (1970) but was soundly rejected by Sloan (1976) and Steinwald and Sloan (1974). Although some of the studies did not reject the hypothesis that the doctor cannot induce demand for his target income, it is almost impossible to distinguish demand shifts resulting from changes in consumer tastes from shifts caused by the physician's manipulation of information to the consumer, or from shifts that are simply responses to changes in time price faced by consumers.

Exogenous Price Ceilings Model

The exogenous price ceilings model assumes that the doctor is a price taker and the price is controlled by either third parties or government agencies; that demand cannot be shifted; and that the market will not clear. This model was considered by Reinhardt (1975) and Pauly (1980). According to this model, doctors would like to produce services at the point where the marginal cost equals the price ceiling, because production beyond this point gains the doctors less profit. Thus, the supply of medical services would consistently fall short of demand if price controls were too strict. There is no empirical support for this model (Newhouse 1988).

ANALYSIS OF DOCTORS' BEHAVIOR IN CHINA

The literature discussed in the previous sections is drawn mostly from studies done in the United States where doctors are traditionally not hospital employees; they work mainly in their own offices but, if a patient needs to be hospitalized, also in hospitals. Medical doctors can also use hospital facilities if a patient needs surgical services that cannot be done in the doctor's office. A patient who receives a doctor's services in the hospital is billed separately from hospital services either by the doctor himself or through the hospital. This is different from

China's situation. To analyze doctors' behavior in China, let us first look briefly at the characteristics of China's doctors and their possible behaviors.

Characteristics of Doctors in China

The first feature of the organization of medical doctors in China is the separation of hospital-based doctors from office-based doctors, the two main categories. Office-based doctors engage in individual or group practice in their offices, and they are not allowed to provide inpatient services in hospitals. They are either salaried employees of institutions or individual private practitioners. Hospital-based doctors are salaried employees of the hospitals, and they engage in both outpatient and inpatient care in the hospital facilities. Some doctors (after working full time in the hospital) are allowed to practice medicine in offices for extra income after hours.

The second feature is the integration of medical services and drug dispensary. Health care providers in China are allowed to dispense drugs while they provide medical consultancy and other medical services. Although prices for labor services are set below cost, drugs are allowed to be sold at mark-ups of between 15 and 40 percent. The private medical doctor usually has a stock of 100 to 200 kinds of Western medicines. If he also practices traditional Chinese medicine, he may stock 200 to 300 Chinese medicines.

Private practice of medicine in China follows the traditional pattern in which the doctor charges no or a very low consultancy fee (private doctors' fees are not strictly regulated), and the doctor's income is generated mostly through drug sales. Salaried, office-based doctors affiliated with an institution may obtain bonuses based on the institution's drug-sale profits. A hospital usually has one or two pharmacy room(s); their profits go into the hospital's financial pool. Generally, the size of the hospital staff bonus, if any, depends on the hospital's financial status.

Possible Behaviors of Different Types of Doctors

Doctors, practicing in different settings and with different incentives, behave in different ways.

Private Office–Based Doctors

Private medical practice was restored in China in the early 1980s, some 15 years after its eradication under the Cultural Revolution of 1966. As table 8.1 indicates, the number of health workers engaged in private practice has been increasing rapidly since the early 1980s. By the end of the 1980s, about 3.3 percent of the health workers above the village level and nearly half of the health workers at the rural village level were engaged in private practice.

Private office–based doctors follow the traditional pattern of medical practice, in which patients pay out of pocket for medical services. Because the Social

TABLE 8.1   The Number of Health Workers Engaged in Individual Private Practice in China, 1982–90

Year	Above village level			At village level		
	Total health workers	Private practice	Private practice as % total	Total clinics	Private clinics	Private clinics as % total
1982	—	—	—	—	—	5.0
1983	4,090,030	49,080	1.2	707,933	221,016	31.2
1984	4,213,646	80,223	1.9	707,168	222,771	31.5
1985	—	—	—	—	—	—
1986	4,495,919	132,424	3.0	795,963	349,792	43.9
1987	4,564,122	138,334	3.0	807,844	363,285	44.9
1988	4,677,512	157,985	3.4	806,497	369,209	45.8
1989	4,786,959	165,966	3.5	820,798	396,431	48.3
1990	4,906,201	162,031	3.3	803,956	381,844	47.5

Source: Chinese Ministry of Health (1991); the *Yearbook* included no data for 1985.

Note: — = not available.

Health Insurance Schemes and the Cooperative Medical System do not reimburse clients for services provided by private office–based doctors, these doctors' clients are not covered by any health insurance scheme. The doctor-patient interaction is a bilateral principal–agent relationship, as indicated in chapter 6. Private office–based doctors can be divided into two types: private village doctors and private doctors in cities or rural township centers.

Private village doctors can be best described as monopolizers of patient demand, limited price setters, and constrained drug sellers. Private office–based doctors are said to be demand monoplizers for several reasons. First, there are usually only one or two doctors in each village. Additional doctors are either not allowed by village authorities or cannot sustain a practice because the village is too isolated or small. Second, villagers are usually reluctant to consult doctors in other villages because of the inconvenience (such as bad transportation and added travel cost) or for fear of offending the patients' village doctor whom the patients need and contact the most frequently. Third, the village doctor is usually familiar with the health conditions of village members. This gives the doctor an advantage over other doctors in diagnosing and treating village residents' diseases. Thus, a village doctor can usually automatically count on most of the village as patients, except for the most complicated cases that are beyond his service capacity.

The government does not regulate private doctors' fees. They set their own prices/fees for consultation, injection, and transfusion. Although private office–based doctors can set their own prices, the level of prices is constrained by several factors. First, the price level is limited by traditional prices, which are generally low, and price increases have to be incremental. Drastic price increases are pro-hibited by public opinion and would tarnish the doctor's reputation among villagers. Second, prices should be set with reference to regulated prices at public health facilities. Any price over the regulated price will be questioned by the public and by the price-management authorities. Third, prices have to be set with reference to the prices charged by other village doctors; the villagers will be reluctant to pay higher prices for the same service. Thus, although private office–based doctors can theoretically set their own prices, they cannot be set without regard to service prices in the medical market.

Private office–based doctors, who are permitted to sell drugs, have been criticized as mere drug sellers. An estimated 90 percent of those doctors' revenue is generated through drug sales (Mao 1995). Although there are other reasons for the high proportion of drug revenue (such as low consultation fees), many researchers doubt that private office–based doctors dispense drugs inappropriately in their own economic interests. However, this hypothesis has never been tested. Selling more and costlier drugs does mean more income for the doctors, but their behavior is subject to some constraints. The first prominent constraint is the patient's ability to pay. The clients of private office–based doctors are predominantly patients who pay out of pocket. Rural peasants' incomes are usually low, and they cannot afford to pay for more, and more expensive, drugs. The doctor's opportunities for misbehavior by inducing patients to use more, and more costly, drugs are limited. The second constraint is the patient's willingness to pay. It is well recognized that service quality of hospital-based doctors is better than that of office-based doctors, and patients are less willing to pay office-based doctors more for their services. This may explain why China's office-based medical doctors are not rich.

Office-based village doctors can capture villagers' demand for primary care, but they may not be able to increase service prices for extra income although they are allowed to do so. Their income is generated mainly by drug sales at a mark-up rate of 15 to 40 percent. Drug prescription and dispensary behavior may be limited by villagers' ability and willingness to pay for drugs. If private office–based doctors were contracted by third parties to serve insured patients, the constraints on the patient's willingness to pay and ability to pay would be removed, and this would result in a different picture of doctors' behavior. Research into the pricing and prescription behaviors of office-based doctors is needed, because there is no empirical evidence in these areas.

Private office–based doctors working in cities or rural township centers are similar to private village doctors in that they rely heavily on drug sales to generate revenue. The main difference is that, within their catchment areas, competition for patients among many private doctors and public health facilities usually constrains their pricing decisions.

Salaried Office-Based Doctors

Salaried office-based doctors are employed by an organizational unit (government, professional institution, industry, or village) to provide primary outpatient care for the unit members who are entitled to coverage under social health insurance schemes or rural cooperative medical systems organized at the organizational level. Usually, a medium-size organization with 500 to 2,000 members in an urban area will hire several doctors and other health professionals and set up a clinic within the organization. The traditional rural cooperative systems are usually based on collective clinics that pay salaries to the doctors. The functions of this clinic are to provide outpatient curative and preventive care to the members of the organization, manage the health funds, and purchase tertiary care for members.

Traditionally, the doctors in the organizational unit are salaried, and salary is their only source of income. The clinic is responsible for providing services and managing health funds, but it is not responsible for the profit or loss of institutional health funds. Surpluses are turned over to the organizational unit, and the organization covers any deficit. The doctor's behavior is guided by well-defined responsibilities and a set number of hours of work; by their intention to gain high status and good reputation among patients; and by a desire for increases in leisure time without any corresponding reduction in salary in the short run. Although doctors may be able to shirk, they have no economic incentive to provide patients with unnecessary care and drugs. The status argument in the doctors' utility function may help them work in the patients' interests.

Contract-related reform in the last several years, however, has changed the context of doctors' behavior. To prevent deficits in their health insurance schemes, most organizations contract the budget to clinics. By contract, the clinic is responsible for providing and purchasing patient care within the allotted budget; the clinic keeps surpluses and bears any losses of the health funds; and the clinic staff can receive bonuses from the surplus at the end of the year. The contract mechanism and the bonus system introduce strong economic incentives for the doctors to save. In addition, the doctors are allowed to provide services to patients outside the organization based on fee for service. Earnings from outside patients are part of their bonus. This policy, instead of providing incentives to save, provides incentive to provide more services and more, and more costly, drugs. Although this kind of reform has been going on for more than 10 years, research in this area is generally lacking.

Salaried Hospital-Based Doctors

Historically (before the 1980s), medical doctors in Chinese hospitals were paid according to national uniform salary standards. Their salaries depended mostly upon their seniority, and the salary was practically their sole source of income. Under this payment system, economic incentives to provide unnecessary care and to prescribe more and more costly drugs were removed, but leisure became relatively important. Leisure and status might be more important arguments of the doctor's utility function. Similarly to the salaried, office-based doctors without bonus payments, the traditional salaried, hospital-based doctors might have had a tendency to seek more leisure, with no reduction in their income, but there was no economic incentive for them to provide less or more care and drugs than thought necessary.

Along with the health care reform initiated in the early 1980s, the bonus system intended to improve internal hospital efficiency was introduced nation-wide as a supplementary way for hospitals to pay medical doctors. Bonuses are now paid to doctors in three ways: (1) the hospital pays individual doctors a flat bonus related to the hospital's profitability, regardless of the volume and quality of the individual doctor's work and the revenue generated by it; (2) the doctors are paid bonuses according to the volume and quality of their work without con-sidering individual doctors' revenue contributions; and (3) a bonus is paid to a doctor in proportion to the revenue generated by his prescriptions and services.

The introduction of different bonus systems introduces economic incentives, with different strengths, for the doctors to work harder in their own and the hospital's economic interests. The flat bonus system may provide doctors with the weakest economic incentive to work productively and in their own economic interests; the work-related bonus system may provide doctors with a moderate economic incentive to work productively and in their own economic interests to the detriment of patients. The revenue-related bonus system may give doctors a strong incentive to increase their productivity, but it also provides a strong incen-tive for them to misbehave in their own economic interests at the expense of their patients. Again, the introduction of the bonus system may change doctors' behavior, which may help increase their productivity but may also increase the possibility that they will write unnecessary prescriptions and perform unnecessary procedures. Strong economic incentives can make doctors into money-generating machines for hospitals. The possible trade-off needs to be examined between hos-pital efficiency (in terms of volume of services produced and revenue generated at a given level of costs) and social efficiency in the health sector (in terms of quan-tity of health care produced at a given amount of medical expenditure).

In addition to the introduction of the bonus system for hospital-based doctors, another change in the last 10 years is that the hospital-based doctors are allowed to earn extra income by engaging in a second position (office-based practice or hospital-based practice in other hospitals) outside the regular working hours. This policy gives the doctor an incentive to refer patients to institutions where he holds a second, better-paid position. Some hospitals even provide kickbacks to doctors from other hospitals for referring patients to them for hospitalization, high-tech tests, and surgery. This practice may distort these doctors' behavior. In these situ-ations, doctors can obtain extra income by opportunistic behaviors without an increase in their efforts. The negative effects of these practices have never been evaluated, and so far there is no effective policy to prohibit these practices.

Summary

The original salary system for paying doctors has been criticized as low productiv-ity (because of the "pig pot" policy of paying the salary regardless of the work). The economic incentive–oriented "reforms" of the last 15 years may change doctors' behavior. Although improved productivity has not been proven, the restoration of private practice, the budget contract between social health insurance funds and salaried office-based doctors, the introduction of the bonus system for hospital-based doctors, and the lack of countermeasures prohibiting kickbacks may provide doctors with incentives to behave against patients' best interests. The system for paying doctors needs to be examined carefully by Chinese policy makers and researchers. Future reforms of the doctor payment system should take into consideration experiences and lessons of the past.

NOTE

This chapter is based on a review of the literature by the authors when Xingzhu Liu was pursuing his PhD under the supervision of Professor Anne Mills at the London School of Hygiene and Tropical Medicine. The initial work was funded by the United Nations Development Programme/World Bank/World Health Organization Special Programme for Research and Training in Tropical Diseases and the Overseas Research Students Awards Scheme in the United Kingdom. The authors are also grateful for the follow-up support provided by the World Bank and Abt Associates Inc., Bethesda, Maryland.

REFERENCES

Baumol, W. 1988. "Price Controls for Medical Services and the Medical Needs of the Nation's Elderly." Paper commissioned by the American Medical Association, March 11. Chicago, IL: AMA.

Brown, D., and H. Lapan. 1979. "The Supply of Physician Services." *Economic Inquiry* 17(2): 269–79.

Chinese Ministry of Health. 1991. *Chinese Yearbook of Health*. Beijing: People's Health Press.

Dyckman, Z.T. 1978. *A Study of Physician's Fees*. Staff report. Washington, DC: Council on Wage and Price Stability.

Eastaugh, S.R. 1992. *Health Economics: Efficiency, Quality, and Equity*. Westport, CT: Greenwood.

———. 1981. *Medical Economics and Health Financing*. Boston, MA: Auburn House.

Evans, R.G. 1974. "Supplier-Induced Demand: Some Empirical Evidence and Implications." In *The Economics of Health and Medical Care,* ed. M. Perlman. London: Macmillan.

———. 1970. *Price Formation in the Market for Physician Services in Canada 1957–1969*. Ottawa: Quenn's Printer.

Feldman, R., and F. Sloan. 1988. "Competition among Physicians Revisited." *Journal of Health Politics, Policy and Law* 13(2): 239–61.

Feldstein, M. 1970. "The Rising Price of Physicians' Services." *Review of Economics and Statistics* 52(2):121–33.

Fuchs, V. 1986. *The Health Economy*. Cambridge, MA: Harvard University Press.

Fuchs, V.R., and M.J. Kramer. 1972. *Determinants of Expenditures for Physicians' Services in the United States, 1948–1968*. National Center for Health Services Research and Development.

Holahan, J., J. Hadley, W. Scanlon, and R. Lee. 1978. *Physician Pricing in California*. Urban Institute Working Paper, Report 998–100. Washington, DC: Urban Institute Press.

Hu, T., and B. Yang. 1988. "Demand for and Supply of Physician Services in the U.S.: A Disequilibrium Analysis." *Applied Economics* 20(8): 995–1006.

Kessel, R. 1958. "Price Discrimination in Medicine." *Journal of Law and Economics* 1(1): 20–53.

Mao, J.W. 1995. "The Operation Status of 3,000 General Hospitals in 1994." *Chinese Hospital Management* 15(5): 5–9.

Newhouse, J.P. 1988. "Has the Erosion of the Medical Marketplace Ended?" *Journal of Health Politics, Policy and Law* 13(2): 263–78.

———. 1970. "A Model of Physician Pricing." *Southern Economic Journal* 37(2): 174–83.

Newhouse, J., and C. Phalps. 1976. "New Estimates of Price and Income Elasticities of Medical Care Services." In *The Role of Health Insurance in the Health Service Sector*, ed. R. Rosett. New York, NY: Watson Academic.

Pauly, M. 1980. *Doctors and Their Workshops: Economic Models of Physician Behavior*. Chicago, IL: University of Chicago Press.

Pauly, M., and M. Redisch. 1973. "The Not-for-Profit Hospital as a Physician Cooperative." *American Economic Review* 63(1): 87–99.

Reinhardt, U. 1975. *Physician Productivity and the Demand for Health Manpower*. Cambridge, MA: Ballinger.

Rice, T.H. 1983. "The Impact of Changing Medicare Reimbursement Rates on Physician-Induced Demand." *Medical Care* 21: 803–15.

Sloan, F. 1976. "Physician Fee Inflation: Evidence from the Late 1960s." In *The Role of Health Insurance in the Health Service Sector*, ed. R. Rosett. New York, NY: Watson Academic.

Steinwald, B., and F.A. Sloan. 1974. "Determinants of Physicians' Fees." *Journal of Business* 47(4): 493–511.

CHAPTER 9

Economic Models of Hospital Behavior

Xingzhu Liu and Anne Mills

Hospital behavior models are studied to explain past hospital behavior, to provide policy-making experiences and lessons for designing and regulating payment to hospitals, and to predict future behavior under changing exogenous factors, including transformation of the payment system. Hospital behavior following change in the payment system can then be predicted with reasonable accuracy and a good payment system worked out. The objectives of this chapter are to review the available models of hospital behavior and to discuss their potential uses in the development of hospital payment systems.

For a model to be applicable to the design of a hospital payment system, it is proposed that five prerequisites must be met: (1) *objective captivity:* the model must be able to include all of the endogenous arguments that are significantly important to the hospital; (2) *argument measurability:* the arguments included in the model should be operationally defined and be measurable with reasonable validity; (3) *trade-off testability:* the trade-offs between arguments must be identified and estimated; (4) *utility estimatability:* the relative importance of the arguments must be quantifiable, namely the marginal utility attached to each argument must be examined; and (5) *effect predictability:* the effect of payment systems and other exogenous factors on the quantity of the arguments and their utility contributions should be predictable. A review of the available models of hospital behavior reveals that none of the models meet these requirements.

INTRODUCTION

The study of hospital behavior models can be used to (1) explain the hospital's past behavior and provide experiences and lessons for policy making regarding hospital regulation and payment to them, and (2) predict future behavior under changing exogenous factors, one of which is the transformation of the payment system. Only if the change in hospital behavior as the payment system changes can be predicted with reasonable accuracy can a good hospital payment system be designed. This is one of the major reasons so many attempts have been made to model and study hospital behavior over the past 30 years.

The objectives of this chapter are to review the available models of hospital behavior and discuss their potential uses in the development of hospital payment systems. Following this brief introduction, types of hospitals are introduced in the second section. The third section describes the possible objectives of hospitals that can set bases for hospital behavior models. The fourth section reviews the available models of hospital behavior. The last section examines possible application of these models.

HOSPITAL TYPES

To model the hospital behavior, what type of hospital it is must be considered, because different types of hospitals may have different goals and be financed differently, and their behaviors may also differ. The categorization of hospitals can provide the basis for considering the appropriateness and the utilization of various available models of hospital behavior. On several dimensions, hospitals can be divided by: *ownership,* into private and public hospitals; *financial objectives,* into for-profit and nonprofit hospitals; *educational responsibilities,* into teaching and nonteaching hospitals; *administration or catchment area,* into primary, secondary, and tertiary hospitals; degree of *service specification* into general and specialized hospitals; and by *employee status of their doctors*, into staff model and nonstaff model hospitals.

Public and Private Hospitals

By ownership, hospitals can be divided into *private hospitals,* invested mainly by private entities, and *public hospitals*, invested by public entities such as governments and collectives (e.g., state enterprises). Private hospitals can be further divided into: *proprietary hospitals,* invested and owned by individual private owners; *partnership hospitals*, invested and owned jointly by several private owners; and *joint-stock hospitals,* owned by all of the stockholders.

Public hospitals can further be divided into pure public and quasi-public hospitals. *Pure public hospitals* are owned and managed by public entities. *Quasi-public hospitals* are owned by public entities and contracted out for management by a private person or company that is responsible for maintaining the public property and providing services with or without a fixed government budget, and which is allowed to distribute profits, if any, at will or according to the contract terms.

For-Profit and Nonprofit Hospitals

The financial goal of the for-profit hospital is generally understood as to earn a profit, while the financial goal of the nonprofit hospital is to break even. But this definition may not entirely capture the nature of these two types of hospitals. There are two major differences between for-profit and nonprofit hospitals (or, more accurately, *not-for-profit hospitals*). (1) Earning a profit is stated as one of management's major goals for the for-profit hospital but not for the nonprofit hospital. This does not mean that nonprofit hospitals do not like to earn a profit.

(2) The second and more important difference concerns the different ways the two entities treat profits.

The for-profit hospital turns over any profits to its owners as private income, while the nonprofit hospital keeps any profit (or "surplus") to expand services or its equity endowment. A nonprofit hospital's profit can never be used as economic return on investment. It would be a mistake, however, to say that the nonprofit hospital does not have an incentive to earn a profit, because with the profit the hospital can grow and pay bonuses to staff, and the managers of the hospital can enjoy their status and managerial achievements. For a nonprofit hospital, a surplus is better than just breaking even, and a loss is prohibitive unless it can be recovered over the long term.

According to the above definition, public hospitals should be classified as nonprofit hospitals. Private hospitals, however, can be either for-profit or nonprofit institutions, depending on the two conditions laid out above. Nonetheless, both public and private nonprofit hospitals have incentives to make profits, but the two types of institutions use their profits differently.

Teaching and Nonteaching Hospitals

The teaching hospital, due to its educational mission, has to have a broad range of services, high technology, high-quality medical doctors, and complicated case mixes. As a result, the teaching hospital can usually deliver high-quality services, and the cost is also relatively high. The higher cost, however, is not due solely to the increased service cost. The increased cost of the teaching hospital can be decomposed into two parts: one part due to the higher technical quality of medical services and the other due to teaching activities. The teaching hospital produces not only medical service products, but also products in the form of trained medical personnel. In theory, the increased cost due to the differential for higher-quality service should be reimbursed by service users or third-party payers if the users are covered by health insurance, and the increased cost due solely to teaching activities should be reimbursed by the trainees or by the government if medical personnel are considered social products. In addition to educational activities, the teaching hospital usually engages in research that may also increase its costs via the production of social products of research.

The above arguments have implications for understanding hospital behavior and reimbursement of teaching hospitals. Whether the hospital engages in teaching activities may make a difference in its utility function arguments and then in its behavior. Who should reimburse the increased cost due to education and research will make a difference in reimbursement policy. For example, the Medicare Diagnosis-Related Group payment system in the United States provides a higher rate for the same services rendered by teaching hospitals (Jacobs 1991). In the United Kingdom, there is a service incentive for teaching, that is, teaching hospitals get top priority in National Health Service budget allocations with separate funding for their educational role.

Hospital Hierarchies

Hospitals can be divided into hierarchical tiers similar to Mills's classification (1990), where hospitals in developing countries are divided into central, general, and district hospitals according to the levels of administration in the planned health care system or the catchment area and the degree of specialization in the market-oriented system. The first tier is the *primary care hospital*. The characteristics of the primary care hospital are the following: the target population is patients within the community; it is staffed by general practitioners (GPs); it provides hospital services and surgical services for common diseases; the number of beds is usually small, fewer than 100; and its diagnostic system and equipment are low technology (e.g., X-ray and B-ultrasound equipment and basic laboratory tests). The *secondary hospital* usually serves the population of a district or county; it is staffed by GPs and specialists; it can provide most hospital services and major surgical services; it has between 100 and 500 beds; and the equipped technology is at a medium level (e.g., computed tomography [CT] imaging and most laboratory tests). The *tertiary hospital* represents the technological level of a province or a country; it is staffed by specialists and often has a teaching role; it mainly provides services to patients who cannot be diagnosed and treated at a lower-level hospital; it usually has more than 500 beds; and it is equipped with up-to-date technology.

The hospital system varies in different countries, and the number of beds may also vary depending on population size and available resources. Hospitals in any country can be divided according to the dimensions used here to classify the hospital levels.

General and Specialized Hospitals

Hospitals can be divided into general hospitals and specialized hospitals. *General hospitals* provide medical services for all kinds of diseases to all types of patients. *Specialized hospitals* provide services for specified diseases (e.g., psychiatric, tumors and cancer, heart and vascular, ear and eye, infectious, parasitic, tuberculosis, schistosomiasis, and so on) to specified groups of patients (e.g., women, children, geriatric, short-term nursing, and so on). The specificity of hospital services may influence the hospital's objectives.

Staff Model and Nonstaff Model

Because most of the literature on hospital behavior models has been developed in the United States, where most doctors are not hospital employees, applying these models to hospitals in which the doctors are hospital employees requires an understanding of their situational differences. The nonstaff model hospitals exist in the United States, Canada, and South Africa. Instead of being hospital staff, the doctors are actually the hospitals' clients, and the hospitals provide the doctors with settings in which they practice hospitalized medicine. While engaging in his or her office-based medical practice, the doctor can refer patients to his affiliated hospital where he provides services for them. This means that a hospital that wants to attract more patients must attract more affiliated-quality doctors by providing high-tech equipment and broad service capacity and scope, depending on the number of doctors and the number of hospitals in the area. Otherwise the doctor will lose business or shift his affiliation to other hospitals to protect his earnings.

Most countries have staff model hospitals, and the doctors are salaried employees. In this case, attracting patient demand will not rely on attracting doctors in the short run, and the financial incentives of the hospital and its doctors are somewhat integrated. For example, the staff model of hospital practice helps to prevent conflicts of interest between a hospital and its doctors under a prospective payment system, because saving is a good thing for both hospital and doctors due to the increased benefit. The case of the nonstaff hospital is different. Under the prospective payment system (assuming prospective payment is just for the hospital and doctors are paid on a fee-for-service basis), the hospital has an incentive to save, while the doctors have an incentive to provide more because more services and longer stays mean more income for them (Jacobs 1991).

HOSPITAL OBJECTIVES

Hospitals thus come in many different shapes and sizes, as can be seen from the combinations of hospital classifications just given. Because different types of hospitals' objectives may vary a great deal, generalizations about their objectives are difficult to make, a representative and typical hospital cannot be identified, and developing a single model for predicting hospital behavior is challenging (McGuire, Henderson, and Mooney 1988). The best approach to understanding the overall picture of hospital behavior may be by listing alternative objectives mentioned in the literature and attempting to relate them to each of the above hospital types.

Profit Maximization

Profit maximization is recognized as the single most important objective of for-profit hospitals (Davis 1971; Feldstein 1979). Indeed, many hospitals are built explicitly to earn a profit and would not otherwise enter the medical market. These hospitals include for-profit proprietary hospitals, private nursing home industries (such as those in the United States), joint venture hospitals, and joint-stock hospitals. For most hospitals, however, profit making is not a stated goal, or at least earning a profit is not their major objective. These hospitals include public hospitals and private nonprofit hospitals.

Although the profit-maximization objective is explicitly stated as an objective, others goals might be important to profit-oriented hospitals, such as quality for tertiary hospitals and the number of trainees for teaching hospitals. Thus, hospital behavior modeling based only on the profit objective may not comprehensively capture hospital behavior. In addition, although profit making is not explicitly stated as an objective for nonprofit hospitals, it may implicitly direct their behavior because money is also important to them. Assuming that profit maximization is the only objective of for-profit hospitals and not an objective for nonprofit hospitals might not fit reality.

Quantity Maximization

By rejecting the hypothesis that profit maximization is the objective for nonprofit hospitals, many health economists support the hypothesis that quantity maximization is the major objective of the nonprofits (Brown 1970; Klarman 1965; Long 1964; Reder 1965; Rice 1966). As a measurement of quantity, Klarman (1965) suggests the number of patients treated, Reder (1965) suggests the weighted number of patients treated, and so on. Indeed, most hospitals want to increase their service volume, but quantity alone may not capture the nature of hospital objectives for two reasons.

First, quantity means different things in different situations. If there is a profit margin for each additional unit of service provision, quantity means profit; if the medical price is regulated below the total average cost level (but more than average variable costs), as in China, quantity means less loss. If public hospitals provide services free of charge, quantity means social welfare. If quantity reflects increased demand because of an increase in quality, quantity means quality.

Second, how the hospital is reimbursed matters a great deal. If the hospital is reimbursed based on case payment, an increase in the number of cases treated means an increase in profitability. If the hospital is paid a fixed budget and is responsible for hospital services, quantity means reduced profitability. If the hospital is reimbursed based on fee for service, an increase in quantity means an increase in profitability. Quantity is important for most hospitals in most situations, but it may not be the hospital's ultimate objective because the hospital may increase the quantity to meet other objectives.

Social Welfare Maximization

The social welfare maximization objective is reported by Feldstein (1961). He states that the nonprofit hospital is to maximize social welfare, subject to the constraint of financial solvency. Although this hypothetical objective is interesting, it is rarely investigated in detail. Most public hospitals and many private nonprofit hospitals seem to pursue this objective explicitly or implicitly. The motto of public hospitals in China, "social benefit first," is roughly equivalent to the social welfare hypothesis. But the hospitals themselves do not know what social welfare means. In economic terms, social welfare means the *total consumers' surplus*, which equals total willingness to pay for hospital care minus the total actual payment (cost) to society as a whole. It is apparent that hospitals do not pursue the total consumer's surplus. There are two other social welfare alternatives for the hospitals to pursue: to maximize the health of treated patients or to maximize the output of hospital services. Both alternatives are subject to financial solvency. Maximizing health seems suitable for public and nonprofit hospitals, but it is a fuzzy goal, considering how difficult it is to measure "health," and it might be inconsistent with achieving the society's real welfare. Maximizing output actually means maximizing the quantity of hospital services.

Sales Maximization

The hospital as a sales-maximizing entity is reported by Steven Finkler (1983) based on Baumol's (1959) theory of sales maximization. Baumol argues that a business always tries to increase the total number of sales (or total revenue) until the breakeven point, while Finkler argues that hospitals will keep expanding their roster of services, even when losing money on them, and that, if there is a breakeven constraint, nonprofit hospitals will not offer products with insufficient demand even without a loss.

The underlying rationales are that the hospital would like more demand for its services, because increased demand can raise total revenue and the hospital can still break even; that demand for a hospital service is limited unless the hospital can attract more affiliated doctors; that one way of attracting doctors is to expand service scope and require more and higher technology; and that, as a result, the hospital gains its maximized sales, even if suffering some loss.

Analysis of these rationales shows that sales maximization is equivalent to maximization of the output of hospital services, namely quantity maximization. Broadening the scope of services means attracting a greater number of affiliated doctors, then increasing demand for the hospital, and then producing the maximum volume of services. This objective is reportedly putting stress on the situation of hospital–doctors separation, as in the United States. It may not be suitable for hospitals in which the hospital and its doctors are one integrated entity.

Capacity Maximization

The capacity maximization objective is implicitly stated by Lee (1971), Newhouse (1970), and Feldstein (1971). According to this hypothesis, hospitals always want to expand the scope of services, acquire more high-tech equipment, attract more quality doctors, and increase service quantity and quality. It is true that any hospital wants capacity expanded, but their reasons for wanting to maximize their service capacity have not been fully analyzed. Possible answers may be that hospitals covet prestige, reputation, and excellence (Lee 1971). For anyone who still wonders why, answers might lie in previously discussed objectives, such as profit maximization, quantity maximization, and so on.

Maximizing Income per Doctor

The hypothetical objective of maximizing income per doctor means that the hospital wants to maximize its revenue per medical doctor. This objective is reported by many authors (Frank 1987; Morrisey et al. 1984; Pauly 1980; Pauly and Redisch 1973; Penchansky and Rosenthal 1965; Shalit 1977). It overlaps with other objectives such as revenue or sales maximization because the maximization of income per medical doctor will automatically maximize the hospital's total income. The model based on this objective is discussed in detail later in this chapter.

Utility Maximization

Supporters of utility maximization argue that hospital behavior is guided by many factors of importance to the hospital. This is reported by several authors (Newhouse 1970; Lee 1971; Goldfarb, Hornbrook, and Rafferty 1980; Hornbrook and Goldfarb 1983). Some of them involve only quantity and quality as arguments of the utility function; others involve many arguments, including profit, number of hospital admissions, emergency capacity, case mix, and quality of care. Utility maximization seems to be the only objective that has a potential to comprehensively cover the objectives of all types of hospitals by adding all possible elements of importance. In practice, however, it may be difficult to conduct empirical tests because many elements in the utility function may be difficult to measure.

Consideration of the alternative objectives reported in the past 30 years reveals no single objective that captures the nature of the whole body of hospitals. This is because (1) hospitals vary a great deal in type and (2) the types and quantity of output differ significantly. As Berki (1972) stated, "if the literature on the objectives of the hospital agrees on a central point, it is that the objectives are vague, ill-defined, contradictory, and sometimes nonexistent."

ECONOMIC MODELS OF HOSPITAL BEHAVIOR

Because there is no consensus on hospital objectives, the models are developed in association with particular hypothesized objectives that fit particular types of hospitals and special applications. The uniform model of hospital behavior that fits, explains, and predicts behavior for all types of hospitals has not yet come into existence. This section reviews the major available models of hospital behavior. It is followed by a discussion about the application of these models and suggestions for future research.

Profit-Maximizing Models

Jacobs's Model

Jacobs (1991) develops a basic model for explanatory purposes. Although he assumes the health care service supplier is a lab that provides a single test service, it is equivalent to the assumption of a hospital that provides a single product. Here it is described as a model of hospital behavior. This model has the following assumptions:

- The hospital's objective is to maximize profit.

- The hospital provides a single product or multiple products measured by a single indicator.

- All the hospital's revenue comes from service charges.

- The hospital is a price taker rather than a price setter because the price is set by an independent administrative agency or because the hospital operates in a competitive situation in which the best price it can get for its product is the price prevailing in the market.

- To produce the product, the hospital incurs both fixed and variable costs, and the average variable cost is assumed to fall initially and subsequently rise as output increases.

With the above assumptions, the central question of this model can be asked: What quantity of output will be supplied taking the hospital as a profit maximizer, what quantity will be chosen, and how will this quantity vary when prices and costs vary?

This model predicts that a profit-maximizing hospital will produce services to the point where the marginal cost (MC) equals the marginal revenue (MR), in this case, the price of hospital service (P). As long as the marginal revenue (price) exceeds the marginal cost, the profit maximizer will always try to expand output, because the additional revenue from the additional output exceeds the additional cost, and the hospital can still earn more profit by expanding the output. The hospital will never expand output to the point where the marginal cost exceeds the marginal revenue, because more output would mean less profit.

The change in the marginal cost will affect the quantity of supply. The increase in the marginal cost for a given amount of output will reduce the quantity of supply, at constant prices, and vice versa. The implication is that a profit-maximizing hospital will reduce its output to raise profits if the input price inflates.

This model also predicts that the hospital will increase both output and output price and decrease output with a decrease in the price, and that the supply curve of the hospital will be the marginal cost curve. The quantity supplied will be where the price equals the marginal cost.

According to the model, if the price is so low that the hospital would be better off producing nothing, the hospital will shut down operations. The criterion the hospital will use to decide whether to continue to produce is not whether it incurs a loss but whether it can minimize its loss. It is assumed that, if the hospital shuts down, it has to incur the loss of its total assets (equal to the total fixed cost). In this case, if the price is lower than the average total cost (ATC) but higher than the average variable cost (AVC), the hospital will incur a loss but will not shut down because the surplus over AVC can still recover some of the fixed cost. If the price is lower than the *AVC*, continuing operations means incurring more loss than only the fixed cost, and the hospital will shut down. Thus, the shut-down point is where the price equals the *AVC*, below which there will be no reason for a profit-maximizing hospital to continue operations.

This model is shown in figure 9.1, from which it can be seen that, at a price of P_2, P_3, and P_4, a profit-maximizing hospital will produce Q_2, Q_3, and Q_4 amounts of service. At these quantities, for which $MR = MC = P$, the hospital can make the maximum amount of profit. If the price is reduced below P_1, where the price equals *ATC*, the hospital can no longer earn a profit, but will not shut down until the price is reduced to P_0, where the price equals *AVC*.

Feldstein's Model

Feldstein (1979) developed one of the simplest models of hospital behavior. In this model, he assumes the following:

- The hospital is a profit-maximization firm.

- The hospital has monopoly power—it controls the price, and the hospital, as a firm, is facing a downward demand curve for its services.

- The hospital produces with a diminishing return on scale—the marginal cost will increase as output increases.

This model predicts that, to maximize profit, the hospital will produce the quantity of output at the point where the marginal cost (*MC*) equals the marginal revenue (*MR*), as indicated in figure 9.2. The maximum amount of production

Figure 9.1   Jacobs's Model: Marginal Costs and Prices

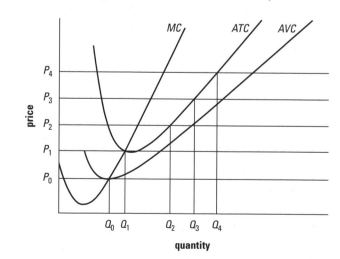

Source: Jacobs 1991.

Figure 9.2   Feldstein's Model: Short-Run Equilibrium under Monopoly

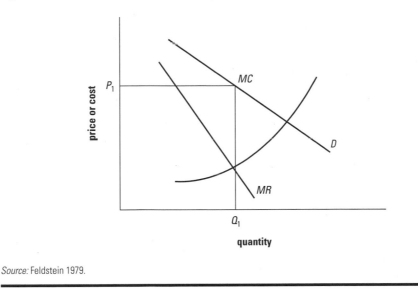

Source: Feldstein 1979.

will be Q_1. The quantity of the output less than Q_1 means giving up the opportunity to earn more profit, and the quantity of output exceeding Q_1 means less profit. Because the hospital has monopoly power, it can set the price at P_1, facing its demand curve, D, for excess profit, subject to clearance by the market.

Feldstein extends this model to a situation in which the hospital is a multi-product firm with different payers. Under these conditions, the model predicts that the hospital will practice price discrimination by charging different prices for different types of services and patients according to the price elasticity of demand for each class of patient and type of service. Assuming there are n classes of patients and k types of service, the following criteria will be observed when deciding the quantity of output and setting prices:

$$MR_{1n} = MR_{2n} = \ldots = MR_{kn} = MC_1 = MC_2 = \ldots = MC_k.$$

Unlike Jacobs's model, the Feldstein model assumes that the hospital is a monopoly and multiproduct firm.

Quantity-Maximizing Models

Jacobs's Model

In this quantity-maximizing model, Jacobs (1991) assumes that the hospital is an output maximizer instead of a profit maximizer, as assumed in his previous model. While the previous model may fit the for-profit hospital, this model is suitable for the nonprofit hospital, the predominant type in almost every nation. Other assumptions are the same as those described in Jacobs's profit-maximizing model, in particular, that the hospital is a price taker.

According to this model, the hospital will expand its output to the point where the firm just breaks even, that is, where the total cost (TC) equals total revenue (TR), or the price (P) equals the total average cost (TAC). The output of a nonprofit hospital that intends to maximize its output to the breakeven point will be higher than the output of a for-profit hospital that intends to maximize its profit. As depicted in figure 9.1, the supply curve for the output maximizer is the TAC curve instead of the MC curve in the case of profit maximization. If the price increases, output will increase accordingly. Any factor that shifts the ATC curve downward (lower unit costs at any level of output) will cause output to increase at any price. If the price is lower than the minimum level of ATC, the hospital will operate in deficit. In this case, the hospital will need an external subsidy to maintain its operation for break even; without a subsidy, the hospital has to shrink. If the price is lower than the minimum average variable cost (AVC), the hospital has to go out of business.

Rice's Model

As developed by Rice (1966), this quantity-maximization model assumes that the hospital (nonprofit) is a quantity maximizer; that it has monopoly power, namely, that it faces a downward demand curve and is a price setter; and that it produces a single homogeneous product.

According to this model as depicted in figure 9.3, the total costs are directly related to output. The slope of the total cost curve increases as output expands, reflecting the effect of diminishing marginal productivity on marginal costs. The revenue curve is drawn with a slope that decreases as output increases. This reflects decreases in the marginal revenue associated with a declining price elasticity of demand, which occurs as the quantity produced and sold increases. The total surplus (TS) or profit is equal to the total revenue (TR) minus the total cost (TC). An inspection of figure 9.3 reveals that the breakeven volume is Q_1 and Q_3, profit is maximized at Q_2, and losses are incurred if the hospital attempts to produce more than Q_3 or less than Q_1. Thus, the hospital with monopoly power as an output maximizer subject to the breakeven constraint will produce Q_3 amount of hospital services.

Staff Income-Maximizing Model

Pauly and Redisch (1973) are the first to emphasize an active role of the physician in a model of hospital behavior (Rosko and Broyles 1988). In this model they assume the following:

- The goal of the nonprofit hospital is to maximize net hospital income per member of the medical staff, subject to the constraints imposed by the hospital production function and demand curve.

- Reimbursement is cost based, and the patient pays the full cost of hospitalization. Thus, the inputs can be employed to the point at which the marginal contribution of each physician's revenue is zero.

Figure 9.3   Rice's Model: Quantity Maximization

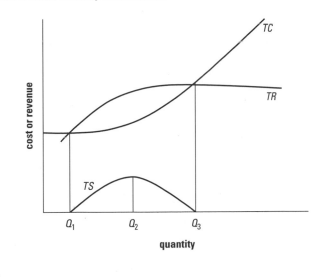

Source: Rice 1966.

As figure 9.4 depicts, the average revenue product (*ARP*) of the medical staff is the maximand of the objective function. It is expressed as

$$ARP = (PQ - K - L)/M,$$

where *PQ* represents total revenue, *K* represents the cost for capital, and *M* represents the size of the medical staff. This equation implies that the difference between total revenue and hospital operating costs (i.e., *K* + *L*) is distributed to the medical staff. Also appearing in figure 9. 4 is the marginal revenue product (*MRP*), which is equal to the change in the total revenue product associated with a one-unit change in the size of the medical staff.

According to this model, if net income can be equally shared by the hospital's closed medical staff, and staff members themselves decide upon their number, the *ARP* will be maximized when M_1 physician is employed by the hospital, because below this number of physicians the *MRP* is greater than the *ARP*, and the additional physician will increase the *ARP*. Above this number of physicians, the *MRP* is less than the *ARP*, and the additional physician can only reduce the *ARP*. This means that the hospital will increase the number of physicians and thus increase the quantity of hospital services to the point where the *MRP* equals the *ARP*.

If the medical doctors are salaried at a wage of *S*, the equilibrium staff size will be M_2, where *MRP* is equal to *S*, because, from M_0 to M_2, a range for which the number of staff is less than M_2, the additional staff member will bring about the revenue contribution to the hospital, and after M_2 the additional physician can only reduce the net revenue of the hospital because the *MRP* is less than *S*.

Figure 9.4   Pauly and Redisch's Model: Physician Equilibrium at Maximized Staff Income

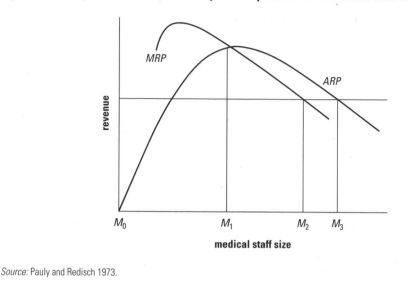

Source: Pauly and Redisch 1973.

If an open staff is assumed (namely, the hospital will decide the number of the staff), the Pauly-Redisch model predicts that the equilibrium size of the medical staff is M_3, where *ARP* equals the wage of the medical staff, *S*. There is no incentive for the hospital to expand the size of its medical staff beyond M_3 because further increases would reduce the physician's average income below a level that could be earned in alternative activities.

Executive-Benefit-Maximization Model

This model has several assumptions as follows (Jacobs 1991):

- The executives or administrators of the hospital have considerable control over hospital behavior, and the behavior of the executive can represent the behavior of the hospital as a whole.

- The behavior of the executive is driven mainly by pecuniary incentives for the executive who works in a for-profit hospital; the hospital's profit can be turned into a take-home pecuniary benefit to the executive. The executive who works in a nonprofit hospital has less pecuniary incentive, because he is paid a fixed salary, and the hospital's profit cannot be translated into the executive's financial benefit.

- The behavior of the executive who works in a nonprofit hospital is driven mainly by nonpecuniary incentives, such as high-grade office furniture, a relaxed work atmosphere, business trips to exotic places, high status due to high quality of care, and so on. The executive who works in a nonprofit hospital is less motivated by pecuniary incentives than one who works in a for-profit hospital.

Because resources are scarce, there will be a trade-off between the executives' nonpecuniary benefit and the hospital's profit. In a for-profit hospital, greater profit can be expected from a smaller commitment of resources for a given amount of output. For a nonprofit hospital the nonpecuniary benefit for the executive is expected at a higher level of costs for a given amount of hospital services, and at reduced profit.

This model predicts that, for the hospital whose executives are motivated mainly by nonpecuniary objectives, more resources would be committed, and productivity and profitability would be lower than in hospitals whose executives are motivated mainly by the pecuniary benefit. The former hospital is expected to have higher service quality and a more complex case mix than the latter hospital, which may want to minimize its cost by reducing quality and weeding out the costly cases.

Revenue-Maximization Model

The revenue-maximization model is reported by Finkler (1983). The following assumptions are associated with this model.

- Nonprofit hospitals pursue a policy of revenue maximization or sales maximization, because its managers or administrators are rewarded on the basis of the firm's revenue rather than its profits. Although sometimes it is said that the managers are rewarded for the quality and quantity of hospital services, that is almost impossible. Quality is difficult to define and measure, and quantity is also difficult to measure due to the hospital's multiproduct nature.

- Hospitals are oligopolistic firms, each faced by a downward-sloping demand curve. It is further assumed that demand for each hospital product is finite, even at a price of zero, because of patients' limited needs and other costs incurred, such as travel and time costs. Finkler argues that a hospital cannot maximize revenue simply by offering to mend an infinite number of broken legs. Demand for that service will eventually be satisfied, and the hospital will have to offer another product to expand revenue.

Demand for or revenue from hospital services are functions of service price and the number of medical doctors affiliated with the hospital. The more doctors affiliated with the hospital, the greater is the demand for that hospital. This is particularly true in the United States where the hospital's inpatients are referred by its affiliated doctors. In addition, the higher the price, the less is the demand for the hospital.

Suppose there are *n* products for a hospital. The hospital will maximize its revenue by maximizing the sum of revenues for all of its products, subject to the breakeven constraint, as follows:

$$Max[P_1Q_1 + P_2Q_2 + \ldots + P_nQ_n]$$

$$S.T. \ [P_1Q_1 + P_2Q_2 + \ldots + P_nQ_n] = C_1 + C_2 + \ldots + C_n],$$

where P_1Q_1 is the revenue from product 1 and P_nQ_n is the revenue from product *n*; and C_1 is the total cost of product 1 and C_n is the total cost of product *n*.

This model predicts that the hospital, as a revenue maximizer, will produce as many types of products and as much of each product as possible, as long as total revenue is maximized and the hospital can still break even, and that some products will be offered at a loss if their effect on demand for other products produces a profit greater than or equal to the loss. The rationales for the latter prediction are that to increase revenue, demand should be increased; to increase demand, the hospital must attract more affiliated doctors; to attract doctors, the hospital has to offer a wide range of services. Although a new product may be offered at a loss, the introduction of this product may increase the profitability of existing products by increasing demand for them and their revenue by attracting more affiliated doctors. This is shown in figures 9.5 and 9.6. It can be seen that the introduction of product 2 (a new product) will create a loss for the hospital (figure 9.5) because the total revenue for this product (TR_2) is less than its total cost (TC_2); that the introduction of product 2 will increase demand for other products (here, product 1), and thus the total revenue curve for product 1 is shifted upward

Figure 9.5   Net Revenue Increase from Other Products after Introduction of New Product at a Loss

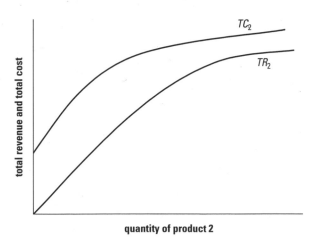

Source: Finkler 1983.

Figure 9.6   Shift in Revenue Curve of Old Product due to Introduction of New Product

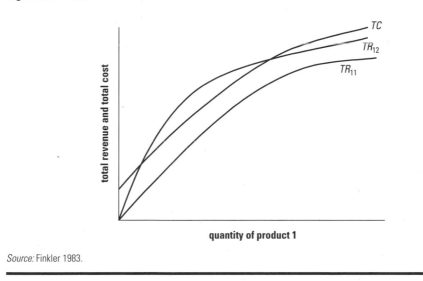

Source: Finkler 1983.

from TR_{11} to TR_{12} (figure 9.6). As a result, the loss $(TR_2 - TC_2)$ due to the introduction of the new product (product 2) is offset by the increased profit for other products (in this case, $(TR_{12 - TC1}) - (TR_{11} - TC_1)$), and the hospital can increase its total revenue without suffering any loss or additional loss in general.

Utility-Maximizing Model

Lee's Model

In Lee's model (1971), it is assumed that the hospital administrators—who direct hospital behavior—are the subject of concern. Lee postulated that hospital administrators attempt to maximize their own utility, which is a function of salary, prestige, security, power, and professional satisfaction. He further argues that the determinants of utility are directly related to the number and types of sophisticated inputs and services used by the hospital. The operation of sophisticated services and the use of high-tech equipment will enhance the hospital administrators' income, security, and prestige. This model predicts that a hospital's pursuit of conspicuous production, as it is assumed, will result in unnecessary duplication of facilities and overhiring of staff.

Feldstein's Model

Different from Lee's model, Feldstein (1971) introduces, in his utility function, a trade-off between the quantity and quality of hospital services. This model, as shown in figure 9.7, is based on the simplified assumption that given a fixed budget, hospital decision makers face the opportunity locus (the product

Figure 9.7   Feldstein's Model: Trade-Off between Quality and Quantity

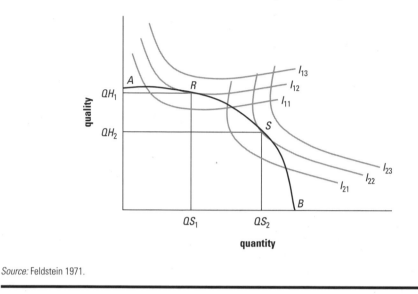

Source: Feldstein 1971.

transformation curve) *AB*. This curve represents a situation in which the hospital faces a trade-off between the quantity and quality of services, with quantity measured by the number of patient days and quality measured by the intensity of care. The opportunity locus in this model is drawn with respect to the origin. This indicates that as the hospital moves from point *B* toward point *A* on the production transformation curve, an increasing amount of service quantity must be sacrificed to obtain each extra unit of quality. This reflects the increasing marginal costs as quality is increased. This model also assumes that the utility of the decision maker is a function of quality and quantity and that utility is indifferent along the indifference curve, *I*. The indifference curve is drawn convex with respect to origin, which reflects the assumption that the administrator's marginal evaluation of quality decreases as the level of quality increases. The model also implicitly assumes that different hospitals will have different sets of indifference curves, reflecting differences in their valuation of the trade-off between quality and quantity. As shown in figure 9.7, the indifference curves I_{11}, I_{12}, and I_{13} are for hospital *C*, and I_{21}, I_{22}, and I_{23} are for hospital *D*. This model predicts that a quality-oriented hospital (which puts more utility on quality) will produce at point *R* where the level of quality is QH_1 and the level of quantity is QS_1, and that a quantity-oriented hospital will produce at point *S* where the level of quality is QH_2 and the level of quantity is QS_2.

Cromwell's Model

Cromwell (1976) extends the Feldstein model by imposing the payment constraint, that is, the prospective payment, based on inpatient days or per case.

As figure 9.8 depicts, before the imposition of the prospective payment system, the opportunity locus facing the hospital is *AEFB*, and to maximize the utility of the hospital it will produce at point *E* where the level of quantity is PD_1 and the level of quality is QH_1. After the imposition of the prospective payment system, the hospital will be paid a reduced fixed amount per case or per inpatient day. The hospital's opportunity locus becomes QH_2GFB because the revenue ceiling imposed by the prospective payment does not allow the hospital to provide care that is more expensive than the value of the inputs needed to provide QH_2 amount of quality per unit of services. At the new equilibrium position, point *F*, the hospital will produce more units of service, but at a lower level of quality. This model predicts that, the imposition of the prospective payment will provide the hospital with incentive to reduce service quality and increase the number of units of services on which the payment is based.

Goldfarb, Hornbrook, and Rafferty's Model

In contrast to the earlier utility models of hospital behavior, Goldfarb, Hornbrook, and Rafferty (1980) explicitly recognize the multiproduct and multigoal nature of the hospital. This model assumes that the hospital decision makers attempt to maximize the utility, which is a function of the number of admissions, case mix, quality, and profit, subject to the constraints of reimbursement policies, technology, patient availability, and general resources. It is also assumed that the hospital decision makers face the trade-offs between the components of the objective function, and that the criterion is to equalize the marginal utility of each of the

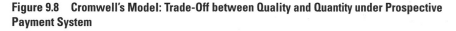

Figure 9.8   Cromwell's Model: Trade-Off between Quality and Quantity under Prospective Payment System

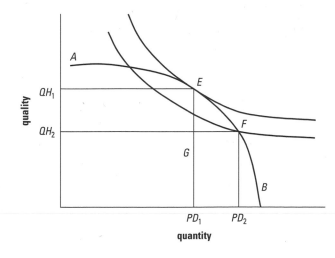

Source: Cromwell 1976.

components of the objective function. Their later publication (Hornbrook and Goldfarb 1983) includes more arguments in the utility function, but the framework is the same.

Rosko's Model

Rosko (1982) extends Cromwell's model by considering marginal slack as an argument in the administrator's utility function. The model predicts that as the slack increases, the quality and quantity of services would decrease and the cost per unit of service would increase. The model also predicts that the imposition of revenue constraints in the form of per-diem prospective payments would result in a reduction in the slack and thus improve the hospital's internal efficiency.

Sloan and Steinwald's Model

Similar to the Goldfarb-Hornbrook-Rafferty model, this model, as developed by Sloan and Steinwald (1980), assumes that the hospital's utility (U) is a function of service composite (X), which incorporates both the quality and quantity dimensions of the output; amenities (Y), including those provided to patients and physicians; and the profit (π), that is:

Maximize $U = U(X, Y, \pi)$.

It is argued that different types of hospitals may place different weights on the objectives. For-profit hospitals may emphasize profit, while nonprofit hospitals may place more weight on X or Y. It is interesting that both the Sloan-Steinwald and Goldfarb-Hornbrook-Rafferty models take profit as an argument for the nonprofit hospitals. Although it is contradictory to the general statement that earning a profit is not the objective of the nonprofit hospital, the fact is that the nonprofit hospital does have an incentive to earn a profit (Rosko and Broyles 1988) because of the changes in the hospital payment system and the trend of hospital corporatization.

THE APPLICATION OF HOSPITAL BEHAVIOR MODELS

One of the major objectives in developing models of hospital behavior is to predict changes in hospital behavior that will occur with the changes in exogenous factors. One of these factors is how and how much the hospital is reimbursed, which will provide scientific information needed to design hospital payment systems.

To be applicable to the design of hospital payment, a model must meet five prerequisites: (1) *objective captivity:* the model must be able to include all of the endogenous arguments that are significantly important to the hospital; (2) *argument measurability:* the arguments included in the model should be operationally defined and measurable with reasonable validity; (3) *trade-off testability:* the trade-offs between arguments must be identified and estimated; (4) *utility estimatability:* the relative importance of the arguments must be quantifiable, namely the marginal utility attached to each argument must be examined; and (5) *effect predictability:* the effect of payment systems and other exogenous factors on the quantity of the arguments and their utility contributions should be predictable. If the five prerequisites can be met, hospital behavior will be predictable. A review of the available models of hospital behavior reveals, however, that none of the models can meet these requirements. The next part of this chapter is a discussion about the five prerequisites listed above, followed by suggestions for further research.

Objective Captivity

The first step in modeling hospital behavior is to decide the hospital's objective function. Generally there are two types of approaches: the single argument approach and the multiargument approach. The single argument approach includes only one endogenous factor in the model. These include the profit-maximization model, the quantity-maximization model, the revenue-maximization model, and so on. The multiargument approach includes mainly different types of utility-maximization models. These two approaches have both advantages and disadvantages. With regard to the single argument approach, one of the most important advantages is that the included endogenous variable is usually relatively easy to measure with validity. For example, the profit-maximization model and the revenue-maximization model recognize profit and revenue, respectively, as the model's only important argument, and they are easy to measure. The second advantage of the single argument approach is that it is relatively easy to put into use because (1) measurement of the utility value of the argument does not have to be considered; if the quantity of the single argument is maximized, the utility contribution of this argument will be automatically maximized; and (2) because the trade-off between endogenous variables need not be considered, as in the case of multiargument models. The single argument models suffer serious shortcomings, one of which is that the single argument is unlikely to capture the nature of the hospitals' objectives. Thus, comes the second disadvantage: that the single argument model may not be able to accurately explain and predict hospitals' behavior due to the lopsided assumption of their objectives. Differing from the single argument approach, the multiargument approach stands a better chance of capturing the nature of the hospital objectives, whereas it has problems meeting prerequisites 2 through 5.

Consensus among the modelers is also lacking on the subject of concern in the formulation of hospital objectives. Generally three groups of people are the possible subjects of hospital objectives: the board of trustees, the hospital administrators, and the medical staff. As Rosko and Broyles (1988) state, "the economic models generally are not clear about to whom the maximand pertains; vague references of trustees, medical staff, and administrators have been made frequently; however the trade-offs that are negotiated by these actors are complex and are likely to differ between organizations." The formulation of hospital objectives is a result of interactions among different stakeholders of the hospital. Failure to recognize this fact will result in failure to capture the nature of hospital objectives. This may be one of the major shortcomings of the previous models of hospital behavior.

Hospitals are much more complex than assumed in the modeling process. The modelers generally recognize the differentiation between nonprofit and for-profit hospitals but fail to consider differences in the objectives of the different types of hospitals classified in the first part of this chapter. The identification of for-profit and nonprofit hospitals is important in formulation of hospital objectives, but this is not to say other classifications of hospitals can be ignored because the objectives of different types of hospitals within each of the two major categories may vary. The financial objectives might be different between public and private hospitals. While the financial objective of the private hospital may be profit maximization if the hospital is for-profit, and financial breakeven if the hospital is nonprofit, the financial objective of the public hospital with public financing might be to recover variable costs in the short term if maintenance of the fixed assets is the government's responsibility, as in many developing countries. While the number of trainees may enter into the utility function of the teaching hospitals, this variable is not a concern for nonteaching hospitals. Case mix and range of services may be an argument of the utility function for general hospitals; it may not be an important argument for specialized hospitals. Although service quality is important for higher-level hospitals, access might be more important for primary care hospitals. Another convincing example is that a publicly funded hospital for infectious disease will not take the number of admissions as an argument of its utility function, because no hospital would like more cases of infectious diseases such as polio.

Although there are large variations in the objectives of hospitals across different types of hospitals and considering the subject of concern, it would be a mistake to say that each hospital has it own unique objective function. To make the hospital behavior model useful, the objective function must be generalized into, if not one, several types. The generalization process should not be based on subjective arguments and assumptions, as in previous modeling processes, but on empirical investigation of the subjects that concern different types of hospitals. The literature might be biased by the U.S. situation and by neglect of likely behavior of publicly funded and owned hospitals.

Argument Measurability

As stated earlier in this chapter, with the increase in the number of arguments of the hospital objective function, more difficulties are likely to arise in the accurate measurement of these variables. Among those included in the models, the most common additional variables are quality and quantity, about which a great deal of concern has been shown.

The definition and measurement of quality is often vague and incomplete. Donabedian (1969) divided quality measurements into the *structure* (mix of inputs offered by the institution), the *process* (the manner in which services are provided), and the *outcomes* (results of care). The available models put more emphasis on the structure dimension of quality such as the availability of high-tech ancillary services. The failure to include other dimensions may constitute a deficiency in the quality measurement. Furthermore, even if all three dimensions were included, the selection of the variables to be measured on each quality dimension would still be problematic. The quality of hospitals at different levels and with different specialties can be measured by using the same idea, but the elements measured should be different. This will pose a problem of comparability between hospitals. In Feldstein's model (1971), *quality* is defined as the intensity of services provided (i.e., the number of inputs per patient day). Unfortunately, Dowling (1976) reported serious difficulties in acquiring reliable and valid measures of intensity. Therefore, quality, in Feldstein's model, pertains to something that can be conceptualized but cannot be measured. In Hornbrook and Goldbarb's (1983) utility model of hospital behavior, quality is measured by diagnosis-adjusted fatality rates. This measure is not only gross, as the modeler states, but also invalid because hospitals can increase the fatality rate by referring-out dying patients.

The problem of quantity measurement comes into existence when a hospital is involved in multiproduct production. A hospital usually provides a broad range of services, such as outpatient services and many sorts of ancillary services besides hospitalization and surgery. The traditional one indicator measurement, such as the number of admissions and the total number of hospital days, is not appropriate because hospitals that provide the same number of admissions or hospital days may vary in the quantity of services delivered due to the possibly large variation in ancillary services provided for the same cases. Finkler (1983) argues that hospital revenue is the normalized quantity of services in monetary terms. This may be so if the prices for hospital services are standardized, but it holds true if the prices for the same services vary across hospitals. Another possible approach is to use the relative equivalent to measure quantity. Each type of service is given a weight, and the quantity is then measured by the weighted indicator such as the hospital-day equivalent. There is no agreement, however, on how and how much weight should be attached to each type of service.

Despite some difficulties in measuring the arguments of the hospital objective function, measurement should be possible. Researchers have to try to develop valid measurements of these arguments; otherwise the model can only be conceptualized, and never validly tested and utilized. The measurements developed might not be perfect, but they must be broadly able to represent the real nature of the arguments, and they must be standardized.

Trade-Off Testability

To maximize its utility, the hospital must fully employ the available resources and know-how to realize its objectives. But sometimes an increase in argument X must come at the expense of argument Y. The best possible combination of X and Y is to yield the highest attainable level of utility. When the objective function involves more than one variable, there would be a need to identify and estimate the trade-offs between these variables. In other words, the opportunity locus between each pair of arguments must be identified and quantified.

A review of the literature reveals that, except for the conceptualization of the trade-off between quality and quantity by Feldstein (1971), little research has been done to identify the trade-offs between other important variables (objectives). The quantitative estimations of opportunity locus have never been investigated. To develop a useful model, just listing the possible arguments and providing a valid measure for each is not enough. The quantitative trade-offs among them must be testable and tested. Unless the trade-offs are quantified, the conceptual multiobjective model alone will provide little value to the prediction of hospital behavior.

Utility Estimatability

The arguments of the hospital behavior model are those variables that are of significant importance to the hospital, but the arguments are not equally important. This comes down to the need for estimating the arguments' marginal utilities and their changes with the changes in quantity of the arguments' value. The trade-offs between the marginal utilities of the arguments should also be estimated. The results of the utility estimation will constitute the indifferent utility curves that are used to decide the best quantity combination of different arguments subject to overall utility maximization. The idea is consistent with microeconomic theory, and it should be right in determining the best combination of the arguments' quantities, but a review of the literature shows that this has never been empirically tested. For a multiargument approach, unless the marginal utilities of each argument (at least the relative value of marginal utilities) and their trade-offs can be empirically estimated, the model cannot be used to predict hospital behavior.

Effect Predictability

One of the important steps in predicting hospital behavior is to predict the effects of exogenous factors on the endogenous factors included as arguments in the model. Besides the previously mentioned prerequisites, the implementation of this step requires that the exogenous factors, especially those that are important to the design of the payment system, should be identified and defined, and that the ways of measuring these factors or variables should be developed. The quantitative relationship between the exogenous and the endogenous variables should then be established and generalized by using the empirical data and econometric methods. This step is not the end of the modeling process. After the relationships are established, the model that specifies the quantitative relationships between the exogenous and the endogenous variables should be used to predict the effect of changes in the exogenous variables on changes in the endogenous variables in general settings. The possible trade-offs of these effects are then analyzed by considering the trade-offs between the utilities of different arguments. Last, the best adjustment and combination of the endogenous factors and the related behavior should be predicted, provided that the adjusted combination of the quantity of endogenous factors can maximize the utility of the hospital. The interrelations between exogenous and endogenous factors were tested by Goldfarb, Hornbrook, and Rafferty (1980) and Hornbrook and Goldbarb (1983), but they failed to go any farther to do the quantitative trade-off analysis and predict the adjusted combination of endogenous factors and the related adjustment behavior.

Suggestions for Future Research

Efforts have been made since the early 1970s to model hospital behavior. Due to the complexity of hospital entities, generalizing about the objective function of the hospital is difficult. The profit maximization models are said to fit for-profit hospitals, but it is generally thought other objectives are also important to hospitals. Although some of the modelers of nonprofit hospitals recognize that the hospital's major objective is to maximize the quantity of service provision subject to the financial breakeven, others argue that more objectives should be included in the hospital's objective function. In addition, the previous models suffer from measurement problems in terms of the valid measurement of variables that describe the hospital's objectives and of the utility values of different arguments in the objective function. In general, studies of hospital behavior modeling are far from conclusive. Continuous efforts are needed to have the models reflect the real-world situation and to make the models be of practical use in predicting hospital behavior.

Based on the literature review, several suggestions for future research can be made.

- First, the identification of the hospital's objective function should be based on investigations of different types of hospitals. All of the subjects that concern hospital objectives (e.g., administrators, board of trustees, medical staff, hospital owner) should be investigated in terms of what is important to each of them. In establishing hospital objective functions, interactions among the subjects of concern, and the various types of hospitals, should be considered. In future research, hospital objective functions should be established, based on empirical investigations rather than subjective judgments.

- Second, further efforts should be made on the measurements of the arguments included in hospital objective functions. If perfect measurements are difficult or impossible to develop, they must be able at least to reflect the concepts with reasonable validity. In addition, efforts should be made to standardize measurements at least at the national level. If one measurement for a variable is not suitable for all hospitals, different measurements of a variable can be developed so that the measurements are appropriate for different types of hospitals.

- Third, the relative utility contribution of each unit of an argument (the endogenous variable) for all included arguments should be investigated. This information can be directly used to roughly predict hospital behavior. For instance, if there are three arguments in the hospital objective function, A, B, and C, and the relative utility contributions of each unit of the three arguments are 1, 2, and 3, then if the change in an exogenous factor is predicted to reduce 3 units of A, the hospital will be expected to produce 1 more unit of C or 1.5 additional units of B, or any combination of B and C to maintain the original level of utility. The related actions (behavior) of the hospital to realize this adjustment can be predicted. This type of analysis assumes that the marginal utility of an argument is stable and that the trade-offs between different arguments and their utilities are ignored.

- Fourth, for the long term, more sophisticated analysis should be conducted, involving the measurement of the dynamic marginal utility of each argument, the trade-off analysis of different arguments, and their utilities. The best quantitative combination of different arguments should maximize the total utility of the hospital, subject to the fact that the quantity trade-off rate of any pair of arguments equals their utility trade-off rate. The solution of the best quantity combination of arguments will involve complicated procedures of linear programming and the construction of simultaneous models. In future studies, this sophisticated model—which could solve the quandary of "the best quantitative combination of arguments"—should be explored.

NOTE

This chapter is based on a review of the literature by the authors when Xingzhu Liu was pursuing his PhD under the supervision of Professor Anne Mills at the London School of Hygiene and Tropical Medicine. The initial work was funded by the United Nations Development Programme/World Bank/World Health Organization Special Programme for Research and Training in Tropical Diseases and the Overseas Research Students Awards Scheme in the United Kingdom. The authors are also grateful for the follow-up support provided by the World Bank and Abt Associates Inc., Bethesda, Maryland.

REFERENCES

Baumol, W. 1959. *Business Behavior, Value and Growth.* New York, NY: Macmillan.

Berki, S. 1972. *Hospital Economics.* Lexington, MA: Lexington Books.

Brown, M. 1970. "Economic Analysis of Hospital Operation." *Hospital Administration* 15(60): 67–74.

Cromwell, J. 1976. "Hospital Productivity Trends in Short-Term General Nonteaching Hospitals." *Inquiry* 11(2): 181–7.

Davis, K. 1971. *Economic Theories of Behavior in Nonprofit, Private Hospitals.* Washington, DC: Brookings.

Donabedian, A. 1969. *A Guide to Medical Care Administration. Medical Care Appraisal—Quality and Utilization.* Vol. 2. Washington, DC: American Public Health Association.

Dowling, W.L. 1976. *Impact of the Blue Cross and Medical Prospective Reimbursement Systems in Downstate New York.* Final report on contract HEW-OS–72–2481. Seattle, WA: Department of Health Services, University of Washington.

Feldstein, M. 1971. "Hospital Cost Inflation: A Study of Nonprofit Price Dynamics." *American Economic Review* 61(5): 853–72.

Feldstein, P. 1961. *An Empirical Investigation of the Marginal Cost of Hospital Services.* Chicago, IL: University of Chicago Press.

Feldstein, P.J. 1979. *Health Care Economics.* New York, NY: John Wiley and Sons.

Finkler, S.A. 1983. "The Hospital as a Sales-Maximizing Entity." *Health Service Research* 18(2): 117–33.

Frank, R., J.P. Weiner, D.M. Steinwachs, and D.S. Salkever. 1987. "Economic Rents Derived from Hospital Privileges in the Market for Podiatric Services." *Journal of Health Economics* 6(4): 319–37.

Goldfarb, M., M. Hornbrook, and J. Rafferty. 1980. "Behavior of the Multi-Product Firm: A Model of the Nonprofit Hospital System." *Medical Care* 18(2): 185–201.

Hornbrook, M., and M. Goldfarb. 1983. "A Partial Test of a Hospital Behavior Model." *Social Science and Medicine* 17(10): 667–80.

Jacobs, P. 1991. *The Economics of Health and Medical Care.* Gaithersburg, MD: Aspen.

Klarman, H. 1965. *The Economics of Health.* New York, NY: Columbia University Press.

Lee, M.L. 1971. "A Conspicuous Production Theory of Hospital Behavior." *Southern Economic Journal* 38(1): 48–58.

Long, M.F. 1964. "Efficiency Use of Hospitals." In *The Economics of Health and Medical Care,* ed. S. Muskin. Ann Arbor, MI: University of Michigan Press.

McGuire A., J. Henderson, and G. Mooney. 1988. *The Economics of Health Care: An Introductory Text.* London and New York, NY: Routledge and Kegan Paul.

Mills, A. 1990. "The Economics of Hospitals in Developing Countries. Part I: Expenditure Patterns." *Health Policy and Planning* 5(2): 107–17.

Morrisey, M.A., et al. 1984. "Hospital Rate Review: A Theory and an Empirical Review." *Journal of Health Economics* 3(1): 25–47.

Newhouse, J. 1970. "A Model of Physician Pricing." *Southern Economic Journal* 37(2): 174–83.

Pauly, M. 1980. *Doctors and Their Workshops: Economic Models of Physician Behavior.* Chicago, IL: University of Chicago Press.

Pauly, M., and M. Redisch. 1973. "The Not-for-Profit Hospital as a Physician Cooperative." *American Economic Review* 63(1): 87–99.

Penchansky, R., and G. Rosenthal. 1965. "Productivity, Price, and Income in the Physician's Service Market—A Tentative Hypothesis." *Medical Care* 3: 240–44.

Reder, M. 1965. "Some Problems in Economics of Hospitals." *American Economic Review* 56(2): 472–80.

Rice, R. 1966. "Analysis of the Hospital as an Economic Organism." *Modern Hospital* 106(4): 87–91.

Rosko, M., and R. Broyles. 1988. *The Economics of Health Care: A Reference Handbook.* Westport, CT: Greenwood Press.

Rosko, M.D. 1982. "Hospital Response to Prospective Rate Setting." Doctoral Dissertation. Philadelphia, PA: Temple University.

Shalit, S. 1977. "A Doctor-Hospital Cartel Theory." *Journal of Business* 59(1): 1–20.

Sloan, F.A., and B. Steinwald. 1980. *Insurance, Regulation, and Hospital Costs.* Lexington, MA: D.C. Heath and Company.

CHAPTER 10

Motivation and Performance-Related Pay

Xingzhu Liu and Anne Mills

Resource allocation will not be improved unless the people responsible for apportioning resources are motivated to do it efficiently. In the health care sector, doctors and hospitals take a major role in allocating resources. Success or failure in resource allocation and use thus depends largely on decisions made by providers, and policies that can influence their behavior are of overarching importance. This chapter provides a thorough review of the theories and methods for motivating providers to improve their performance, particularly through performance-related pay. The practice of performance-related pay in developed and developing countries is also reviewed.

INTRODUCTION

A major concern of health economics policy is what should be done to improve the health of populations, using the least resources, and to maximize health outcomes, using the available resources and allocating them in the most efficient way *(optimal allocation)*. Because resources are managed by people, the optimal resource allocation will not be achieved unless these individuals are so motivated. In the health care sector, doctors and hospitals play a major role in the allocation of health resources. It is estimated that 70 to 80 percent of health resources are affected by medical doctors' decisions (Reinhardt 1985) and that the hospital sector absorbs 30 to 50 percent of health care expenditure in developing countries (Mills 1990) and more in developed countries. Thus, success or failure in the allocation and the use of these resources depends to a large extent on provider decisions, and policies that can influence their behavior are of overarching importance. Because providers' decisions are known to be driven by their motivations, the payment system focuses on ways of inducing them to use all their resources wisely.

In the next section, the relevant theories of motivation are reviewed in an effort to develop an understanding of ways of motivating providers to improve performance. Concepts and methods of performance-related pay are discussed in the third section to see how it can be used to motivate people to achieve performance targets. The fourth and last section is a literature review of the application of performance-related pay in the health care sector.

MOTIVATION THEORIES

Motivation refers to the driving forces that determine the direction and strength of goal-oriented behaviors. This definition means that the goal of an individual or an organization is established based on related needs and that behaviors for achieving the goal, and the intensity with which the goal is pursued, may vary with different kinds of motivation.

Motivation Concepts

Motivation can be intrinsic or extrinsic. *Intrinsic* motivation refers to the self-generated factors that influence people to behave in a particular way or move in a particular direction. These factors include the perception of responsibility, the existence of interests, and the perception of the performed activities' long-term benefit. *Extrinsic* motivation refers to what is done to or for people to encourage or discourage them to behave in a particular way and direction. This includes rewards (such as increased pay), praise, promotion, and punishment (such as disciplinary action, pay withholding, and negative criticism). Extrinsic motivators can have an immediate, powerful effect, but it might not last long. Intrinsic motivators are likely to have a deeper and longer-term effect because they are inherent in individuals, not imposed from the outside.

Motivation Theories

Motivation theories posit that people can be induced to behave by needs and incentives.

Instrumentality Theory

Instrumentality theory assumes that people work only for money and that a person will be motivated to work if monetary rewards and penalties are tied directly to his or her performance. The instrumentality theory emerged in the second half of the nineteenth century and is rooted in the scientific management methods of Taylor (1911), who wrote: "It is impossible, through any long period of time, to get workmen to work much harder than the average men around them unless they are assured a large and permanent increase in their pay."

Motivation strategy based on this approach has been widely adopted, is still in use, and can be successful in some circumstances. But it is based exclusively on a system of external controls and fails to recognize a number of other human needs.

Needs Theory

Needs theory assumes that all behaviors are motivated by unsatisfied needs. An unsatisfied need creates a state of disequilibrium. To restore balance, a goal that satisfies the need will be identified, and a behavior pathway leading to the achievement of the goal will be selected. This theory states that not all needs are equally important to a person at any one time. Some needs may provide more powerful impetus toward a goal than others, depending on an individual's background and present situation. This theory also recognizes that the same need can be satisfied by a number of different goals and that one goal can satisfy a number of needs. Within this basic outline, there are three versions of the needs theory. Maslow's "hierarchy of needs" is the earliest and the most famous needs theory.

Maslow (1954) suggests that there are five major need categories that apply to people in general, starting with the basic physiological needs (oxygen, food, and water) and leading through a hierarchy of psychological needs: *safety* (protection against danger and risk), *social* (love, affection, and group acceptance), *esteem* (self-esteem and prestige), and *self-fulfillment* (potentialities and skills). This theory states that, when a lower need is satisfied, the next highest becomes dominant, and the individual's attention turns to satisfying this higher need. The need for self-fulfillment can never be satisfied. The most important point of this theory is that only an unsatisfied need can motivate a behavior and that the dominant need is the prime motivator. One of the implications of Maslow's theory is that the higher-order needs for esteem and self-fulfillment provide the greatest impetus to motivation, and these may not have a link to money.

Expectancy Theory

Vroom (1964), who developed the expectancy theory, defines *expectancy* as a momentary belief concerning the likelihood that a particular act will be followed by a particular outcome. This theory states that motivation is likely only when a clearly perceived relationship exists between performance and outcome and satisfies the need. This theory can explain why extrinsic financial motivation works only if the link between effort and reward is clear, and the value of the reward is worth the effort.

This theory was further developed by Porter and Lawler (1968). They suggest that two factors determine the effort people put into their jobs: the *value* of the reward (in terms of the degree of need satisfaction) and the *probability* (expectation) that rewards will depend on effort as perceived by the individual. Thus, the greater the value a set of rewards, and the higher the probability that receiving each reward depends on the effort, the greater will be the effort put forth. Put in economic terms, effort (EF) will depend on the expected utility (EV) of the reward, which equals the total utility (TU) of the reward multiplied by the probability (P) that the effort will be linked to the reward, that is:

$$EF = f(EV) \text{ and } EV = TU \times P.$$

Goal Theory

The *goal theory* was developed by Latham and Locke (1979). This theory states that motivation and performance are higher under three conditions. First, individuals set specific goals. Efforts without clearly defined goals cannot be expected to motivate good performance. Second, goals are difficult and challenging to achieve, but people accept them and make commitments to achieving them. Third, feedback on performance allows the individual to rate his or her performance in relation to the goal, so that any necessary adjustments in effort can be made.

Reactance Theory

The *reactance theory* was formulated by Brehm (1966). This theory assumes that people are aware of their needs and the behavior necessary to satisfy these needs. If they have the freedom to behave as they wish, they will choose the behavior that maximizes their need for satisfaction. If their freedom to act is threatened, however, people will react to avoid the loss of freedom. According to this theory, individuals are not passive receivers and responders. Instead, they actively strive to make sense of their environment and to reduce uncertainty by seeking to control factors that influence rewards. The implication of this theory is that motivation methods may not work unless peoples' own values and orientations are understood, and the motivation methods are based on and aligned with that understanding.

Equity Theory

The *equity theory* was first reported by Adams (1965). This theory states that people will be better motivated if they think they are being treated fairly and demotivated if they think they are being treated unfairly. This theory is concerned with the people's perceptions about how they are treated as compared with others. Here, equity involves feelings and perceptions, and it is always a comparative process. It is different from *equality*, which means treating every person the same; this would be "inequitable" if they deserve to be treated differently.

Self-Efficacy Theory

The *self-efficacy theory* was developed by Bandura (1982). It is concerned with an individual's self-belief that he will be able to accomplish certain tasks, achieve certain goals, or learn certain things. According to this theory, people are more likely to be motivated to do a better job if they believe they are able to do so.

Social Learning Theory

The *social learning theory* was developed by Bandura (1977). This theory combines both expectancy theory, as described above, and *behavioral theory,* which emphasizes that behavior is determined by past experiences and plays down the significance of internal factors that affect people's motivation. Social learning theory recognizes that people's behavior is determined by past experiences that reinforce the behavior through repeated actions, as well as by internal psychological factors, especially expectations about the value of goals. It recognizes that while the situation will affect individual behavior, individuals will simultaneously influence the situation. This theory implies that people's motivation is determined by both internal and external factors and that incentive schemes that manipulate only the external factors and ignore the internal ones may not be effective in motivating people.

Attribution Theory

The *attribution theory* is concerned with how performance is explained after efforts have been expended on a particular task (Armstrong 1995). Four types of explanation may be used to account for either successes or failure: ability, effort, task difficulty, and luck. If the success or failure is explained in terms of effort, then high motivation may follow. If the success or failure can be explained by task difficulty or luck, the result may be a loss of motivation. This theory implies that success or failure may be affected by other factors besides effort. If the performance is highly related to other factors, such as luck and task difficulty, the outcome-related reward will be distorted, and motivation cannot be provided in this case. The reasonable reward can be based only on effort and ability.

Role Model Theory

Role model theory recognizes that people are more likely to be motivated if a high-performing role model can be provided, because they want to emulate the model to get things done. This theory implies that motivation schemes can be more effective if an ideal performance can be copied, and it provides information about the possibility of achieving a better performance and the necessary behavior to do it.

A Summary of the Motivation Theories

According to the above theories, people will be better motivated if rewards can be provided to motivate them both intrinsically and extrinsically; incentive schemes are designed by making use of their understood needs and wants; the rewards are linked to efforts; the performance goal is challenging and individuals accept and are committed to it; the rewards are perceived to be equitable; people feel confident they can perform better; the incentive schemes are in line with both expectations and the individual's goals and values; the incentive scheme design takes into consideration outcome uncertainty that may be unrelated to the effort contribution; and a model of positive leadership can be provided in the process of performance.

Financial Incentive, Motivation, and Performance

Payment in the form of money is the most obvious extrinsic reward. It provides the means of achieving a number of different ends and is a powerful motivating force because it is directly or indirectly linked to the satisfaction of many needs.

First of all, money can satisfy the basic needs for survival and security. With money coming in regularly, a person can buy goods and services to satisfy basic needs. Without money, most people cannot survive. Second, money can help satisfy the need for self-esteem, because money is usually regarded as a sign of status and can sometimes be used to gain prestige (e.g., through charitable donations). Third, increasing the remuneration related to people's performance helps them feel they are valued and provides a tangible sign of recognition.

One of the crucial questions is, Do financial incentives motivate people? The answer is yes for individuals who are strongly motivated by money and whose expectations of financial reward are high. The answer may be no for individuals who consider other motivators more important and to whom the marginal utility of money per unit of effort is less than the marginal utility of other gains per unit of effort. As Herzberg and Mausner (1957) point out, although the lack of money can cause dissatisfaction, having money does not confer lasting satisfaction. Apart from financial remuneration, other things may also be important. As Armstrong (1995) stated, "These include the equitable payment system, real opportunities for promotion, considerate and participative management, a reasonable degree of social interaction at work, interesting and varied tasks and a high degree of control over work pace and work methods. The degree of satisfaction obtained by individuals, however, depends largely on their own needs and expectations, and the environment in which they work."

In general, the effectiveness of the financial incentive varies with the individual and with the same individual at different times and in different situations. A good incentive scheme should be based on a thorough understanding of the targeted people and the situation in which people value the financial reward.

The major assumption of incentive schemes is that the financial reward will motivate people and the motivation will lead to better performance. However, whether better performance can be achieved depends on whether the financial reward does, in fact, motivate the targeted people. Performance quality is determined by motivations from numerous internal and external factors, and the financial incentive is only one of them. Human being's objectives encompass much more than money earnings. Designing incentive schemes to motivate high work performance is all well and good, but the test is in performance. Some incentives work in some contexts; some do not work in any context. But one thing is sure: an incentive scheme design that emphasizes financial incentives to the exclusion of all the other ways of motivating people is incomplete and headed for obsolescence.

CONCEPTS AND METHODS OF PERFORMANCE-RELATED PAY

Performance-related pay (PRP) is a method of payment in which additional payment or payment progression is directly linked to performance and contribution. Individuals and organizations can use PRP to pay individuals, groups of people, or other organizations. *Performance* means how well or poorly a task is executed against a set target; thus it is a measure against the performance target.

Traditionally, payments in the private sector are divided into two major categories: payment based on *time* and payment based on *results*. A time-based payment may be adjusted for seniority, skill, and competence. Results-based payment refers to all types of pay based on performance schemes: the PRP, individual piecework, work-measured schemes, measured daywork, group incentive schemes, executive bonus systems, gainsharing, profit sharing, and profit-related pay. Pay for performance is a much broader term than the performance-related pay, which is only one type of pay for performance.

There are some differences in PRP, bonus (a single, lump-sum payment), and merit pay (payment when performance exceeds the prescribed performance level), but they can be taken as synonyms because all entail an additional payment linked to performance as measured against some target (Appelbaum and Mackenzie 1996). There is, however, one exception: the PRP is sometimes used as a method for deciding increases in base salary.

Armstrong (1995) identifies the arguments for and against PRP. The arguments for PRP include: (1) rewarding people according to their contribution is just and equitable; (2) PRP provides a tangible means of recognizing achievement; (3) PRP is a means of ensuring that everyone understands an organization's performance imperatives; and (4) PRP works as an incentive because money is usually the best motivator. The arguments against PRP include the following: (1) there is little evidence that people are motivated by their expectations of the rewards they will get from PRP, especially as these are often quite small; (2) less-confident employees will not be motivated, because they do not expect to receive the reward; (3) individual performance is difficult to measure objectively, and performance is therefore likely to be unfairly assessed; (4) people are encouraged to focus narrowly on the tasks that can earn them extra money and therefore become less concerned about longer-term issues, such as quality and innovation; if undue emphasis is put on individual performance, teamwork will suffer; and (5) PRP is likely to lead to payment drift (pay rises faster than performance) without appropriate controls.

Operation

The operation or implementation of performance-related pay includes setting the targets for performance, measuring and evaluating performance, relating payment to the level of performance, and introducing performance-related pay through a number of implementation steps.

Setting Targets

Performance-related pay requires the organization to set specific targets for performance in relation to the organization's overall objectives. The target-setting process may be an independent work component of the PRP, or it may be linked to the whole body of performance management or management by objectives, a management method developed in the 1960s (Humble 1970). Because the objectives are different from organization to organization, the targets vary. Even for organizations with the same objectives, specific targets may vary a great deal, because the targets are based on specific situations within each organization.

What, then, is a target? A *target* describes something that has to be accomplished. It defines what an organization, department, team, or individual is expected to achieve. Targets, according to their nature, can be divided into work targets and development targets. A *work target* refers to the result to be achieved or the contribution to be made by individuals, teams, and organizations. A *development target* describes progress that should be made in performance or skills, knowledge, and competence related to improved performance. The target can be *qualitative* or *quantitative,* according to the measurability of the target and to specific situations.

Targets can be divided into different levels. The organizational target can be set by the organization itself for managerial purposes, or it can be set by an agency above the organization to determine rewards (including payment) and punishments to the organization. Departmental or team targets are the breakdowns of the organizational target, and the department or team target can be further broken down into individual targets. One requirement in the breakdown process is that the achievement of lower-level targets should automatically result in the achievement of higher-level targets.

Setting targets is the first step in PRP design, and it is of key importance. A good work target should be able to meet the following seven requirements: (1) *consistency*—the specific targets of the organization should be consistent with its overall objectives, and lower-level targets should be consistent with higher-level targets; (2) *challenge*—the target should be high enough to stimulate high standards of performance and to encourage progress; (3) *measurability*—the target must be precise, clear, well-defined, and related to the quantitative or the qualitative performance measures; (4) *achievability*—the target should be within the control of the targeted people and within achievement capacities in terms of resources (such as personnel, money, time, and equipment); (5) *acceptance*—the target must be accepted by the individuals called upon to achieve it, and these people must be committed to making the effort to achieve it; (6) *time frame*—the target should be related to a defined time scale; and (7) *teamwork orientation*—the target should be couched in terms that emphasize teamwork as well as individual achievement.

Evaluating Performance

PRP requires measurement of performance against the set targets. According to the targets, measures can be divided into several types: (1) *money measures*—include profit, revenue, cost reduction; (2) *time measures*—include performance against timetables, the amount of backlog, the rate of absence, and the length of work; (3) *work measures*—include the quantity and the quality of work; (4) *effect measures*—the outcome of the efforts or of the work done, such as the attainment of certain standards or changes in staff and client behavior; and (5) *reaction measures*—the subjective responses by the relevant people, such as the ratings provided by peers and clients.

The measurement of performance can use single or several measures or a weighted index of multimeasures. The measurements can describe individual performance, group or team performance, or organizational performance, depending on whether the payees are individuals, teams, or organizations. To evaluate performance under PRP, in addition to targets and performance measurements, also needed are a good information system to provide enough reliable data and an appraisal task force with the necessary expertise. The evaluation of performance is more an art than a science. No standard approach is suitable in every situation. A well-designed performance evaluation depends on properly defined targets and measurement tools that correctly reflect the degree to which targets are reached.

Relating Pay to Performance

After the performance of the payee has been appraised, the results should be correlated with the amount of additional payment. Three questions need to be answered to relate performance to rewards:

- How many people (if the payees are individuals) are expected to receive the PRP? This question is associated with the scope of the PRP.

- How much should be paid? This question is associated with the depth of payment.

- What should be the payment gap, that is, the difference between the highest and lowest bonus?

The answers to these questions depend on several considerations, including the organization's ability to pay, the total payment relative to the market rate, and the objectives of PRP schemes. If the PRP budget is limited, the incentive-payment scheme usually cannot guarantee that everyone can get a bonus, meaning that the scope of the PRP is small. If the market rate is higher, the scheme must expand the scope of payment and ensure that everybody in the organization is paid equitably. Otherwise, the organization cannot attract and motivate people. If the main objective of the scheme is to attract high-tech people, the scope of payment may be limited to only those individuals, and the amount of payment may be very high.

Some rules of thumb govern the size of payment. During the 1960s, it was generally believed that bonuses below 15 percent of the base payment are usually too low to encourage increased effort, while bonuses above 35 percent are often classed as "run-away" incentives (Mangum 1964). Recently it was suggested that a 10 to 15 percent merit-based increase over the basic pay is likely to have some impact on employee motivation (Beaumont 1993). Armstrong (1995) suggests that high performers may deserve and expect rewards of at least 10 percent and more; people whose level of performance is well above average may merit an increase of between 8 and 10 percent; average performers may expect an increase of between 5 and 7 percent of their base pay; an increase of between 3 and 5 percent may be justified for individuals who are making steady progress. Armstrong also suggests that a performance-related increase of less than 3 percent is hardly worth giving.

Introducing Performance-Related Pay

Armstrong (1995) outlines an eight-step process for introducing PRP.

- *Step 1. Assess the reasons for PRP.* Why is PRP wanted? What are the objectives for introducing it?

- *Step 2. Assess the readiness for PRP.* Is PRP acceptable to the employees according to the culture of the organization? Is the requisite performance management process in place for successful PRP? Are the necessary resources and skills available for PRP? Is implementing PRP cost-effective?

- *Step 3. Decide whether or not to introduce PRP.* Does the result of the Step 2 assessment indicate that PRP is right for this organization? If yes, can the objective be realized (i.e., improving the performance, delivering the message about performance expectations, focusing attention on key issues, maintaining a competitive pay position)?

- *Step 4. Involve the employees.* After deciding to introduce PRP, employees should be involved. How should the employees be informed of the organization's objectives in introducing PRP? How can the organization minimize employees' concerns about PRP? How should employees be consulted and involved?

- *Step 5. Design the scheme.* What are the criteria that determine the rewards (input, process, and output)? How should performance be measured against these criteria? How many people are expected to get the reward? What are the amounts of rewards in relation to the degrees of performance? How is the scheme managed?

- *Step 6. Brief and train the staff.* How will the organization brief and train the scheme managers? How will the employees be briefed about the benefit of PRP and the way it will work?

- *Step 7. Implement the scheme.* Should the scheme be piloted before full introduction? How will the implementation be monitored?

- *Step 8. Evaluate the scheme.* Are the performance targets well established in terms of their measurability? How will continuous monitoring and evaluation be carried out? Who will do it?

In addition to these eight steps, there are several criteria, including six "golden rules" for mounting a successful PRP scheme (Ferris, Rowland, and Buckley 1990; Armstrong 1995; Beaumont 1993). First, individuals and teams need to be clear about the targets and the required standards of performance. Second, they must be able to influence their performance by changing their behavior. Third, performance should measurable, and individual performers should be ranked. Fourth, people should be clear about the rewards they will receive for achieving the required end results. Fifth, the rewards should be meaningful enough to motivate people to make enough effort to reach the targets, which will make the whole effort to implement the PRP worthwhile. Sixth, the bonus formula should be easy to understand.

The Existence of PRP in Nonhealth Sectors

Motivation has been a challenge as long as the employer-employee relationship has been around. Payment systems using pay to motivate performance came into existence at the end of the 19th century as part of a scientific management movement. During World War II, incentive-payment systems developed rapidly because of the need to increase production of war wares. Since then, various incentive-payment systems have been continuously refined as methods for motivating performance and production improvements (Mangum 1964; Marriott 1968).

PRP, as one of these incentive-payment methods, has become a major method for determining pay progression and has now largely replaced the fixed-incremental system introduced in the private sector during the income-policy era in the 1970s. A survey conducted in the United Kingdom shows that 40 percent of organizations introduced PRP in the 10 years prior to 1992 (Cannell and Wood 1992). According to a study in the United States, 68 percent of 2,000 large U.S. companies polled in 1993 offered incentive compensation to all of their salaried employees, up from 47 percent in 1990.

Although PRP was expanded in the past two decades, views on its success conflict. Some studies show that the PRP improved performance (Cameron 1995), other studies show that it failed to realize the goal of implementing the system (Kohn 1993). Bevan and Thomson's (1991) study of performance management found no strong link between pay and improved company performance. Cannell and Wood (1992) could find no perceived relationship between pay, motivation, and either individual or organizational performance. A U.S. study by Berlet and Cravens (1991) demonstrated a random relationship between executive pay and company financial performance for 163 firms between 1987 and 1989. In October 1990, *Personnel Today* magazine[1] reported that only 11 percent of the organizations surveyed believe that their schemes delivered improved performance. A U.S. review concluded that even if the incentive schemes were related to improved performance, it was difficult to attribute this to the nature of the schemes because many other changes were taking place at the same time (Martin 1994). It is not clear whether the PRP failed because of the bad design and poor implementation or because of the scheme per se (because pay is not a good motivator).

Despite the lack of any definitive evidence that PRP has led to improved performance in the private sector, the introduction of the PRP into the public sector—education, mail service, and police services, for example—is becoming increasingly widespread (Armstrong 1993; Procter 1993; Brown 1994). In recent years, the spread of the PRP arrangement into the public sector has been particularly notable in a number of countries. For example, in Britain some 400,000 out of a total of 585,000 civil servants in 1989 had some part of their pay determined by performance appraisals (Beaumont 1991). Another example is the Functional Position System, introduced in Indonesia in 1980 and linking pay with performance for certain occupational categories of civil servants (Chernichovsky and Bayulken 1995). The spread of PRP in the public sector has certainly not been without difficulties and controversies. For example, the operation of the PRP in Britain's Inland Revenue department has been criticized for setting confused targets and allowing inadequate time for satisfactory performance appraisal, and a workforce survey suggested that only a small minority believe that the scheme enhanced their job motivation and performance (Beaumont 1993). A review of PRP in the public sector indicates little empirical support for the link between pay and performance (Marsden and Richardson 1994).

PERFORMANCE-RELATED PAY IN THE HEALTH CARE SECTOR

Generally speaking, PRP in the health sector was introduced from the private and other public sectors at the end of the 1980s. Its application is now spreading rapidly to many areas of the health sector.

The Existence of PRP in the Health Sector

PRP is used as a method for paying health care managers, nurses, dentists, hospital-based doctors, office-based doctors, and lab technicians. The PRP for managers was reported by the United Kingdom at the end of the 1980s. A report in the *Health Service Journal* in Britain states that, in the United Kingdom, 1,400 general managers and board-level mangers in regions and districts within the National Health Service system were covered by PRP schemes in 1988 and that 7,000 additional middle-level managers would be entitled to PRP coverage in later years (Davies 1988). The PRP for nurses and nursing executives was widely reported in North America and the United Kingdom (Buchan 1993a; Buchan 1993b; Castledine 1993; Buchan and Thompson 1993). Scola (1990) reported on the introduction of PRP to the dental practice in the United Kingdom after three years of experience. Application of PRP to hospital-based doctors was reported in the United States (Bledsoe, Leisy, and Rodeghero 1995;

Berwick 1995) and in the United Kingdom (Lewis 1990; Bloor and Maynard 1992; Bloor, Maynard, and Street 1992; Griffin 1993; Hern 1994; Macara 1995; Smith and Simpson 1994). In some cases, office-based doctors are rewarded based on performance either by a third party (Hutchison 1996; Schlackman 1993) or by their employer (Hemenway et al. 1990). Winkelman, Aitken, and Wybenga (1991) reported on the utilization of PRP in hospital clinical laboratories in the United States.

The Arguments for and against PRP in Health Care

Although PRP is increasingly important in health care, there is no definitive evidence endorsing its effectiveness. Arguments for and against PRP are identified in the literature.

Several benefits are claimed for the PRP. First, it can be used to reward a good contribution (combined effort and capability). Second, it enables managers to send people powerful messages about whether they want them to stay. Third, it forces managers to evaluate their staff. The most important benefit claimed is that it does motivate people to perform better (Boyce and Morris 1992). Although PRP is increasingly being put into practice, little successful experience has been reported. The experience in U.S. nursing suggests that such schemes can be developed successfully, but there is little research evidence to demonstrate their effectiveness (Faulkner 1991).

While health care administrators and managers are keen to introduce PRP schemes, academics show a great deal of opposition. They claim that health care lacks the basic requirements to undertake PRP (Griffin 1993). First, according to expectancy theory, employees must believe that improved performance will be rewarded. It means that the health care organization must have the financial capacity to compensate employees for better performance, and the pay must be equitable. But, due to limitation in resources and cost-control pressures, health care employers have to choose whether to reward a handful of high performers or spread performance payments more thinly across the whole workforce. The first choice will undermine the majority of employees' confidence about the link between performance and reward, while the second choice will lead to almost equal distribution of the bonus budget and provide little incentive to better performance.

Second, performance must be measurable and clearly attributable to individuals. In health care, however, cooperation between medical staff is needed for better quality; better performance is usually the outcome of joint efforts; and the performance of the medical staff is difficult to measure. In a number of jobs, what can be measured is not meaningful, and what is meaningful cannot be measured. For example, the number of night shifts taken over by a doctor may represent his work efforts, but it may not necessarily mean better performance and better quality. The patient's health outcome is the soundest evidence of better performance, but outcome is usually difficult to measure.

Third, rewards must be large enough to be valued by the medical staff. In a developed nation where doctors are already well paid and the labor cost of medical care accounts for the main part of the medical expenditure (75 percent of NHS cost in the United Kingdom [Bloor, Maynard and Street 1992]), added pay will further inflate costs. In a developing country where doctors are paid almost equally to other comparable disciplines, additional pay will raise medical doctors' earnings but their performance may not increase significantly. Griffin (1993) argues that payment is just one of the factors that motivate the medical profession. Participation, job enrichment, recognition, decision-making authority in resource allocation, working environment, and other intangibles can be equally important sources of motivation.

Contrary to the general belief, Martin (1994) offers little comfort for managers and others who wish to introduce a form of individual PRP into nursing, simply because the prerequisites for a successful PRP scheme do not exist. Reviewing the literature, Lemieux-Charles (1994) states that the nature of the performance to be evaluated in medical care is ambiguous and that there are still challenges of developing standards, guidelines, and clinical policies as well as defining quality in relation to performance.

Cases of Performance-Related Pay

PRP has been implemented in many countries. In this section, summaries of the cases of the implementation of PRP are provided, including those in the United Kingdom, the United States and Canada, and Indonesia.

Merit Award in the United Kingdom

The merit-award system was born at the start of the National Health Service (NHS) in the United Kingdom in 1948. Aneurin Bevan, the minister of health, recognized that retaining the service of the best doctors takes money, and the merit award was designed to attract the best medical consultants (salaried hospital-based doctors). Financial rewards are based on consultants' distinguished contributions to their profession through clinical excellence, teaching and training, and research and innovation; outstanding management was added later (Hern 1994). These contributions, judged by peer review, are not linked to any tangible individual or organizational objective (Lewis 1990). The NHS merit-award system is being used as an example of PRP, although it does not exactly fit the previous definition, because the evaluation is a rank-order process and is not related to set targets.

In practice, candidates are nominated by hospital peers, and a nationwide evaluation is organized each year. The awards are divided into four levels: A^+, A, B, and C. The award for A^+ is about £46,000 (equivalent to US$69,000 at an exchange rate of £1 to US$1.50), £35,000 for A, £20,000 for B, and about

£10,000 for C. The award is in addition to the consultant's annual base salary of about £40,000. Many consultants also have private practices, earning from this source alone an average of £40,000 annually (Bloor and Maynard 1992). Thus, the award makes up one third to one half of the doctor's income. About one third of the consultants hold an award, and more than 60 percent receive one before retirement.

Tobias (1994) claims the merit-award system is effective. During the first half of the 20th century, one of its more remarkable features was that the most outstanding individuals were indeed attracted to stay within the NHS, usually working as consultants in large hospitals.

Criticism of the merit-award scheme has increased, however, since the 1990s. It is criticized for "stuffing their mouths with gold," and the merit pay's efficacy is believed to be based more on faith than hard evidence (Griffin 1993). Hern (1994) claims that the merit-award system is biased because of the difficulties of measuring excellence in clinical practice, teaching, and research contributions. Several health economists at the Centre for Health Economics at York University in the United Kingdom consider such a merit award outdated and noncompliant with the Department of Health guidelines that say increases in medical pay should be only sufficient to recruit, retain, and motivate staff of the right caliber. Critics suggest that payments to hospital-based doctors should be based on their targeted performance (Bloor, Maynard, and Street 1992).

PRP in the United Kingdom

Minister Bevan's merit award was more on the cutting edge of payment practices than he realized at the time. During the 1990s, PRP became one of the "buzz" concepts in the health sector, and many of the people challenging the effectiveness of merit pay suggested its replacement with PRP. Throughout the history of the NHS, hospital-based doctors have been paid salaries and given raises based on their experience and seniority. Later it was suggested that PRP should be based, at least in part, on actual performance against performance targets. The desire to move toward PRP was expressed in the Citizen's Charter in the United Kingdom, which proposed that pay for public sector employees should be more closely related to performance (Smith and Simpson 1994). Following the practice of PRP for NHS managers and other public sector employees, the government decided to introduce PRP for medical consultants and nurses in the early 1990s. The introduction of PRP meant the end of nationally consistent pay scales for doctors and the end of the related review body (Smith and Simpson 1994). The Review Body on Doctors' and Dentists' Remuneration substantially accepted the government proposal for introducing locally determined PRP for consultants.

The U.K. government's PRP proposal in the early 1990s met immediate resistance from the medical profession and some academics. Four hundred doctors struggled to get to London on a rail-strike day in a bank holiday week to vent their feelings at a special conference of the British Medical Association, and many more wrote individually to their member of parliament to explain why the policy would be so disastrous for the NHS. The doctors reportedly opposed the proposal in the belief that PRP would be biased because their performances are difficult to measure and they worried about payment reductions (Macara 1995).

Several publications stated that widespread introduction of PRP into the NHS would have, at best, no impact on individual and organizational performance and, at worst, would result in a decline in morale and motivation (Griffin 1993; Smith and Simpson 1994). At the time of this writing, the authors are not clear about whether the government proposal of the PRP will be implemented.

PRP in North America

PRP is fairly new in health care in North America, but it is spreading rapidly. Across the United States, medical businesses are rethinking the way performance is rewarded (Flarey 1991), and today's nurse executives are challenged to design a management compensation system that rewards achievement, performance, and contribution. According to a membership survey of the American Organization of Nurse Executives, a growing number of nurse executives receive compensation bonuses based on the criteria of budget performance, patient satisfaction, and relations with physicians and other nurses (Bell 1991). According to two benefit and compensation surveys in the United States, in an effort to obtain the greatest possible return on their investment in physician employees, many health care organizations are linking physician pay and benefits to improved performance (Bledsoe, Leisy, and Rodeghero 1995).

The reported effectiveness of PRP schemes in the United States is not, however, conclusive. Some observers state that preliminary results show performance improvements (Hopkins 1995), while others claim that some features of the PRP schemes are toxic to systemic improvement, that contingent rewards doled out by supervisors cause decreased focus on customer needs and decreased innovation, and that "pay for performance" may mark a naive understanding of the complexities of human motivation (Berwick 1995).

While most of the PRP schemes implemented are targeted at quality and performance improvement, some of them are revenue oriented. Hemenway et al. (1990) report on a case of revenue-oriented incentive payment in the United States, Health Stop, a chain of investor-owned, ambulatory, primary care centers. Founded in 1983, Health Stop became the largest chain of its kind, with 120 centers in 11 cities. Until 1985, physicians working for Health Stop were paid a flat rate of US$28 an hour. In the middle of 1985, a payment system involving bonus incentives was introduced, according to which physicians would receive either a flat fee or a percentage (24 percent up to US$24,000 and 15 percent thereafter) of the gross monthly charges they generated, whichever was higher. During Hemenway's study period, the physicians increased the number of laboratory tests performed per patient visit by 23 percent and the number of X-ray films per visit by 16 percent. Total charges per month, adjusted for inflation, grew 20 percent, mostly as a result of a 12 percent increase in the average number of patient visits per month. The physicians' wages increased about 19 percent. Hemenway et al. conclude that substantial monetary incentives based on individual performance may induce a group of physicians to increase the intensity of their practice, even though not all of them benefit from the incentives. This case shows that taking revenue as an indicator of performance may provide incentives for doctors to provide unnecessary care and induce patient demand. The organization's financial performance may improve, but at the unnecessary cost of the patients and purchasers.

Canada is one of the earliest countries to introduce PRP to nursing (Wasylak 1991), but no literature on PRP for doctors was found.

PRP in Developing Countries

PRP schemes in the health sector in developing counties were to come into existence in the early 1990s together with other reforms, such as decentralization, ownership-management separation in public health facilities, and privatization of health care provision. However, only a few publications on the introduction of PRP are available, and they deal mainly with two countries, China and Indonesia. Because PRP schemes in China are examined in chapter 8 of this volume, only the PRP scheme in Indonesia is discussed here, based mainly on Chernichovsky and Bayulken (1995).

Payment to medical doctors in publicly owned health facilities in Indonesia was traditionally based on consistent salaries. Promotions and related salary increases were based on experience and seniority. This payment system, characterized by low and fairly uniform pay, leads to low morale in public service. While engaged in public service, doctors usually also maintain private practices for extra earnings. In the early 1990s, after implementation of PRP schemes for civil servants in other sectors, the PRP scheme for civil doctors, the Functional Position System, was introduced nationwide. Under this arrangement, doctors are evaluated against three groups of factors: *knowledge*—education, training, and experience; *performance*—the main tasks of the job; and *professional development*—teaching, scientific work, seminars, and membership in specific teams and professional organizations. Points are allocated for each factor. The accumulation of these points leads to promotion on a professional or technical ladder and to financial rewards. The higher the position, the more additional points are needed for the next promotion. Doctors who achieve the required rating in two years can then be promoted. If an individual's rating exceeds the minimum score required, the balance is credited toward the next promotion. An individual who does not achieve the minimum rating within two years can keep accumulating points toward the basic requirement but cannot be considered for promotion until the next promotion period.

In this PRP scheme, the evaluation of a doctor's performance leads to two types of rewards: one is promotion related (once promoted, he will get a higher salary); the other is a bonus linked to the performance score. This system is expected to achieve better career development, performance, and policy goal attainment by manipulating the scores allocated to these factors. The study conducted by Chernichovsky and Bayulken reveals that this system is ineffective, however, because of several shortcomings. First, the performance measure disregards effort, time inputs, and quality indicators and consequently fails to provide incentives for professional excellence and career development. Second, the system fails to provide enough resources to reward people and induce the doctors to expend more effort in their civil service activities. Third, the system does not achieve the intended policy objectives. Still, Indonesia's payment reform is said to be bold and innovative, and it is an example of how to develop new types of payment systems for both developed and developing countries as a substitute for or supplement to salary, fee for service, and capitation payment. Because system development is a gradual maturation process, further adjustment and modification may lead to success.

Problems and Future Research

Since the early 1990s, performance-related pay for health care providers has been a hot topic in health policy and management. From a review of the literature, however, several problems worth mentioning stand out. First, the concept of PRP in health care is being introduced from the private sector and other public sectors without definitive evidence that it works. It is generally believed that health care is less suitable for PRP than the industrial sector and some public sectors such as education and police services, simply because medical performance is difficult to measure. Considering the 50:50 success and failure rate in the introduction of PRP in the private sector, the blind introduction of PRP to health care is bound to carry a higher risk of failure and, with failure, heavy costs.

Second, while many commentators argue the pros and cons of PRP in health care, sound, scientific evaluations of PRP schemes are generally lacking. So far, it is not clear whether the failure of some PRP schemes signals a fundamental problem, such as that money is not a major motivator, or whether it is a design and implementation problem that can be solved. PRP is ultimately a practical issue, and its effectiveness should be tested empirically. At present, researchers seem to be devoting their energy to arguing against and for PRP in health care, while putting little effort into testing the effectiveness of the many PRP schemes that are being put into practice. Policy makers and health care managers are basing their decisions to go ahead with PRP on ideology rather than scientific evidence. For lack of convincing empirical evidence, researchers' appeals have not been able to stop this movement.

Third, PRP is both a managerial and a health economics and policy issue. But in the debate, its health economics and policy aspects are being neglected, as evidenced by the dearth of literature by health economists on PRP.

PRP is a managerial issue because it is regarded as a reward-management system that an organization can use to motivate its employees to achieve its managerial goals. It is a health economics and policy issue for two main reasons. First,

PRP to providers is closely related to their behavior, which is highly relevant to the allocation and utilization of health care resources. Second, PRP schemes can be conducted as government policy on the national or regional levels, as in the United Kingdom and Indonesia. When doctors (as hospital employees) are paid by the hospital, there are economic and policy implications in the ways the PRP schemes are designed. The hospital, its doctors, and its patients constitute a double agency relationship in which a doctor serves as agent for both hospital and patients. The way the hospital pays the doctor will affect his provision behavior to patients. For example, if the hospital bases payment to doctors on their performance as measured by the revenue generated by each (Hemenway et al. 1990), the doctors will provide more care, and even unnecessary care, for extra income. In that case, more resources will be allocated to less cost-effective care when the resources could be put to better alternative uses. Thus, the introduction, design, and implementation of the PRP schemes, particularly those under national policy, should be considered in the context of health economics and policy. The role of health economists in the design, implementation, and evaluation of PRP schemes cannot be ignored with impunity.

Facing these problems, health policy researchers should direct their attention to the rapid emergence of PRP schemes in both developed and developing countries. Research into the following questions is suggested:

- When policy makers and health care managers decide to introduce PRP, what is the context and what are their intentions?

- How are the successes and failures of PRP related to their design and implementation?

- In what situations and to what extent does the money motivator in PRP work and not work?

- What effects does PRP have on doctors' behavior in providing health care to patients—and on the allocation efficiency of health care resources?

It is expected that as PRP schemes in the health sector develop, health economists and health policy researchers will take an active role in their formulation. The benefits resulting from their involvement would be enormous.

NOTES

This chapter is based on a review of the literature by the authors when Xingzhu Liu was pursuing his PhD under the supervision of Professor Anne Mills at the London School of Hygiene and Tropical Medicine. The initial work was funded by the United Nations Development Programme/World Bank/World Health Organization Special Programme for Research and Training in Tropical Diseases and the Overseas Research Students Awards Scheme in the United Kingdom. The authors are also grateful for the follow-up support provided by the World Bank and Abt Associates Inc., Bethesda, Maryland.

1. Wyatt Consultants, *Personnel Today* 1990 (October): 28–31.

REFERENCES

Adams, J.S. 1965. "Injustice in Social Exchange." In *Advances in Experimental Psychology*, ed. L. Berkowirtz. New York, NY: Academic Press.

Appelbaum, S.H., and L. Mackenzie. 1996. "Compensation in the Year 2000: Pay for Performance?" *Health Manpower Management* 22(3): 31–39.

Armstrong, M. 1995. *A Handbook of Personnel Management Practice*. London: Kogan Page.

———. 1993. *Management Reward System*. London: Open University Press.

Bandura, A. 1982. "Self-Efficacy Mechanism in Human Agency." *American Psychologist* 37: 122–47.

———. 1977. *Social Learning Theory*. Englewood Cliffs, NJ: Prentice-Hall.

Beaumont, P.B. 1993. *Human Resource Management: Key Concepts and Skills*. London: Sage Publications.

———. 1991. *Public Sector Industrial Relations*. London: Routledge.

Bell, E. A. 1991. "Pay for Performance: Motivating the Chief Nurse Executive." *Nursing Economics* 92: 92–96.

Berlet, K.R., and D.M. Cravens. 1991. *Performance Pay as a Competitive Weapon: A Compensation Policy Model for the 1990s*. New York, NY: John Wiley.

Berwick, D.M. 1995. "The Toxicity of Pay for Performance." *Quality Management in Health Care* 4(1): 27–33.

Bevan, S., and M. Thompson. 1991. "Performance Management at the Crossroads." *Personnel Management* (November): 36–39.

Bledsoe, D.R., W.B. Leisy, and J.A. Rodeghero. 1995. "Tying Physician Incentive Pay to Performance." *Healthcare Finance and Management* 49(12): 40–44.

Bloor, K., and A. Maynard. 1992. *Rewarding Excellence? Consultants' Distinction Awards and the Need for Reform*. Discussion Paper No. 100. York, United Kingdom: University of York, Centre for Health Economics.

Bloor, K., A. Maynard, and A. Street. 1992. *How Much Is a Doctor Worth?* Discussion Paper No. 98. York, United Kingdom: University of York, Centre for Health Economics.

Boyce, J., and T. Morris. 1992. "Performance-Related Pay for Hospital Doctors." *British Medical Journal* 305(6846): 131–32.

Brehm, J. W. 1966. *A Theory of Psychological Reactance*. New York, NY: Academic Press.

Brown, D. 1994. "Payroll Pitfalls." *The Health Service Journal* 20: 24–26.

Buchan, J. 1993a. "Performance Pay: Reviewing the Options." *Nursing Standard* 8(10): 29.

———. 1993b."Performance-Related Pay and NHS Nursing." *Nursing Standard* 7(25): 30.

Buchan, J., and M. Thompson. 1993. "Pay and Nursing Performance." *Health Manpower Management* 19(2): 29–31.

Cameron, M. 1995. "Rewarding for Performance: Any Real Progress?" *Journal of Compensation and Benefits* 10(5): 60–63.

Cannell, R.B., and S. Wood. 1992. *Incentive Pay: Impact and Evolution*. London: Institute of Personnel Management.

Castledine, G. 1993. "Can Performance-Related Pay Be Adapted for Nursing?" *British Journal of Nursing* 2(22): 1120–21.

Chernichovsky, D., and C. Bayulken. 1995. "A Pay-for-Performance System for Civil Service Doctors: The Indonesian Experiment." *Social Science and Medicine* 41(2): 155–61.

Davies, P. 1988. "Extending the Flexible Spine of Pay." *Health Service Journal* (December): 1442.

Faulkner, J. 1991. "Salary Equals Performance for Community Health Nurses." *Nursing Management* 22(6): 342–45.

Ferris, G.R., K.M. Rowland, and M.R. Buckley. 1990. *Human Resource Management: Prospective and Issues*. Boston, MA: Allyn & Bacon.

Flarey, D.L. 1991. "Management Compensation: A Reward Systems Approach." *Journal of Nursing Administration* 21(7): 39–46.

Griffin, R.P. 1993. "Why Doesn't Performance Pay Work?" *Health Manpower Management* 19(2): 11–13.

Hannon, K. 1994. "Variable-Pay Programs: Where the Real Raises Are." *Working Woman* 19(3): 17–27.

Hemenway, D., A. Killen, S.B. Cashman, C.L. Parks, and W.J. Bicknell. 1990. "Physicians' Responses to Financial Incentives." *New England Journal of Medicine* 322: 1059–63.

Hern, J.E. 1994. "What Should Be Done about Merit Awards? *British Medical Journal* 308: 973–74.

Herzberg, F.W., and B. Mausner. 1957. *The Motivation to Work*. New York, NY: Wiley.

Hopkins, M.E. 1995. "Gainsharing: Providing Incentive for Process Improvement." *Radiological Management* 17(4): 46–51.

Humble, J. 1970. *Management by Objectives in Action*. Maidenhead, UK: McGraw-Hill.

Hutchison, B., et al. 1996. "Do Physician-Payment Mechanisms Affect Hospital Utilization? A Study of Health Service Organizations in Ontario." *Canadian Medical Association Journal* 154(5): 653–61.

Kohn, A. 1993. "Why Incentive Plans Cannot Work." *Harvard Business Review* 71(5): 54–63.

Latham, G.P., and E. Locke. 1979. "Goal Setting—A Motivation Technique that Works." *Organization Dynamics* 3(Autumn): 68–80.

Lemieux-Charles, L. 1994. "Physicians in Health Care Management: 2. Managing Performance: Who, What, How and When?" *Canadian Medical Association Journal* 150(4): 481–85.

Lewis, E. 1990. "Rewarding Performance." *The Health Service Journal* (December): 1435.

Macara, S. 1995. "Appraisal of Doctors in the NHS: Merit Awards and Performance-Related Pay." *British Journal of Hospital Medicine* 53(3): 111–12.

Mangum, G. 1964. *Wage Incentive Systems*. Berkeley: University of California, Institute of Industrial Relations.

Marriott, R. 1968. *Incentive Payment Systems: A Review of Research and Opinion*. London: Staples Press.

Marsden, D., and R. Richardson. 1994. "The Effects of Merit Pay on Motivation in a Public Service." *British Journal of Industrial Relations* 32(2): 243–62.

Martin, G. 1994. "Performance-Related Pay in Nursing: Theory, Practice and Prospect." *Health Manpower Management* 20(5): 10–17.

Maslow, A. 1954. *Motivation and Personality*. New York, NY: Harper and Row.

Mills, A. 1990. "The Economics of Hospitals in Developing Countries. Part I: Expenditure Patterns." *Health Policy and Planning* 5(2): 107–17.

Porter, L.W., and E.E. Lawler. 1968. *Managerial Attitudes and Performance*. Homewood, IL: Dorsey Press.

Procter, S. 1993. "Performance-Related Pay in Practice: A Critical Perspective." *British Journal of Management* 4(3): 153–60.

Reinhardt, U. 1985. "The Theory of Physician Induced Demand: Reflection after a Decade." *Journal of Health Economics* 4: 187–93.

Schlackman, N. 1993. "Evolution of a Quality-Based Compensation Model: The Third Generation." *American Journal of Medical Quality* 8(2): 103–10.

Scola, C.M. 1990. "Keeping Your Staff. Part 2. Performance Related Pay in Practice." *British Dental Journal* 169(10): 334–36.

Smith, J., and J. Simpson. 1994. "Locally Determined Performance-Related Pay: Better Levers Exist for Improving Performance in a Health Service with Disparate Values." *British Medical Journal* 309: 495–96.

Taylor, F.W. 1911. *Principles of Scientific Management*. New York, NY: Harper.

Tobias, J. 1994. "In Defence of Merit Awards." *British Medical Journal* 308: 974–75.

Vroom, V. 1964. *Work and Motivation*. New York, NY: Wiley.

Wasylak, T.P. 1991. "Pay for Performance." *Canadian Nurse* 87(4): 30–31.

Winkelman, J.W., J.L. Aitken, and D.R. Wybenga. 1991. "Cost Savings in a Hospital Clinical Laboratory with a Pay-for-Performance Incentive Program for Supervisors." *Archives of Pathology and Laboratory Medicine* 115(1): 38–41.

CHAPTER 11

Payment Mechanisms and Provider Behavior

Xingzhu Liu and Anne Mills

Payment mechanisms concern how and how much health care providers are paid. The way providers are paid can create powerful incentives that influence their behavior; and changes in behavior affect the efficiency, quality, and quantity of health care. The hypothetical and empirical linkages between the alternative payment methods, the provider's behavior, and the consequences in terms of efficiency, quality, and quantity of health care services are described in this chapter in an attempt to provide information for designing a reasonable payment system.

An ideal payment system should provide incentives for cost containment, quality assurance, and internal efficiency (productivity) and offer no incentives for over- or underprovision of services. Above all, it should be feasible. However, no existing payment mechanism meets these criteria. Recent studies generally conclude that there will never be a panacea for the payment system and that combining various payment methods may be the best approach.

Developing innovative payment systems will require efforts on both theoretical and empirical studies. Only after providers' objective functions are made clear can their behavior be predicted; and only after their behavior becomes predictable does an ideal payment system become possible. Any recommended payment system should pass scientific tests that demonstrate their effects on provider behavior and performance.

INTRODUCTION

Because payment mechanisms influence provider behavior in delivering health care, and therefore, outcomes, great attention has been devoted to designing health care payment systems within the context of social health insurance schemes and escalating health care costs.

A good payment system is incentive-compatible between payers and providers and promotes efficiency. Thus, its design should be based on an in-depth understanding of provider utility functions and the accurate prediction of provider behavior. Although payment systems appeared with the advent of modern medicine in the 19th century, they did not receive policy attention until the second half of the 20th century when rapid increases in the costs of social health insurance schemes all over the world became a strong driving force for modifying traditional payment systems and developing new systems. New payment methods have come into existence to meet urgent policy needs, but provider utility functions are not yet fully understood, and provider behavior cannot be accurately predicted. A review of current payment methods and a discussion of their pros and cons in terms of provider behavior and its consequences can provide some useful information for designing and choosing appropriate payment systems.

Following this brief introduction, current methods of payment are classified. The third section is a review of these systems and their hypothetical and empirical consequences. In the last section, possible improvements in health care payment systems are discussed.

TAXONOMY OF PAYMENT SYSTEMS

Payment systems can be categorized in several ways. The first and most common method of classification is by the payment base or payment unit. If the payment unit is based on itemized services, it is called *fee-for-service payment*. If the payment unit is based on the number of individuals registered with a service provider, it is a *capitation payment*. If the provider (doctor) is paid based on the time of work, the payment is called *salary*. If based on the number of days a patient stays in the hospital, the payment is a *per diem* or *daily payment*. If based on the number of visits for outpatient services or the number of admissions for inpatient services, it is called a *case payment*. If based on periodic (usually yearly) appropriation of funds from either a flexible or fixed budget and from either a global or itemized budget, it is called a *budget payment*. If an additional payment is provided based on achievements (evaluated against set targets), it is called a *bonus*. The types of payment classified by payment bases are listed in table 11.1.

The second method of classification is related to the timing of the payment or commitment—before or after services are rendered. If prior to service, the payment is called a *prospective payment;* if after services are rendered, a *retrospective payment*. According to these definitions, fee-for-service, salary, and bonus payments are retrospective payments; daily payment, case payment, capitation, and budget are prospective payments.

The third method of classification concerns whether the provider is paid directly by the payer *(direct payment);* otherwise, it is called an *indirect payment*. For example, if the insured patient pays for the services and receives reimbursement from his or her insurer, this is an indirect payment. If a third party pays the provider directly for services rendered to the insured, the payment is a direct payment. Health funds in Germany are an example of indirect payment: the health fund pays a medical association to manage a negotiated budget and to pay providers.

The fourth method of classification is based on the subject of payment, that is, the party paying for the care. The payment can be made out of pocket by patients, by a health fund, or by a third party, which can be a government. In addition, in the case of salaried doctors employed by a hospital, the party paying is the hospital.

TABLE 11.1   Payment Types Classified by Payment Bases

Type of payment	Payment base or unit of payment
Fee for service	Itemized services
Capitation	Individuals registed (number)
Salary	Unit of time worked (e.g., month)
Daily	Hospital stay (number of days)
Case	Visits or admissions (number)
Budget	Yearly appropriation of funds
Bonus	Set performance goals

Source: Authors.

The fifth method of classification considers the object of payment, the party receiving the payment—a doctor or a hospital. The doctor's payment can be divided into payment for office-based doctors and payment for hospital-based doctors.

THE CURRENT PAYMENT SYSTEMS

Payment types according to different payment bases are discussed next in relation to other methods of classification.

Fee for Service

Fee-for-service payment is defined as a method for paying for specific items of medical services, for example, a doctor consultation, specific tests, or specific surgeries. In broad terms, fee-for-service payments also include itemized charges for medical products and drugs, which are often provided together with medical labor services. Fee-for-service payment is similar to the traditional piecework payment, in that the payment is made for each service or product (piece or item). Piecework began in the earliest days of employment; fee-for-service payment for medical services began when the first professional medical practice came into existence (Clarke and Gray 1994).

Fee-for-service payment can be further divided into three subgroups: the open-ended fee, the negotiated fee schedule, and the regulated fee schedule (Ron, Abel-Smith, and Tamburi 1990). The traditional fee-for-service payment consists of *open-ended fees,* charged by doctors according to what the market will bear. This was the main type of payment in the days when medical care was less organized, regulated, and planned than it is today. Fee-for-service payment is still popular in countries such as Canada, the Republic of Korea, and the United States, but elsewhere its importance has been shrinking since the early 20th century. Private practitioners in some countries also charge a market rate, as in the United Kingdom.

The *negotiated fee schedule* came into existence with the establishment of health insurance schemes. To reduce service costs, third parties (social health insurance schemes or private health insurance companies) often negotiate with providers or their associations a set of standard charges for specified services. Countries such as Belgium, France, and Germany use negotiated fee schedules (Normand and Weber 1994), and the United States and Canada are increasingly using them for their social health insurance programs.

The *regulated fee schedule* is a set of standard fees managed by the government. This practice exists in China and many other countries with centrally planned health care systems.

The fee-for-service payment is a method used by patients and third parties to pay office-based doctors, hospital-based doctors, and hospitals. For example, hospital services in China and the Republic of Korea (Ron, Abel-Smith, and Tamburi 1990) are broken down into more than 2,000 items. The regulated fee for these items will be charged to the third party, if a patient is insured, or directly to an uninsured patient. Fee for service can be used to pay hospital-based doctors. In the United States, for example, the vast majority of office-based doctors in many specialties are paid a fee for each service by the patient or the third party (Steinwald 1983). Service fees can be paid directly by the third party (as in France, the Netherlands, and Switzerland) or indirectly by the patients who are reimbursed by the sickness funds (as in Belgium). Service fees can also be paid indirectly by an agent between sickness funds and medical doctors (e.g., the medical association in Germany, exercising the roles of negotiator and manager of its budget for doctors' services) (Glaser 1991).

Fee-for-service payment has advantages. First and most important, it reflects the work actually done and efforts actually made (Ron, Abel-Smith, and Tamburi 1990). Thus, this method of payment encourages providers to work efficiently, hence increasing the productivity (internal efficiency) of the providers. The second advantage is related to the fee schedule in which the fees can be priced above cost to encourage the provision of cost-effective services and below cost to discourage the provision of inefficient services. For example, the South Carolina Preferred Personal Care Plan pays physicians $675 for a colonoscopy in an outpatient setting and $515 for the same procedure performed in a hospital (Jacobs 1991).

Fee-for-service payment also presents serious disadvantages that have been the focal point of payment-system discussion since the second half of the 20th century. The first disadvantage is that it provides a strong economic incentive for doctors to provide unnecessary services, particularly when the workload is low, treatment options are ambiguous, and the fees are set at a profitable level (Ron, Abel-Smith, and Tamburi 1990; Pontes 1995). The second disadvantage is that doctors may try to increase the quantity of service by reducing the length of time spent with each patient or by delegating work to less-qualified workers, particularly if the workload is heavy. Because of this provider misbehavior, the quality of care may suffer. The third disadvantage is the relatively higher cost of administration (Normand and Weber 1994). In general, the fee-for-service system is recognized as favoring the provider's internal efficiency to the detriment of social efficiency, from the consumer's point of view.

Empirical studies focus mainly on testing whether fee-for-service payment results in the overprovision of care due to the direct linkage between provider income and service volume. A review of the literature discloses strong evidence demonstrating the connection between increased utilization of services and the fee-for-service system. One of the earliest studies (Bunker 1970) shows that in the United Kingdom, where surgeons are paid either a salary or some combination of salary and capitation, the rate of surgical operations per capita was about half of that in the United States where surgeons are paid on a fee-for-service basis. Several studies in the United States show that variation in geographic rates of surgery seems to be best explained by the number of surgeons in each geographic area (McPherson et al. 1981). According to research by Hilman et al. (1990), primary care physicians who use their own imaging equipment in their offices order more than four times as many imaging examinations as physicians who refer patients to radiologists for examinations. The link between utilization rates and the fee-for-service system is further demonstrated by evidence from various health systems in Western Europe and Canada, as well as the United States (Broomberg and Price 1990). Under this system, doctors often respond to a drop in real earnings over time by increasing the number of services delivered per capita (Evans 1974, 1986; Eisenberg 1985; Rice 1983; Langwell and Nelson 1986). Medical expenditures by health maintenance organizations (HMOs)— with their salaried or capitated doctors—are 10 to 40 percent lower than medical expenditures by insurers with fee-for-service payments (Broomberg and Price 1990). Due to measurement problems, no conclusions can be reached about whether supplier-induced demand exists, but it is apparent that the quantity of provision under fee-for-service payment is significantly higher than under other payment systems.

Despite strong objections to fee-for-service payment, this system has not yet been abandoned. The first reason for this is that doctors, who have a great deal of political power in the developed world, prefer this system because it affords them autonomy for medical decisions and allows them to earn a higher income. Payment tradition is the second reason. Countries such as China, Germany, and the United States have traditionally based provider payment on fee for service. A revolutionary change may be difficult, especially in the first two democratic countries where reforms can be made only if based on negotiations among different stakeholders. The third reason is that the fee-for-service system works well in Canada, Germany, and Japan, where it is combined with a total budget for physicians' services. The fee schedule provides a relative value or reference point for each service item. The monetary value of each point depends on the total budget and the quantity of service provided. Because the total budget is fixed, greater service volume means a lower price for each item of service. This provides an incentive for the doctors to reduce the quantity of services. This mechanism works better if a cap is put on physician income, as in Canada (Rochaix 1993; Vayda 1994).

The major suggested solutions for the overprovision of services under the fee-for-service system include: adjusting the fee schedule and making selected services less attractive; combining fee for service with the budget cap; copayment for the medical services under concern; and claims monitoring (Ron, Abel-Smith, and Tamburi 1990).

Capitation

Capitation is a method of prospective payment in which the provider is paid a periodic fixed amount per insured person and accepts responsibility for delivering a defined package of health services when the insured needs a covered service. Capitation payment is used in Denmark, Italy, the Netherlands, and the United Kingdom and is being introduced in Costa Rica, Indonesia, and in HMOs in the United States (Ron, Abel-Smith, and Tamburi 1990). This type of payment transfers the economic risk from third-party payers to health care providers. Here, the provider can be an office-based doctor or a hospital (Barnum, Kutzin, and Saxenian 1995). The capitated office-based doctor is usually responsible for providing only primary care (as in Hungary) or, in addition, for purchasing hospital care (e.g., the general practitioner [GP] fundholder in the United Kingdom). The capitated hospital is responsible for providing inpatient care or, in addition, outpatient care (e.g., a hospital contracted by the social health insurance scheme in Thailand). The capitation fee can include both services and drugs (e.g., some HMOs in the United States) or only consultant services, as in most countries (Ron, Abel-Smith, and Tamburi 1990). The capitation can be either a flat fee for each provider or a risk-adjusted fee, based on the relative risk of the registered population. For example, the capitated fee is adjusted in Germany by five variables: age, gender, disability in a working-age patient, family size, and income (Barnum, Kutzin, and Saxenian 1995).

The most important advantage of the capitation payment is that unlike the fee-for-service system, it offers no overprovision incentive to providers and thus helps control health care costs. Because the provider is responsible for providing the contracted package of services for the fixed payment, the provider may look for ways of lowering delivery costs, for example, through cost-reducing technology, use of lower-cost alternative treatment settings, and providing cost-effective care. The second advantage is that the capitation payment provides an incentive for the provider to conduct preventive care. For example, in the United States, 80 percent of women ages 50 to 74 enrolled in the Kaiser Permanente Plan of Northern California, in which doctors are paid capitated fees, had received mammography screening, compared to 25 percent of women in this age group in the population as a whole; and pediatric immunization rates were more than 90 percent in Kaiser plans, compared to the national average of 37 percent (Barnum, Kutzin, and Saxenian 1995). The third advantage is related to low administrative costs.

While the capitation payment provides no incentive for unnecessary care, it may provide an incentive for cutting back on necessary care. The first disadvantage is that the provider will try to select low-risk clients and reject those at high risk if the capitation payment is not adjusted for individual risk. For example, according to evidence from the United States, HMOs have had healthier enrollees than the rest of the population, suggesting they have selected favorable risks to some extent (Congressional Budget Office 1994).

The second disadvantage is that the provider may reduce the quality of care to reduce costs. This can be done by skimping on the office environment and equipment, reducing the number of necessary tests, decreasing time spent with patients, and accepting too many registrants, resulting in a longer waiting list. The third disadvantage is the likelihood of unnecessary referrals to a specialist or a hospital, because referring more patients out means lower costs for the capitated provider. For example, capitated payments to family physicians in Hungary covered only their services, and excluded specialist services (Barnum, Kutzin, and Saxenian 1995). This resulted in a higher referral rate since the more patients the family physician referred to specialists, the lower the medical costs were for the family physicians. Consequently, with fixed capitation payment, the family physicians received a higher level of financial surplus.

Several possible solutions have been suggested and tried out in the practice of the capitation payment. To deal with the adverse-risk selection, individual risk adjustment for the capitation fee has been much discussed in the last decade. Colombia, Germany, the Netherlands, and many other countries are starting to use simple formulas to adjust the risk. As Barnum, Kutzin, and Saxenian (1995) state, however, simple formulas may work better when benefit packages are limited; more complex formulas may be needed for comprehensive packages. Experience to date shows that the ideal risk-adjustment method has not yet come into existence. To protect the quality and volume of health services under the capitation system, competition is suggested in many countries and has been tried out in the United Kingdom where clients are allowed to choose their GPs. To protect their economic interests, GPs have to compete for patients by ensuring reasonable quality and the necessary quantity of services. In addition, to ensure quality, the number of registrations is limited by regulation in the United Kingdom.

To deal with unnecessary referrals, the capitation fee should include both primary and secondary services. There are generally two different practices for removing the incentive for unnecessary referrals. One is GP fundholding, invented in the United Kingdom: the GPs are responsible for providing primary care and purchasing the covered specialist and hospital care, both with the capitated payments. Another practice is found in Thailand and China, where social health insurance schemes pay contracted hospitals capitation fees for providing both primary and secondary services. Both approaches remove the unnecessary-referral incentive but give providers an incentive to keep patients at the primary level even if referrals are needed. The latter incentive, a disadvantage for patients, can be limited by using patients' choice to heighten competition among providers.

Capitation payment and GP fundholding are basic to health care reform in the United Kingdom. The reform creates incentive for GPs to provide care that was originally provided by secondary care institutions. As a result, primary care is substituted for secondary care in terms of minor surgery and chronic disease management. However, evidence on whether the substitution is cost-effective is scarce and therefore inconclusive (Scott 1996).

Salary

Salary is a retrospective payment to doctors based on the time of work—part time or full time. The salary payment to doctors is common in planned health care systems. For example, all hospital-based doctors in China and the United Kingdom are salaried. Doctors who take care of patients in outpatient health centers are often salaried in Finland, Greece, India, Indonesia, Israel, Portugal, Spain, Sweden, the former Soviet republics, Turkey, and many countries in Latin America (Ron, Abel-Smith, and Tamburi 1990). Doctors can be employed by health funds or insurance institutions, independent hospitals, independent outpatient clinics, and other nonhealth organizations (such as universities and industries).

One of the most important advantages of salary over fee-for-service and capitation payments is that it does not provide an economic incentive for overprovision, as in the case of fee for service, or for underprovision, as in the case of capitation. The second advantage is that it makes health care planning easier, because the doctors' salary is known in advance (Culyer, Donaldson, and Gerard 1988). The third advantage is that the salary system encourages doctors to conduct group consultations needed in complex cases to make a diagnosis and work out an appropriate treatment plan because their work is not directly related to their payment. Group consultations are hard to arrange under fee for service because the work and the related payment are not easily shared by a group of doctors. The fourth advantage is related to lower monitoring and administrative cost than under the fee-for-service and capitation payments.

Several authors mention the disadvantages of the salary payment (Rosen 1989; Ron, Abel-Smith, and Tamburi 1990; Culyer, Donaldson, and Gerard 1988). The major disadvantage is that the fixed salary does not provide incentives for the doctors to work productively and to use resources efficiently to lower the cost of care. The second disadvantage is the morale problem, especially for hard-working and talented doctors who might think their good work is not being rewarded. As a result of these two disadvantages, the salary payment may result in low-quality care, which is the third disadvantage. The fourth disadvantage is the danger that low-paid doctors may seek or accept illegal payments from patients and gain under-the-table money from kickbacks provided by pharmaceutical companies and high-tech equipment owners.

Despite its many disadvantages, the salary payment is still the most popular payment method around the world. In the United States and other countries where fee for service is popular, salaries are rising along with integration between physicians and hospitals and between third parties and physicians. One proponent of the salary payment (Pontes 1995) argues that the salary payment is a desirable way of lowering health care costs and that the disadvantages of low productivity, low morale, and less cost awareness can be overcome by partial ownership of a medical facility by physicians and by properly designed and implemented bonus systems.

Daily Payment

The *daily* or *per diem payment* is a fixed amount paid to an institution for each day of inpatient care, regardless of the actual use of services, drugs, and medical products. In theory, it is applicable to all inpatient services including long-term care in nursing homes. In practice, it is used only by third parties to pay hospitals (Normand and Weber 1994). In the U.S. literature, the daily payment and the case payment are classified as prospective payments (Jacobs 1991). This type of hospital payment is commonly used in continental Western Europe and is being tried out in China and Indonesia in their social insurance schemes.

The per diem provides incentives for hospitals to increase the total number of inpatient hospital days by prolonging stays and increasing the number of admissions, while reducing the intensity of care. Thus, technical quality may suffer due to insufficient services and drugs, although perceived quality, such as doctors' attitudes toward patients, may increase for making the patient's stay longer.

This system may work well when there is a budget cap on hospital services. Both the quality of care and the length of hospital stay can be monitored by a peer doctor, but monitoring costs are high. Whether the per diem payment can reduce the cost of hospital care depends on whether the payers can control the length of stay. Whether this payment can improve social efficiency depends, in addition to controlling the length of stay, on whether the payers can effectively monitor the hospital to see that it provides the needed services and drugs.

Case Payment

Using the *case payment method,* third parties pay an inclusive fixed amount per case, regardless of the actual cost of providing services. Case payment can be used for both outpatient care (being tested in China as part of its social health insurance reform) and inpatient care (e.g., the Diagnosis-Related Grouping [DRG] used in the United States), and for both physician care (as suggested by Mitchell 1985) and hospital care. The case payment method can be based on a single flat rate per case, regardless of the diagnosis, or on a schedule of diagnoses. The most popular type of case payment is the DRG payment for hospital services used in the U.S. Medicare program and tested in Indonesia, Taiwan (China), and some other countries and regions. The case payment method is used only by third-party payers, not by individual patients. It is classified as a prospective payment in the U.S. literature (Lave 1984).

The theory for the case payment is that costs among cases within one group should be as similar as possible and that the administrative cost should not be beyond the available capacity. In the judgment of the trade-off, case groups can be as simple as a single group and as complex as 478 groups in the United States; Indonesia and other countries may fall between the two extremes (Jacobs 1991; Ron, Abel-Smith, and Tamburi 1990.

As a more sophisticated instance of the case payment, the DRG is explored in greater detail. The idea of DRG was invented by Fetter (1980) of Yale University and introduced by the U.S. government as a new prospective payment system for Medicare hospital patients. Patients were grouped through cross-hospital studies of the average costs for each type of diagnosis, and the factors affecting costs were identified for each diagnosis. The major factors selected were principal diagnosis, secondary diagnosis, principal procedure, secondary procedure, discharge destination, gender, age, and length of stay. According to these factors, patients are divided into groups that reflect differences in resource utilization during hospital care. In the DRG payment system, payments are made for DRG cases according to their indices of case-weighted admissions, a series of relative values reflecting treatment costs for different DRG groups. The monetary value of each DRG point is called "the standardized amount," established in relation to the Medicare program budget and the cost of the requisite hospital services. Payments are adjusted for hospital location (urban or rural), educational responsibility (teaching or nonteaching), and outlier (length of stay and cost per DRG case that exceeds the norm). In addition, capital costs (fixed asset depreciation) and the cost of direct education (interns' and residents' salaries) are passed on, that is, paid by Medicare, whatever they are. These costs vary widely from facility to facility, and efforts to incorporate them in the DRG rate have been met with resistance from facilities with higher capital and educational costs.

A major advantage of the case payment system is that it removes the economic incentives for hospitals to provide as many items of service as possible—present in fee-for-service payment—and to stretch outpatients' hospital stays—present in the daily payment. The second advantage is that the reduction of unnecessary services can improve the quality of care (Lave 1984, 1989). The third advantage is that it is easy to operate, and the administrative cost is low if the providers are paid a single, flat rate per case.

Assorted disadvantages are predicted. The first is *DRG creep,* which means that the hospital would like to code the patient into a group with a higher point (or index) for higher payment. The second disadvantage is *cost shifting,* which means that while the costs for DRG patients are controlled, the reduced costs will be shifted to non-DRG patients, and, as a result, the total cost to society is not reduced. In another type of cost shifting, the provider may increase the quantity of preadmission tests and discharge patients prematurely. As a result, the costs are shifted to outpatient services, home care, and nursing home care. In still another type of cost shifting, the provider may skim the costly cases and shift the costs for treating these costly cases to other providers. Hospitals will want the cases with the highest payment rates relative to costs (Omenn and Conrad 1984).

The third disadvantage of the case payment system is that it offers a provider incentive to make unnecessary admissions and readmissions. This may increase the total cost of health care and decrease the quality of care through interruptions. The fourth disadvantage is the likelihood of reduced quality, caused by holding back on necessary care, including the length of stay, services, and drugs. For example, under DRG, hospital administrators usually put pressure on physicians to order fewer lab tests and examinations (Young and Saltman 1982). Effective implementation of case payment clearly depends on whether payment policies can ensure the assignment of cases to the right diagnosis group, prevent needless transfer of patients from one provider to another, and maintain a respectable level of quality (Normand and Weber 1994). The implementation of DRG payment can shorten hospital stays and reduce daily costs (Rosko and Broyles 1987), but whether it improves social efficiency in terms of the costs for society as a whole is less clear.

Budget

The *budget* is a prospective payment method in which health care providers are paid an amount per given period (usually a year) for specified service provision responsibilities. A budget can be either variable or fixed. A *variable budget* is only a reference value of spending for the budget period, and it can be further divided into an open-ended budget and a target budget. Under an *open-ended budget,* if the budget is exceeded, the payer will provide additional funds, and the budget for the next time period will be increased accordingly. Under a *target budget,* if the budget is exceeded, the payer will provide additional funds but they will be debited against the budget for the next period as a penalty (Glaser 1993). The *fixed budget* is also called a "budget cap" or "ceiling," meaning that after the amount of budget has been set it will not be changed.

The budget can be either a line-item budget or a global budget. A *line-item budget* is broken down into categories, such as salaries, drugs, equipment, maintenance, and the like. Rules and regulations prohibit managers from switching funds across line items without approval from the funding agency. Under a *global budget,* health care providers are given an inclusive budget for the defined responsibilities, and the use of the budget is delegated to the managers of the health providers. The literature often refers to the global budget as the fixed global budget. Thus, the global budget, the fixed global budget, and the budget cap or ceiling are synonymous.

The budget can be either full or partial. A *full budget* is provided to cover the entire cost of providing services. This is the usual budget when a third party pays providers for the total cost of services. A *partial budget* covers only a portion of the cost of providing services, the rest of the costs must be covered by private donations and service charges. An example of the partial budget comes from China. The government provides public hospitals with a partial budget that covers only the basic salary of the hospital staff and part of the expenditures for the fixed assets (at one time it also covered labor costs and expenditures for buildings and equipment). The rest of the costs must be covered by service charges to the social health insurance schemes and uncovered, self-paying patients.

Budgets can be provided by governments to their affiliated health facilities; by third parties to their own health institutions; and by third parties to independent providers. The budget may cover only physician services or only hospital services or both types of services. It may cover only outpatient services or only inpatient services or both.

A budget can be established in many different ways. It can be based on negotiations between third-party payers and providers, or their association, as in Germany, where the budget is negotiated yearly between the health funds and the medical association representing the providers. The budget can also be based on a prenegotiated formula that reflects variations in medical costs. The yearly budget is then calculated according to this formula without yearly budget negotiations, as in the United Kingdom. The budget can also be regulated by the government as a compulsory budget policy that involves little negotiation, as in China.

The bases on which the budgets are made vary, and each type of base offers different incentives to providers. If the budget is based on the previous year's expenditure (adjusted for inflation and changes in utilization), it provides the inertia that tends to lock in the existing pattern of resource use and offers providers no incentive to save because overspending one year means more budget the next year (Wiley 1992). If the budget is based on a fixed input such as cost per hospital bed, it will provide an incentive to add capital input in order to increase the budget, thus leading to excess capacity in the long run. If the budget is related to performance criteria, the incentive depends on the indicators used to measure performance. In Hungary prior to case-payment reform, hospital budgets were based on occupancy rates, which promoted long hospital stays (Barnum, Kutzin, and Saxenian 1995). In Israel, budgets based on age-adjusted capitation led to a reduction in lengths of stay and increases in use of lower-cost alternatives to hospitalization.

Different types of budgets have different advantages and disadvantages. The global budget (fixed global budget) is increasingly popular. It makes the cost of health care predictable and provides a strong incentive for providers to reduce the costs of services, thus improving the internal efficiency of health services. But the global budget transfers all the risk to providers and gives them incentives to underserve patients and reduce the quality of care. The line-item budget, used less and less, provides an incentive to spend everything by the end of the budget year. Its rigid spending pattern provides no incentive to improve internal efficiency, but it can control inappropriate spending due to poor management, often an advantage in some developing countries. The variable budget, in contrast to the fixed budget, transfers no risk to providers and offers providers an incentive to increase the quality and the quantity of output subject to the breakeven constraint, but it provides no incentive to minimize the cost of care.

The global budget, due to its successful history of controlling costs in Canada, Germany, and the United Kingdom, is gaining attention in other parts of the world (Ron, Abel-Smith, and Tamburi 1990). It was adopted as a cost-control strategy in the health care reform plan of the Clinton administration in the United States (Holahan, Blumberg, and Zuckerman 1994). Although it is effective in controlling the cost of care, social efficiency cannot be achieved unless quality of care and access to necessary care can be ensured.

Bonus Payment

The *bonus* is a payment method that awards the payee extra money for achievement in association with established indicators of objectives. Bonuses are intended to provide financial incentive for the actors to behave in the interests of the payers. The objective may be economic in nature (e.g., profit and revenue objectives) or managerial (performance goals). The objectives can also be related to health policy objectives such as targets related to childhood immunization rates and incidence rates of some infectious diseases. If the objective is concrete (revenue, profit, service quantity), the bonus can be paid according to a single indicator. For example, an outpatient clinic can pay its salaried doctors a bonus linked to extra visits provided over the normal standard. Abstract or multiple objectives are usually broken down into a set of indicators, and bonuses can be paid for achieving them. For example, if the bonus is quality related, the quality objective should be broken down into several indicators related to each dimension of quality. Bonuses can also be paid according to the summarized score of service quality.

Bonuses may be paid by a third party to health service providers, by a health service institution to its employees, and by the government or health authority to affiliated health institutions. The party receiving a bonus can be an individual *(individual incentive system)*, a group of people as a unit *(group incentive system)*, or an organization *(organizational incentive system)*. The bonus can be paid as a lump sum at the end of the year, or it can be paid periodically within the year. It can be paid independently of the basic payment, or it can be paid along with the basic payment according to specific conditions of the bonus system.

Bonus systems are used frequently in the health sector. According to the available cases, the bonus system in health care can be divided into several types. The first type of bonus system in health care is the *revenue-related bonus,* by which the bonus is provided according to a revenue target or a certain proportion of the revenue. For example, in the United States, around 3 percent of hospital-based physicians (including anesthesiologists, pathologists, radiologists, cardiologists, and emergency room physicians) are paid on a salary-plus arrangement, in which salary is the major part and a percentage of the department revenue is added (Steinwald 1983).

The second type is the *savings-related bonus,* by which the provider is paid a portion of the total savings. One example of this is the financial incentive scheme on prescribing in nonfundholding general practices in the United Kingdom (Bateman et al.1996). The health funds set a target for prescription savings for each GP group, whose practitioners are paid on the capitation basis, with an additional payment of part of the savings if they meet the targets.

The third type is the *quality-related bonus,* an additional payment for achieving predetermined quality standards. An example of this is the quality compensation plan in some HMOs in the United States, where providers are paid by capitation, with an additional payment for meeting some quality measures such as quality review components, comprehensive care components, and utilization components (Schlackman 1993).

The fourth type is the *quantity-related bonus,* an extra payment geared to the amount of work performed. For example, in the United Kingdom, GPs are paid capitation fees and bonuses based on the quantity of preventive services delivered by the GP.

The fifth is the *performance-related bonus* ("performance-related pay" in the literature), used by health institutions as an incentive payment to their employees. Performance-related pay can also be used to pay groups and organizations. As mentioned in chapter 10, performance-related pay is an outcome-related payment provided according to a set of outcome indicators. The National Health Service in the United Kingdom introduced performance-related pay for hospital-based doctors (Griffin 1992) and nurses (Martin 1994). Canada was one of the earliest countries to introduce performance-related pay for salaried nurses (Wakylak 1991). The Indonesian government introduced performance-related pay for civil service doctors in the early 1990s (Chernichovsky and Bayulken 1995).

This is not an exhaustive list of bonus system types. The design of bonus systems is an art, each system with its own characteristics, but some general patterns can be discerned. In theory, the bonus system can be based on multidimensional indicators that reflect the payer's utility function, but no such complicated bonus system has been found in the published literature. Although performance-related pay is becoming increasingly popular, few studies in the health sector analyze the theoretical bases and practical effectiveness of this system.

The bonus system is likely to be abused when the payer's objective conflicts with the patient's or society's objective. For example, the savings-related bonus, as in the United Kingdom for nonfundholding GPs, will induce a behavior of underprescribing even some essential drugs. In this case, although the health funds (principal) and the providers (agent) are both satisfied economically, the patients may suffer. A study in the United States examined how physicians' prescribing behavior was affected by ambulatory care centers' introduction of the revenue-related monetary incentive to generate more business. The findings revealed a substantial increase in the quantity of services (Hemenway et al. 1990). Another example of overprovision behavior linked to the revenue-related bonus occurs in China, where some hospitals pay their doctors bonuses proportionate to the revenue they bring in. Although the hospitals (principals) and the doctors (agents) are both satisfied, patients and third-party payers may suffer.

These hypotheses are rarely tested, however, and little is reported in the international literature regarding the impact of bonus systems on the internal (productive) and external (social) efficiency of health services.

TOWARD A BETTER PAYMENT SYSTEM

The development of ideal payment systems is a challenging task, but it is always possible to improve the current payment systems to get the best value for the money. The payment system designers will need to (1) keep in mind the criteria for an ideal payment system so that any payment systems designed should be compared against these criteria; (2) combine different payment systems so that the disadvantages of one payment system can be limited by another payment system; and (3) strengthen theoretical studies for the innovation of new payment systems and obtain evidence of existing payment systems via rigorous evaluations.

Criteria for an Ideal Payment System

For several decades, the search has been on for an ideal payment system in health care. Capitation, case payment, daily charge, and global budget constitute the major innovations in health care policy and management. Empirical evaluation of these payment methods, however, finds that any method presents advantages and disadvantages and that, at present, there is no panacea for paying health care providers. At this point, the reader may wonder what criteria would constitute an ideal payment system. In general terms, an ideal payment system should meet six conditions. It should provide incentives for *cost containment, quality assurance,* and *internal efficiency* (productivity); offer no incentives for *over- or underprovision of services*; and should be *feasible*. Table 11.2 presents a comparison of the existing payment systems in terms of these six requirements.

Cost containment is certainly the most important requirement for any payment system, and galloping increases in health care costs are a main motivator of people's efforts to develop good payment systems. Among the payment systems now in use, fee-for-service and open-ended budget payments are the two worst ways of controlling costs, while capitation and the fixed global budget do this well. Salary, daily payment, and case payment may also have some effect on costs, but the degree depends on the way they are implemented. The bonus may increase or decrease health care costs, depending on the purpose of the bonus scheme. For example, the revenue-related bonus will increase costs, and the savings-related bonus will decrease them.

There are trade-offs between quality and cost containment. Payment systems that inflate costs, such as fee for service and the open-ended budget, can ensure quality of care, while systems that effectively control costs are more likely to impair quality, especially technical quality or intensity of care, which correlates with cost of care.

TABLE 11.2   Payment Systems Compared by Cost Containment, Quality Assurance, Overprovision, Underprovision, Internal Efficiency, and Administrative Feasibility

Type of payment	Cost containment	Quality assurance	No incentive for over-provision	No incentive for under-provision	Internal efficiency	Administrative feasibility
Fee for service	− − −	+ + +	− − −	+ + +	+ + +	− −
Capitation	+ + +	−	+ + +	− − −	+	+ +
Salary	+ +	+	+ +	+ +	− − −	+ +
Daily	+	− −	−/+	−/+	+ +	−/+
Case	+ +	−	+ + +	− − −	+ +	− − −
Open-ended budget	− − −	+ + +	+	+	− − −	−
Fixed global budget	+ + +	−	+ + +	− −	+ + +	+ +
Bonus	−/+	−/+	−/+	−/+	+ +	+

Source: Authors.

Note: The number of "+" signs refers to the degree of goodness; the number of "−" signs refers to the degree of badness; and the number of "−/+" pairs indicates it depends on the specific design.

Removing the incentive for overprovision is one of the driving forces for seeking alternative methods of payment. Capitation, case payment, and the fixed global budget remove the incentive for overprovision. Fee for service and the open-ended budget give providers incentives to deliver more care. The daily payment can remove the incentive to provide more care per day, but the incentive remains to provide more days of care.

Removing the incentive for overprovision is usually accompanied by the introduction of an incentive for underprovision. The existence of the incentive for overprovision reduces the risk of underprovision. For example, capitation, case payment, and fixed global budget methods are more likely to give providers incentives to deliver less care than necessary, while the fee-for-service, salary, and open-ended budget methods do not seem to have this problem.

The internal efficiency of the provider will be high under fee-for-service and fixed global budget payments but low under salary and open-ended budget payment. Internal efficiency under capitation, daily, case, and bonus payments is generally good, but the degree of efficiency depends on monitoring and management.

The administrative feasibility includes the cost of monitoring provider behavior, the cost of operating the payment system itself, and the availability of technology and skills. Capitation, salary, and fixed global budget are easy to manage, but case payment (particularly the DRG) and the fee for service are difficult. For judging the administrative feasibility of any system, the context within which the payment system is introduced, and the complementary systems used, are important considerations.

Combining Payment Systems

From this discussion, it can be seen that any payment system has advantages and disadvantages. Despite the efforts directed toward finding an ideal provider payment system, none is in sight. Several authors have suggested combining payment systems so that each provides remedies for the deficits of the others (Normand and Weber 1990; Barnum, Kutzin, and Saxenian 1995; Pontes 1995). Pontes (1995) strongly recommends salary as a method of paying physicians and suggests adding bonuses to motivate medical staff productivity. The GP payment system in the United Kingdom seems to work well; the doctors are paid capitation fees, supplemented by fees for special services (such as night calls, maternity services, and adult immunization), and bonuses for preventive service. The fee-for-service method works well in Canada and Germany, where it is combined with the global budget or the budget cap. The daily payment is combined with the case payment in Indonesia, where major surgical procedures and costly cases with definite diagnosis are paid by case, and others are paid on daily charges. Although different combinations have been suggested, the open-ended fee for service and the open-ended budget are rejected—at any rate by academics.

Suggestions for Future Work

Current debate seems to focus on the evaluation of the existing payment systems, but little effort is being devoted to inventing new payment systems. It is philosophically correct to say that there can be no panacea for payment systems, but this conclusion does not mean the end of the road. Continuous efforts should be made toward a better payment method. Besides modifying the systems in use, efforts should be directed to inventing new ones. A revolutionary breakthrough in the payment for health care cannot be expected without the belief that there must be one and that it can be found. Efforts to develop innovative payment methods should be encouraged.

Some payment systems, such as the DRG and capitation, have been implemented before any sound evidence of their effectiveness has been found and before policy makers and researchers have reached a consensus. Decisions seem likely to be based on hypotheses rather than on empirical studies. For example, despite the lack of any firm evidence that performance-related pay actually improved performance in the private sector, the government of the United Kingdom decided to implement it in health care at the end of the 1980s. Such a practice carries a high risk of failure, which might make things worse. Here, the suggestion is that while studies can continue to focus on evaluating and modifying the existing payment methods to prevent failure, researchers should do something to further scientific decision making by undertaking practical research that provides the information needed for policy making. In addition, academics should advocate against arbitrary policy making.

While efforts on the practical side unfold, theoretical consideration of the payment system cannot be neglected. Theory can be produced in the process of practice and can, in turn, guide further practice that leads to a new theory. Thus, the process of evaluating current systems will give scientists a chance to understand the provider utility function, the basis for predicting provider behavior. A review of the existing literature discloses that predictions of provider behavior are based implicitly on profit maximization or revenue maximization. In fact, provider utility is much more complicated than assumed. As indicated in chapter 7, only after the utility function or objective function is made clear can behavior be accurately predicted. And only after provider behavior becomes predictable, can an ideal payment system become possible. The importance of the suggestion that future research should be directed to studying the providers' utility function and to predicting their behavior is clear.

NOTE

This chapter is based on a review of the literature by the authors when Xingzhu Liu was pursuing his PhD under the supervision of Professor Anne Mills at the London School of Hygiene and Tropical Medicine. The initial work was funded by the United Nations Development Programme/World Bank/World Health Organization Special Programme for Research and Training in Tropical Diseases and the Overseas Research Students Awards Scheme in the United Kingdom. The authors are also grateful for the follow-up support provided by the World Bank and Abt Associates Inc., Bethesda, Maryland.

REFERENCES

Barnum, H., J. Kutzin, and H. Saxenian. 1995. "Incentive and Provider Payment Methods." *International Journal of Health Planning and Management* 10: 23–45.

Bateman, D.N., M. Campbell, L.J. Donaldson, S.J. Roberts, and J.M. Smith. 1996. "A Prescribing Incentive Scheme for Nonfundholding General Practices: An Observational Study." *British Medical Journal* 313(7056): 535–38.

Broomberg, J., and M. Price. 1990. "The Impact of the Fee-for-Service Reimbursement System on the Utilization of Health Services." *South Africa Medical Journal* 78(4): 130–32.

Bunker, J.P. 1970. "Surgical Manpower: A Comparison of Operations and Surgeons in the United States and in England and Wales." *New England Journal of Medicine* 282: 135–44.

Chernichovsky, D., and C. Bayulken. 1995. "A Pay-for-Performance System for Civil Service Doctors: The Indonesian Experiment." *Social Science and Medicine* 41(2): 155–61.

Clarke, R., and C. Gray. 1994. "Options for Change in the NHS Consultant Contract." *British Medical Journal* 309: 528–30.

Congressional Budget Office. 1994. "Effects of Managed Care: An Update." CBO memorandum. Washington, DC.

Culyer, A.J, C. Donaldson, and K. Gerard. 1988. *Financial Aspects of Health Services: Drawing on Experience*. Working Paper No. 3. York, United Kingdom: University of York, Centre for Health Economics.

Eisenberg, J. 1985. "Physician Utilization." *Medical Care* 23: 461–83.

Evans, R.G. 1986. "Finding the Levers, Finding the Courage: Lessons from Cost Containment in North America." *Journal of Health Politics, Policy and Law* 11(4): 585–615.

———. 1974. "Supplier Induced Demand: Some Empirical Evidence and Implications." In *The Economics of Health and Medical Care*, ed. M. Perlman. London: Macmillan.

Fetter, R.B. 1980. "Construction of Diagnosis-Related Groups." *Medical Care* 18(2): 5–20.

Glaser, W.A. 1993. "How Expenditure Caps and Expenditure Targets Really Work." *The Milbank Quarterly* 71(1): 97–127.

———. 1991. *Health Insurance in Practice: International Variations in Financing, Benefits, and Problems*. San Francisco, CA: Jossey-Bass Publishers.

Griffin, R.P. 1992. "Why Doesn't Performance Pay Work?" *Health Manpower Management* 18(4): 31–33.

Hemenway, D., A. Killen, S.B. Cashman, C.L. Parks, and W.J. Bicknell. 1990. "Physicians' Responses to Financial Incentives." *New England Journal of Medicine* 322: 1059–63.

Hilman, B.J., C.A. Joseph, M.R. Mabry, J.H. Sunshine, S.D. Kennedy, and M. Noether. 1990. "Frequency and Costs of Diagnositic Imaging in Office Practice: A Comparison of Self-Referring and Radiologist-Referring Physicians." *New England Journal of Medicine* 323(23): 1604–8.

Holahan, J., L.J. Blumberg, and S. Zuckerman. 1994. "Strategies for Implementing Global Budgets." *The Milbank Quarterly* 72(3): 399–429.

Jacobs, P. 1991. *The Economics of Health and Medical Care*. Gaithersburg, MD: Aspen.

Langwell, K.M., and L.M. Nelson. 1986. "Physician Payment Systems: A Review of History, Alternatives and Evidence." *Medical Care Review* 43: 5–58.

Lave, J.R. 1989. "The Effect of the Medicare Prospective Payment System." *Annual Review of Public Health* 10: 141–61.

———. 1984. "Hospital Reimbursement under Medicare." *The Milbank Quarterly* 62(2): 251–68.

Martin, G. 1994. "Performance-Related Pay in Nursing: Theory, Practice and Prospect." *Health Manpower Management* 20(5): 10–17.

McPherson, K., P.M. Strong, A. Epstein, and L. Jones. 1981. "Regional Variations in the Use of Common Surgical Procedures: within and between England and Wales, Canada and the United States of America." *Social Sciences and Medicine* 15A: 273–88.

Mitchell, J.B. 1985. "Physician DRGs." *New England Journal of Medicine* 313: 670–75.

Normand, C., and A. Weber. 1994. *Social Health Insurance: A Guidebook for Planning*. Geneva: World Health Organization.

Omenn, G.S., and D.A. Conrad. 1984. "Implication of DRG's for Clinicians." *New England Journal of Medicine* 311: 1314–17.

Pontes, M.C. 1995. "Agency Theory: A Framework for Analyzing Physician Services." *Health Care Management Review* 20(4): 57–67.

Rice, T.H. 1983. "The Impact of Changing Medicare Reimbursement Rates on Physician-Induced Demand." *Medical Care* 21: 803–15.

Rochaix, L. 1993. "Financial Incentives for Physicians: The Quebec Experience." *Health Economics* 2: 163–76.

Ron, A., B. Abel-Smith, and G. Tamburi. 1990. *Health Insurance in Developing Countries: The Social Security Approach.* Geneva: International Labour Office.

Rosen, B. 1989. "Professional Reimbursement and Professional Behavior: Emerging Issues and Research Challenges." *Social Science and Medicine* 29(3): 455–62.

Rosko, M.D. and R.W. Broyles. 1987. "Short-Term Responses of Hospitals to the DRG Prospective Pricing Mechanism in New Jersey." *Medical Care* 25: 88–94.

Schlackman, N. 1993. "Evolution of a Quality-Based Compensation Model: The Third Generation." *American Journal of Medical Quality* 8(2): 103–10.

Scott, A. 1996. "Primary or Secondary Care? What Can Economics Contribute to Evaluation at the Interface?" *Journal of Public Health Medicine* 18(1): 19–26.

Steinwald, B. 1983. "Compensation of Hospital-Based Physicians." *Health Service Research* 18(1): 17–47.

Vayda, E. 1994. "Physicians in Health Care Management: Payment of Physicians and Organization of Medical Services." *Canadian Medical Association Journal* 150(10): 1583–88.

Wakylak, T.P. 1991. "Pay for Performance." *Canada Journal of Nursing* 87(4): 30–31.

Wiley, M.M. 1992. "Hospital Financing Reform and Case Mix Measurement: An International Review." *Health Care Financing Review* 1(4): 119–33.

Young, D.W., and R.B Saltman. 1982. "Medicare Practice, Case Mix, and Cost Containment." *Journal of the American Medical Association* 247: 801–5.

CHAPTER 12

Supplier-Induced Demand and Unnecessary Care

Xingzhu Liu and Anne Mills

Health policy makers and researchers are increasingly concerned about the association between financial incentives and provider behavior, as well as about ways of controlling misbehavior and motivating good behavior. *Misbehavior* in this context means a provider recommendation for more health care than is necessary or more than is demanded by well-informed patients. The former involves the concept of unnecessary care (UNC); the latter concerns the concept of supplier-induced demand (SID).

The major purpose of this chapter is to provide methodological information on how to measure SID and UNC. It first introduces a conceptual framework that defines and helps clarify relevant concepts. It then reviews the empirical evidence on the existence of SID and UNC. The chapter closes by identifying problems and suggesting recommendations for future research.

INTRODUCTION

Medical doctors provide two types of services. One is medical information about the need for medical services and the types of services needed for specific conditions. The other type is medical care itself. In other words, the medical doctor is both the recommender and the provider of medical services, because the patient does not have the medical knowledge to diagnose a condition and select a course of treatment without a doctor's advice.

The concern here is that, if the provision of a medical service is connected with the interests of the doctor, the doctor may have incentives to provide more and costlier care that might not improve the health outcome and the patient's welfare. But this hypothesis cannot be tested unless SID and UNC are operationally defined and are measurable. This chapter, therefore, focuses on providing methodological information about measuring SID and UNC.

THE CONCEPTUAL FRAMEWORK OF SID AND UNC

This section first provides definitions for *supplier-induced demand, unnecessary care,* and *need.* Then, it expands on the concepts of SID and UNC using the framework that specifies the interactions between need, demand, and provision.

Definition of *Supplier-Induced Demand*

Supplier-induced demand is an economic term in health care. Most health economists (Jacobs 1991; McGuire, Henderson, and Mooney 1988; Scott 1996; Hemenway and Fallon 1985) define it as the provision of services that consumers would not demand were they fully informed. SID's predominant concern is overprovision. Although overprovision may occur if more services means more gain to the provider (as in the case of fee-for-service payment), underprovision may occur if delivering less service is in the provider's interests (as in the case of capitation payment). The doctor can induce the patient to use more or fewer services, depending on the direction of the incentive. Both overprovision and underprovision behaviors are related to demand inducement. Thus, supplier-induced demand can be more accurately defined as the difference between the actual provision of services and the true demand for services if the patient is fully informed. If the difference takes a positive sign (the actual provision is more than the true demand), the incentive must be directed at overprovision. If the difference takes a negative sign (the actual provision is less than the true demand), the incentive must be directed at underprovision. In an environment of escalating health care costs, people's concerns have been focusing on the overprovision side of SID. To be in accord with the published literature, the traditional definition of *supplier-induced demand* is used in this chapter: overprovision and its opposite, underprovision.

Definition of *Unnecessary Care*

Mark Pauly (1979), a well-known health economist, states that a surgery or any other procedure would be judged necessary if a fully informed consumer would choose it and as unnecessary if a fully informed consumer would not choose it. Joanna Coast (1996), a health economist at the University of Bristol in the United Kingdom, states that unnecessary care is being given if the same amount of health care could be produced using less medical care input. It seems that Pauly's statement defines SID and Coast's statement defines efficiency of medical care utilization. SID, UNC, and the efficiency of medical care utilization are interrelated, but they are different concepts.

Different from SID, which considers patient preference, *unnecessary care* is not by nature an economic term, although it is related to the economic analysis of health care. It concerns the quantity of service actually used in excess of the health care needed, that is, *overutilization.* Overutilization is one of the two types of inappropriate care. The other, *underutilization,* can be defined as the quantity of medical care that is medically needed but not actually utilized. For the reason of cost control, major concerns have concentrated on unnecessary care, and little literature on underutilization is available. Although the terms *underutilization* and *underprovision* and *overutilization* and *overprovision* are used interchangeably in the literature, for the purposes of clarification in this chapter *overprovision* (SID) and *underprovision* are defined as the two types of demand manipulation; and *overutilization* (UNC) and *underutilization* are defined as the two types of inappropriate care.

Currently, the most acceptable definition of unnecessary care is that the care is considered unnecessary if it does not benefit the patient (Leape 1989). In other words, the care is unnecessary if it does not do what it purports to do or, at most, confers benefits so small that they are outweighed by the costs in terms of risk, morbidity, disability, and pain. To be more operational, care is unnecessary when, for an average group of patients presenting to an average physician, the expected health benefit cannot exceed the expected negative consequences by a sufficiently wide margin, excluding the consideration of monetary costs (Hopkins 1993).

Definition of *Need*

The concept of need for health care comes into existence when considering that health care services should be equitably distributed and that access to health care when needed is a basic right of all people. While the concept of the health care need now seems straightforward, it was strongly debated in the 1970s (Feldstein 1987). In health service research, the health care need of a population is often defined by the prevalence and severity of illness, but it may not reflect the nature-of-need concept. The most acceptable definition of *health care need* is the capacity to benefit from treatment (Mooney 1994). According to this definition, if a patient has disease A and another patient has disease B, which is more serious than disease A, and if both diseases are curable, the second patient will have more health care need than the first because the second patient can get more benefit from the treatment. If a patient has a serious illness, but there is no means of dealing with it, there will be little need for health care, simply because the patient cannot benefit from any treatment. The question of whether there is a need for health care, and the level of need, can be answered only by medical professionals. Thus, the evaluation of need for health care should be based on the judgment of medical professionals.

Interrelations between Need, Demand, and Provision

The concepts of UNC and SID can be concretely explained by figure 12.1, which shows the interrelations between the health care need, the true demand for health care, and the actual provision (equivalent to utilization). It is assumed that there is a sick person. His or her need for health care can be evaluated by a neutral (nonincentive to provide less or more care or not responsible for providing care) and capable doctor based on a firm diagnosis and the doctor's perception of the effectiveness and the negative consequence of care (not on its monetary cost). The amount of need can be represented by *Circle B* (*Circle B = PDN + PN + DN + N*). *Circle A*, which equals *PDN + PD + DN + D*, refers to the true demand, which is the demand for health care if the patient has the same knowledge as the doctor. *Circle C* denotes the actual provision to or actual utilization by the patient (*Circle C = PDN + PD + PN + P*).

By putting together these three circles (which are not necessarily equal in size), the concepts discussed above are clarified. In figure 12.1, *P + PN* represents SID, which is the health care actually provided by the doctor but not demanded by the perfectly informed patient; *D + DN* represents the underprovision, which is the health care demanded by the informed patient but not actually provided by the doctor. It is important to note that SID and underprovision can exist simultaneously. This is most likely if the fees are set at different levels related to the costs of care. For services that are priced at profitable levels, SID or overprovision is more likely to occur. For services priced at unprofitable levels, underprovision is more likely to occur.

The simultaneous existence of overprovision and underprovision has implications for the measurement of SID. First, SID does not equal the actual provision (*Circle C*) minus the total true demand (*Circle A*). It should be equal to the actual provision minus the part of actual provision that the informed consumer will

Figure 12.1   The Interrelations between the Need and Demand for Health Care and Its Provision (Utilization)

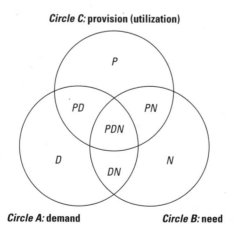

Source: Authors.
Note: P= an area of provision that can satisfy neither demand nor need; D= demand that is neither translated from professionally defined need nor satisfied by actual provision; N= need for health care that is not met by actual utilization and not related to demand; PD= satisfied demand that is not related to need; PN= satisfied need that is not related to demand; DN= demand translated from need but not met by actual provision; PDN= an area in which provision can meet both need and demand.

demand, that is, SID = *Circle C − (PDN + PD)*. Second, the underprovision does not equal the true demand (*Circle A*) minus the actual provision (*Circle C*). It should be equal to the true demand minus that part of demand that is satisfied by actual provision, that is, underprovision = *Circle A − (PDN + PD)*. While the theoretical statement of SID and underprovision are easy, the empirical measurement of them is quite difficult, because the true demand (*Circle A* and *PDN + PD*) is hard to measure and is complicated by subsidized medical care. Quite a few approaches have been tried to measure SID during the last two decades (and are introduced in detail in the second part of this chapter).

The concepts of UNC and underutilization can be explained in terms of the relationship between the need for health care and the actual utilization. In figure 12.1, *P + PD* represents UNC, which is that part of actual utilization beyond the professionally defined need for health care; *DN + N* represents the underutilization, which is that part of the need not satisfied by the actual utilization. Similar to the measurement of SID and underprovision, UNC is not equal to the actual utilization (*Circle C*) minus the total need (*Circle B*). Instead, UNC can be measured by the actual utilization minus the part of actual utilization that meets the need for health care, that is, *UNC = Circle C −(PDN + PN)*; the underutilization can be measured by the total need minus the satisfied need, that is, underutilization = *Circle B − (PDN + PN)*. Measuring UNC and underutilization is not easy, simply because the need (*Circle B* and *PDN + PN*) is difficult to measure. A tremendous body of literature provides approaches for measuring UNC. These are discussed later in this chapter.

There are two extremes for the relationship between provision (*Circle C*), need (*Circle B*), and true demand (*Circle A*). One extreme is that the three circles fully overlap. In this case, all the need is translated into demand; all the demand is satisfied; all of the provision goes to satisfy both the demand and the need; there is no SID and underprovision; and there is no UNC and underutilization; and the health care services are efficiently used in both economic and medical profession terms. Probably, this extreme is the theoretical direction of health care policy, although the issue of payment or subsidization of medical care complicates things.

In the other extreme, the three circles are independent of each other, and there is no overlap between any two of them. In this case, provision is completely away from demand and need; no need is translated into demand; all of the provision is SID and UNC (SID and UNC being equal in this case); all of the demand is underprovision; and all of the need is underutilization. This extreme represents the worst health care situation, in which the heath care services are used to satisfy neither demand nor need, and the resources are wasted completely. The discussion of these two extremes is for illustrative purposes. In fact, the full overlap and the full separation of the three circles can never happen. All the situations are different degrees of partial overlap among need, demand, and provision.

The overlap between the three circles divides the whole picture into seven interrelated areas, each carrying a unique meaning. *P* is an area of provision that can satisfy neither demand nor need. *D* refers to demand that is neither translated from professionally defined need nor satisfied by actual provision. *N* is need for health care that is not met by actual utilization and not related to demand. *PD* is satisfied demand that is not related to need. *PN* is satisfied need that is not related to demand. *DN* is demand translated from need, but not met by actual provision. *PDN* represents an area where provision can meet both need and demand.

The implications of these divisions are the following: (1) both economists and health professionals hold that *PDN* should be increased and *DN* should be decreased; (2) in the view of health economists, *PD* should be increased and *PN* should be decreased; (3) in the view of health professionals, however, *PN* should be increased and *PD* should be decreased; (4) to economists, *P* and *D* should be decreased, and *N* may be a concern if there is underdemand due to lack of income; and (5) to health professionals, however, *P* and *N* should be reduced and *D* is not a concern. Health economists and health professionals disagree regarding *PD* and *PN*, and *N* and *D*. Because of these conflicts, the ideal provision would mean different things to both groups if demand and need do not fully overlap. Health economists would like to make an effort to pull *Circle C* down and to the left so that both SID and underprovision can be reduced; while health professionals would like to pull *Circle C* down and to the right so that both UNC and underutilization can be reduced. Agreement will be reached when demand (*Circle A*) and need (*Circle B*) are coextensive. In this case, both health economists and health professionals would like to pull *Circle C* downward so that SID, UNC, underprovision, and underutilization can be minimized.

The above discussion puts the concepts of SID and UNC into a broader context. This can help clarify the framework for the estimation of SID and UNC, explored below.

SUPPLIER-INDUCED DEMAND

According to standard economic theory, an increase in supply is expected to be followed by a decrease in the suppliers' earnings and in the prices of their services. Although this can explain most markets, it cannot explain the market for health care.

A Brief History

As early as 1959, Roemer and Shain found that an increase in the supply of beds was followed by an increase in the utilization of hospital services. They stated that "a built bed is a filled bed," which is sometimes referred to as Roemer's Law (Roemer and Shain 1959). Ten years later in 1969, Lewis found significant variations in surgical utilizations across geographic areas in the United States, part of which he attributed to differences in surgeon-population ratios (Lewis 1969). In

1970 Bunker found that England and Wales, with a national health service, had a surgeon-population ratio only one half as large as the ratio in the United States and performed one half the number of operations, with no discernable detriment to health status (Bunker 1970). In 1972 Fuchs and Kramer found that the physician-population ratio was more important than consumer income, price, or insurance coverage in explaining variations in the number of visits per capita (Fuchs and Kramer 1973). In 1974 Evans found a positive relationship between medical prices and physician-population ratio in some Canadian provinces (Evans 1974). In 1981, Mitchell and Cromwell found a strong positive relationship between surgeon density and surgical fees (Mitchell and Cromwell 1981).

A hypothesis that may explain these phenomena is that physicians have the power to alter consumer demand. The underlying reasons are that because of the lack of information about health status and the effect of medical care on health, consumers of health care often rely heavily on physicians to act as their agents and inform them about these variables; that physicians can often provide information about these variables that will allow patients to form a demand curve; and that in their own interest, physicians can influence the demand curve for medical care by providing information that is not wholly accurate. These provide the theoretical basis for the SID hypothesis.

Intense debate about whether physicians can create demand for health services started in the early 1970s. Throughout the past two decades, health economists have tried to formulate a SID theory, develop a method for estimating SID, and provide empirical evidence regarding the presence and absence of SID.

Theory of Supplier-Induced Demand

The SID theory reported by Evans (1974), Reinhardt (1978), and Jacobs (1991), predicts doctors' behavior when the price is set at different levels. The number of doctors in an area increases under both fixed and unfixed medical prices.

Basic Assumptions

The theory has two major groups of basic assumptions. The first group is the demand-side assumptions: (1) demand for health care depends on consumer tastes and income and on service prices; (2) consumer tastes for medical care depend on the marginal utility of health ($\Delta U/\Delta H$), the marginal effect of medical care on health ($\Delta H/\Delta M$), and the individual's health status; (3) the demand curve for medical care will slope downward with respect to price, because the marginal utility of medical care will decline with the increase of medical care; and (4) when any of $\Delta U/\Delta H$, $\Delta H/\Delta M$, or the initial health status change, individual tastes will change, and the change in tastes will cause the demand curve to shift.

The second group is the supply-side assumptions: (1) each physician faces a demand curve that is dependent on market demand and the number of physicians for a given population; (2) as the number of physicians increases relative to the population, each physician's demand curve shifts inward; (3) each physician can induce a change in the patient's tastes and hence an outward shift in demand for that physician's services by influencing the patient's perceived values of H and $\Delta H/\Delta M$; (4) there is a limit to the degree to which this demand generation or inducement can occur, first, because the physician is not the only source of information and, if the patient perceives that the physician's information is too far from reality, the patient will switch to another doctor, and second, because inducement can yield disutility to the physician. In either case, generating too much SID will make the physician worse off; and (5) with regard to cost behavior, it is assumed that physicians have the upward-sloping marginal cost (MC) curves, that is, as more services are provided, marginal costs increase.

The Level of Fixed Price and SID by the Doctor as a Profit Maximizer

In addition to the above basic assumptions, physician behavior may vary depending on the doctor's objective function. In this first case, the doctor is a profit maximizer and the medical price is fixed. As figure 12.2 indicates, if the price is fixed at P_1, the true demand curve is D_0, and the marginal cost curve is MC, the doctor will provide Q_1 amount of services. The doctor will not provide more than Q_1 because more services means less profit. If the price is set at P_2, the doctor would shift the demand curve from D_0 to D_1 for more income, and he can produce as much as Q_2 amount of services. If the price is set at P_3, the doctor has to produce Q_3 instead of Q_4 amount of services because the doctor is reluctant to shift demand further. D_2 will be the limit beyond which the doctor will be worse off.

The conclusions of this simple model are that with the most selfish of physicians, the quantity demanded and the degree of demand generation will depend on the given price of medical care. The higher the price, the more likely is the doctor to induce demand. This model predicts, first, whether SID exists; how much it depends on the level of true demand and the level of the fixed price. SID happens only if more demand can generate more profit, and SID is below the limit. Second, an increase in the physician-population ratio will lead to a reduction in demand for an individual doctor, and the doctor will shift demand out only if SID is less than the limit. Third, while the increase in per capita provision following an increase in the physician-population ratio means SID, holding other factors constant, the nonchange in per capita provision with an increase in this ratio does not mean there is no SID because demand may already be induced to the limit.

SID by the Doctor with Income Target under Fixed Price

In the second case, the doctor's objective is to reach his target income level, and the price is fixed. Suppose that the set price is P_2 and the true demand is D_1 As shown in figure 12.2, the quantity of service provided will be Q_2. At this production point, Y amount of net income will be generated for the doctor. The doctor

Figure 12.2   The Price, Marginal Cost, and Supplier-Induced Demand

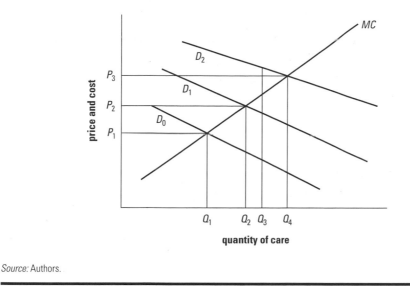

Source: Authors.

will not shift the demand curve to D_2, because his income is already at the target income level, Y. If the number of physicians in this area increases significantly, the doctor will face a reduced true demand (assuming demand is equally distributed among doctors in this area), and the true demand curve will shift from D_1 to D_0, and the doctor's income will be reduced accordingly. To maintain his original target income, the doctor has to maintain the level of demand by inducing the patients' willingness to pay, so that demand will not fall as a result of the increase in the number of physicians in this area. The demand curve will be kept at D_1, although the true demand curve is D_0. The conclusions of this prediction are the following: for a doctor facing a fixed price with the target income, if the physician-population ratio increases and true demand decreases, the doctor will try to maintain demand by inducement to reach the target income; and if the fixed price decreases (or increases), the quantity of provision will increase (or decrease) for the target income.

SID with Price Increase

Contrary to standard economic theory, which predicts a price decrease following an increase in supply, in some cases an increase in the supply of doctors is followed by an increase in medical fees if the fees are not regulated (Evans 1974). The model is shown in figure 12.3.

In this figure, D_1 represents an initial demand level; S_1 an initial supply level; the equilibrium price will be P_1; and the equilibrium quantity will be Q_1. The initial

Figure 12.3   Supplier-Induced Demand under a Nonfixed Price

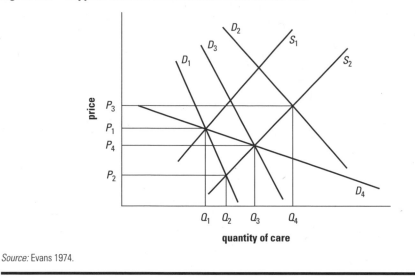

Source: Evans 1974.

supply level corresponds to an initial physician-population ratio. If the physician-population ratio increases, the supply curve will shift out to S_2. According to standard economic theory, a new equilibrium will be formed, the price will fall to P_2, and the equilibrium quantity will rise to Q_2. But this prediction does not square with the alleged empirical fact that price increases with an increase in the physician-population ratio. To square the theory with facts, a number of health economists have contended that suppliers can shift out the demand. Suppose that the supplier can shift the demand curve from D_1 to D_2, the equilibrium price increases to P_3 ($P_3 > P_1$) and the equilibrium quantity to Q_3 ($Q_3 > Q_1$) when supply increases from S_1 to S_2. This prediction concludes that if the doctor can shift demand and if the price of medical care is not fixed, then both the price and the quantity can increase. The increase in price and quantity means the existence of SID only if the increase cannot be explained by other factors that may influence demand. This constitutes a major difficulty in estimating SID, which is discussed in detail later in this chapter.

SID with Price Decrease

Differing from the case stated above, SID may not necessarily lead to an increase in price. Suppose, for instance, that after an increase in supply from S_1 to S_2, as shown in figure 12.3, the doctor can shift the demand only from D_1 to D_3. In this case, the equilibrium price and quantity will be P_4 and Q_4. As a result of the demand inducement, the quantity increases from Q_1 to Q_4, but the price decreases from P_1 to P_4. If this phenomenon occurs in the real world (i.e., the quantity increases and the price decreases after an increase in supply), the existence of SID cannot be considered proven because this phenomenon can be explained by an alternative reason. Because the true demand curve is not known, whether the true demand curve will be D_1 or D_4 is not certain. If the true demand curve is D_4, the phenomenon can be explained by the competitive economic model. Thus, a fall in price when supply increases is consistent with both the competitive and the SID theories. The conclusion here is that if a decrease in price and an increase in quantity are observed after an increase in supply, the existence of SID can neither be denied nor granted.

Measurement Methods and Empirical Evidence

"It takes two to tango." As stated early in this chapter, SID can only be measured directly if true demand and actual provision are both measurable. But in practice, only the actual provision is measurable, and SID cannot be measured directly by using the equation, *SID = Provision – (PDN + PD)*. Although SID is not directly measurable, it may be inferred through additional technical analysis. A number of different methods have been tried in the past two decades and are summarized below.

Correlation Analysis Using Aggregated Data

The idea behind this method is that if there is a positive relationship between the total number of provisions (dependent variable) and the physician-population ratio (independent variable) across geographic areas or between the fee (dependent variable) and the physician-population ratio (independent variable) across geographic areas, and if other factors cannot explain or cannot fully explain the difference in provisions, SID will exist.

The aggregated-data approach means that the observation units are geographic areas, and the data are collected at area levels. Aggregated data can either be cross-sectional or time-series. The cross-sectional data are collected at a given point in time across various areas, as in Fuchs and Kramer (1973), Fuchs (1978), and Cromwell and Mitchell (1986). The time-series data are collected at various points in time for each area of the study sample, as in Feldstein's study (1970). In either case, regression analysis (or other types of analysis) can be conducted to test whether there is a positive relationship between the dependent variables (fee level and aggregated provision) and the independent variables including the physician-population ratio and other possible variables. Although some of the studies find a positive relation between physician-population ratio and per capita provision (Fuchs and Kramer 1973; Fuchs 1978; Mitchell and Cromwell 1982), and some of the studies find a positive relation between physician-population ratio and fee level (Evans 1974; Mitchell and Cromwell 1981), some of them do not find these positive relationships (Feldstein 1970; Dyckman 1978).

Using the aggregated data to test the existence of SID encounters several methodological problems. The first is the "identification problem," that is, the studies fail to identify other factors that may be correlated with the fee level and the quantity of provision (Pauly 1980; Ramsey 1981; Auster and Oaxaca 1981), such as tastes, income, insurance coverage, and health status of the population. Because almost all the studies of this type use data that are collected for other purposes than for testing the SID hypothesis, some of the variables mentioned above cannot be included in the analysis. The increase in per capita use and medical price may be caused by change in consumer tastes, increase in insurance coverage, increase in income, and change in health status of the population. Thus, attributing the positive relationship between per capita use or price and the physician-population ratio exclusively to the supplier inducement is not valid.

The second problem related to aggregated data is the invalid measurement of the dependent variable—the per capita quantity of services. In aggregated data studies, per capita use is calculated by the total quantity of service provided in an area divided by the total number of people in this area. Error will exist if people from other areas use services in this area, or if people in this area use services in other areas. Sloan and Feldman (1978) call this phenomenon "border-crossing." This problem becomes less severe as the definition of the geographic area becomes larger.

Wilensky and Rossiter (1983) point out another problem: that the observation units (areas) should represent a specific medical market, and the areas should be the same size in terms of the market they represent. In almost all the studies of this kind, however, the areas are selected for other purposes and they may not represent the medical market. In addition, because the sizes of the market areas are not similar, their contributions to the relationship between the physician-population ratio and per capita use or price are different. Statistical analysis in this case should consider the different weights that should be attached to the observation units by using the weighted least-square method. But, as Wilensky and Rossiter state, this has rarely been the practice.

Correlation Analysis Using Disaggregated Data

Differing from the aggregated data approach, the studies based on disaggregated data collect data from either individual patients or individual physicians. The relationship between the physician-population ratio and the fees or the quantity of care has been tested. The quantity of care is measured by the number of visits, physician-initiated visits, procedures, and physician-initiated expenditure. The advantage of this type of study is that the data regarding other factors that may affect the dependent variables—such as the reimbursement rate, characteristics of the physician or patient, insurance coverage, and patient income—can be collected. This allows the researchers to do micro-analysis of any causality relationship between the physician-population ratio and the fees or quantity of services.

The studies using data collected from individual physicians have generally found some evidence to support a causal relationship between the physician-population ratio and induced demand. Evans (1974), a recognized proponent of the physician-induced demand hypothesis, demonstrated higher individual physician fees and gross billings in areas with a higher physician-population ratio and concluded that SID is a significant factor in the Canadian health care system. Steinwald and Sloan (1974), using individual physician data, found a positive relationship between physician density and internists' and obstetricians' fees, but a negative relationship for general practitioners. Pauly and Satterthwaite (1981), using individual physician data, identified a positive relationship between physician density and physician fees, but they found an alternative explanation to SID. They postulated that physicians are able to become increasingly monopolistic as physician density increases because information sharing among consumers is more difficult when there are many physicians. This theory expects higher fees in physician-dense areas. Woodward and Warren-Boulten (1981), after analyzing the relationship between physicians' net income and physician density, concludes that physicians may be able to generate demand for their services.

Patient-based studies, however, generally find little evidence of SID. May (1975) reports a positive correlation between physician density and the number of visits, but it was explained as the result of increased availability instead of SID. Pauly (1980) investigates the relationship between physician density and medical price (measured by whether the patients carry insurance), and concludes that physician-induced demand is an issue that can safely be ignored.

Wilensky and Rossiter (1983) reported on multivariate studies testing the relationship between physician-initiated utilization and expenditure. In addition to physician supply, the studies take into consideration related factors, such as physician characteristics, patient characteristics, insurance, and reimbursement. The relationships revealed between physician density and inducement are mixed after controlling for other factors. Although these studies show a positive relationship between physician density and physician-initiated ambulatory care, the number of physician-initiated visits, and the amount spent on these visits, physician density does not affect the likelihood of surgery or total physician-initiated expenditure.

Review of the disaggregated data approaches shows that even more microanalysis cannot enable a firm conclusion about the existence of SID. In addition, when this type of analysis uses data on physician-initiated utilization and expenditure, problems appear because physician-initiated demand and SID are not the same concept. Physician initiation is inducement only when services recommended are above and beyond what the patient would buy if he knew as much as the physician. Because how much of the initiation is beyond the patient's true demand is generally unknown, SID is still an untestable concept.

Natural Experiment

The idea of natural experiment is based mostly on the target income hypothesis of SID. According to this hypothesis, if the payment rate for the physician services decreases, the physician will increase his service provision to maintain his original income; if the payment rate increases, the quantity of service provision is expected to decrease. Contrary to the previous approaches, the natural experiment takes the change in the payment level as a natural intervention and examines whether it results in a reverse change in provision. The inverse relationship between output and reimbursement is consistent with the notion of SID (Rice 1987).

This type of study is characterized by a retrospective, longitudinal approach. Data are collected before and after the payment change. The study may be based on either a simple before-and-after comparison or a more sophisticated control study in which data are collected for both a test group (with intervention) and control group (without intervention). A major advantage of this type of study is that it is able to control for many other factors and remove the variable omission problem that exists in the previous method of correlating physician density with measures of output. Another advantage is that the measurement problem is minimized because data are usually collected from the third-party claim file. It generally believed that this natural experiment approach can yield more valid conclusions than the correlation approaches.

Rice (1987) and Scott and Hall (1995) review several natural experimental studies and come to almost the same conclusion. When there is an exogenous change in the payment rates, physicians respond in a consistent manner: the reduced payment results in increased output, and the increased payment leads to lower output. Typically, output responses are in the form of increased intensity of visits and provision of more ancillary services.

Analyses by Rice (1983) and Barer, Evans, and Rice (1988) indicate that reductions in the level of remuneration lead to increases in provision and service intensity, while controlling for other factors. Hadley, Holahan, and Scanlon (1979), using longitudinal billing data from random samples of physicians in California in the United States, test the effect of fee controls between 1972 and 1975. The results show that the number of billed Medicare services increases when controls are in place and, when the controls are lifted, utilization levels off. Gross physician payments are unaffected. Although most of the studies provide support for the SID hypothesis, some studies find little evidence. For example, Hughes and Yule (1992) test the effect of changes in fees on the quantity of maternity and cervical cytology services over a 22-year period in the United Kingdom by using secondary data sources. They find that the annual changes in real fees do not influence the quantity of services provided.

Although the natural experiment has advantages over correlation methods, the validity of conclusions from the natural experiment is also limited for several reasons. First, as stated by Scott, most studies are opportunistic in nature and use secondary data collected for other purposes. In this case, it is impossible to include all the possible variables that might explain variations in the dependent variable. For example, Hadley, Holahan, and Scanlon (1979) and Mitchell, Wedig, and Cromwell (1989) failed to control for important confounding factors because of the data availability problem. Second, comparability between control groups is questionable because the observation subjects are not randomly distributed to the groups. Thus, the change in the dependent variable may not be caused by the intervention, but rather by the original and natural variation between experiment and control groups. Third, because the conclusions cannot be replicated in some situations and the research results are not fully consistent, studies of this type are unlikely to settle the issue of SID. They do, however, offer an attractive alternative to the conventional approaches.

Informed-Uninformed Consumer Comparison

Informed-uninformed consumer comparison studies focus directly on the information gap between physician and patient by comparing the quantity of service provision to patients who are physicians with the quantity of services provided to other professionals. It is argued that if physicians induce the demand, less health service will be provided to them and their family members than to other professionals and their family members with similar demographic and socioeconomic status but lacking the same medical knowledge. By measuring the difference in provision to informed consumers and to relatively uninformed consumers, this approach provides a method of attempting to directly estimate SID.

Bunker and Brown (1974) reported the first study of this type. They compared the provision of seven surgeries performed on physicians and their spouses and on their nonmedical counterparts. They found that the physician patients and their spouses had 20 to 30 percent higher total rates of operations than the general population, and the differences were statistically significant. Their conclusion provides no support for the SID hypothesis.

Later, Hay and Leahy (1982) reported the second study of this type and provided critiques of Bunker and Brown's study. The first shortcoming of the study is that the sample was not representative of a national population because it was not a random sample and the sample was small. The second important shortcoming is that in Bunker and Brown's study, the price of the surgical study was not controlled. Physicians' families may well have more comprehensive health insurance coverage, receive more "professional courtesy" medical care, and pay a lower price for medical services than patients outside the medical profession. If so, the true demand of physician families should be higher, and as a result, the difference in provision may reflect a difference in true demand, not in SID. Third, a history of high health risk in the family may have influenced a medical doctor's choice of profession; his family members may have a higher demand for services because of a predisposition to health problems; and their true demand should naturally be higher, other things being equal. This third shortcoming poses another comparability problem. Hay and Leahy attempt to overcome these shortcomings and examine the differences between informed (physician patients) and relatively uninformed patients. They conclude that medical professionals and their families are as likely, if not more likely than other people, to visit physicians, controlling for the sociodemographic factors, price factors, access to care, and perceived health status.

Some 10 years later, a study conducted by Domenighetti and others (1993) in Switzerland, where there are strong financial incentives for doctors to over-provide, reveals a different conclusion. This study measures by questionnaire the standardized consumption of seven common surgical procedures. Except for appendectomy, the age- and gender-standardized consumption of each of the common surgical procedures is always higher in the general population than for the gold-standard physician patients. This study suggests that, contrary to prior research, doctors have much lower rates of surgery than the general population and that, in a fee-for-service heath care market without financial barriers to medical care, the less-informed patients are greater consumers of common surgical procedures.

Although this method provides an approach that can almost directly measure SID, the inconsistent conclusions and the comparability problems existing between the informed and uninformed consumers put a cloud of doubt on this method. In addition, according to the condition of coexistence of overprovision and underprovision, even if the true demand of physicians and general patients is the same, the measurement of SID is still difficult, because the inducement can only be measured by considering both the overprovision and the underprovision. Although services are less likely to be overprovided to physician patients, they are also less likely to be underprovided. Differences in the actual provision between physician patients and general patients are meaningless unless both overprovision and underprovision can be measured.

Hypothetical Case Method

An interesting method is reported by David Hemenway at the Harvard School of Public Health, the hypothetical case method. According to this method, designed hypothetical cases are presented to doctors from areas with different physician densities. The doctors are asked to propose treatment. If physicians from high physician-density areas propose more services than physicians from low-density areas, it means that SID is more likely. Hemenway's study shows that physician density is significantly and positively correlated with the aggressiveness of the proposed treatment. This result lends support to the induced demand hypothesis.

One of the advantages of this approach is that it can hold all the consumer factors constant and eliminate many of the confounding factors on the part of the patients. Another advantage is that the physician characteristics can be collected, and they can be incorporated into analysis. One of the disadvantages is that the proposed treatment may not represent the real behavior of the doctors, and the proposed treatment may be biased toward the interest of the patient because the doctors know this is a "test." Another disadvantage is that the proposed treatment is not equal to the actual provision, because the patient may not use the proposed services after the recommendation. In addition, variations in the proposed treatment may be explained by uncertainty about the effectiveness of the treatment and by differences in patient preferences. Thus, this method can be used to develop the hypothesis, not to test the hypothesis of SID.

Experimental Study

Phelps (1986) suggests a social laboratory experiment method, but he does not recommend any particular design for this approach. No literature on the experimental study for testing the SID hypothesis has been found by the present authors.

The proposed method can take one of three forms. (1) Patients with specified diseases are educated on the appropriate care, and the actual provision can be compared between before and after the education and/or between the experiment and the control groups, into which individual patients are distributed randomly. If educational intervention reduces the actual provision, then SID will be supported. (2) Patients with the same diseases and other characteristics (such as insurance coverage) are randomly distributed to physicians in different areas with different physician densities, and the service provided for a period of time can then be compared between patients visiting areas with different physician densities. (3) At the most extreme, the inducement laboratory (Phelps 1986) can be created in which similar physicians and similar patients are selected and randomly distributed into the experiment group and the control group. Intervention can be changed in fee levels, education of the patient, or manipulation of the physicians' workload. Although the experimental study is difficult to undertake and has never been conducted, it may provide the only method toward a firm conclusion of SID.

UNNECESSARY CARE

The study of UNC begins with the recognition of geographic variations in the utilization of health care services.

Geographic Variation in Utilization

Early studies of geographic variation reported differences in the utilization of surgical services among small areas (counties or hospital catchment areas), but later studies showed impressive variations in the variety of services between large areas (regions, provinces, and countries). From the beginning, geographic variation has been regarded as evidence of UNC.

One of the earliest studies was conducted by Lewis (1969). He compared the utilization of six common surgical procedures by Blue Cross enrollees among 11 health planning regions in Kansas, United States. Variation in utilization ranged from 2.3 times for inguinal hernia to 3.8 times for appendectomy. He noted a correlation of surgical rates with the number of hospital beds and the number of surgeons.

Later, Wennberg and Gittelsohn (1973) studied variations in the performance of the same six operations and some other surgeries among 13 hospital service areas in Vermont, also in the United States. They found that the number of procedures performed per 10,000 persons ranged from 13 to 151 for tonsillectomy, 10 to 32 for appendectomy, and 30 to 1,141 for dilation and curettage. In 1975, they found similar variations in the utilization of these same operations among 42 Health Service Areas in Maine, United States (Wennberg and Gittelsohn 1975). These became known as the "Wennberg Variation."

In 1982 McPherson and others found that hysterectomy was performed nearly 3 times as often in the United States as in England and Wales, and prostatectomy 2.5 times as frequently (McPherson et al. 1982). In 1984 Vayda and others found a more than fourfold variation in cesarean-section rates and a more than ninefold variation for colectomy among counties in Ontario, Canada (Vayda et al. 1984).

Several other studies involve the geographic difference in utilization of other health care services, including the length of hospital stay (Chassin 1983; Deason et al. 1979), hospital admissions for medical conditions (Connell, Day, LoGerfo 1981; Knickman and Foltz 1984), office visits (Chassin and Brook 1989), and home health visits (Hammond 1985).

Theory of Geographic Variation

Some authors note that the variation could result from statistical problems of sampling (Diehr 1984), but the consistency of variations over time and across regions from multiple studies provides abundant evidence that the variations are real. What then are the reasons for these variations?

Possible Explanatory Factors

A number of variables have been studied as possible explanations for geographic variation in the utilization of health care. These include the supply of beds and physicians, patient characteristics, physician characteristics, and the health care system itself.

The supply variables, such as the number of beds per 1,000 population and physician density, have been studied thoroughly under the hypothesis of supplier-induced demand, previously discussed. Generally speaking, although there is much evidence that more beds (Lewis 1969; Stockwell and Vayda 1979; Wennberg and Gittelsohn 1973) and more physicians (Lewis 1969; Bunker 1970; Wennberg, Barnes, and Zubkoff 1982) will be followed by more provision (or utilization), some authors do not find this positive relationship. For example, Roos (1984) finds no relationship between geographic variation in the performance of hysterectomy and the availability of hospital beds. Two studies refute the positive relationship between physician density and the quantity of provision of tonsillectomy and cholecystectomy, the highest rates being found in regions with the lowest number of physicians performing the operations. Roos, Roos, and Henteleff

1977; Cageorge, Roos, and Danzinger 1981). The case for the SID hypothesis is still inconclusive.

While studies show that some patient characteristics such as age, gender, income, education, and health status influence the rate of utilizations, they have little link with geographic variations (Leape 1989).

With regard to the health care system, although at the national level the health care financing system is correlated with utilization rates (e.g., Britain versus the United States), there is little link at the regional level between the geographic variation and the ability to find a doctor (Roos and Roos 1982); the method of payment (Leape 1989); and participation in a health maintenance organization (HMO) (Manning et al. 1984).

Another group of factors that may affect utilization rates across geographic areas are related to the practice style or philosophy of the physicians. Bunker (1970) noted long ago that U.S. surgeons were more aggressive than their overworked British counterparts. Vayda (1973) found similar differences in comparing Canadian surgeons to those in England and Wales. Wennberg and Gittelsohn used the term "surgical signature" to refer to surgical decision patterns in small areas (Wennberg and Gittelsohn 1982). They consider differences in the physician's propensity to employ surgical treatment the most important variable explaining regional variations. Now, additional questions arise: why are the doctors' decisions different and do the geographic variations indicate the existence of unnecessary care? Three theories compete to explain the geographic variations: the unnecessary care theory, the uncertainty theory, and the enthusiasm theory.

Unnecessary Care Theory

The earliest theory to explain the geographic variations in health care services is the unnecessary care theory. This theory predicts that variations in utilization among areas are caused by variations in the degree of unnecessary care; the higher utilization rates in some areas result from greater overutilization. This theory was proposed as soon as the geographic variations in utilization were recognized in the early 1950s (Lembcke 1952), and it was later developed in the 1970s and 1980s. One of the shortcomings of this theory is that it ignores the possibility that, although the variations may be caused by overutilization in high-use areas, they may be caused by underutilization in low-use areas. Probably driven by cost-control forces, the problem of underutilization is rarely addressed.

Some evidence points to the existence of unnecessary care, for instance that feedback to doctors on their performance can reduce the utilization rate. Wennberg (1984) shows that, when practitioners were informed that their rates were substantially above state averages, their rates subsequently dropped. In some cases, the results were dramatic: a 50 percent decrease in the rate of hysterectomy and a 90 percent decrease in the rate of tonsillectomy. The logical conclusion from this experience is that the surgeons recognized that some of the previous operations had been unnecessary.

Another piece of evidence is that the second-opinion program in the United States helps reduce the rate of utilization. The famous "SSO" (second surgical opinion) study conducted by McCarthy and Widmer (1974) led to congressional hearings in the United States held by the Subcommittee on Oversight and Investigations of the House Committee on Interstate and Foreign Commerce. Based on McCarthy's unconfirmed estimation, the committee reported that in 1975, 2.4 million unnecessary operations had been performed, with 11,900 deaths and at a cost of US$3.9 billion (Leape 1989). During the following decade, the second-opinion program expanded gradually. By the mid-1980s, the program was implemented nationwide for elective surgeries by both commercial and social health insurance schemes. Although there were many design problems in the studies conducted during the 1980s, as reviewed by Leape (1989), the 10 to 30 percent reduction in the rates of surgery suggests that unnecessary care exists to a large extent.

More evidence is that HMO enrollees use fewer medical services than insured persons with fee-for-service payment, and there is also some evidence that this reduction in utilization is not associated with impaired health outcomes (Manning et al. 1984; Ware et al. 1986). This suggests that there might be overutilization under the fee-for-service system.

Still more evidence comes from the 2.3 percent reduction in unnecessary surgery and unnecessary admissions after the U.S. Congress established the peer review organizations in 1984 (Leape 1989). Peer review organizations are independent contractors, charged with reviewing doctors' medical recommendations for Medicare patients. When a surgeon proposes an operation, approval must be obtained before the patient can be admitted to the hospital or have the operation performed. The reduction in hospital and surgical utilization by Medicare patients also suggests the existence of UNC.

There is some evidence of the existence of UNC but little evidence on whether geographic variation in utilization can be explained by the variation in UNC. Two early studies conducted by Roos, Roos, and Henteleff (1977) directly addressed this issue. In these studies, practice standards were developed and used to evaluate the existence of UNC for several operations. They found high percentages of unnecessary use but no correlation of unnecessary use with the utilization rates. Another prestigious study, conducted by the RAND Corporation and the University of California at Los Angeles (UCLA), drew a similar conclusion (Chassin, Kosecoff, and Park 1987). The researchers examined the presumption that high rates mean inappropriate use, using elaborate methods (which are introduced later). They found high percentages of inappropriate use but failed to find significant differences between high- and low-use areas in the percentage of operations performed for inappropriate reasons.

According to the available information, it seems likely that UNC is not an explanation for geographic variation in the use of care. The variation puzzle still needs further investigations. One thing is almost conclusive: based on solid evidence, UNC does exist. This raises another question, why does UNC exist? This question is discussed next.

Uncertainty Theory

Scientists made little headway with the puzzle until Wennberg, Barnes, and Zubkoff (1982) proposed the theory of uncertainty (Wennberg 1987). This theory states that physicians face great uncertainty concerning which health services are effective under which clinical circumstances. Proponents of this theory maintain that the great lack of data on effectiveness permits reasonable physicians to come to different conclusions regarding when to use various health services. This theory implies that whereas physicians may agree on indications for procedures that are clearly appropriate and on those that are clearly inappropriate, much disagreement exists over the large gray area in the middle. This theory would predict that for a procedure with higher professional uncertainty, the geographic variation will be greater than for one with high certainty, and vice versa; and that there will be a greater proportion of equivocal cases in high-use areas than in low-use areas.

Some empirical studies show some evidence that procedures with higher uncertainty are more likely to vary. Inguinal hernia and fractured hip are good examples of conditions with low uncertainty. In all geographic-variation studies, these two conditions show a small degree of variation (Wennberg 1986; Chassin and Brook 1989). Conversely, the indications for carotid endarterectomy are highly controversial, and there are wide variations in its use (Chassin et al. 1986). Unfortunately, the second prediction is not proved. Neither the large-area studies (Chassin, Kosecoff, and Park 1987) nor the small-area studies (Leape, Park, and Solomon 1990) find a positive relationship between the level of use and the proportion of equivocal cases. The power of the theory of professional uncertainty to explain geographic variations seems inconclusive.

Enthusiasm Theory

The enthusiasm theory was proposed by Mark Chassin, one of the investigators in the RAND/UCLA project (Chassin 1993). This theory suggests that differences in the utilization of specific care across areas are caused primarily by the variability in the prevalence of physicians who are "enthusiastic" about the use of a service that varies in use. Differing from the uncertainty theory, this theory suggests that enthusiasts are not uncertain; they are believers. Chassin argues that the up-to-date data are consistent with the hypothesis that geographic differences arise when large numbers of physicians in one area become enthusiastic about a procedure. He states:

> This enthusiasm maybe originated in a major local physician training program, in which a particularly influential teacher communicates enthusiastic views to residents and fellows. The enthusiasts must then persuade the primary care physicians who refer patients that their views are correct. If the enthusiasts are successful, large differences in the use of procedures can be created simply because one area has a greater number of enthusiasts than another.

Chassin examined this theory by using carotid endarterectomy as an example and found the high-use area had approximately sixfold the number of enthusiasts

as the low-use area, as measured by surgeons who did at least 10 carotid endar-
terectomies in 1981. He suggests that the evidence on this theory is preliminary
and that further studies need to be undertaken to test it, but no literature on
further studies was found by the present authors.

Explaining Unnecessary Care

A great deal of effort has been made to explain the geographic variations in
utilization, but relatively little has been done to study the factors that influence
the degree of UNC, which is more relevant to efficiency improvement and cost
control.

The economic incentive is the most important of all the factors that may
influence a doctor's decision. Although the characterization of physicians as
income maximizers is overly simplistic, in a society where income determines
both status and the standard of living, income maximization is surely a rational
behavior. The evidence that patients in fee-for-service systems have more operations overall than those in prepaid plans has been widely accepted as evidence
that the economic incentive leads to increased provision of services. In addressing the question of whether the economic motivation can lead physicians to
provide UNC, another look at SID, agency theory, and the utility function of the
doctors is useful (chapters 5 and 6 in this volume). Although few studies establish a linkage between economic incentive and UNC, if professional uncertainty
is considered, the economic incentive such as fee-for-service will lead a physician to decide to provide more care with uncertain effectiveness.

At this point, the concepts of SID and UNC may converge. Unnecessary care
(overutilization) and supplier-induced demand (overprovision) are different concepts, but they carry the same meaning—waste. Economists consider this waste
the actual provision in excess of true demand, and other researchers consider it
the actual utilization in excess of need. If the relationship between the economic
incentive (or any other factor related to policy intervention) and SID cannot
be tested, due to the difficulty of measuring SID, can the relationship between
those factors and UNC be tested? The answer to this question depends on the
measurability of UNC, discussed next.

Methods of Measurement

The measurement of UNC is closely related to health service utilization review,
intended to ensure quality and reduce health care costs. The utilization review
was developed in the United States and later was used in European countries
(Coast 1996). Two quality assurance studies in the early 1930s first addressed
the problem of measuring the appropriateness of hospital care (Payne 1987),
but identification of unnecessary care did not receive wide attention until World
War II, during the wartime hospital bed shortage. Increases in health care costs
due to the implementation of social health schemes in the United States in the

1960s speeded up the development of utilization review programs. By the end of 1979, 90 percent of U.S. hospitals had put in place utilization review programs (Gertman et al. 1979). To measure unnecessary care, these programs need a method that is standardized, reliable, valid, and widely accepted. Generally speaking, there are three types of methods: implicit criteria, explicit diagnosis-independent criteria, and explicit diagnosis-specific criteria.

Implicit Criteria

In the *implicit criteria method,* a group of physicians reviews the entire patient record and makes summary judgments about whether the care provided is appropriate and necessary. In the review process, the researcher specifies neither the information to be used in making the judgment nor the process for weighting the various aspects of the information. The validity of the method therefore depends entirely on the knowledge, skill, and judgment of the reviewer. For example, in one study of this type (Morehead 1967), reviewers are briefed on the purpose of the study, and their general role in it, and are asked to use their clinical judgment in assessing the quality and the appropriateness of the medical care provided. The entire medical record is available for their review, and no instructions are provided on how to weigh the various aspects of the review.

Payne (1987) discussed the advantages and disadvantages of this method. The first advantage is that all relevant information about patient care can be included for the reviewer to consider in his review. The second advantage is that the development of the criteria is relatively inexpensive. The most important disadvantage is the bias that results from differences in reviewers' abilities and judgments. This problem is shown by the low agreement rates (low reliability) across reviewers. This problem can be reduced by selecting and training reviewers carefully, but it is unlikely that the bias can be eliminated. In addition, these practices represent a departure from totally implicit, unstructured methods toward an intermediate method between implicit and explicit criteria. The second disadvantage is that the reviewers must be physicians, and so reviews are costly.

Explicit Diagnosis-Independent Criteria

The explicit diagnosis-independent criteria method provides the reviewers with a set of specific criteria for the types of diagnoses and spells out the review process in detail. Ideally, these criteria should be objective, verifiable, and uniform across different hospitals, physician specialties, and types of patients and diagnoses. The earliest diagnosis-independent criteria for the assessment of appropriateness of care were developed by Goldberg and Holloway 1975). Based on their work, the Appropriate Evaluation Protocol (AEP) was developed at Boston University in the early 1980s (Gertman and Restuccia 1981). The AEP assesses the appropriateness of timing and care level of adult medical, surgical, gynecological, and obstetric patients and noninfant pediatric patients, and the medical need for selected medical and surgical procedures. The review instrument can focus on either specific services or hospitalized patients, but not on specific diagnoses. The AEP needs information from the patient's record and is designed to be used by nonphysician reviewers. The AEP includes generic criteria lists that are applied to all patients. For example, there are 16 criteria for admission, and if one of them is met, the admission is deemed appropriate; there are 26 criteria for a day of care, and if one of them is met the day is appropriate (Payne 1987).

The advantages of this method are the following: (1) it needs relatively few criteria, compared with the explicit diagnosis-specific criteria; (2) the criteria can be standardized and transferred from one institution to another; (3) it can be applied by trained nonphysician reviewers, and the practice is relatively inexpensive; and (4) the validity of the assessment does not depend on the accuracy of diagnosis. The first disadvantage is that it costs more to develop explicit criteria than implicit criteria. The second is that the criteria may not include all indicators. If a decision cannot be made for lack of information, final judgment has to rely on the judgment of individual physicians. In this case, bias may occur.

Explicit Diagnosis-Specific Criteria

In the *explicit diagnosis-specific criteria method,* distinctive guidelines are established for categories of patients with specified diagnoses or signs and symptoms. This method requires much more complex instruments and a more structured review process than the implicit criteria method because of the large number of possible diagnoses and treatments, the wide range of patients' medical responses, the variations in the treatments for the same disease, and the advances in technology. The challenges facing the developers of the diagnosis-specific method, as stated by Payne (1987), are to identify each situation that the reviewer might encounter and to develop methods that can be implemented and readily adapted to technology changes. Although this method dates to 1956 when Lembcke developed the first protocol for assessing the appropriateness of care (Payne 1987), the most sophisticated one was developed by the RAND Corporation and UCLA (Brook et al. 1986; Chassin, Kosecoff, and Park 1987).

The RAND/UCLA method of assessing appropriateness was developed in the mid-1980s to test the hypothesis that geographical and institutional variations in the rates of use of specific procedures could be explained by variations in the proportions of appropriately delivered care. The research team developed a systematic method for generating explicit criteria for appropriateness that could be applied evenhandedly to interventions performed in different institutions. It entails a review of the literature and the generation of catalogs of all conceivable indications (usually hundreds of them) for using a particular procedure.

A panel of nine expert clinicians is appointed. Each panelist is sent a copy of the literature review and the catalog of potential indications and asked to rate the appropriateness of performing the procedure for each potential indication on a scale from 1 (extremely inappropriate) to 9 (extremely appropriate). The panel then meets. Each panelist is reminded of the way they rated each indication and given an anonymous breakdown of the other panelists' ratings for each indication. After discussing areas of disagreement, panelists anonymously rerate the entire set of indications. For each indication, a mean score and a measure of the panel's agreement is calculated. Where the mean score for an indication is 1 to 3, there is broad agreement the indication is classified as inappropriate. When the mean is 7 to 9, there is an agreement the indication is classified as appropriate. If the mean is 4 to 6 or if there is a disagreement among the panel, then the indication is classified as equivocal. It is so far the most sophisticated method and has been used by many insurance companies in the United States to determine the appropriateness of care.

The major advantages of this method are the following: (1) the appropriateness of care is assessed by considering all relevant information specified by the indicators; (2) this method can be applied by trained nonphysician reviewers; and (3) once developed, it can be used in different types of institutions and providers. Generally, the disadvantages are these: (1) the instrument is more expensive to develop and update; (2) the assessment process is much more time consuming than the implicit method and the explicit diagnosis-independent criteria; and (3) errors in diagnoses will result in misclassification in terms of appropriateness and inappropriateness.

With regard to the RAND/UCLA method, things are never perfect. Several shortcomings are mentioned by Hicks (1994). First, the definition used by the RAND/UCLA method is not precise and clear. It defines care as *appropriate,* when for an average group of patients presenting to an average U.S. physician, the expected health benefit exceeds the expected negative consequences by a sufficiently wide margin, excluding the consideration of monetary costs. Hopkins (1993) argues that the RAND/UCLA definition omits two important determinants of appropriateness: resources and the individuality of the patient. A decision on the appropriateness of care cannot be made without considering the cost of care. If the costs of care outweigh the benefit, the care cannot be considered appropriate. In addition, because different people value benefit and cost differently, different patients with the same treatment for the same condition may differ in their appropriateness of care.

Second, the RAND/UCLA definition fails to make explicit the intended outcome of the intervention, and the process for generating the criteria does not require the panelists to make the intervention objectives explicit as they rate each indication. This is important because different people may legitimately have different aims and expectations for care, even in identical clinical circumstances. It cannot necessarily be assumed that each of the nine panelists rating an indication has in mind the same intended outcome. This makes it hard for the users of the appropriateness ratings to understand them.

Third, the method asks the panelists to estimate the benefit and risk of the procedure, but what is meant by risk and benefit is not clearly defined. Thus, bias is likely to occur because different panelists will probably take into account different benefits and different risks.

Fourth, the method fails to consider the treatment alternative(s). When procedure A for a patient is assessed appropriate, if another procedure, say procedure B, is much better for the patient, procedure A should be not be provided. The RAND/UCLA method would rate procedure A as appropriate although there is a better alternative.

Fifth, the method takes the point of view of the doctors. If the patients' point of view or society's view is considered, the assessment result may be different.

Finally, bias may occur if (1) the literature review is not thorough; (2) there is little published information to guide the physicians' rating; (3) the panelists are not selected carefully; or (4) the role of the chairperson is not neutral, and the chairperson tries to influence the rating results.

TOWARD BETTER EFFICIENCY OF CARE

While most health economists agree on the existence of SID and predict that it is related to the economic incentive introduced by different payment systems, they are neither available to test the magnitude of SID nor able to confirm its existence. The major difficulty for the measurement of SID stems from the fact that *true demand,* defined as demand by the informed consumer, is not measurable. Fortunately, the studies on health care appropriateness in the past several decades provide many methods for measuring UNC. Although geographic variation studies cannot prove that the variations are caused by UNC, they do prove that UNC exists to a considerable extent. The estimated rates of inappropriate treatment have ranged from about 15 to 30 percent, but up to 40 percent for particular procedures at individual institutions (Phelps 1993). Some studies estimated a rate of 16 percent for inappropriate hysterectomy in seven HMOs (Bernstein, McGlynn, and Siu 1993), 24 percent for inappropriate days spent in a Canadian children's hospital (Gloor, Kissoon, and Joubert 1993), and 23 percent for inappropriate hospitalizations for measles (Havens et al. 1993). Brook, a leader in the studies of medical appropriateness, states (1989: 3027), "If one could extrapolate from the available literature, then perhaps one fourth of hospital days, one fourth of procedures, and two fifths of medications could be done without."

Although there is no consensus on the degree of inefficiency, due to its variations with differences in the situation, it is conclusive that health services are not used efficiently. At this point, the meaning of *efficient use of health services* should be clarified. As discussed in the first section of this chapter, according to the economists' point of view, inefficiency occurs if services (with no positive externality and no public goods) are provided beyond the true demand of the patient, because the benefit from the utilization can be evaluated only by individual patients. According to the point of view of health professionals, inefficiency occurs if utilization of health care exceeds the needs, because the services beyond the needs will not improve health. The economists' view is related to the concept of SID and the health professionals' point view involves the concept of UNC. SID and UNC are twin and partially overlapping concepts, as depicted in figure 12.1. If patients' utility gains from health care depends only on the health outcome, as many health economists say, the informed patient will make health care choices based on the potential health benefit. In this case, SID and UNC become similar concepts.

The review of the literature identifies several problems in the course of efficiency improvement.

- First, proponents of both SID and UNC rarely explicitly express the efficiency concept from the viewpoint of society (Hicks 1994). If the objective of health care is to improve the health of people as stated by the World Health Organization, many other international health care organizations, and various national government bodies, the *efficiency of health services* should be defined as the achievement of the population's maximum health with a given amount of health services. According to this concept, efficiency will occur if the health benefit outweighs the cost of health service, and the marginal health gains from each alternative health service are equal. Thus, the provision of necessary care will not mean efficiency if there is an alternative, less costly treatment with the same benefit; if the supplier-induced demand is not necessarily inefficient; or if the services belong to public goods or goods with a positive external effect.

- Second, while scientists put a great deal of effort into trying to estimate UNC (overutilization) and SID (overprovision), relatively little effort is being made to reduce the extent of underprovision and underutilization. In an era of health care cost control with capitation payment and case payment, the "under" problem should be emphasized. If overutilization and overprovision are taken as utilization and provision of inefficient care, underutilization and underprovision are the failure to provide and utilize efficient care. To improve overall health care efficiency, SID and UNC have to be reduced while, at the same time, preventing underprovision and underutilization. To work on both sides to improve efficiency, underprovision and underutilization need to be estimated and reduced. Cost control and money saving may not necessarily lead to efficiency improvement, unless the necessary services are ensured and the true demand is satisfied.

- Third, while health economists have been enthusiastic about testing the difficult-to-test hypothesis of SID in the last three decades, relatively little effort has been devoted to the practical measures to reduce the extent of inefficiency evidenced by widely identified inappropriate care. In addition, health economists are likely to explain the concept of unnecessary care in economic terms (Pauly 1979), and as a result confusion occurs between the concepts of SID and UNC. If SID is not testable in the foreseeable future, can health economists borrow the idea of UNC, as defined by health professionals? They could then study the factors that may explain differences in UNC, such as the economic incentive, and try to work out policy measures to improve the efficiency of health care services.

NOTE

This chapter is based on a review of the literature by the authors when Xingzhu Liu was pursuing his PhD under the supervision of Professor Anne Mills at the London School of Hygiene and Tropical Medicine. The initial work was funded by the United Nations Development Programme/World Bank/World Health Organization Special Programme for Research and Training in Tropical Diseases and the Overseas Research Students Awards Scheme in the United Kingdom. The authors are also grateful for the follow-up support provided by the World Bank and Abt Associates Inc., Bethesda, Maryland.

REFERENCES

Auster, R.D., and R.L. Oaxaca. 1981. "Identification of Supplier-Induced Demand in the Health Care Sector." *Journal of Human Resources* 16: 327–42.

Barer, M., R.G. Evans, and T. Rice. 1988. "Fee Control and Cost Control: Tales from the Frozen North." *Milbank Quarterly* 66: 1–64.

Bernstein, S.J., E.A. McGlynn, and A.L. Siu. 1993. "The Appropriateness of Hysterectomy: A Comparison of Care in Seven Health Plans." *Journal of the American Medical Association* 269: 2398–2402.

Brook, R.H. 1989. "Practice Guidelines and Practicing Medicine: Are They Compatible?" *Journal of the American Medical Association* 262: 3027–130.

Brook, R.H., M.R. Chassin, D.H. Solomon, J. Kosecoff, and R.R. Park. 1986. "A Method for Detailed Assessment of the Appropriateness of Medical Technologies." *International Journal of Assessment of Health Care* 2: 53–63.

Bunker, J.P. 1970. "Surgical Manpower: A Comparison of Operations and Surgeons in the United States and in England and Wales." *New England Journal of Medicine* 282(3): 135–44.

Bunker, J., and B. Brown. 1974. "Physician-Patient as an Informed Consumer of Surgical Services." *New England Journal of Medicine* 290: 1051–55.

Cageorge, S.M., L.L. Roos, and R. Danzinger Jr. 1981. "Gallbladder Operations: A Population-Based Analysis." *Medical Care* 19(5): 510–25.

Chassin, M.R. 1993. "Explaining Geographic Variations: The Enthusiasm Hypothesis." *Medical Care* 31(5): YS37-YS44.

———.1983. *Variations in Hospital Length of Stay: Their Relationship to Health Outcomes.* Publication No. OTA-HCA-24. Washington, DC: Office of Technology Assessment.

Chassin, M.R. and R.H. Brook. 1989. "The Appropriateness of Selected Medical and Surgical Procedures: Relationship to Geographic Variations." Ann Arbor, MI: Health Administration Press.

Chassin, M.R., R.H. Brook, R.E. Park, J. Keesey, A. Fink, J. Kosecoff, K. Kahn, N. Merrick, and D.H. Solomon. 1986. "Variations in the Use of Medical and Surgical Services by the Medicare Population." *New England Journal of Medicine* 314(5): 285–90.

Chassin, M.R., J. Kosecoff, and R.E. Park. 1987. "Does Inappropriate Use Explain Geographic Variations in the Use of Health Care Services?" *Journal of the American Medical Association* 258: 2533–37.

Coast, J. 1996. "Appropriateness Versus Efficiency: The Economics of Utilisation Review." *Health Policy* 36: 69–81.

Connell, F.A., R.W. Day, and J.P. LoGerfo. 1981. "Hospitalization of Medicaid Children: Analysis of Small Area Variations in Admission Rate." *American Journal of Public Health* 71: 606–9.

Cromwell, J., and J.B. Mitchell. 1986. "Physician-Induced Demand for Surgery." *Journal of Health Economics* 5: 293–313.

Deason, R., J. Lubitz, M. Gurnick, and M. Newton. 1979. "Analysis of Variations in Hospital Use by Medicare Patients in PSRO Areas, 1974–1977." *Health Care Financing Review* 1: 79–107.

Diehr, P. 1984. "Small Area Statistics: Large Statistical Problems." *American Journal of Public Health* 74(4): 313–14.

Domenighetti, G., A. Casabianca, F. Gutzwiller, and S. Martinoli. 1993. "Revisiting the Most Informed Consumer of Surgical Services: The Physician-Patient." *International Journal of Technology Assessment in Health Care* 9(4): 505–13.

Dyckman, Z.T. 1978. *A Study of Physicians' Fees.* Staff report. Washington, DC: Council on Wage and Price Stability.

Evans, R.G. 1974. "Supplier-Induced Demand: Some Empirical Evidence and Implications." In *The Economics of Health and Medical Care,* ed. M. Perlman. London: Macmillan.

Feldstein, M.S. 1970. "The Rising Price of Physicians' Services." *Review of Economics and Statistics* 52: 121–33.

Feldstein, P. 1987. *Economics of Health Care.* New York, NY: John Wiley and Sons.

Fuchs, V. 1978. "The Supply of Surgeons and the Demand for Operations." *Journal of Human Resources* 1: 231–34.

Fuchs, V.R., and M.J. Kramer. 1972. *Determinants of Expenditure for Physicians' Services in the United States 1948–1968.* National Center for Health Services Research and Development.

Gabel, J., and T. Rice. 1985. "Reducing Public Expenditures for Physician Services: The Price of Paying Less." *Journal of Health Politics, Policy, and Law* 9: 595–609.

Gertman, P., and J. Restuccia. 1981. "The Appropriateness Evaluation Protocol: A Technique for Assessing Unnecessary Days of Hospital Care." *Medical Care* 19(8): 855–71.

Gertman, P.M., A.C. Monheit, J.J. Anderson, J.B. Eagle, and D.K. Levenson. 1979. "Utilization Review in the United States: Results from a 1976–1977 National Survey of Hospitals." *Medical Care* 17(8): 1–148.

Gloor, J.E., N. Kissoon, and G.I. Joubert. 1993. "Appropriateness of Hospitalization in a Canadian Paediatric Hospital." *Paediatrics* 91: 70–74.

Goldberg, G.A., and D.C. Holloway. 1975. "Emphasizing Level of Care over Length of Stay in Hospital Utilization Review." *Medical Care* 13(6): 474–85.

Hadley, J., J. Holahan, and W. Scanlon. 1979. "Can Fee-for-Service Reimbursement Coexist with Demand Creation?" *Inquiry* 16: 247–58.

Hammond, J. 1985. "Analysis of County-Level Data Concerning the Use of Medicare Home Health Benefits." *Public Health Report* 100(1): 48–55.

Havens, P.L., J.C. Butler, S.E. Day, B.A. Mohr, J.P. Davis, and M.J. Chusid. 1993. "Treating Measles: The Appropriateness of Admission to a Wisconsin Children's Hospital." *American Journal of Public Health* 83(3): 379–84.

Hay, J., and M. Leahy. 1982. "Physician-Induced Demand: An Empirical Analysis of the Consumer Information Gap." *Journal of Health Economics* 1: 231–44.

Hemenway, D., and D. Fallon. 1985. "Testing for Physician-Induced Demand with Hypothetical Cases." *Medical Care* 23(4): 344–49.

Hicks, N.R. 1994. "Some Observations on Attempts to Measure Appropriateness of Care." *British Medical Journal* 309: 730–33.

Hopkins, A. 1993. "What Do We Mean by Appropriate Health Care?" *Quality in Health Care* (2): 415–22.

Hughes, D., and B. Yule. 1992. "The Effect of Per-Item Fees on the Behavior of General Practitioners." *Journal of Health Economics* 4: 413–38.

Jacobs, P. 1991. *The Economics of Health and Medical Care*. Gaithersburg, MD: Aspen.

Knickman, J.R., and A.M. Foltz. 1984. "Regional Differences in Hospital Utilization." *Medical Care* 22: 971–78.

Leape, L. 1989. "Unnecessary Surgery." *Health Services Research* 24(3): 351–407.

Leape, L.L., R.E. Park, and D.H. Solomon. 1990. "Does Inappropriate Use Explain Small-Area Variation in the Use of Health Care Services?" *Journal of the American Medical Association* 42: 276–285.

Lembcke, P.A. 1952. "Measuring the Quality of Medical Care through Vital Statistics Based on Hospital Service Areas. I. Comparative Study of Appendectomy Rates." *American Journal of Public Health* 42: 276–85.

Lewis, C.E. 1969. "Variations in the Incidence of Surgery." *New England Journal of Medicine* 281: 880–84.

Manning, W.G., A. Leibowitz, G.A Goldberg, W.H. Rogers, and J.P. Newhouse. 1984. "A Controlled Trial of the Effect of a Prepaid Group Practice on Use of Services." *New England Journal of Medicine* 310(23): 1505–10.

May, J.J. 1975. "Utilization of Health Services and the Availability of Resources." In *Equity in Health Services: Empirical Analysis in Social Policy,* ed. R. Andersen, R.J. Krauits, and O. Anderson. Cambridge, MA: Ballinger.

McCarthy, E.G. and G.W. Widmer. 1974. "Effects of Screening by Consultants on Recommended Elective Surgical Procedures." *New England Journal of Medicine* 291(25): 1331–35.

McGuire, A., J. Henderson, and G. Mooney. 1988. *The Economics of Health Care: An Introductory Text*. London and New York, NY: Routledge & Kegan Paul.

McPherson, K., J.E. Wennberg, O.B. Hovind, and P. Clifford. 1982. "Small-Area Variations in the Use of Common Surgical Procedures: An International Comparison of New England, England and Norway." *New England Journal of Medicine* 307(21):1310–14.

Mitchell, J.B., and J. Cromwell. 1982. "Physician Behavior under the Medicare Assignment Option." *Journal of Health Economics* 1(3): 245–64.

———. 1981. *Physician-Induced Demand for Surgical Operations.* Health Care Financing Grant and Contracts Report. Pub. No. 03086. Washington, DC: Health Care Financing Administration.

Mitchell, J.B., G. Wedig, and J. Cromwell. 1989. "The Medicare Physician Fee Freeze." *Health Affairs* 8: 21–32.

Mooney, G. 1994. *Key Issues in Health Economics.* London: Harvester Wheatsheaf.

Morehead, M. A. 1967. "The Medical Audit as an Operational Tool." *American Journal of Public Health* 57: 1643–56.

Pauly, M. 1980. *Doctors and Their Workshops: Economic Models of Physician Behavior.* Chicago, IL: University of Chicago Press.

———. 1979. "What Is Unnecessary Surgery?" *Milbank Quarterly* 57(1): 95–117.

Pauly, M.V., and M.A. Satterthwaite. 1981. "The Effect of Provider Supply on Price." In *The Target Income Hypothesis and Related Issues in Health Manpower Policy.* No. 80. Washington, DC: Bureau of Health Manpower.

Payne, S.M. 1987. "Identifying and Managing Inappropriate Hospital Utilization: A Policy Synthesis." *Health Service Research* 22(5): 709–69.

Phelps, C. 1986. "Induced Demand—Can We Ever Know Its Extent?" *Journal of Health Economics* 5: 355–65.

Phelps, C.E. 1993. "The Methodology Foundation of Studies of the Appropriateness of Medical Care." *New England Journal of Medicine* 329(17): 1241–45.

Ramsey, J.B. 1981. "An Analysis of Competing Hypotheses of the Demand for and Supply of Physician Services." *The Target Income Hypothesis and Related Issues in Health Manpower Policy.* No. 80. Washington, DC: Bureau of Health Manpower.

Reinhardt, U.E. 1978. "The Physician as the Generator of Health Care Costs." *Health Care in the American Economy: Issues and Forecasts.* Chicago, IL: Health Service Foundation.

Rice, T. 1987. Comment on "Induced Demand—Can We Know Its Extent?" *Journal of Health Economics* 6: 375–76.

———. 1983. "The Impact of Changing Medicare Reimbursement Rates on Physician-Induced Demand." *Medical Care* 21: 803–15.

Roemer, R., and M. Shain. 1959. "Hospital Cost Related to the Supply of Beds." *The Modern Hospital* 92: 72–73.

Roos, N.P. 1984. "Hysterectomy: Variations in Rates across Small Areas and across Physicians' Practices." *American Journal of Public Health* 74(4): 327–35.

Roos, N.P., and L.L. Roos. 1982. "Surgical Rate Variations: Do They Reflect the Health or Socioeconomic Characteristics of the Population?" *Medical Care* 20(9): 945–58.

Roos, N.P., L.L Roos, and P.D Henteleff. 1977. "Elective Surgical Rates—Do High Rates Mean Lower Standards?" *New England Journal of Medicine* 297(7): 360–65.

Scott, A. 1996. "Agency, Incentive and the Behavior of General Practitioners: The Relevance of Principal-Agent Theory in Designing Incentives for GPs in the UK." Discussion Paper No. 3. Aberdeen, United Kingdom: University of Aberdeen, Health Economic Research Unit.

Scott, A., and H. Hall. 1995. "Evaluating the Effects on GP Remuneration: Problems and Prospects." *Health Policy* 31: 183–95.

Sloan, F.A., and R. Feldman. 1978. "Competition among Physicians." *Competitions in the Health Care Sector: Past, Present and Future.* Washington, DC: Federal Trade Commission.

Steinwald, B., and F.A. Sloan. 1974. "Determinants of Physician's Fees." *Journal of Business* 47(4): 493–511.

Stockwell, H., and E.Vayda. 1979. "Variation in Surgery in Ontario." *Medical Care* 17(4): 390–96.

Vayda, E. 1973. "A Comparison of Surgical Rates in Canada and in England and Wales." *Manpower* 289(23): 1224–29.

Vayda, E., J.M. Barnsley, W.R. Mindell, and B. Cardillo. 1984. "Five-Year Study of Surgical Rates in Ontario's Counties." *Canadian Medical Association Journal* 131(15): 111–15.

Ware, J.E., R.H. Brook, W.H. Rogers, E.B. Keeler, A.R. Davies, C.D. Sherbourne, G.A. Goldberg, P. Camp, J.P. Newhouse. 1986. "Comparison of Health Outcomes at a Health Maintenance Organisation with Those of Fee-for-Service Care." *Lancet* 1 (8488): 1017–22.

Wennberg, J.E. 1987. "The Paradox of Appropriate Care." *Journal of the American Medical Association* 258: 2568–75.

———. 1986. "Which Rate Is Right?" *New England Journal of Medicine* 314(5): 310–11.

———.1984. "Dealing with Medical Practice Variations: A Proposal for Action." *Health Affairs* 3(2): 6–31.

Wennberg, J.E., and A. Gittelsohn. 1982. "Variation in Medical Care among Small Areas." *Scientific American* 246(4): 120–34.

———. 1975. "Health Care Delivery in Maine I: Patterns of Use of Common Surgical Procedures." *Journal of the Maine Medical Association* 66(5): 123–49.

———.1973. "Small Area Variations in Health Care Delivery." *Science* 182: 1102–1108.

Wennberg, J.E., B.A. Barnes, and M. Zubkoff. 1982. "Professional Uncertainty and the Problems of Supplier-Induced Demand." *Social Science and Medicine* 16: 811–20.

Wilensky, G.R., and L.F. Rossiter. 1983. "The Relative Importance of Physician-Induced Demand in the Demand for Medical Care." *Milbank Quarterly* 61: 252–77.

Woodward, R.S., and F. Warren-Boulton. 1981. "Physician Productivity, Remuneration Method, and Supplier-Induced Demand." In *Issues in Physician Reimbursement,* ed. N. Greenspan. Publication No. 03121. Baltimore, MD: Health Care Financing Administration.

CHAPTER 13

The Organization of Publicly Financed Health Care Services

William Jack

I t is widely acknowledged that there is a role for public financing of medical care and insurance, derived both from market failures and redistribution. However, there is much less consensus on how public resources should be used to reach efficiency and equity goals.

This chapter addresses these kinds of questions in a general framework in which organizational forms are characterized by alternative allocations of control and cash-flow rights. It then briefly reviews the experience of a number of countries in light of this theory.

INTRODUCTION

There is widespread acknowledgment of a role for public financing of medical care and insurance, derived both from market failures (particularly in the insurance sector) and redistribution. There is considerably less consensus, however, over how public resources should be used to attain efficiency and equity goals. Should attention focus on relatively cheap and predictable primary health care or on more expensive and less widely used hospital care? Should publicly funded health providers be public employees? Should the ministry of health perform the administrative functions of resource allocation within the sector, or should some of these functions be delegated to autonomous agencies. If so, should these agencies be for-profit or nonprofit?

These kinds of issues have been characterized in terms of three generic choices: what to buy; how to pay for it; and from whom to buy (Preker and Langenbrunner 2005). These three choices are not mutually exclusive, but separate investigation along these lines may help focus public debate. This chapter addresses the last of the three choices, from whom to purchase.[1]

An obvious, and simple, answer to this question is that governments should purchase services from providers who deliver high quality at low prices. There is likely to be a trade-off between the two, and choosing the appropriate quality-price pair is essentially a matter of cost-benefit analysis. This chapter does not revisit this literature. Instead, it examines in detail the alternative institutional relationships between suppliers and the purchaser, focusing on the allocation of control rights and financial or cash-flow rights. It also distinguishes between two different tasks that need to be performed—the performance of medical functions and the coordination of such functions across providers. The allocation of control and cash-flow rights associated with these two functions provides a rich description of alternative organizational designs.

The next section identifies two primary functions in the health sector—things doctors do and things insurance companies do. Both kinds of functions need to be assigned to institutions (e.g., the ministry of health, insurance companies, health care management organizations, public hospitals, private clinics). A taxonomy of organizational arrangements, based on the allocation of control and cash-flow rights, is provided in the third section. This taxonomy can apply equally to providers of insurance and administrative services and to providers of medical care. In the fourth section, the ideas behind this taxonomy are applied to the organization of the two types of functions. The next section briefly reviews some theoretical work on nongovernmental organizations (NGOs) that complements the allocation of rights literature of the previous sections. Some experience with contracting in developing countries in Latin America and South and Southeast Asia is then reviewed, and the last section presents some conclusions.

PURCHASING MEDICAL CARE AND COORDINATING SERVICES

A key starting point is the observation that medical care is a multidimensional product, whose individual components are supplied by different individuals (e.g., general practitioners, specialists) in different environments (e.g., doctors' offices, hospitals). The critical feature of medical care is that individual consumers are unlikely to understand the ways in which these components should be combined. In current parlance, someone who facilitates the appropriate use of different kinds of care is said to provide an *integrated service*.

In terms of the allocation of this coordinating role, from whom should health care be purchased? Three simple models can be envisaged.

1. Under an *integrated model,* the government contracts with a provider consortium (PC) of some kind[2] to provide integrated care. The consortium forms contracts with providers and hospitals and sets rules for communication and cooperation between them (e.g., referral protocols, gate-keeping rules). The "contracts" set up by the consortium can range from salaried employment of physicians and outright ownership of facilities to more arm's length arrangements.

2. Under a *direct purchase model,* the government contracts directly with providers and hospitals, and itself determines rules governing treatment and allocation of patients. As in the case of managed care, the "contracts" employed by the government can vary. They might look like public ownership (e.g., public hospitals), or explicit contracts with either nonprofits (or NGOs) or for-profit

hospitals. The difference is that the government itself (or at least the ministry of health) retains the role of determining rules by which patients are allocated in the system. (One of these rules could be "free choice of doctor," so there is no restriction to government assignment of individuals across providers.)

3. In a *mixed system*, the government could contract with PCs and directly with providers. Natural questions that arise include the following:

   • How should consumers be allocated to the different parts of the mixed system? Should they be permitted to choose between signing with a PC and seeing a "public" provider? Maybe the allocation is geographic, determined mainly by technological constraints (e.g., rural areas have public providers, urban area residents must enroll in a PC). Individuals could be allocated on the basis of income—for example, in Colombia the better-off must join a PC-equivalent, but the poor can choose to see a public provider. The situation is similar in Chile.

   • What about the decisions of providers? Should they be permitted to work for a PC (that has a public contract), while also working in the direct purchase arm of the system (i.e., as a public provider)?

The questions of whether to allow free choice of provider (by consumers) and free choice of organizational form (by providers) highlight the need to include in the description of the environment the relative prices and wages associated with these decisions. These considerations open up the possibility of quality differentials, especially in a targeting environment, which leads us to think about procurement design—the how-to-buy question.

ALLOCATING CONTROL AND CASH-FLOW RIGHTS

This section adapts a framework—suggested by Shleifer and Vishny (1994) for the analysis of privatization of state-owned enterprises in transition economies—for considering questions of public ownership, corporatization, and privatization in the health care sector. Full public ownership is undesirable if public managers and providers make decisions that are not in "the public interest." Maybe politicians derive some personal or political benefits from interfering in the way hospitals are run, or maybe union power puts some constraints on the strength of incentives that can be provided to public employees vis-à-vis contract workers. These fundamental issues of political economy are not addressed here but instead the discussion is limited to investigating the implications of self-interested public sector decision makers.

Consider a base contractual arrangement between a public purchaser and a medical provider (e.g., a hospital). For our purposes, *cash-flow rights* refer to the power of financial incentives for the provider, which can be thought of as the share of surplus generated that accrues to hospital management. Public sector managers on fixed salaries therefore have little or no cash-flow rights, in that their discretion over the use of financial resources earned by the facility is limited. Managers on performance-based contracts have greater cash-flow rights, since higher facility-level financial receipts translate into greater personal incomes.

Control rights refer to the allocation of decision-making authority. The idea is, when it is easy for a politician or bureaucrat to interfere in hospital decisions, he or she holds the relevant control rights. Alternatively, when the hospital is under independent management, politicians relinquish control rights to managers.

Practical experience with contracting for health services seems to support our focus on control and cash-flow rights. For example, Loevinsohn (2000a) observes that "[i]mpediments to managerial autonomy include: (i) line item budgets; (ii) imposition of strategies or approaches that don't have a very strong scientific basis; (iii) requiring that the purchaser pre-approve innovations suggested by the contractors;[3] and (iv) purchasers introducing new programs or activities without extensive discussion with contractors."

Table 13.1 distinguishes between four organizational structures, common in the health sector, according to the allocation of cash-flow and control rights.[4]

Actions specified in the base contract must be distinguished from other activities that, when dictated by the government, look like interference. The distinction can be made by appealing to the literature on incomplete contracts,[5] wherein some variables can be included in a contract, while others cannot.[6] Some examples of government interference in hospital decisions include staffing ratios, referral procedures, drug use protocols, and hours of operation.

The interaction between cash-flow and control rights determines the outcomes under the different organizational structures. In all cases, political interference is assumed to impose extra costs on the provider (relative to the costs it would have incurred without interference). The extent to which the provider can be made to bear the full burden of these costs is limited by the requirement that the provider willingly accept the interference, subject to the allocation of control rights.

For example, consider the case in which the government has control rights. When hospital management has no cash-flow rights and thus little discretion over

TABLE 13.1   Taxonomy of Organization by the Allocation of Control and Cash-Flow Rights

Cash-flow rights	Control rights	
	Government	Management
Vested in government	Public provision (mild intervention)	Autonomous (little intervention)
Vested in management	Regulated private (significant intervention)	Corporatized/privatized[a] (little intervention)

Source: Adapted from Shleifer and Vishny 1994.

a. See endnote 4.

financial resources, the costs of government interference cannot be imposed on the provider. This constrains the incentives to interfere. But when the base contract includes high-powered incentives and corresponding positive profits, these can be used to pay for the costs of interference, and the politician's incentives to interfere are greater. Shleifer and Vishny (1994) thus predict that a regulated private firm will be subject to more political interference than a public firm.[7]

Handing over control rights to providers essentially means that the government must fully finance any cost-increasing interference.[8] This implies that the extent of interference will typically decrease and that it will be independent of the allocation of cash-flow rights (independent of the strength of financial incentives in the base contract). Thus, both autonomous and corporatized or fully privatized providers experience reduced interference to the same degree.

Roland (2001) notes that this prediction seems at odds with evidence from the nonhealth sector in transition economies (where state-owned enterprises that were given broad autonomy behaved differently from private firms). Autonomous and corporatized and privatized providers might yield different outcomes because, by giving up control rights, the government exacerbates the moral hazard problem. When cash-flow rights match control rights, the effects on incentives are arguably less important. But when the government retains cash-flow rights, as under autonomization, hospital-level moral hazard may increase. A particular manifestation of this problem is the softening of budget constraints, wherein hospitals and other facilities that fail to perform are bailed out (Dewatripont and Maskin 1995).

The extent of public interference in provider decisions has been examined under different institutional settings. The assumption of Shleifer and Vishny's generic model is that such interference is socially undesirable and costly to the firm. In the context of the delivery of health services, however, some kinds of interference may be desirable. For example, the requirement to "inefficiently" provide primary care services to the poor free of charge seems supportable within a poverty-focused public expenditure regime. Similarly, requiring an insurer or NGO to *community rate* (charge all comers the same price) as a matter of equity need not be seen as socially undesirable. Conversely, requiring the purchase of nongeneric drugs because of kickbacks earned by the minister of health is less benign.

Given this range of both socially costly and socially desirable interventions, the appropriate institutional setting seems to hinge on the type of function being purchased (e.g., medical care versus administration and coordination) and the need to restrain or facilitate public intervention in the activities of the supplier. The next section considers the appropriate institutional design of both medical and coordination functions on the basis of the allocation of control and cash-flow rights.

ALLOCATING AUTHORITY OVER COORDINATION AND MEDICAL FUNCTIONS

From the foregoing discussion, the two basic purchasing models can be recharacterized and further broken down in terms of the allocation of control and cash-flow rights. In all cases, think of three players: the government, a provider consortium (i.e., administrator/coordinator/insurer), and a hospital.

Direct Purchase versus Managed Care

Under the *direct purchase model*, the providers of administrative functions have low-powered incentives (little cash-flow rights) and are public employees (have no control rights). Mild intervention in noncontracted insurance and administrative decisions (e.g., between the ministry of finance and the ministry of health) is then predicted to occur (table 13.1). This organization of purchasing is *direct* in that the government deals directly with medical providers. The relationship between providers and the government can take on any of the forms in table 13.1, however, with associated incentives for government intervention and interference.

If most relevant hospital and facility-level decision variables are easily written into a contract, it would seem that the relationship between providers and the government should be such as to limit interference. Table 13.1 indicates that control rights should then be assigned to the hospital or facility either through autonomization or through corporatization or privatization. Autonomization, however, has the draw-back associated with soft budget constraints, mentioned above.

If many hospital and facility decisions are difficult to specify contractually, the government may wish to leave itself room to intervene, suggesting control rights be held by the government. Depending on the extent of intervention expected to be necessary (say because of the severity of limits on contracting), either public ownership or regulated private provision are desirable.

Within this framework, the *managed care model* admits three alternative organizational forms, wherein either one or both of control and cash-flow rights are held by the body overseeing the administration and coordination of health insurance services (generically, a PC). Now the relevant question is, "What proportion of the coordinating body's decisions can be easily included in a managed care contract between the government and the PC?" If contracting is thought to be more or less exhaustive, it is likely that both control and cash-flow rights should reside with the PC, so as to limit intervention by the government. If important actions cannot be contracted and a significant degree of public sector influence is envisaged, the PC should have cash-flow, but not control, rights.[9]

What Kinds of Important Decisions Are Noncontractible in PCs and Hospitals?

PCs serve the roles of bringing people into the formal health insurance and health care system, say through outreach programs and coordinating the activities of providers. When one of the goals of public policy is to expand coverage to populations that are difficult to get to or costly to serve, PCs may skimp on the necessary outreach activities. However, coordinating services can potentially mean constraining the quality of care so as to save on costs. Both of these activities might be difficult to specify in contracts, suggesting the desirability of leaving the door open for government intervention in the decisions of the insurer. In turn, this suggests adopting either a public insurance system or a regulated private one with control rights under either system vested in the government.

Even harder to specify and enforce is a requirement of PCs to target resources to certain groups, particularly the poor. In other words, *selective expansion* may be difficult to contract. In particular, for the same reasons it is difficult for governments to target resources efficiently (notably, selection constraints), contractors may not be able to comply with ambitious quality and targeting requirements without incurring high administrative costs. Incentives to misrepresent outcomes (i.e., by falsely claiming to have covered the poor) might be intense, particularly when the poor themselves are unable to effectively voice their concerns. The scope for public intervention is then expanded under the proviso that it is intended to ensure access of the poor to services.

At the provider level the trade-off is less clear. Again, quality is difficult to specify contractually, but the potential for costly public interference seems greater. For example, if medical profession unions are powerful, public interference may take the form of excess labor requirements or above-market wages. The political influence of drug companies could also lead to costly public interventions in the form of expensive drug protocols. If the risk of such abuses of public office are high, allocating control rights to hospitals and facilities via autonomization, corporatization, or privatization is desirable.

CONTRACTING WITH NONGOVERNMENTAL ORGANIZATIONS

The preceding sections have interpreted the identity of a supplier with its organizational characteristics, specifically in terms of the allocation of control and cash-flow rights. In the health sector, for-profit providers are frequently distinguished from nonprofit providers, most often represented in developing countries by NGOs. Building on the work of Glaeser and Shleifer (1998), Jack (2001b) interprets NGO status in terms of limitations put on a firm's use of revenues. If the NGO has control over internal decisions, its status is similar to the autonomous form examined above.

Limiting the uses to which providers can put funds means that higher financial transfers will need to be made from purchaser to provider. However, reducing the value of financial resources (by limiting their use) can be shown to effect noncontractible decisions over cost-reducing effort and quality. In fact, under certain conditions, effort and quality can both increase as more restrictions are placed on the use of revenues.[10] The benefits of these changes in provider incentives must be traded off against the additional financial costs that arise because a dollar given with strings attached (limitations on the use of funds) is worth less to the provider than a dollar in cash. This trade-off will be optimally made at different points (at different degrees of "NGOness") depending on the extent to which the provider inherently values the output. Providers that inherently value the output more should demonstrably be contracted with as NGOs; those that do not should be treated as for-profit firms. Thus, the kinds of contracts, and the prices paid, may vary across providers; contracting with both types remains optimal.

In the context of developing countries, the distinction between international NGOs and grassroots NGOs may also be important. Which type should a government use, if either, to provide health services? A second model in Jack (2001b) incorporates the role of external finance (from donors and international financial institutions) to evaluate this question. It finds that if a donor and a government share similar objectives, an international NGO may be the preferred vehicle for delivering services, but when their objectives differ enough, a local grassroots NGO may be the better choice.

SOME EXAMPLES OF CONTRACTING

Experience with contracting for health care services has grown recently, as countries seek to improve quality and extend coverage through changes in the way service providers are compensated. A brief review of experience suggests that to change the way services are purchased—the "how" of medical care procurement—it is often necessary to change the provider—the "from whom?" In most cases, formerly publicly provided services are contracted out to NGOs, and at the same time performance-based incentives are instituted. It is then difficult to attribute any change in outcomes to performance-based pay versus the nature of the provider.

One study of reforms in Haiti, supported by the U.S. Agency for International Development (Eichler, Auxila, and Pollock 2001), kept the institution fixed (NGO delivery) and increased the power of the incentive payment by stipulating immunization and family planning targets. The unsurprising result was improved performance in these areas. An ongoing pilot project in Cambodia (Loevinsohn 2001) has the potential to shed light on the effects of the institutional nature of the provider. In that project, participating district health systems operate under one of three alternative regimes: a contracting-out regime (in which an NGO is given full autonomy over hiring and firing, payments, drug procurement, and the like); a contracting-in regime (in which an NGO is contracted to manage ministry of health workers, within the constraints of the civil service, although with some scope for incentive pay and bonuses); and a comparison or control group. This control group is split into two subgroups, one that receives additional funding equal to that received by the contracting-in NGOs, and one that receives no funding increase.

A similar distinction between contracting for provision of services and their management has arisen across some Latin American countries. In Panama, Honduras, El Salvador, and Ecuador, ministries of health have implemented various contractual arrangements directly with medical providers (often NGOs). Guatemala, however, has chosen to contract with an NGO to manage ministry of health providers. Evaluation of these experiments is, however, at the early stages.

Loevinsohn (2000b) reports the experience of two contracting projects in Bangladesh, the Bangladesh Integrated Nutrition Project (BINP) and the Urban Primary Health Care Project (UPHCP). Both projects use NGOs to provide services to specified populations, but they differ in a number of relevant respects. Under the BINP, nongovernmental organizations were chosen on the basis of technical proposals that did not include price bids, while under the UPHCP applicants were required to competitively submit price-quality bids (with an associated scoring rule to determine the winners). One interpretation is that, to compensate for the lack of price competition at the bidding stage, more stringent administrative controls were implemented in the BINP, while providers in the UPHCP were granted relatively more managerial autonomy.

However, following the control and cash-rights framework described above, it is useful to concentrate on the ex post stage, that is, the relationships between the government and the NGOs after bids have been evaluated and winners chosen. In the BINP project, performance-based bonuses (paid from government to the NGOs) were rare, suggesting that the government effectively retained cash-flow rights. The authorities also seem to have maintained control over a number of dimensions of NGO activity in the form of budgetary line items, excessive specifications, and the requirement for prior approval (Loevinsohn 2000b). Under the UPHCP, financial incentives for NGOs were higher powered—payment was linked more often to performance—allowing NGOs to potentially exercise greater cash-flow rights. At the same time, they were granted broader authority over input decisions and permitted wider discretion. Thus, in terms of the framework, the BINP nongovernmental organizations acted in an environment similar to a public provider (table 13.1, upper left corner), while the operating environment of the UPHCP nongovernmental organizations was more like an unregulated private sector (table 13.1, bottom right corner).[11]

At this early stage, it is difficult to tell which alternative is preferable, as public interference in itself may not be undesirable, say if noncontractible quality variables are positively influenced by such intervention. Loevinsohn's discussion suggests, however, that intervention was administratively costly and had, at best, unidentified effects on quality.

CONCLUSIONS

In purchasing health services, a government must decide which suppliers to use and how to pay them. In a fundamental sense, both dimensions reflect the fact that incentives have to be provided to suppliers. Such incentives can be given explicitly in the form of contracts (how to pay), and implicitly through the design of the institutional environment in which suppliers operate. The choice of institutional environment has been identified with the decision about from whom to purchase.

Four types of institutional arrangement—public, regulated private, autonomous, and corporatized or private—can be defined according to the allocation of control rights and cash-flow rights between the government and the provider. The allocation of control rights determines how easy it is for the government to interfere with production decisions, while the allocation of cash-flow rights determines who finances the additional costs imposed on providers by such interference. Furthermore, interference can be "good" (demanding coverage of the poor, ensuring quality of care) or "bad" (imposing inefficient labor or wage policies or expensive drug protocols). The typical government interference in the coordination and insurance functions are, on balance, of the "good" variety, so these functions should be undertaken either through a public authority or a regulated private one. However, there seems to be more room for "bad" intervention in the provision of care, inducing a preference for autonomous or corporatized or private provision. These conclusions are necessarily tentative, subject to more detailed modeling of the political preferences of, and constraints on, governments.

Finally, recognizing the importance of NGO activities in many developing countries, especially in the health sector, the author reviewed two models of contracting that allowed a choice between for-profit and nonprofit providers or a choice between international and grassroots NGOs. Nonprofit status may lead to higher quality and cost-reducing effort (although it need not), but it is financially more expensive. International NGOs might be preferred to domestic ones when donors and governments share similar policy objectives.

NOTES

Thanks to Jack Langenbrunner for his comments.

1. For a discussion of what to buy, see Preker and Langenbrunner (2005). Bentz, Grout, and Halonen (2001) interpret the what-to-buy decision in terms of whether the government should buy assets with which to produce services (i.e., public hospitals) or purchase the services directly (e.g., from private hospitals). On how to pay, see Jack (2001a).

2. A *provider consortium* is any organization that itself forms relationships with medical providers. HMOs present one example.

3. This is exactly the modeling assumption of Hart, Shleifer, and Vishny (1997) in distinguishing between public and private employees.

4. Under both corporatization and full privatization, the facility retains both control and cash-flow rights. The distinction between the two is that the physical assets of corporatized facilities (particularly hospitals) remain under public ownership. Control rights are thus somewhat less than completely held by a corporatized facility, as the government, through ownership, presumably has the right to remove hospital management. However, in practice, corporatization is meant to transfer control over management decisions to managers and away from government. Ownership is retained by

the government sometimes because of the nonnegligible costs of bringing the facility to market and arranging the financial transaction. Corporatization is similar to privatization but with passive (nonvoting) government ownership of facilities. See Preker and Harding (2003) for a related discussion of autonomous and corporatized hospitals.

5. This literature grew out of earlier work on institutions by Williamson (1985), including Grossman and Hart (1986), Hart and Moore (1990), and Hart (1995).

6. Contractual incompleteness stems less from *informational asymmetries* (when one party to a contract knows more than the other) than from the inability of a third party (e.g., a court) to enforce the terms of a contract (in which case, the contract itself is of little value). This may be an especially appropriate assumption in countries in which the executive and judicial branches of government are not separated, so that the "third" party is effectively the same as one of the contracting parties (the government purchaser).

7. In the incentives literature (e.g., Holmstrom 1979), the reason managers are not typically given complete cash-flow rights is that this will expose them to excessive risk. Such concerns are important with small-scale providers, who might face highly stochastic case mixes, and so on. Having larger cash-flow rights would not necessarily monotonically increase the certainty-equivalent wealth of such providers, in which case the effects on equilibrium interference would be less robust. For larger facilities, smaller case-mix variability would mitigate the risk exposure effect, and the impact of the assignment of cash-flow rights would be as described.

8. In the incomplete contracts literature, control rights typically are associated with outside options within a bargaining context. Thus, having control rights is the same as being in a good bargaining position, which translates into being able to push costs onto the other party.

9. If only a minor degree of intervention is expected to be desirable, the HMO should be part of the public sector—this is the *direct purchase model*.

10. Jack (2001a) shows that, if the cost of achieving quality q, given effort e, is $c(e,q) = g(e)h(q)$, where $g(e) = k/e$ and $h(q) = k'q^n$, then both quality and cost-reducing effort are higher for an NGO than for a for-profit firm.

11. It is important to recognize that the extent to which UPHCP nongovernmental organizations were unregulated was in terms of public interference not included in the initial contract bid specifications. Adherence to criteria specified by the government under the original criteria would have to be monitored and enforced.

REFERENCES

Bentz, A., P. Grout, and M. Halonen. 2001. "What Should the State Buy?" CMPO Working Paper Series No. 01/40. Bristol, United Kingdom: University of Bristol, Bristol Institute of Public Affairs, Centre for Market and Public Organisation.

Dewatripont, M., and E. Maskin. 1995. "Credit and Efficiency in Centralized and Decentralized Economies." *Review of Economic Studies* 62: 541–55.

Eichler, R., P. Auxila, and J. Pollock. 2001. "Performance-Based Payment to Improve the Impact of Health Services: Evidence from Haiti." Arlington, VA: Management Sciences for Health, Center for Health Reform and Financing.

Glaeser, E., and A. Shleifer. 1998. "Not-for-Profit Entrepreneurs." NBER Working Paper 6810. Cambridge, MA: National Bureau for Economic Research.

Grossman, S., and O. Hart. 1986. "The Costs and Benefits of Ownership: A Theory of Vertical and Lateral Integration." *Journal of Political Economy* 94: 691–719.

Hart, O. 1995. *Firms, Contracts, and Financial Structure.* New York, NY, and Oxford, United Kingdom: Oxford University Press.

Hart, O., and J. Moore. 1990. "Property Rights and the Nature of the Firm." *Journal of Political Economy* 98(6): 1119–58.

Hart, O., A. Shleifer, and R.W. Vishny. 1987. "The Proper Scope of Government: Theory and an Application to Prisons." *Quarterly Journal of Economics* 112(4): 1127–61.

Holmstrom, B. 1979. "Moral Hazard and Observability." *Bell Journal of Economics* 10(1): 74–91.

Jack, W. 2001a. "Contracting for Medical Care: Providing Incentives and Controlling Costs." Resource Allocation and Purchasing Paper. Washington, DC: World Bank, Health, Nutrition, and Population Group.

———. 2001b. *Public Policy toward NGOs in Developing Countries.* World Bank Policy Research Working Paper, No. 2639. Washington, DC: World Bank.

Loevinsohn, B. 2000a. "Checklist for Contracting of Health Services." Washington, DC: World Bank.

———. 2000b. "Contracting for Health Services: Lessons from Two Large Projects in Bangladesh." Washington, DC: World Bank.

———. 2001. "Contracting for the Delivery of Primary Health Care in Cambodia: Design and Initial Experience of a Large Pilot Test." Washington, DC: World Bank.

Preker, A.S., and A. Harding, eds. 2003. *Innovations in Health Service Delivery: The Corporitization of Public Hospitals.* Washington, DC: World Bank.

Preker, A.S., and J.C. Langenbrunner, eds. 2005. *Spending Wisely: Buying Health Services for the Poor.* Washington, DC: World Bank.

Roland, G. 2001. *Transition and Economics: Politics, Markets, and Firms.* Cambridge, MA: MIT Press.

Shleifer, A., and R. Vishny. 1994. "Politicians and Firms." *Quarterly Journal of Economics* 109: 995–1025.

Williamson, O. 1985. *The Economic Institutions of Capitalism: Firms, Markets and Relational Contracting.* New York, NY: Free Press.

CHAPTER 14

Contracting for Medical Care: Providing Incentives and Controlling Costs

William Jack

T he question of how to purchase medical care is important because in many
societies there are multiple real and financial links between the provider of
care and the final consumer. Designing a purchasing arrangement amounts
to establishing the institutional relationships between various actors—including
consumers, physicians, insurance pools, managers, and government ministries,
as well as specifying the contingent financial flows among them. The specification of financial flows between parties is the subject of contract theory and
mechanism design. The design of institutions, and relationships among them,
can be studied drawing on the theory of transaction cost and the property rights
literature. In this chapter, these tools are used to understand the way medical
care services might best be purchased.

INTRODUCTION

How to purchase medical care is an important question because in many societies
there are multiple real and financial links between the provider of care and the
final consumer. To address the normative question of optimal purchasing arrangements, it is important to understand the special nature of medical care services
that makes the use of an intermediary agent (like a middleman) desirable. Designing a purchasing arrangement then amounts to establishing the institutional relationships between the various actors, as well as specifying the contingent financial
flows among them. The specification of financial flows between parties is the subject of contract theory and mechanism design. The design of institutions, and
relationships among them, can be studied drawing on the theory of transaction
cost and the property rights literature. Here, these tools will be used to understand
the way medical care services might best be purchased.

This chapter is not specifically about the role of government in the allocation
of medical care resources, although often the government or a public institution fulfills the role of middleman. Instead, it identifies roles for intermediaries
even in predominantly private systems of care and asks how these might be
organized in a socially desirable way. In particular, institutions might develop
endogenously to correct failures of private markets: these could look similar to

public institutions in some countries but may represent other mechanisms for implementing collective action. The same kinds of issues of incentives, risk allocation, and even equity arise in the design of both public and private resource allocation mechanisms.

In a similar vein, this chapter goes beyond an analysis of what might be considered the planning function of a ministry of health. Standard project evaluation techniques such as general cost-benefit analysis or more specific incidence analysis (for poverty targeting) are suitable for setting public spending priorities. Indeed, often the author takes the medical care service to be provided as given and asks, What is the best way to procure it? Thus the tricky problem of valuing the social benefits of the service is avoided.) The chapter concentrates on organizational issues, and specifically the links between such decision-making institutions and providers of health services.

The next section provides a brief review of some financing mechanisms employed in the health care sector. The third section examines in detail models in the principal–agent paradigm that allow analysis of trade-offs between incentives and risk or between incentives and rent extraction. A primary goal of this section is to investigate the determinants of the "power" of optimal incentive schemes. The fourth section provides examples of the principal–agent approach in the pricing of medical care. The fifth section discusses the roles of competition and regulation in controlling costs. The final section presents brief conclusions.

TYPES OF HEALTH CARE FUNDING MECHANISMS

Many countries have experimented with alternative ways of paying providers of health care services. This section illustrates some of the different methods and suggests some of the advantages and limitations of each. The following sections provide a general theoretical framework for evaluating the alternatives.

Oxley (1995) characterizes the financial relationship between funders (i.e., purchasers) and providers of health services in three categories. He identifies the *reimbursement approach* as one in which providers are funded retrospectively for services actually delivered. Under this open-ended fee-for-service model, the agents who determine the nature and quality of health service (i.e., the patients and the physicians) face little in the way of financial consequences. Cost control is difficult for the purchaser in this case.

Oxley's *contract approach* is seen as involving some kind of prospective agreement between the purchaser and the provider regarding the terms and conditions of payments. Of course, such an ex ante agreement exists under the reimbursement approach, if only implicitly, in terms of the fee schedule adopted. The idea of the contract approach is that more explicit specifications of the amount and quality of care are included in the agreement.

Finally, an *integrated approach* to health system design combines the roles of purchaser and provider under a single institutional umbrella (often a local or central government). Under this model, personnel services (e.g., those of physicians) are reimbursed on a salary basis, and other costs are "bulk funded." Perhaps the best way to interpret these arrangements is in terms of a very incomplete contract regarding the nature of tasks to be fulfilled by doctors and other personnel. The responsibility for assigning activities and tasks among staff is allocated to a manager ex ante, who makes such decisions ex post. Incentives for staff to carry out these tasks are then provided either by the threat of termination of employment (as opposed to explicit incentive payments) or by the implicit promise of future rewards (e.g., promotions).

This characterization of payment mechanisms can be applied to both hospital and physician funding. For example, hospitals are funded in a variety of ways including block grants, fee for service, per case payment, and payments on the basis of occupied beds. While this kind of classification has some use, to properly assess the implications of these alternative payment mechanisms, a model of hospital behavior is needed, one simple enough to be tractable but general enough to allow the effects of each kind of mechanism to be modeled.

Similarly, the ways in which physicians are paid range from fee for service to capitation, with some kinds of services paid for specifically (e.g., immunizations) and others covered by general income sources. Again, to properly evaluate the benefits of alternative payment mechanisms, a model is needed that admits outcomes of interest (quality of care, cost, targeting to the poor) vary according to the financing alternative employed.

An obvious question that might occur to an observer is, Why can't a purchaser just buy the services he or she wants from hospitals and doctors? If the services can be fully specified in an enforceable contract, it might be possible to purchase them directly, but the financial cost and allocation of risk associated with such a contract might be undesirable. However, there are good reasons to believe that any contract specifying services to be provided will be inherently incomplete. In both cases, the issue of incentives is core. The models in the following sections provide the framework in which to think about these issues and are followed by some illustrative models of hospital and physician financing.

CONTRACTING AND ASYMMETRIC INFORMATION

Writing a contract for the delivery of services can be problematic if it is difficult to confirm delivery of the service or to tell how much the service should have cost to deliver. Examples of each of these contracting problems occur throughout the health care sector, especially in the provision of services, but also in interactions between consumers and purchasers (e.g., insurance companies). Specifically, when some physician inputs (efforts) are difficult to observe and verify, and observable outcomes are determined both by these inputs and by other exogenous and uncertain elements, efficient purchasing is generally precluded. *Moral hazard* occurs when the uncertainty is resolved after the provider acts. When uncertainty is resolved before the provider acts but the purchaser does not share this information, there is *adverse selection.*

In the case of moral hazard, in order to induce a provider to deliver inputs that are not easily observed (generically identified as effort), payment must be made conditional on other correlated outputs or indicators.[1] Because of stochastic elements in the link between effort and indicators, the incentives provided are not as strong as, and allocate risk less efficiently than, those under a contract based directly on effort. For example, a capitation payment for a physician might induce the correct level of effort (because the physician is the "residual claimant") but exposes him to risk that arises from uncertain case loads. Cost reimbursement, which relates payment to cost but not effort, exposes the physician to little risk, but it provides weak incentives to engage in effort.

In the case of adverse selection, uncertainty about observable outcomes derives not from a stochastic effect outside the relationship but from the purchaser's imperfect knowledge about the circumstances of the provider such as the health needs of her clientele. In this case, a purchaser who observed high costs of care would not be able to tell if these were due to high underlying needs coupled with efficiently delivered care, or low needs coupled with wasteful and cost-padded delivery. The trade-off now is between incentives and rent extraction. Using the example in the previous paragraph, a physician who knows the case load she would encounter under capitation would have good incentives to exert effort. But if the purchaser does not share this information, she will need to set the capitation rate high enough to ensure that a provider with a high case load is willing to participate. This means that physicians with low case loads (who get paid the same amount) earn rents, which are costly to the purchaser. These rents can be eliminated by simply reimbursing realized costs, but again, only at the expense of incentives, as the provider would exert no effort to control costs. The optimal payment mechanism in this case is characterized by nonnegative rents (profits) that decrease the underlying cost (so very low-cost providers make high profits).

Related to adverse selection is the issue of what can be called *active selection.* When underlying cost differences across providers are due to technical ability, those who earn profits can just be considered lucky (i.e., lucky enough to have high ability). However, when they are due to case mix, any payment mechanism under which rents accrue to lower-cost providers will induce providers to target low-cost patients. They might do this by actively seeking low-cost patients (say through advertising and sales techniques) or by manipulating the quality of care provided.[2] This could reduce the cost financed by the purchaser, due to lower-cost patients and lower-quality care, but would not be desirable, as high-cost patients went unserved, quality fell, or both. The payment mechanism may have to be adjusted to reduce this selection incentive.

In health economics, the term *moral hazard* is most often associated with overconsumption of subsidized care, not with shirking by a physician. In fact, this situation is better described as a context of hidden information (Holmstrom and Milgrom 1987) or *costly verification* (Dixit 2002). Dixit's terminology is used.

The distinction between costly verification and both moral hazard and adverse selection can be understood in terms of the timing of information acquisition, as illustrated in figure 14.1. In the insurance context, assuming a homogeneous pool of known risk, an insurer and a consumer sign a contract under conditions of symmetric information (like under moral hazard). Next, an illness occurs, the nature of which is private information to the consumer. The "appropriate" level of care, given the illness, is also private information to the consumer.[3] The consumer then chooses a level of medical expenditure, which is observed by the insurer, and reimbursed in accordance with the terms of the contract (i.e., net of any copayments, deductibles, and coinsurance).

A fully optimal insurance contract would base the transfer to the consumer on the illness he has, thus ensuring he faces the full (social) cost of care at the margin, while being protected against risk through a lump-sum payment. However, when it is costly to verify the illness state, insurance payments are based on endogenous expenditures, and so introduce a distortion inducing the patient to use more care that he otherwise would.[4] The same overconsumption of care occurs if the physician is thought to be making choices of care, as long as he acts in the interests of the patient.[5]

One policy response to (physician shirking) moral hazard is to try to monitor physician actions more closely, and thus approach the ideal of purchasing effort directly. Withholding payment for doctors who do not show up for work and paying bonuses for outstanding service are examples, but of course, these are likely to be imperfect measures of underlying effort. Similarly, a response to adverse selection is to monitor the underlying cost conditions that individual providers experience, so as to avoid giving away rents to those with low costs. The use of diagnosis-based payments for hospital treatments (most often in the form of transfers based on Diagnosis-Related Groups [DRGs]) can be understood in this way. However, just requiring the provider to *report* the underlying cost condition (as summarized, for example, by the diagnosis) does not resolve the

Figure 14.1   Moral Hazard, Adverse Selection, and Costly Verification

					➤ Time
Moral hazard	Sign contract	Take action	Uncertainty resolved	Outputs, payment	
Adverse selection	Uncertainty resolved	Sign contract	Take action	Outputs, payment	
Costly verification	Sign contract	Uncertainty resolved	Take action	Outputs, payment	

Source: Author.

adverse selection problem, since the provider will have an incentive to misrepresent his private information (see below). Finally, to curb overspending due to costly verification, utilization review procedures can be used, essentially as a means of verifying the health care needs of patients.

The foregoing discussion has highlighted the effect of various types of asymmetric information on the form of explicit incentive mechanisms or payment schemes. All of these schemes link payments to outcome, some observable (by both parties) and verifiable (by a third party who enforces the contractual agreement). However, it is often difficult to make payments contingent on health outcomes, especially when they are difficult to verify in court. A purchaser might rely then on *implicit incentives*, as provided by dynamic considerations.

Holmstrom (1999) provided the first formal model of implicit incentives in what he labeled a model of *career concerns*. This model (generalized by Dewatripont, Jewitt, and Tirole 1999a) has both moral hazard and adverse selection components and relies on repeated interaction between potential buyers ("the market") and a seller. The simple idea is that competition among purchasers at future dates provides incentives for effort early on: effort improves performance, and hence causes the market to update its belief about the underlying cost and efficiency of the provider. Competition in later periods bids up the price paid to the provider, validating the provider's exertion of first-period effort. This kind of model is better suited to conditions in which the provider's cost efficiency is a function of its capability (perhaps the quality of its physicians, or the flexibility of its management team) than to conditions in which it is determined by the mix of patients. In the latter case, a provider will have an incentive to shirk early on, in order to incur high costs and convince a purchaser that the case mix is unfavorable. Because of this, the career concern model is likely more useful in describing the way physicians should be paid by their employers rather than the interactions between purchasing and provider institutions.

High- versus Low-Powered Incentives under Conditions of Moral Hazard

How high-powered should incentives be? This question has been addressed most convincingly in the case of moral hazard (Holmstrom and Milgrom 1987, 1991), so start with this context.[6] In a generic agency model, a worker exerts effort e in producing observable output x. Uncertainty about the production process means that knowledge of x is not sufficient for the (risk-neutral) principal to infer effort. A simple example is $x = e + \varepsilon$, where ε is, say, normally distributed with mean zero and variance σ^2. Effort is costly to the agent, and the marginal cost is increasing, $c(e) = ke^2/2$. With this simple formulation, Holmstrom and Milgrom (1991) show that the optimal payment mechanism is

$$t(x) = a + bx,$$

where $b = 1/(1+rk\sigma^2)$, and r is the agent's coefficient of absolute risk aversion.[7] The parameter a can be thought of as the salary component of the agent's compensation, while b is the share of output that the agent gets to keep. The payment mechanism provides high-powered incentives if b is close to 1, and low-powered incentives if it is close to zero. If $b = 1$, the agent is a residual claimant. This is optimal only when the agent is risk neutral ($r = 0$), effort is costless ($k = 0$), or there is no uncertainty. When the agent is very risk averse, when effort is very costly, or when the information contained in the signal (output) is very uninformative about effort (σ^2 very large), the agent should be paid primarily in the form of a fixed salary.

It is important to be specific about how easily this model can be applied to the context of inducing effort from a health care provider. The model might seem of limited use if the output, x, is considered to be health status, because it is difficult to imagine making payments contingent on it, let alone giving the corresponding ownership rights to someone other than the patient. More usefully, x might be interpreted as a measure of cost savings, which can be stochastically increased through effort. The profit-sharing parameter b then determines the proportion of cost savings that accrue to the provider. Thus, suppose some benchmark or standard cost of treating a patient, c_0, is established and that by exerting effort, the provider can reduce the cost by $x = c_0 - c$. Then the above payment schedule becomes

$$t(x) = a + bc_0 - bc$$

or equivalently

$$t(c) = a' - bc,$$

where $a' = a + bc_0$. Paying the provider on a capitation basis means setting $b = 1$, in which case all cost savings accrue to him. This is the same as saying that the provider is responsible for covering all realized costs of care out of the capitation payment or budget a', that is, the provider is a U.K. National Health Service–style fundholder. Providers who do not mind being exposed to risk, for whom effort is inexpensive, or for whom risk is small, should be paid in this way. Otherwise, at least some of the realized costs of care should be shared with the purchaser.

An immediate concern is that providers will reduce costs by skimping on quality. To incorporate such a possibility into the simple model above, quality has to be introduced as a second outcome measure. A first step in that direction is to assume there are two types of effort, one that affects (unit) costs, and the other that affects quality (per unit cost). Thus, for $i = 1,2$, let

$$x_i = e_i + \varepsilon_i,$$

where x_1 is cost savings and x_2 is quality. Dixit (2002) parameterizes the cost of effort as

$$c(e_1, e_2) = k[e_1^2 + 2\gamma e_1 e_2 + e_2^2],$$

where γ is between -1 and $+1$, and measures the degree of complementarity ($\gamma < 0$) or substitutability ($\gamma > 0$) between the efforts. Holmstrom and Milgrom (1987) show that, if the stochastic shocks are distributed with variance-covariance matrix $\Sigma = [\sigma_{ij}]$, the optimal payment mechanism is of the form

$$t(x) = a + b_1x_1 + b_2x_2,$$

with the sharing parameters b_I given by

$$\begin{pmatrix} b_1 \\ b_2 \end{pmatrix} = [I + rc_{ij}\Sigma]^{-1}\begin{pmatrix} 1 \\ 1 \end{pmatrix},$$

where c_{ij} is the second derivative matrix of the cost function. As a special case, Dixit (2002) assumes the shock terms ε_i are identically and independently distributed ($\sigma_{ij} = 0$), in which case

$$b_1 = b_2 = 1 / [1+(1+\gamma)rk\sigma^2].$$

Thus, both outcome measures should be rewarded with incentives of the same power, but the power is reduced (increased) compared with the single-effort case above if the efforts are substitutes (complements).

Of perhaps more interest is the case when one dimension of output (say quality) is difficult to measure precisely for contracting purposes. Thus, suppose σ_2^2 is very large (approaching infinity in the limit), but that realized cost is observable with a finite error (i.e., $\sigma_1^2 < \infty$). Then it is possible to show that $b_2 \to 0$ and

$$b_1 \to (1 - \gamma)/[1 + 2kr\sigma_1^2(1-\gamma^2)].$$

When the two efforts are perfect substitutes (i.e., $\gamma = 1$), the optimal contract is characterized by $b_1 = b_2 = 0$. That is, no incentive is provided at the margin for quality (which is too hard to measure), and none is provided at the margin for cost reduction, because, if it were, it would lead to complete substitution out of quality-improving effort into cost containment.

Thus, the basic interpretation of this multitask model is that, when it is difficult to provide incentives for a subset of tasks, the incentives optimally provided for others will be altered: if the tasks or efforts are substitutes, incentives will be weakened; if they are complements, incentives will be made stronger. It seems likely that, in the case of medical care, the marginal effort cost of controlling pecuniary costs would increase with the quality of output, suggesting the inputs are substitutes, and hence pointing toward relatively low-powered incentives.

An alternative interpretation of the two tasks can provide insights into how the power of optimal incentives is correlated with asset ownership. For example, suppose quality is fixed and that the two tasks are reducing current costs and, by maintaining equipment and facilities, controlling future costs. If it is difficult to provide explicit incentives for maintenance (say because it is hard to verifiably update the economic value of physical assets over time), and if current cost containment and maintenance are substitutes, incentives for current cost containment should be weak. Holmstrom and Milgrom (1991) have suggested that this can explain why employees should be given weak incentives, but those for outside contractors (who own their own tools) should be higher powered. Thus, public hospitals might be funded more under a cost-reimbursement mechanism than private hospitals that provide publicly financed services. These hospitals would act more as residual claimants.[8]

Yet another application of these ideas is to the question of allowable activities—for example, should physicians in public hospitals be permitted to see private patients on the side (moonlighting)? Milgrom (1988) studies a situation in which an agent can undertake a range of tasks (Y), but only a subset of these (Z) is of value to the principal. As Dixit (2002) discusses, if the tasks in Z are all relatively easy to measure, high-powered incentives can be given to them directly, thus limiting the agent's desire to engage in outside activities. If some of the tasks in Z are difficult to measure, as above, this might mean that explicit incentives provided for all Z-tasks need to be weak. In this case the agent should be explicitly forbidden to engage in outside activities.

In the context of medical care, one would expect to see a correlation between the power of explicit incentives and the authority to engage in outside practice. Providers who are paid as residual claimants should be permitted to engage in outside activities, while those who have their costs reimbursed should face restrictions.

In a similar vein, the theory suggests that incentives can better be provided if tasks with similar observability (i.e., similar outcome variances) are grouped together and assigned to agents. This could suggest why general practitioners might be paid on a salary basis, thus facing weak incentives, but specialists could face higher-powered incentives, if it could be argued that the outcomes associated with the services provided by specialists could be more easily observed than those of general practitioners.

Another determinant of optimal task assignment derives from the career concerns model. Dewatripont, Jewitt, and Tirole (1999b) generalize Holmstrom's (1999) model to a multitask environment and show that, if an agent is required to perform a number of tasks, the impact of effort on market perceptions may be weak, and so the implicit incentives to provide effort, ineffectual. Narrowing the agent's focus can improve the market's inference about his ability and increase the return on effort. This suggests a role for specialized centers rather than institutional providers with broadly defined tasks and goals. It also suggests that implicit incentives in the form of future career options may be stronger for specialist physicians than for general practitioners.

A final rationalization of weak formal incentives occurs in situations in which there is a delay between the agent's action and the outcome upon which he is compensated. This is a better model of interinstitutional contracting than of the payment of individual providers. The idea is that if the delay is significant, the agent and the principal will have an incentive to renegotiate an initial incentive contract, since exposure to future risk now has no effect on incentives. Indeed, the principal will offer full insurance and pay the agent a fixed payment independent of the outcome. Anticipating this, the agent will provide no effort initially, even if a high-powered incentive contract was agreed upon. Fudenberg and Tirole (1990) show that effort can be induced by allowing the agent to choose between alternative contracts after she has put in her effort. Because the principal cannot observe which action was chosen, she cannot offer full insurance to her without losing money on average. Thus, she effectively commits to maintaining the incentives of the original contract.

The Power of Incentive Schemes under Adverse Selection

The theory determining the power of incentive schemes under adverse selection has been most thoroughly examined and documented by Laffont and Tirole (1993) in their book on procurement and regulation. The model developed there is most suitable for thinking about a contractual relationship between a purchaser and a firm, rather than at the provider level. This makes it useful for thinking about purchasing decisions in the context of government contracting out to private hospitals or contractual relationships between insurance companies and physician groups.

The basic set-up (Laffont and Tirole 1993, p. 55) involves a supplier who can produce the good (e.g., hospital service) at a realized cost $C = \beta - e$. β is a parameter that describes the firm's efficiency (so a lower β corresponds to a more efficient firm), and e is an effort input supplied by the firm that reduces costs. The purchaser cannot observe β or e, so must make payments to the firm conditional on C only, according to a schedule $T(C)$.[9] The purchaser knows that β is distributed on an interval $[\beta_0, \beta_1]$.

As discussed above, a fixed fee of the form $T(C) = T_F$ gives the firm strong incentives to exert cost-reducing effort, while full cost-reimbursement of the form $T(C) = C$ leads to little cost containment. The authors show that the optimal way of paying the firm is with a schedule $T(C)$ satisfying the following properties:

1. $T(C) \geq C$, with equality only for the highest possible realized cost, so all firms but the most costly earn a positive rent.

2. $\pi(C) = T(C) - C$ is decreasing in C, so more efficient firms earn higher rents.

3. $T(C)$ and $T'(C)$ are increasing in C.

The particular shape of the payment schedule will be a function of the distribution of efficiency parameters and the social cost of forgone rents, but in general, the optimal payment mechanism will look something like that shown in figure 14.2.

It is tempting to hope that the rents associated with this payment schedule could be reduced by asking the firm to report its true efficiency (its value of β), then instructing it to provide services at the first-best realized cost (i.e., to choose effort e^* satisfying $\psi'(e^*) = 1$, where $\psi(e)$ is the cost of effort incurred by the provider, and to produce at cost $C = \beta - e^*$. This kind of payment rule is referred to as a *direct mechanism,* in which payment is a function of a report by the firm instead of an endogenously determined cost. It is, more or less, what a diagnosis-based payment attempts.

Figure 14.2   Optimal Cost-Based Payment under Adverse Selection

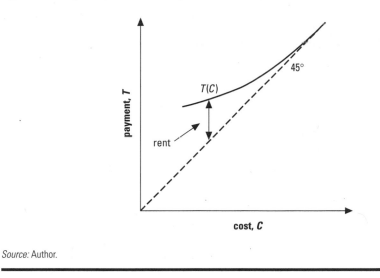

Source: Author.

To see this, let β be a measure of the underlying cost of treating a patient, which varies with the patient's condition. A diagnosis is meant to serve as a report of this underlying determinant of cost. Of course, making a payment contingent only on the patient's reported condition would lead the hospital to always claim high underlying costs (i.e., severe cases). As a check, the purchaser may require verification of the actual (pecuniary) cost incurred, to ensure that the hospital does not abuse the mechanism.

But this check is not enough, as the need to provide incentives to report the true value of underlying cost must be recognized. For example, if the payment is structured so that the hospital makes zero profit whenever it truthfully reports the value of β, it will have an incentive to over-report the parameter—that is, to engage in overdiagnosis. To see this, suppose that the true underlying cost parameter (patient condition) is β and that the hospital reports a value $\beta' > \beta$. According to the purchaser's naive payment rule, the hospital is paid $T(\beta') = (\beta' - e^*) + \psi(e^*)$ as long as its realized cost is $\beta' - e^*$. But now let $e' < e^*$ satisfy $\beta' - e^* = \beta - e'$. The hospital can overreport its cost parameter ($\beta' > \beta$), put in less effort ($e' < e^*$), and receive the same transfer. Thus, revenues are unaffected but effort costs are reduced, confirming that the mechanism does not induce truthful reporting.

McClellan (1997) provides evidence of increased costs under the DRG-payment method in the U.S. Medicare program. These stem from the fact that hospitals are paid not just on the basis of diagnosis but also on the intervention chosen. This is in effect a means of fine-tuning the "report" the hospital makes: use of a more intensive treatment signals a more severe condition. Hospitals have increased their use of such treatments in the same way they would have by over-reporting the condition of patients, as suggested above.[10] To induce hospitals to report the true value, they must be given an incentive to do so, say in the form of a bonus for reporting low-cost patients. This, however, is exactly the same as the rent π defined by the optimal cost-based payment scheme above.[11]

The convexity implied by point 3, above, means that, instead of presenting such a nonlinear schedule to a firm, the purchaser could allow the firm to choose from a menu of linear contracts of the form

$$T_\beta(C) = a_\beta + b_\beta C$$

where a_β is increasing in β and b_β is decreasing in β. Faced with this choice, a firm with greater efficiency (lower β) chooses a higher-powered linear incentive scheme that has a larger fixed fee (a_β) and smaller cost sharing rate (b_β). Indeed, when firms expect to have low costs, they are observed to bargain with procures for higher-powered incentive schemes than when they expect to have high costs. This basic model suggests that, when contracting-out with a private hospital, for example, the government (purchaser) should offer the hospital management a choice between high- and low-powered incentive payments.

As in the case of moral hazard, purchasers are not just concerned with cost reduction. The basic model of Laffont and Tirole (1993) assumes that the *quality* of the service produced is contractible, so there is no question about whether cost-reduction incentives will lead to low-quality care. If quality can be easily observed and verified, it does not affect the power of the optimal incentive scheme. However, if it is difficult to write quality requirements into a contract, and when the service in question is an "experience good," incentives must be provided through the promise or threat of future consequences.[12] In a static one-period model with noncontractible quality, a firm or hospital will have little incentive to improve the quality of an experience good. Only the threat of future punishment, in the form of reduced purchases by consumers or switching of suppliers by the purchaser, can provide incentives for quality.

Here the distinction between the purchaser (perhaps an organization) and consumers (individuals) becomes important. It may be easier for consumers to monitor hospital performance and to switch to alternative providers (if they exist) when quality is low. If the hospital is paid independently of the number of patients it sees, this sales effect has little impact on quality incentives. Making payments sensitive to admissions (or, more efficiently, cases) allows consumer demand to motivate quality supply.[13] However, if the hospital has a fixed contract with the purchasing agency, the threat of future review, with the prospect of the contract's being awarded to an alternative provider *(second sourcing)*, provides current-period incentives for quality.[14]

However incentives for quality provision are implemented, the power of incentives for cost reduction should respond to the social value of quality relative to cost. For example, if the social value of quality increases, the one-period incentive scheme should be less high powered. This is because in a high-powered scheme, the cost of quality is large, as perceived by the provider, since effort focused on quality is diverted from cost reduction, itself a high-return activity. To reduce the incentive to concentrate effort on cost control, the incentive mechanism should be less high powered. There are obvious parallels with the multitask moral hazard model described in the first part of this section.

The discussion above takes the identity of the provider as given, with the insight that even if the provider has low costs, if this information is not available to the purchaser, it will give up some rent in procuring the services. The possibility of *competition among hospitals for government contracts* means that some of these rents might be clawed back by the purchaser. One question that has been asked is, How is this reduction in rents manifested? It turns out that all of the rent reduction accrues to the purchaser in the form of a lump-sum payment. The incentive scheme used when there is just one potential contractor, $T(C)$, is simply shifted down when there is an auction *(open bidding)* to allocate the service contract. That is, the winner at the bidding phase is subject to a schedule $T(C) - T_0$, for some constant T_0. The implication is that competition for contracts does not alter the incentive power of the contract awarded, conditional on the efficiency of the winning provider.[15]

If the purchaser wishes to provide quality incentives by putting the existing contract up for potential second sourcing at a future date, it becomes necessary to account for investment incentives of the initial provider. Laffont and Tirole (1993) examine two cases: transferable and nontransferable investments. The idea is that some kinds of investments (transferable ones)—for example, improving consumer health consciousness or developing new diagnostic and curative techniques that are not patentable—can yield benefits for future competitors, while the returns to others (nontransferable ones) are fully appropriated and internalized by the investing party.

If the initial supplier undertakes transferable investments, at the second stage it should be favored in the bidding competition: even if its bid is somewhat higher than another firm's, the incumbent should have its contract extended. This increased chance of winning later rounds reduces the effect of the potentially positive externality in investment. Also, conditional on having its contract extended, the power of the incentive scheme faced by the provider should be higher in the second stage than in the first. This ensures that, early on, the incumbent perceives the net cost of investment as low (because there is a large cost-reimbursement element to the contract), encouraging investment. Also, in later periods, it bears a large proportion of its cost, which itself increases the incentive to make cost-reducing investments early on.

When the investment is nontransferable, no external effect induces the purchaser to favor the incumbent at the second stage or alters the strength of incentives across periods. In this case the purchaser should favor the competitor in the second round of procurement. This is because, on average, the cost of the incumbent firm will be lower than its competitors' since it has had the opportunity to make (nontransferable) cost-saving investments. The general theory of auctions tells us that, in an auction with *asymmetric bidders* (bidders with differently distributed costs), those with higher average costs should be favored so as to increase the competitive pressure on low-cost firms to bid aggressively. Thus, the intertemporal evolution of the power of incentives depends crucially on the nature of investment decisions.

A final influence on the power of incentives in adverse selection models is *cost padding* (misreporting of expenses). Up until now it has been assumed that realized costs were ex post observable and that contractual payments could be based on these. But often costs are reported to the purchaser through an accounting process that can be at best confusing and often opaque. The potential for inflating costs by cost padding seems great, especially when collusion between the primary provider and his input suppliers is possible. Laffont and Tirole (1993) report the intuitive result that, as cost padding becomes more difficult to detect, the power of incentive schemes should increase. This can be understood most easily by noting that a provider that is paid a fixed fee has little reason to inflate costs, while one that is paid an increasing function of reported cost will be induced to do so.

APPLYING CONTRACT THEORY TO THE PURCHASE OF HEALTH SERVICES

The previous section outlined the theoretical determinants of how providers of services should be paid within the principal–agent paradigm. The benefits of high-powered incentives had to be balanced against the potential costs, including exposure to risk, the misallocation of rents, and the diversion of effort to alternative activities. Implications of the theory for the purchase of medical care were also highlighted, but this section explicitly addresses three particular contracting problems in the health sector, employing the tools of the previous section.

The first issue is how capitation rates should be set, and adjusted, for hospitals. The next issue is the use of comparative performance schemes in normalizing reimbursement schedules for physician services. And finally, there are the mechanisms to sort physicians with different opportunity costs, in order to reduce financial transfers while maintaining supply.

Hospital Funding

It is probably fair to say that the need to provide incentives when purchasing hospital services stems primarily from either adverse selection or costly verification problems, and not moral hazard per se. Basing payments on health outcomes (e.g., whether the patient recovered) would present a true moral hazard problem, since the outcome would still be uncertain after physician effort had been supplied. In most countries, such explicit outcome-related payments are rare (although Leonard [2003] documents their use in the market for traditional healers in Africa). Consider a purchaser contracting with a hospital for the provision of health services to cover a given population. Adverse selection may be operative if hospitals have better ex ante information about the costs of undertaking this task (including knowledge of both the unit costs of various treatments and the prevalence of such conditions in the population). Costly verification characterizes a situation in which this information is learned by the hospital ex interim, after the contract is signed but before it acts.

It can be argued that adverse selection and costly verification will likely occur under different contracting approaches, depending on the unit of analysis. For example, if a purchaser writes a contract with a hospital to supply health care services for a given population for a year, Laffont and Tirole's (1993) adverse selection model seems appropriate. As long as the hospital is large enough, the uncertainty associated with the case load will be small, so the hospital should have a good idea of the underlying cost (β in the procurement model above) of fulfilling the contract terms. The analysis of the previous section suggests both block grants and full cost-reimbursement are suboptimal, and that a cost-plus contract would be warranted.

However, suppose a purchaser writes a contract under which a hospital is paid on the basis of each episode of illness (instead of getting paid just on the basis of providing care to the population). If the contract is signed at the beginning of the year, for example, each patient presents the hospital with a new underlying cost realization. Now the payment made for treating *each patient* should have a cost-plus characteristic.

These cost-based payment mechanisms are designed primarily to control costs (i.e., restrict rents while providing cost-reducing incentives). However, instead of basing payment on cost realizations, many hospital payment mechanisms relate payment to volume measures. But it turns out that volume-based payments must make the same kinds of trade-offs between incentives and rent allocation as cost-based mechanisms, for the simple reason that service volume is an endogenous choice made by the hospital.

To see this, recall that the motivation for the cost-plus contract is that observable pecuniary cost, C, is a function of underlying efficiency β, and effort e, that is, $C = \beta - e$. The idea of this model is that the hospital produces the appropriate service but that the cost may be higher than necessary if effort is not provided. The incentive problem is to encourage effort while restricting rents. However, the model can be reformalized in terms of health outcomes and the level or volume of care and investigate the trade-off between correct volume choices and rent appropriation.

To this end, suppose that the health effects of treatment are captured by the function $h(v,\beta)$, with $h_\beta > 0$, and $h_{v\beta} > 0$—that is, greater health needs increase the health effects of care both absolutely and at the margin. β now denotes the health needs of the hospital's patients—β is either the population health status if the hospital is paid for providing services to the whole population, or it is a given patient's health status if it is paid on a per patient basis.

Medical care volume is measured in units so that the unit price of care is 1. The *appropriate* level of care maximizes net benefits of intervention, $h(v,\beta) - v$, and is denoted $v^*(\beta)$ satisfying $h_v(v,\beta) = 1$.

However, the hospital chooses volume in pursuit of its objectives. One extreme assumption is that the hospital cares only about money (less the cost of care, v), so that if it is paid an amount $t(v)$, it will choose v such that $t'(v) = 1$. Alternatively, if the hospital cares about health outcomes (for ethical or competitive reasons), its objective will be to maximize $\alpha h(v,\beta) + t(v) - v$, where α is the weight it puts on health outcomes relative to income. It thus chooses $v(\beta)$ to satisfy $t'(v) + \alpha h_v(v,\beta) = 1$. The hospital is induced to provide the appropriate volume of care only if it is paid with a schedule $t(.)$ that satisfies $t'(v) = (1 - \alpha) h_v(v^*,\beta)$. To ensure the hospital is willing to accept the contract, the actual transfer function would need to be

$$t(v) = t_0 + (1 - \alpha) h_v(v^*,\beta)$$

where t_0 is a lump-sum payment. If the hospital must cover all its costs with transfers from the purchaser, then $t(v) = v(\beta)$. If the transfer must only ensure zero net surplus to the hospital, it satisfies $t(v) = v(\beta) - \alpha h(v,\beta)$.

Only when the hospital fully values the health effects of its services ($\alpha = 1$) is a pure capitation or fixed budget payment optimal. The less the hospital values health benefits, the higher the marginal payment for volume must be. (Similarly, applied to physician care, this analysis suggests that a fundholder model is optimal only under special conditions.)

In any case, to implement the two-part tariff above, the purchaser needs to know the value of β, even when $\alpha = 1$. In this case, while a lump-sum payment is optimal, the optimal level of this lump-sum payment depends on β. In particular, if the purchaser wants to minimize the rents the hospital receives (because it is costly to raise revenue), it will want to pay as low a lump sum as possible. However, if it pays too low a lump sum, hospitals with high costs will either refuse to sign the contract (adverse selection) or provide insufficient care (costly verification).

Reimbursing all costs—paying the hospital $t(v) = v$, for all t—would ensure the participation of the hospital, whatever its cost, but would result in large rents earned by hospitals with low underlying costs. As in the standard procurement model, the optimal trade-off between rents and incentives is to pay the hospital an amount that increases in volume, with $t(v) > v$ for low volumes, but with the net rent $t(v) - v$ decreasing as volume increases. This payment schedule is qualitatively similar to that of figure 14.2, with volume on the horizontal axis. (A similar schedule, including an additional marginal payment, characterizes the optimum when $\alpha < 1$.)

One implication of this analysis is that paying hospitals a constant price per unit of care is unlikely to be optimal. One approach adopted by some purchasers is to employ elaborate mechanisms for calculating care volumes in terms of points—these being weighted sums of medical procedures, the weights corresponding to some notion of relative input costs. This provides a one-dimensional measure of volume—like the one assumed above, v—but to reimburse this aggregate volume linearly is optimal only if there is no adverse selection or costly verification problem and if the hospital does not care fully about the health effects of its actions. (If it cares fully about them, the optimal payment is a lump sum.)

In the same way that Laffont and Tirole's (1993) cost-plus incentive scheme can be implemented by allowing a provider to choose from a menu of linear cost-sharing rules, in this model a hospital may be allowed to choose from a menu of linear volume contracts. Such contracts would consist of a lump-sum payment plus a price per point, but the price would (usually) be less than the marginal cost (one). In this sense, paying hospitals a price per point may be part of an optimal reimbursement scheme, with the condition that the hospital would be required to choose from a menu of such prices ex ante. This would appear to be more operational when the hospital is paid annually (with its annual budget determined by its annual volume of services provided), rather than per patient.

Relative Performance Schemes for Doctors

More than 20 years ago, Shleifer (1985) applied the idea of yardstick competition to Medicare payment mechanisms in the United States. The simple intuition of this model is that, if providers have correlated private information, comparative performance schemes can make it cheaper for a purchaser to generate incentives. These ideas apply both to situations of moral hazard (as formulated by Holmstrom 1982) and adverse selection.

Consider then the compensation of physicians, and suppose that the realized cost of treating a population of patients over the course of a year is $C = \beta - e$. (Here the model reverts to that in the third section, taking the quality of care as fixed.) It was seen in that case that a lump-sum payment would induce efficient effort choice but that choosing the level of the payment was difficult if β were unknown. In that case, a cost-based payment traded off the incentive to control cost with the appropriation of rents by the physician.

The important property of a lump-sum payment is that it is independent of the action of the physician. Now suppose there are two physicians, $i = 1,2$, and that they both face the same underlying cost (i.e., case mix) β. Consider a contract for physician 1 of the form $t_1 = \psi(e^*) + C_2$. Physician 1's objective is to maximize $t_1 - C_1 - \psi(e_1)$, and taking the behavior of physician 2 as fixed, physician 1 therefore chooses the efficient level of effort (satisfying $\psi'(e^*) = 1$). If physician 2 is given the symmetric contract (being paid physician 1's costs), he too chooses the efficient effort level. However, the net profit (rent) of physician 1 is $t_1 - C_1 - \psi(e_1) = 0$, so the purchaser is able to eliminate the rent paid though unable to observe the underlying cost directly. More generally, when there are many providers, the reimbursement of one physician can be contingent on the average costs incurred by other physicians.

The example above shows that when underlying efficiency parameters are the same for different providers, the purchaser can obtain as good an outcome as it could if they were observable. This intuition can be carried over to a more general case in which providers' costs are not perfectly correlated. For example, if the underlying efficiency parameter of firm i takes the form $\beta_i = \beta_0 + \varepsilon_i$, where β_0 is a common shock and ε_i is idiosyncratic, a cost-plus incentive scheme can be written that induces the same outcomes as could be achieved if the purchaser knew the common shock. In particular, the rents given up under such a comparative performance scheme would be smaller than if otherwise optimal independent incentive schemes were used (Laffont and Tirole 1993: 85).

A mechanism similar to this, for paying physicians, has been devised by a private insurance company in the Czech Republic (Jack 2000a). There, physicians receive bonus payments when their costs are lower than average and are taxed when they are higher.[16]

Sorting Contracts

Most of the discussion so far has assumed that underlying cost differentials stem from case-mix variations across physicians or across hospitals. But cost variability may also arise because of differences in opportunity costs, due to differences in ability and skill of physicians. This may be particularly important in the case of specialist care.

A similar analysis to the foregoing applies in this kind of situation: a purchaser, attempting to procure the services of specialists with differing underlying costs would rationally wish to price discriminate among them, paying a premium for the higher-quality providers. But if this quality is difficult to observe, or to contract upon, the only way to pay different providers different amounts is to induce self-selection: to offer alternative contractual arrangements that induce lower-quality specialists to accept one kind of contract, and higher-quality providers to accept another.[17]

This approach has been adopted in the Czech Republic. Specialists are permitted to choose between receiving a high price per procedure (measured in points) with a cap on the number of points they can charge for and a lower price without limit. While this is not quite an optimal arrangement (an optimal pair of contracts would likely involve open-ended, two-part tariffs), it suffices to sort specialists with different opportunity costs, thereby saving resources for the purchaser.

Ownership and Implicit Incentives

The discussion of explicit payment mechanisms above focused on how financial relationships between parties should be designed so as to allocate risk and rents while maintaining incentives. Some of the results of this literature can provide insights into how financial transfers should be structured in different institutional settings. For example, it was seen that due to the difficulty of providing explicit incentives for maintenance, outsourcing contracts might be higher powered than contracts for internal employees due to a difference in asset ownership. While this suggests certain correlations between the strength of formal incentives and organizational structures, it is less useful in predicting which of the possible combinations should be observed in practice, or which kinds of arrangements should be adopted or supported by public decision makers.

Hart (1995, paper 1) provides a useful examination of these issues, and shows how transaction cost economics (e.g., Williamson 1985) arose to deal with them within the context of the theory of the firm. The idea of this literature is that contracts of the form analyzed in the principal–agent paradigm are more costly to write than that theory assumes. The additional costs include planning costs (each party has to figure out what it wants from the relationship, and this can take time and effort), negotiating costs (they have to haggle over the terms), and actual writing costs (even when each knows what it wants, and they have both agreed, it might be difficult for the parties to write this information down in a way that a court could later interpret in mediating a dispute). The theory of the firm as elaborated in the transaction cost literature predicts that transactions will occur within the boundaries of a firm in order to economize on these costs, perhaps giving up some benefits of the higher-powered incentives that could accompany arms' length relationships.

Exactly why transaction costs should be lower within a firm than outside it was not made explicit in the early literature. The more recent formal *property rights theory* notes that, because of transaction costs, actual contracts will be incomplete, especially when the environment in which the players interact is changing often and in unpredictable ways. Incompleteness means that, in some contingencies, the required actions of the parties and the transfers between them will not be contractually specified, and they will need to negotiate over them. These negotiations may be costly, but even if they are not, their mere existence means that the returns to investments made early in the relationship will be distributed between the parties according to their relative ex post bargaining power, not on the basis of ex ante (contractual) agreements. This is the *hold up problem*. Hart's insight was that by assigning authority to make decisions in unspecified contingencies (implemented, perhaps, through the allocation of asset ownership), the allocation of bargaining power, and hence the strength of ex ante incentives, can be altered. Within this framework, it is possible to conduct a normative analysis of the assignment of decision-making authority.

The basic set-up of the property rights model includes two parties and one (or more) physical asset(s). In addition to the physical asset, ownership of which can be assigned to either party, each party can invest in nonallocable (i.e., human) capital. Who owns this is not a decision variable. Total surplus is a function of the two stocks of human capital, as well as the physical capital.

The assignment of ownership rights to the physical asset permits the owner to choose how to use it in contingencies not specified in an initial contract between the two—that is, ownership bestows control rights. The asset accords the owner enhanced bargaining power if and when the parties renegotiate, because the owner's outside option is improved: the owner can threaten to quit the relationship and continue using the asset. An important assumption is that the parties are always better off together (i.e., jointly using the physical asset and their human capital assets) than apart, but the threat of leaving is more credible for the party with the better outside option.

This improved bargaining power gives the owner greater incentive to invest in the complementary human (nonallocable) capital, while the incentives of the other party for such investment are reduced. Ownership should thus go to that party whose investment in human capital is relatively elastic and important (in terms of joint surplus generation).[18] Hart finds that joint ownership, in the context of two profit-maximizing parties, is never optimal.

In the context of medical care, it is convenient to think of the physical asset as a hospital. Consider then two parties: a financing intermediary that is responsible for arranging the delivery of medical care to a specified population and a group of physicians (or a professional hospital administrator). Delivery of care is improved if the intermediary invests in knowledge of the needs of the population, matches needs with resources well, acts promptly, and so on (these are the nonallocable assets of the intermediary). It is also improved if the physician group/administrator keeps abreast of professional developments, improves management oversight, and so on. The question that incomplete contract theory seeks to address is, Which of the two parties should own the hospital?

In either case, financial resources will flow from the intermediary to the physician group. However, if the physician group/administrator owns the hospital, then it looks like a contracting-out arrangement, in which the financing intermediary "purchases" services from the physician-owned hospital. But, if the financing intermediary owns the hospital, it appears more likely that it is a labor contract, in which the intermediary employs physicians to work at its hospital. A final alternative is that both parties jointly own the hospital; this looks something like a physician-owned insurance company.

According to the theory of the (private sector) firm, which the theory of incomplete contracts supports, joint ownership is never optimal: either the financing intermediary should own the hospital outright, or it should purchase services from a privatized (or at least financially autonomous) hospital. A less extreme statement of the same result is that highly complementary assets should be owned by a single party, and not split between two. This suggests that partnerships, defined as joint ownership of physical assets, are unwise.

However, when applied to the health sector, this argument loses some of its force. Recently, Besley and Ghatak (2000) and Jack (2000b) have examined the allocation of asset ownership in the design of a health system. The essential feature of these papers is that, if the parties were to not reach an agreement when unforeseen contingencies arose, they would each continue to engage in costly effort. In the simple model of private enterprise, the returns to each party in this case are internalized. However, when the return accrues at least partly in kind, say as the health status of a population, then it has the nature of a public good (as defined vis-à-vis the two parties). Even under joint ownership then, the parties would continue to have incentives to invest ex ante, and jointly these incentives might outweigh those that could be sustained under single ownership.[19]

This discussion allows us to begin to formalize the trade-offs between different organizational structures. Ownership of a facility by a purchasing intermediary is illustrative of publicly owned and financed hospitals that have employment contracts with physicians. Provider-owned hospitals financed from an outside source suggest a contracting-out model, in which the purchaser is the government or a private sector insurer. Finally, joint ownership is suggestive of a physician-insurer–owned health system—what might be called an integrated health system, not dissimilar to a health maintenance organization (HMO).

It should be noted that ownership is used to generate incentives for the parties to *invest* in the relationship—i.e., to improve the environment in which they jointly operate. In addition, incentives for *current* performance may still be needed. In the simple incomplete contract model, it is assumed that contracts are so incomplete they are absent. In practice, however, contracts will be only partially incomplete, and responsibilities and contingent transfers will be specified, if imperfectly. Thus, the insights of the principal–agent paradigm can still be used to predict the strength of formal incentive mechanisms that will be adopted by the parties.

It is thus expected that the contract between a publicly owned and financed hospital and its employees will be relatively low powered if incentives for maintenance and the like are important. Similarly, physician services may be multidimensional in other respects, meaning explicit incentives cannot be too strong. There might be restrictions on the ability of employees to see private patients in this case.[20] Under a purchaser–provider split, the same reasoning as above suggests somewhat higher-powered formal incentives may be appropriate. Under full integration, explicit incentives between purchaser and provider relating payment to current performance might be expected to be intermediary (although this is speculative at this stage).

COMPETITION AND REGULATION

Most of the discussion until now has been about how incentives can be provided in situations of bilateral monopoly—that is, how services should be purchased and how relationships between purchaser and provider should be structured. One of the strongest instruments for inducing performance at low cost is competition among agents. This section discusses the forms in which competition can take place, the likely welfare properties of each, and the scope for regulation.

Provider Competition

For reasons of imperfect information, travel costs, and other transaction costs, medical care is usually thought of as being supplied within a not-fully competitive market. A commonly adopted model is that of monopolistic competition, in which providers exercise some local market power over consumers. Also, apart from providers' being able to sustain prices above marginal cost, they compete on other, nonprice, attributes of care and service. When competition is not perfect, its net benefits are not always unambiguously positive, so the choices of whether to introduce it, and how to structure the market in which it takes place, are nontrivial.

A purchaser might introduce competition among providers to generate cost savings or to provide quality incentives. To examine these issues, Che and Gale (1997) have developed a model of buyer alliances—that is, purchasing cooperatives—in which providers (HMOs) compete over quality and price in a spatial model. The purchaser chooses the number of providers from which to buy and the format the competition should take. Under "sponsor-driven competition," the purchaser chooses the number, and spatial distribution, of firms, and negotiates price and quality contracts. Under individual-driven demand, the sponsor plays a more passive role, selecting the firms but leaving decisions about prices and quality up to the providers and consumers. Sponsor-driven competition is closer to what Enthoven (1993) termed *managed competition*.

In a related paper, in the context of the United Kingdom's quasi-market reforms (Le Grand 1991), Halonen and Propper (1999) show that by requiring providers to compete for patients, a purchaser can induce quality provision, but with the consequence that costs may rise. Their model is one of tax-financed universal care, so individual-driven competition arises as consumers respond to quality differentials between providers. When competition has little effect on quality (either because physicians enjoy providing it, or because demand is unresponsive to quality changes), or when the distortionary or political costs of taxation are high, the purchaser prefers a single agency over a quasi-market.

A number of authors have noted that competition in the health sector—either between hospitals and other providers of care, or between insurance companies—can have negative consequences when the population of consumers has heterogenous costs. Cream skimming and dumping incentives (Ma 1994) lead providers to either engage in costly screening procedures, or manipulate product quality, or both. The purchaser then must trade off the incentives that competition provides for internal productive efficiency (i.e., using the appropriate techniques, including unobservable effort, in producing services) against the potential social costs of wasteful underwriting (e.g., marketing to the healthy), undersupply to some groups, or both. For example, a sure-fire way to reduce active selection incentives is to reimburse the provider for all costs incurred, thus making him indifferent between serving a high- or low-cost consumer. However, this policy provides very weak incentives for cost control.

In analyzing this problem, modeling the nature of competition between providers is important, because for active selection to be operative, some degree of pooling (i.e., cross-subsidization from low-cost to high-cost individuals) must be sustained in equilibrium. Newhouse (1999) introduced costs of writing insurance contracts into Rothschild and Stiglitz's (1976) model of perfect competition with adverse selection to generate such pooling equilibria, then used the tools of Laffont and Tirole (1993) to examine selection incentives. Jack (2001b) used a model of horizontal product differentiation, and was able to explicitly evaluate alternative cost-sharing policies within the context of competition-induced active selection. In that model, selection incentives can be removed simply by disallowing individual-driven competition (i.e., consumer choice) through the exogenous assignment of individuals to providers. The selection effects of competition can be partially mitigated by using a cost-sharing formula between purchaser and provider, but it is possible that the cost-sharing rate should actually be negative.

Purchaser Competition

A purchasing intermediary is meant to act on behalf of consumers. But, as noted in the first part of this chapter, providing incentives for this agent may be as important as inducing providers of care to act efficiently. Many of the issues that arise in the analysis of competition between (imperfectly competitive) providers of care continue to be relevant in the purchasing market. Consumer responsiveness to changes in price and quality of the services offered by the purchaser may be weak, endowing each purchaser with some local market power. Entry into the market may be excessive, depending on the cost structure of purchasers (e.g., the size of fixed costs).

An important competitive issue in the purchasing market that may not arise in the provider market is the issue of vertical restraint. Unrestrained competition would permit a provider to contract with multiple purchasers, just as a retail store might contract with multiple goods suppliers, even for similar goods. One view of restrictive practices, such as exclusive dealing arrangements under which a provider of care contracts with only one purchaser, is that they are agreements between "consenting adults" and are therefore efficiency enhancing (since the parties would not agree unless each was better off). Indeed, restraints can be efficiency enhancing if they help correct externalities. For example, if the purchaser provides promotional services to attract customers on behalf of a provider, the provider might sign a side contract with another purchaser to induce individuals to switch. The possibility of this kind of contractual competition between purchasers for the services of a single agent (the "common agency" problem, e.g., see Martimort, 1996) can both reduce the power of incentives provided through the contracts (e.g., see Dixit 2002), and reduce the promotional services provided by the purchaser.

Vertical restraints can have less benign effects. Some have argued that they might constitute a barrier to entry in the up-stream (i.e., purchaser) market (Tirole, 1988, pp. 185–86). Exclusive dealing contracts force new entrants into the purchasing market to set up their own provider networks, increasing the fixed costs of entry. Similarly, vertical restraints might soften upstream competition, for example, by making collusion among purchasers easier.

Alternatives to Competition

Competition is effective when individuals can, and do, exercise choice. In some cases, the large fixed costs associated with the delivery of particular services (e.g., hospital services) mean that making this choice available is costly. The policy maker then must judge whether regulation is more effective than costly competition, or indeed if some other mechanism can be used to ensure accountability.

Many of the purchasing questions addressed above in the context of the design of incentive mechanisms are regulatory in nature. Indeed, one can think of regulation as affecting the environment in which a firm (e.g., hospital) works, while leaving operational decisions in the hands of managers. The same kinds of issues of moral hazard and adverse selection will naturally emerge, and the tools described in the third section, above, are applicable.

An alternative disciplining mechanism that has received some attention recently is the idea of "voice." Consumers are not given the choice of switching providers, but they are given the opportunity—either through the media or through administrative review procedures—to complain when services are not in accordance with their expectations. One can think of a number of shortcomings of this kind of incentive mechanism, including the free-rider problem (one voice may not make much of a difference, but many will), a commitment problem (harsh punishments cannot be credibly threatened without formalized institutional rules such as a constitution), and political distortions (mob rule could punish the wrong person for poor performance).

However, when economies of scale are significant (so building two hospitals is unfeasible), and when formal regulatory institutions are inoperative due to resource or corruption constraints, voice may be the best mechanism for providing incentives.

SOME CONCLUSIONS

This chapter has asked how medical care services should be purchased. This question can be usefully divided into two: What institutional arrangements should exist between providers, purchasers, and consumers? and How should financial flows among them be conditioned on observable and verifiable information? Central to the whole analysis was the idea that purchasing arrangements must generate incentives for performance. The chapter had little to say about what kinds of medical care—for example, curative versus preventative—should be purchased. These decisions must be made on the basis of weighing social benefits against costs: alternative purchasing mechanisms generate different incentives and hence different costs and benefits (say through quality or distribution), so understanding the effects of these mechanisms is a necessary step to addressing the question of which health interventions should be financed.

A purchasing agency will often need to trade the provision of incentives off against risk and rent appropriation, suggesting a role for cost-sharing mechanisms of some kind. These design issues are well understood, both in the general principal–agent literature, and in the health care provider payment literature as well. The allocation of authority and/or ownership between purchaser and provider has been somewhat less fully explored, relying as it likely will, on more recent theoretical developments. Finally, the appropriate roles of competition (market discipline) and regulation (external discipline) can be judged only when proper account is taken of the nature of competition and regulatory constraints.

NOTES

1. Ma and McGuire (1997: 688) interpret *effort* as "any costly activity that affects the patient's valuation of the services received, including dimensions of convenience, comfort, communication about medical conditions, as well as some narrowly defined 'clinical' quality of care."

2. See Newhouse (1999) for a general review of selection incentives, and Jack (2001a) for a model of quality-based active selection in health insurance markets.

3. This information might be transmitted to the consumer by a physician. At this stage, assume the physician undertakes no communication with the insurer. Ma and McGuire (1997) illustrate the effects of relaxing this assumption in a model that jointly determines optimal payments to providers by consumers.

4. For more analysis of the costly verification issue, and its interaction with adverse selection, see Zeckhauser (1970), Jack and Sheiner (1997), and Jack (2001b).

5. Ellis and McGuire (1986) examine the implications of the physician-patient agency relationship for provider payment mechanisms.

6. Dixit (2002) offers a useful and readable review.

7. In general the optimal payment scheme need not be linear or even monotonically increasing in output. However, Holmstrom and Milgrom (1987) show that when effort must be provided continuously over time, the optimal scheme is linear (as long as there are no wealth effects, which occur when the principal and agent have utility functions exhibiting constant absolute risk aversion).

8. This observation is about how incentives and ownership might be correlated but does not inform us as to which allocation of asset ownership and incentives yields the better outcome.

9. The full cost to the firm is $C + \psi(e)$, where $\psi(.)$ is the nonpecuniary cost of effort (i.e., the cost directly borne by the provider). It is useful to think of the pecuniary cost, C, as representing the costs the provider incurs in purchasing inputs on a spot market. This is the only component of total costs that is observable by the purchaser.

10. McClellan (1997) quotes the 1991 Annual Report to [the U.S.] Congress of the Prospective Payment Assessment Commission as reporting that "[t]he most important influences on the overall level of PPS payments is the increase in the case mix index" suggesting a ratcheting up of diagnoses in response to the DRG-payment mechanism.

11. This argument is an application of the Revelation Principal (Myerson 1979). Chalkley and Malcomson (1999) show how the DRG system—which bases payments solely on reported diagnosis—can be improved by also linking payment to realized costs.

12. An *experience good* is one whose quality is difficult to discern before purchase. Medical care seems an obvious candidate for such a definition.

13. This is sometimes referred to as allowing "the money to follow the patient."

14. Chalkey and Malcomson (1998) examine the effects of provider preferences on the power of incentives when demand is not responsive to quality.

15. If introducing competition meant a more efficient provider won the contract, the power of the optimal implemented incentive scheme would increase. (See the earlier discussion on menus of linear contracts.) The point here is that competition among providers at the procurement stage reduces rents but does not alter the strength of the incentives the winner makes at the margin.

16. Glazer and McGuire (2000) apply the ideas of Cremer and McLean (1985) on correlated information to show that, in some contexts, a purchaser can extract all the information rents from providers even when underlying costs are only imperfectly correlated. The mechanisms that implement such first-best outcomes can require very large transfers, however, bringing their applicability into question. Laffont and Martimort (2000) show that, when collusion between providers is taken into account, this kind of mechanism cannot implement the first best.

17. See Hammer and Jack (2001) for a relevant model.

18. See Hart (1995: 45–46) for statements and explanations of these and other results.

19. This point was in fact addressed by Hart (1995: 68–69), although it was motivated from a slightly different perspective.

20. An aspect of multidimensionality examined by Halonen and Propper (1999) derives from the necessity of dealing with routine (i.e., mundane) procedures and more exotic and challenging cases.

REFERENCES

Besley, T., and M. Ghatak. 2000. "Public-Private Partnerships for the Provision of Public Goods: Theory and an Application to NGOs in Developing Countries." London: London School of Economics.

Chalkley, M., and J.M. Malcomson. 1999. "Cost-Sharing in Health Service Provision: An Empirical Assessment of Cost Savings." *Journal of Public Economics* 84(2): 218–50.

———. 1998. "Contracting for Health Services When Patient Demand Does Not Reflect Quality." *Journal of Health Economics* (17)1: 1–19.

Che, Y-K., and I. Gale. 1997. "Buyer Alliances and Managed Competition." *Journal of Economics and Management Strategy* 6(1): 175–200.

Cremer, J., and R. McLean. 1985. "Optimal Selling Strategies under Uncertainty for a Discriminating Monopolist When Demands Are Interdependent." *Econometrica* 53: 345–61.

Dewatripont, M., I. Jewitt, and J. Tirole. 1999a. "The Economics of Career Concerns. Part I: Comparing Information Systems." *Review of Economic Studies* 66(1): 183–98.

———. 1999b. "The Economics of Career Concerns. Part II: Application to Missions and Accountability of Government Agencies." *Review of Economic Studies* 66(1): 199–217.

Dixit, A. 2002. "Incentives and Organizations in the Public Sector: An Interpretative Review." *Journal of Human Resources* 37(4): 696–727.

Ellis, R., and T. McGuire. 1986. "Provider Response to Prospective Payment: Cost Sharing and Supply." *Journal of Health Economics* 5(2): 129–51.

Enthoven, A.C. 1993. "The History and Principles of Managed Competition." *Health Affairs* 12 (Supp. 1): 24–48.

Fudenberg, D., and J. Tirole. 1990. "Moral Hazard and Renegotiation in Agency Contracts." *Econometrica* 58(6): 1279–319.

Glazer, J., and T. McGuire. 2000. "Optimal Risk Adjustment in Markets with Adverse Selection: An Application to Managed Care." *American Economic Review* 90(4): 1055–71.

Halonen, M., and C. Propper. 1999. *The Organisation of Government Bureaucracies: The Choice between Competition and Single Agency.* Working Paper No. 99/010. Bristol, United Kingdom: Bristol University, Centre for Market and Public Organisation.

Hammer, J., and W. Jack. 2001. "The Design of Incentives for Health Care Providers in Developing Countries: Contracts, Competition, and Cost Control." Research Working Paper No. 2547. Washington, DC: World Bank, Development Economics Research Group, Public Economics.

Hart, O. 1995. *Firms, Contracts, and Financial Structure.* Oxford, United Kingdom: Oxford University Press.

Holmstrom, B. 1999. "Managerial Incentive Problems: A Dynamic Perspective," *Review of Economic Studies* 66 (1): 169–82.

———— 1982. "Moral Hazard in Teams." *Bell Journal of Economics* 13: 324–40.

Holmstrom, B., and Paul Milgrom. 1987. "Aggregation and Linearity in the Provision of Intertemporal Incentives." *Econometrica* 55(2): 303–28.

————. 1991. "Multi-Task Principal-Agent Analysis: Incentive Contracts, Asset Ownership, and Job Design." *Journal of Law, Economics, and Organization* 7 (Special issue): 24–52.

Jack, W.G. 2001a. "Controlling Selection Incentives When Health Insurance Contracts Are Endogenous." *Journal of Public Economics* (80)1: 25–48.

————. 2001b. "Equilibrium in Insurance Markets with Ex Ante Adverse Selection and Ex Post Moral Hazard." *Journal of Public Economics.*

————. 2000a. "Decentralizing the Provision of Health Services: An Incomplete Contracts Approach." Policy Research Working Paper 2395. Washington, DC: World Bank, Development Economics Research Group.

————. 2000b. "Health Insurance Reform in Four Latin American Countries: Theory and Practice." World Bank Policy Research Paper 2492, Washington, DC.

————. 2000c. "The Purchase of Medical Care in the Czech Republic: Provider Payment Mechanisms in Practice." Washington, DC: World Bank.

Jack, W., and L. Sheiner. 1997. "Welfare-Improving Health Expenditure Subsidies," *American Economic Review* 87(1): 206–21.

Laffont, J-J., and D. Martimort. 2000. "Mechanism Design with Collusion and Correlation." *Econometrica* 68(2): 309–42.

Laffont, J-J., and J. Tirole 1993. *A Theory of Incentives in Procurement and Regulation.* Cambridge, MA: MIT Press.

Le Grand, J. 1991. "Quasi-Markets and Social Policy." *Economic Journal* 101(405): 1256–67.

Leonard, K. 2003. "African Traditional Healers and Outcome-Contingent Contracts in Health Care." *Journal of Development Economics* 71(1): 1–22.

Ma, C-T. A. 1994. "Health Care Payment Systems: Cost and Quality Incentives." *Journal of Economics and Management Strategy* 3(1): 93–112.

Ma, C-T. A., and T. McGuire. 1997. "Optimal Health Insurance and Provider Payment." *American Economic Review* 87(4): 685–704.

Martimort, D. 1996. "Exclusive Dealing, Common Agency, and Multiprincipals Incentive Theory." *RAND Journal of Economics* 27(1): 1–31.

McClellan, M. 1997. "Hospital Reimbursement Incentives: An Empirical Analysis." *Journal of Economics and Management Strategy* 6(1): 91–128.

Milgrom, P. 1988. "Employment Contracts, Influence Activities, and Efficient Organization Design." *Journal of Political Economy* 96(1): 42–60.

Myerson, R. 1979. "Incentive Compatibility and the Bargaining Problem." *Econometrica* 47(1): 61–74.

Newhouse, J. 1999. "Reimbursing Health Plans and Health Providers: Efficiency in Production Versus Selection." *Journal of Economic Literature* 34(3): 1236–63.

Oxley, H. 1995. "New Directions in Health Care Policy." Paris: Organisation for Economic Co-operation and Development.

Rothschild, M., and J. Stiglitz. 1976. "Equilibrium in Competitive Insurance Markets: An Essay on the Economics of Imperfect Information." *Quarterly Journal of Economics* 90(4): 629–49.

Shleifer, A. 1985. "A Theory of Yardstick Competition." *Rand Journal of Economics* 16: 319–27.

Tirole, J. 1988. *The Theory of Industrial Organization*. Cambridge, MA: MIT Press.

Williamson, O. 1985. *The Economic Institutions of Capitalism: Firms, Markets, and Relational Contracting*. New York, NY: Free Press.

Zeckhauser, R. 1970. "Medical Insurance: A Case Study of the Tradeoff between Risk Spreading and Appropriate Incentives." *Journal of Economic Theory* 2(1): 10–26.

CHAPTER 15

Measuring Efficiency in Purchasing

Xingzhu Liu and Anne Mills

The concept of efficiency seems straightforward at first glance, but soon becomes complicated when considering the definition and measurement of outputs, the relationship between social efficiency and organizational efficiency, and the measurements of efficiency concepts. The output can be health or quantity of services or the total satisfaction of the users. Using different output measures to define efficiency will produce different concepts, and thus their measurement also differs. Organizational efficiency does not necessarily mean social efficiency, because the quantity of services can be maximized through the provision of unnecessary care, which is contrary to social efficiency.

For these reasons, the concepts of efficiency must be clarified and methods for measuring them must be provided for research related to the formulation of resource allocation policy and the design of motivational strategies for health care providers. This chapter clarifies the concepts underlying different definitions of efficiency in the health care sector and provides various methods for measuring the existence and the extent of efficiency or inefficiency under different efficiency concepts.

INTRODUCTION

Health economics is concerned with the efficient use of health care resources. This concern is important because only a limited amount of scarce societal resource is allocated to health sector. People always hope that the use of these limited inputs can yield the maximum amount of output. Achieving efficient use of health care resources, however, is not easy. It requires, at the macro level, that the social health resources can be allocated among different health sector fields (e.g., curative care and preventive care) so that the marginal outputs of the resource inputs to different fields are equal or similar; that within each field the resources can be allocated among different projects properly so that the ratio of marginal cost to marginal output is equal across projects. At the micro level, the efficient use of health resources requires that health sector organizations can allocate their budgets in a way that allows different types of inputs to be combined properly and results in the use of the best combination of organizational inputs to yield the maximum amount of output. In the health sector, efficiency cannot be achieved unless governments can formulate and implement appropriate policies and health care providers and users are motivated to provide and use health care efficiently.

Due to the increasing cost pressures in the health sector, policy makers in different governmental bodies and relevant researchers have been trying to develop (1) policies to guide resource allocation among different health sector fields and projects within each field, and (2) ways to motivate the health care organizations to improve their productive efficiency. At first glance, the concept of efficiency seems straightforward, but soon becomes complicated when considering the definition and measurement of outputs, the relationship between social efficiency and organizational efficiency, and the measurement of efficiency concepts. The output can be health or quantity of services or the total satisfaction of the users. Using different output measures to define efficiency will result in different concepts, and thus the measurement of these concepts differs. Organizational efficiency does not necessarily mean social efficiency, because the quantity of services can be maximized through the provision of unnecessary care which is contrary to social efficiency. For these reasons, the concepts of efficiency must be clarified and methods for measuring them must be provided for research related to the formulation of resource allocation policy and the design of motivational strategies for health care providers.

The objectives of this chapter are to clarify the concepts of different definitions of efficiency in the health care sector and to provide alternatives for measuring the existence and the extent of efficiency or inefficiency under different efficiency concepts. In the second part, the concepts of efficiency are addressed. The third section reviews different ways of measuring organizational efficiency. The last section is a discussion of measuring the social efficiency of health care services.

CONCEPTS OF EFFICIENCY

Efficiency is generally defined by the quantitative relationship between input and output. It can be expressed by the ratio of output/input. The larger the ratio, the more efficient the activity will be. If the activity is based on a given input, *perfect efficiency* means that the output is maximized. If the activity is based on a given output, perfect efficiency means that the input is minimized. *Inefficiency* will occur if output can be increased without an increase in the input, and if the input can be decreased without a decrease in the output.

General Concepts of Efficiency

Economists often divide efficiency into technical and allocative efficiency (Rosko and Broyles 1988). *Technical efficiency* means that the output can be maximized by using a given set of inputs. For example, a public hospital is provided with a fixed combination of inputs in terms of the types of inputs and the amount of each input. If the hospital can produce the maximum amount of output by using these sets of inputs, the hospital can be called "technically efficient." Technical efficiency is explained graphically in figure 15.1.

If a firm produces by using two types of inputs—capital and labor—and the two can substitute for each other, a given amount of production can be made with less labor and more capital or with more labor and less capital. As shown in figure 15.1, to produce 1,000 units of output efficiently, the firm needs many possible sets of combinations of inputs, which are shown by isoquant curve I. For example, both combination A and combination B can produce 1,000 units of output. If the firm is technically efficient, given the sets of input combinations indicated by curve I, it must produce 1,000 units of output, because more output is impossible and less output means inefficiency. In summary, a technically efficient firm will produce at the production possibility frontier with the given sets of inputs. Technical inefficiency occurs if the output can be increased without an increase in any input of the combination of inputs.

Allocative efficiency means that the production is made at the best combination of inputs so that the cost of production can be minimized. *Allocative inefficiency* occurs if the cost for producing a given amount of output can be reduced by changing the combination of inputs without changing the output, or if the output can be increased by adjusting the combination of inputs without increasing the total cost.

Allocative efficiency can be shown graphically. In figure 15.2, TC_1, TC_2, and TC_3 are isocost lines along which the combination of inputs (capital and labor) changes, but the total costs remain equal. If a firm is technically efficient and produces an output of 1,000 units, the total cost of production can be reduced by adjusting the combination of inputs to point A, where the total cost for producing

---

Figure 15.1   Isoquant Curve and Technical Efficiency

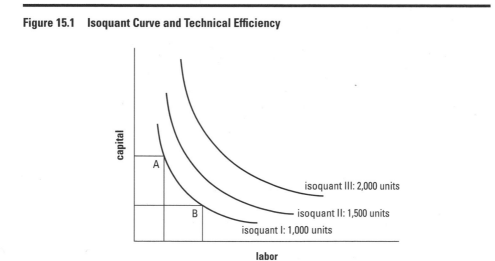

Source: Authors.

Figure 15.2   Isocost, Isoquant, and Allocative Efficiency

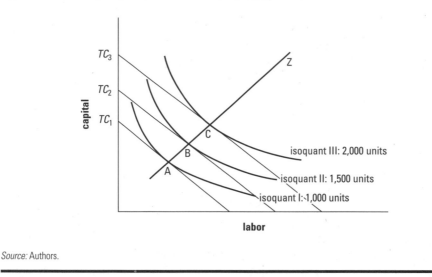

Source: Authors.

1,000 units of output can be minimized. Point A is the point of tangency between the isoquant curve and isocost line where the slope of the isoquant curve equals the slope of the isocost line. The slope of the isoquant curve is called the *marginal rate of technical substitution* (MRTS), which indicates how many units of capital must be increased with one unit reduction in labor, holding the quantity of output constant. The slope of the isocost line is called the *market rate of substitution* (MRS), which means how many units of capital must be increased with one unit reduction in labor, holding the total cost of production constant. Similarly, points B and C are also the best combinations for producing 1,500 and 2,000 units of output. A firm is said to be allocatively efficient if it can produce along line Z, which shows the best combination of inputs for various levels of output. Allocative inefficiency occurs if the combination of inputs departs from the best input combination line.

Production efficiency requires production to be both technically and allocatively efficient. That production is technically efficient does not mean it is allocatively efficient because the output is maximized at the given sets of combination of inputs and the input combination is not necessarily the least costly input combination. Neither does allocative efficiency equate with technical efficiency because the combination is optimized; the firm may be unable to maximize its output, given the set of the best combination of inputs.

Efficiency Concepts under Different Output Measures

Input can be expressed in monetary terms, but expressions of output are different. Output can be health services, health status, monetary value of health, and the total utility derived from health services.

The immediate output of the health sector is health services (Feldstein 1993). If the output is measured by the quantity of health services, the concept of efficiency will be that the quantity of health services is maximized at the least cost. Take, for example, the case of two hospitals. If the ratio of service quantity/cost for hospital A is larger than that for hospital B, hospital A is relatively more efficient. Perfect efficiency will occur if the hospital can produce at its production possibility frontier with the best combination of inputs.

The advantages of using service quantity as the output for measuring efficiency are that the service quantity is easy to measure and that there is a direct link between the quantity of health services and the input. This means that the output is specific to the input. There are, however, several disadvantages. The first disadvantage is that the measurement problem emerges when the production unit involves several types of services, as it usually does in hospital production. A valid efficiency comparison is difficult to make unless the services are weighted and a single output indicator is developed. The second disadvantage is that, if the quality of health services varies among the observation units, the comparison of the ratio of service quantity/cost is not meaningful. A valid comparison cannot be made unless the quantity of services can be adjusted by quality. The third disadvantage is that problems may exist if some of the quantity of services is unnecessary care. If the proportions of the unnecessary care are different between the two hospitals, the quantity/cost ratios in themselves are less meaningful for comparing the efficiency of the two hospitals.

Due to the disadvantages of taking the quantity of services as output, people have to seek other alternatives for measuring output. One of these is the health outcome, which is said to be the ultimate output of the health sector input (Feldstein 1993). Thus, efficiency can be measured by the ratio of health outcome/cost. Perfect efficiency means that the best combination of health inputs can lead to the highest of health status. There is a tremendous body of literature on measuring the health of individuals and the population (Kind and Gudex 1994; Bowling 1991; Schillemans, et al. 1990). In general, health outcome can be measured by the unidimensional scale and the multidimensional scalar index. The examples of unidimensional measurements are lowering blood pressure by x mm Hg, the length of life in years, mortality, morbidity, and life expectancy. Examples of multidimensional measurements are quality-adjusted life years (QALYs) (Zweifel and Breyer 1997) and quality of life (EuroQol Group 1990). The major advantage of taking health outcome as the output of health input is that it allows removal of the problem connected with using the quantity of service as output. But it suffers from several disadvantages. Health outcome has a character of uncertainty and it is not specific to health input. This means that the improvement in health status does not necessarily result from health input, and that a number of other factors influence the level of health outcome, such as environmental factors, education, and economic status. Unless the net effect of health input on health can be specified, efficiency of health input cannot be evaluated with reasonable validity. The second problem is that the uniform measurement of the health status is generally lacking and that QALYs and the like involve tremendous amount of work. Efficiency cannot be evaluated by using inconsistent and inefficient tools.

The previous two approaches of output measurement suffer from a common problem: that efficiency evaluation must be based on comparison of more than two units of observation or alternatives. It cannot answer the question of whether an activity is worth doing. Health economists suggested and developed a method for measuring the output of health input by monetary value. This is called *benefit-cost analysis,* according to which, if the benefit/cost ratio is greater than 1, the activity is worth doing. In this case, perfect efficiency means that the maximum benefit (health in terms of money) can be achieved by using the best combination of health input. Although this definition can provide a direct monetary measurement of efficiency, it is usually difficult to convert the health outcome into a monetary value, and the problem of specification of input to output remains.

Another concept indicating the output is *consumer utility.* The utility here refers to total consumer satisfaction with a health care service, gained from not only health improvement but also the process of service utilization. According to this concept, *efficiency* can be defined as consumer satisfaction maximized at the least cost to society (Donald and Gerard 1993). This concept is comprehensive, but tools have not yet been developed to measure it.

The Concepts of Organizational and Social Efficiency

While efficiency can be defined in terms of various definitions of output, it can also be defined in terms of the perspective of either the organization or society as a whole. Generally, *organizational efficiency* means that an organization can produce the maximum amount of output with minimized input (Sherman 1984). But how it is defined by the organization depends on the organization's objective function. In terms of hospitals, their objectives may be to maximize the quantity of services, the revenue generated from services, and the profit. Thus, hospital efficiency can be measured by each of the following alternatives. One is *productivity,* operationally defined as the ratio of service quantity/input. The input here can be measured by the monetary term (e.g., cost per item of service) or the nonmonetary term (e.g., number of hospital days per doctor). Different methods for measuring productivity are provided in the next section.

Another approach to efficiency measurement is *profitability,* defined as the difference between total revenue minus total cost divided by total cost. It, in fact, measures the rate of net economic return. If it is zero, the hospital can break even; if it is negative, the hospital suffers a loss; if it is positive, the hospital earns a profit. Still another method of measurement is the ratio of total revenue/total cost. If it is equal to 1, the hospital can break even; if it is less than 1, the hospital suffers a loss; and if it is more than 1, the hospital earns a profit. The last two approaches are widely used by hospitals to evaluate their financial status, although there are problems in measuring the cost of the hospital (specifically the depreciation cost) due to the lack of a uniform method of depreciation.

Social efficiency is defined in the perspective of society as a whole as the social output maximized at the least social cost (Chernichovsky 1995; Ortun-Rubio and Rodriguez-Artalejo 1990). Depending on the purpose of efficiency evaluation, the input and the output in social efficiency measurement are more inclusive than those in the organizational efficiency measurement. For example, to evaluate the efficiency of a health program, all the costs and outputs should be included. To measure the social efficiency, *output* can be defined in a number of ways. For example, it can be the quantity (or quality-adjusted quantity) of health services, improvement in the health status, increased social wealth (production or gross national product) due to health investment, and *social welfare* defined by the total willingness to pay, minus the total social cost. Specific methods of measuring the social efficiency are discussed in the last section of this chapter.

Differing from the concepts of technical efficiency and allocative efficiency, which are not mutually exclusive (the increase in technical efficiency affects the increase or the decrease in allocative efficiency), organizational efficiency and social efficiency may be mutually exclusive, but not always. For example, an increase in the total quantity of hospital services with a fixed amount of inputs means improvement in the hospital's organizational efficiency. But, if the increase in quantity is largely due to the provision of unnecessary care and reduction in the quality of care, the costs are actually shifted to the service users. As a result, the improvement in the hospital's organizational efficiency is based on the reduction in its social efficiency. The inconsistency between organizational efficiency and social efficiency sets the basis for designing the payment system to hospitals to motivate them to behave so that both organizational and social efficiency can be achieved. The hospital's main interest is to improve its organizational efficiency. A hospital is less likely to behave in a way that improves its social efficiency unless it is motivated to do so.

MEASUREMENT OF ORGANIZATIONAL EFFICIENCY

Organizational efficiency can be measured by each of the following methods: unidimensional ratio analysis, multidimensional weighted ratio analysis, production function analysis, cost function analysis, and data envelopment analysis. The mechanisms of these methods and their strengths and weaknesses are discussed in this section.

Unidimensional Ratio Analysis

In *unidimensional ratio analysis,* the earliest form of hospital efficiency analysis, the relationship is calculated between two variables: the output variable and the input variable (Farrell 1962). The indicators of this analysis are usually the cost per inpatient day, the cost per hospital admission, the personnel full-time equivalents per patient, the number of inpatient days per doctor, the number of outpatient visits per doctor, the hospital bed occupancy rate, the number of admissions per bed, and so on.

This type of analysis has been widely used by hospitals, third-party payers, and government hospital administrations because of its several advantages, including the following: (1) the indicators are easy to calculate and they do not involve any sophisticated mathematical method; (2) the data related to the calculation of the indicators are usually available from the regular statistics of the hospitals, and the calculation of these indicators does not mean significant extra work and cost; (3) this type of analysis can reflect change in a hospital's efficiency over time (for example, if the number of inpatient days per doctor is more this year than last year, and other indicators remain unchanged, it means improvement in hospital efficiency); and (4) this analysis can be used to evaluate efficiency across similar (comparable) hospitals, and the result of comparison can help the hospital managers identify and try to solve efficiency shortcomings. Because of the last two advantages, this type of analysis can provide hospitals with information for improving their managerial efficiency.

Though simple, this method suffers from several problems. The first and most serious problem is the inconsistency between different indicators and among hospitals. For example, one group of ratios is better one year than for the previous year, while another group of ratios may be worse. In this case, whether the hospital's efficiency improved or decreased cannot be said. In addition, one hospital may appear relatively efficient on one group of ratios and inefficient on another; another hospital may have the opposite result for the same ratios. In this case, which hospital is more efficient cannot be said. Second, in most cases, a ratio lacks comparability between hospitals. By nature, each ratio is limited to one output and one input and cannot accommodate a multi-output and multi-input situation. For example, if hospital A has a lower cost/patient day ratio than hospital B, a conclusion that hospital A is more efficient than hospital B will be biased simply because of the difference in quality of care and case mix between the two hospitals. Third, this analysis is based on the idea of relative efficiency. The improvement in a ratio for a hospital reflects the improvement in its efficiency in this aspect, and the hospital with a better ratio than the mean may be more efficient than the average, but it says nothing about whether the hospital is operating at the efficiency frontier and achieving its best efficiency.

Multidimensional Weighted Ratio Analysis

The multidimensional weighted ratio analysis is designed to solve the first two problems of the unidimensional ratio analysis, namely inconsistency and incomparability. It tries to capture all types of outputs and inputs and to develop a single indicator for measuring hospital efficiency (Sherman 1984). The general idea of this approach is that outputs are measured by using one indicator, derived by converting all types of outputs into an output equivalent, and that the inputs are measured by using either the total cost measure or an input equivalent. To derive the single output measure, a series of relative weights need to be worked out for all types of service outputs, based on one type of output. For example, if the outputs are to be measured by using hospital day equivalents, other types of output must be converted into hospital day measures by deciding their values relative to a hospital day. If quality is considered, one type of service can be broken down into several categories according to the severity of diseases and their resource use, and the relative value will be assigned to each of the categories. The single measure of output can then be measured by using the following equation:

(1) $\qquad OE = \sum_{i=l}^{n} W_i Q_i$,

where OE refers to the output equivalent; W_i is the relative value of the ith type or category of output; and Q_i is the total quantity of the ith type or category of output. The final quantity of output will be measured by a relative quantity that is based on the type or category of service with a relative value 1, which is the base of the output measurement. Inputs can be measured in the same way. An input equivalent, a full-time doctor equivalent, for instance, can be used as an input measure, and all of the inputs must be converted into this measure by weighting other inputs relative to a full-time doctor. If the inputs are measured by using the total cost of an institution, the input measure seems straightforward. It simply equals the operation expenditure (variable cost) plus the depreciation costs (fixed costs). Thus, hospital efficiency can be measured by either of the two equations. One equation is

(2) $\qquad HE = \dfrac{\sum_{j=1}^{m} W_j I_j}{\sum_{i=1}^{n} W_i Q_i}$,

where HE indicates hospital efficiency; W_j refers to the relative value of the jth input; and I_j is the quantity of the jth input. This equation measures the quantity of input equivalent per unit of output equivalent. And the other equation is

(3) $\qquad HE = \dfrac{OE + \sum_{j=1}^{m} DR_j FA_j}{\sum_{i=1}^{n} W_i Q_i}$,

where OE refers to the operation expenditure; DR_j refers to the depreciation rate of the jth type of fixed asset; and FA_j is the purchase cost of the jth fixed asset. This equation measures the monetary cost per unit of output equivalent.

The inconsistency and incomparability problems can be partially remedied by using multidimensional ratio analysis, but it still cannot tell anything about whether the relatively efficient hospital is operating at its efficiency frontier. In addition, the usefulness of this approach is limited by the facts that the uniform efficient relative weights for outputs and inputs are not available due to the difficulty of establishing an agreed-upon set of weights, and that what are the uniform bases of input and output equivalents are generally not known. Using the total cost as the input measure is also problematic because there is no uniform depreciation method, due to difficulties in specifying the rates of inflation of the fixed assets, one of the bases for specifying the replacement cost, depreciation period, interest rate on debt, and foreign exchange rates if the equipment is imported.

Production Function Analysis

Production function analysis has been used by economists to study efficiency since the 1930s and is one of the econometric methods most often used by health economists (Eastaugh 1992). With regard to the production function, first the concept is described; then model specification, output and input measurement, and use for measuring hospital efficiency are discussed.

The Production Function Concept

Production function refers to the physical relationship between an organization's input of productive resources and its output of goods and services per unit of time. The production function can be presented as

$$(4) \qquad Q = f(X_1, X_2, \ldots, X_n) ,$$

where Q is the quantity of output per period of time with specific combinations of input X_1, X_2, . . ., X_n (Rosko and Broyles 1988). While the general form of production function is such, the specification of the model differs.

Specification of Models

Two models are commonly used in the estimation of hospital production function (Rosko and Broyles 1988): the Cobb-Douglas model and the transcendental logarithmic (translog model). A simple case of the Cobb-Douglas model involves only two inputs. The model can be expressed as

$$(5) \qquad Q = AL^{\alpha}K^{\beta} ,$$

where Q represents output; A is a constant term; L refers to the quantity of labor; K is the quantity of capital; α is the output elasticity of labor; and β is the output elasticity of capital. The property of this model is (Walters 1963): (1) If $\alpha + \beta > 1$, there are increase returns to scale; if $\alpha + \beta = 1$, there are constant returns to scale; and if $\alpha + \beta < 1$, there are decreasing returns to scale. (2) The marginal physical productivity of labor declines if $\alpha < 1$, and the marginal physical productivity of capital declines if $\beta < 1$. (3) The elasticity of input substitution is unity. The general model of this type can be presented as (Eastaugh 1992)

$$(6) \qquad Q = (\prod_{i=1}^{n} X_i^{\beta_i})\beta_0 e^{\varepsilon} ,$$

where X_i represents the ith input; β_i represents the output elasticity of the ith input; e^ε is residual which equals $u + v$, and u is the inefficiency term which follows a half normal distribution, and v is the random error which follows a normal distribution with 0 mean and variance of δ^2; and β_0 is a constant term.

A typical translog function form is derived from the above model, by adding the terms of interaction between any two types of input. The translog function, as specified by Berndt and Christensen (1973), can be expressed as

$$(7) \qquad \ln Q = a_0 + \sum_{i=1}^{n} a_i \ln X_i + \sum_{i,j} b_{ij} \ln X_i \ln X_j + u + v,$$

where Q represents output; a_0 is a constant term; a_i represents the output elasticity of the ith input; X_i represents the ith input; b_{ij} is the substitution elasticity between the ith and jth inputs; and u and v are the inefficiency term and random error.

In comparison with the Cobb-Douglas model, the translog function model has a number of advantages. First, this model assumes that the output elasticities and substitution elasticities are dependent on the level of input utilization. The Cobb-Douglas model, however, is based on a less realistic assumption that output elasticities are independent of the level of inputs. Second, the translog function adds the effects of interactions between inputs. The Cobb-Douglas model, in contrast, omits these effects and assumes the elasticity of substitution is unity, which is less realistic. Research results showed that the coefficient of multiple regression of the translog function was much higher than that of the Cobb-Douglas model (Hellinger 1975). Thus, most of the hospital production function studies have used this flexible translog function form (Rosko and Broyles 1988; McGuire 1987).

Definition and Measurement of the Output

Using the production function to measure hospital efficiency requires use of a single indicator to measure hospital output. The alternatives that can be considered are the health outcome, the monetary expression of health improvement, the monetary expression of the output (gross revenue of the hospital), total utility derived from health service utilization, and the quantity of health services. Because of measurement difficulties, the health outcome, the monetary expression of health improvement, and the total utility derived from health service utilization have never been used as output measures in the estimation of the organizational production function. The gross revenue generated from service provision can be used as an aggregated-output measure. Gross service revenue can be used as an output measure for two reasons. The first is that all the hospital services can be immediately transferred into the gross revenue (except for bad debts and services provided free of charge). The second reason is that health economists had used service cost as an adjuster to develop the single measure of hospital output (Feldstein 1968). In this case, one unit of service will equal a certain amount of service revenue if the fee schedule is set at cost levels. If it is supposed that one unit of revenue (£1 or US$1) represents one unit of standardized service, the revenue measure can be used as an output measure. One of the basic requirements for using gross service revenue as an output measure is that it should be perfectly correlated to the quality-adjusted real output of the hospital. The literature review shows, however, that it has never been used by health economists to measure hospital output.

Production function studies so far have used the quantity of hospital services as the only measure of hospital output. The major problem in measuring the hospital output stems from the multi-output character of hospital production. The variation in quantities of services of different types in terms of case mix and resource use reflects differences in the quality of care. The outputs of hospital services are measured without considering that quality difference will lead to a biased measurement. Hospital services need to be adjusted and developed into one aggregated measure.

Rosko and Broyles (1988) provide a review measuring hospital output. Though done years ago, it still represents the state-of-the-art measurement method. Feldstein (1968) dealt with the output heterogeneity problem in two ways. He used relative costliness to weigh the output measure, hospital discharges, and he included independent variables for the proportion of patients in various diagnostic groups. Goldman and Grossman (1983) used similar procedures to estimate the production functions for community health centers. The output was measured by the sum of patient care encounters with primary care doctors, specialist physicians, and mid-level practitioners and nurses, weighted by their relative costliness. Their right-hand-side output adjustment includes a vector of case mix variables—age groups. Jensen and Morrisey (1986) used the relative costliness of Diagnosis-Related Groups (DRGs) to weight their output measure. Hellinger (1975) defined output as a cost-weighted combination of patient days of routine services, X-rays, laboratory procedures, and operations. The weight given to a particular service was based upon the average cost of all hospitals in the sample. Montfort (1981) measured the output, based on regulated service charges rather than on average costs.

Although most studies attempted to reflect the multiproduct nature of the hospital, it is doubtful that the output adjustments were adequate to eliminate the product heterogeneity problem. As stated by Rosko and Broyles (1988), there is likely to be substantial heterogeneity within case-mix measures, even refined ones such as DRGs. This may result in a biased estimation of production function parameters.

Definition and Measurement of Inputs

The inputs are the right-hand-side variables of the production function. Hospital inputs can be broadly classified into labor, capital, and supplies. Within each category, there are many items. The labor input includes medical doctors, nurses, pharmaceutical personnel, technicians, hospital managers, other nonmedical technical staff such as accountants and engineers, and nontechnical staff such as cleaners. The capital input includes the consumed portions of different fixed assets such as buildings and equipment of various types. Supplies include all types of materials, reagents, and drugs directly consumed in the delivery of services.

All inputs must be specified and included in the process of estimating the production function. A review of the literature finds, however, that most of the production function studies failed to do so. Instead, most of the studies specified the inputs in very broad categories, and some of the inputs are seriously omitted (Rosko and Broyles 1988). For example, Hellinger (1975) omitted the physician input, and Feldstein (1968) and Montfort (1981) entered the physician inputs in the form of broad aggregates. The number of beds has been used as a surrogate for capital; and in most of the studies, supplies are omitted. Hospital depreciation costs have been used as the capital inputs, but it is less meaningful if the depreciation method varies among hospitals. Drugs are an important input, accounting for more than 50 percent of the hospital input in developing countries, but it was omitted in the available developed country studies. The failure in the specification of input will comprehensively bias the estimation of production function parameters.

Measurement of Hospital Efficiency

The production function can be used to estimate (1) the output elasticity from which scale effects can be derived; (2) elasticity of the input substitution that can be used to measure allocative efficiency in combination with the input prices; and (3) efficiency.

The economy of scale or the production structure can be indicated by the characteristics of returns on scale. The types of return on scale can be ascertained by summing the output elasticity coefficients for each input. A sum greater than 1 indicates the increasing return on scale; a sum equal to 1 means a constant return on scale; and a sum less than 1 reflects a decreasing return on scale. The input substitution elasticity can be interpreted as the percentage change in the ratio of two inputs for a 1 percent change in the marginal rate of substitution of the two inputs. The sign of the coefficient of input substitution indicates whether the inputs are complements (positive coefficient) or substitutes (negative coefficient). The magnitude of this coefficient measures the ease with which one input can be replaced by another, holding constant the rate of output and the levels of other inputs.

Elasticity analysis provides a direct method of measuring hospital efficiency. For example, if the sum of the output elasticity coefficients is less than 1, a 1 percent proportional increase in the input will result in a less than 1 percent increase in the output. Another example pertains to the elasticity of input substitution. If the sign of the input substitution coefficient between bed and nurse is positive and the two inputs are complements, an increase in the number of beds has to correspond to an increase in the number of nurses provided that the existing nurses are perfectly efficient. Otherwise, efficiency will be reduced. If the sign of the input substitution coefficient between nurses and nursing aids is negative and these two inputs are substitutes, an increase in the number of nursing aids has to correspond to a decrease in the number of nurses, holding other things constant. Otherwise efficiency will suffer.

The allocative efficiency (the best combination of inputs) can also be indirectly estimated by considering the prices of inputs and the marginal rates of substitution derived from the input substitution elasticity. Goldman and Grossman (1983) used the information about the local input prices and the production function estimates to derive an inefficiency index. In their study, they computed an index for inefficiency in the use of aids relative to physicians (EPA) in community health centers, which was expressed as: $EPA = MRTS_{PA} - 1/PR_{PA}$, where the price ratio PR_{PA} represents P_P divided by P_A; and $MRTS_{PA}$ is the marginal rate of technical substitution of physician (P) for aids (A). Since the optimal employment of inputs occurs when $MRTS_{PA} = PR_{PA}$, an increase in the value of EPA indicates less-efficient input combination.

The direct measurement of efficiency using the production function takes two forms. One is to measure technical efficiency and the other is to measure allocative efficiency. Each of them has specific assumptions. Most of the literature on the measurement of technical efficiency takes the following assumptions: (1) hospitals are cost minimizers; and (2) hospitals are able to monitor input combination so that the cost of producing a given amount of output can be minimized by adjusting the input combination. Under these assumptions, the variation in the output with a given amount of cost is due to the variation in technical efficiency. The hospital production frontier with a given amount and a combination of inputs can be estimated by regression analysis using the translog model specified by equation (7). Hospital inefficiency can be measured by the residual term u. Since it is assumed that the error term v follows a normal distribution with a mean equal to zero, when a large sample of hospitals is used for the regression, u can be computed with

$$(8) \qquad u = \ln Q - \left(a_0 + \sum_{i=1}^{n} a_i \ln X_i + \sum_{i \leq j} b_{ij} \ln X_i \ln X_j \right),$$

where u is an inefficiency term that can be interpreted as the percentage difference between the frontier output and the observed output; $\ln Q$ is the logarithm of the estimated production frontier; and the other part of the right-hand side of the equation is the predicted mean output (in logarithm form) of the sample hospitals.

The technical inefficiency of an individual hospital can be estimated by specifying the relationship between the predicted production frontier of the hospital by using the estimated production equation and the actual production of the hospital (Eastaugh 1992). Suppose that the hospital's actual production is Q, and the predicted production frontier (maximum output, Q^*), the technical inefficiency of the individual hospital can be measured by the index of divergence (D), which is calculated by the following equation:

(9) $D = (Q^* - Q)/Q^*$,

in which Q can be directly available based on the measurements of the outputs of individual hospitals; and Q^* for each hospital can be estimated by using the parameters estimated through the regression analysis based on the translog model ($Q^* = \ln^{-1} (\ln Q)$, and $\ln Q$ can be calculated by using the estimated equation). The magnitude of the technical efficiency is straightforward, which is the inverse of the inefficiency measure.

The allocative efficiency of hospitals is measured under the following assumptions: (1) hospitals are output maximizers, which means that they will automatically produce the maximum amount of hospital services by using the given input amount and combination; and (2) hospitals are unable to adjust the input combination because of the existing distribution of property rights or because the inputs are not adjustable in the short run. Under these assumptions, the hospitals are assumed to be automatically and technically efficient, and all inefficiency in existence is due to the poor combination of inputs, namely allocative inefficiency.

A typical study of allocative efficiency using the production function is reported by McGuire (1987). He assumes that the objective function of the hospital is output maximization under constraint that is related to factors such as the distribution of property rights within the hospital sector, and the techniques of contracting the enforcement and the utility maximization behavior of the individual agents within the hospitals. Under these conditions, he states the only efficiency issues are allocative. Based on the translog model of the production function depicted in equation (7), his study develops the models that the shares of the inputs in the total cost of all inputs are functions of different inputs, expressed as

(10) $S_i = \alpha_i + \sum_{j=1}^{n} \gamma_{ij} \log X_j, i, j = 1, 2, \ldots, n$,

where S_i represents the share of the ith input in the total cost of production, which equals $P_i X_i / Q$ (P_i is the price if the ith input); and X_j represents the jth input. The parameters of these equations are estimated using regression analysis. The error term is taken as the deviation of observed cost shares from the theoretical optimum. That is, the error term captures the effects of allocative inefficiency. By estimation of the parameters, the allocative inefficiency can be estimated; the observed factor input ratios can be compared with the optimal ratio; and the observed mean cost amounts and the combination of the hospital sample can be compared with the implied optimal.

Although using the production function to measure a firm's efficiency has been tried since the 1930s (Eastaugh 1992), the methodology has still not matured. Besides the problems regarding the measurements of input and output discussed earlier, three additional problems are prominent. First, allocative efficiency and technical efficiency are estimated under different assumptions. It is doubtful that these assumptions reflect the real-world status of the hospital's objective function and behavior which health economists have long argued without reaching a consensus. The second problem is that technical and allocative inefficiencies likely exist simultaneously among hospitals. Previous studies failed to decompose the hospital's overall inefficiency into these two types of inefficiency. Since the existence and magnitude of the technical and allocative inefficiencies mean different countermeasures to improve hospital efficiency, the failure on their clear-cut separation may hinder the usefulness of policy and managerial suggestions for improving efficiency. The third problem is that least-squares regression techniques result in the estimation of average relationships, which are not necessarily the efficient relationship. Regression techniques will reflect the efficient relationship only when all the observations are themselves efficient. Thus, the estimated inefficiency using regression analysis is likely to be biased.

Cost Function Analysis

Since efficiency specifies the relationship between cost (input) and production (output), input and output are the two sides of the same coin, and the cost function is the duality of the production function. The *cost function* is defined in classical economic theory as the description of the relationship between costs, quantities, output mix, and input prices. Health care cost function studies have extended the basic cost function model to include internal characteristics (such as the ownership and teaching orientation) and environmental factors (such as location and extent of regulation). With regard to the cost function, first the specification of the model is discussed, followed by the utilization of the model for estimating hospital efficiency.

Model Specification

The cost function models that have been used vary a great deal. The models can be classified by different dimensions, namely, specification of dependent variables; types of independent variables included; and the functional form of the model.

The dependent variables can be the total cost, total variable cost, and average cost per unit of service. The model using average cost as a dependent variable typically estimates the relationship between the average cost per case day and the various variables assumed to influence the costs. The main objectives of these studies are to explain variations in the average costs among hospitals and to try to develop interventions to improve hospital efficiency. The model using the total cost as a dependent variable is a long-run cost function type that assumes that the capital cost of the hospital can be adjusted over a long time period. The model using total variable cost as a dependent variable tries to test the relationship between the short-run cost and the various independent variables. The major reasons for using the short-run model are that it assumes that the hospitals must take the capital cost as given and that it cannot adjust the capital cost in a short period of time (Scott and Parkin 1995).

According to the types of independent variables included in the models, the models can be divided into structural models, behavioral models, and quasi-technical models. The *structural models* are also called the technical or neoclassical cost functions. In these models, the total cost is used as the dependent variable, and the input prices and the output quantities constitute the only independent variables (Conrad and Strauss 1983). The *behavioral models* usually use many independent variables to explain variations in hospitals' short-run costs. The independent variables include market demand conditions (ability to pay and the need for hospital care), input prices, fixed capital stock (e.g., beds), case mix and severity of diseases, hospital characteristics (teaching activities and ownership), and regulation environment (hospital rate setting and capital control) (Sloan and Steinwald 1980). The *quasi-technical models* are added variables depicting hospital characteristics in the structural or the technical models (Pauly 1978).

According to the forms of the models, they can be divided into three types. The first use the logarithm of cost as the dependent variables and the natural measure as the independent variables. The general form of these models is

$$(11) \qquad \log C = \beta_0 + \sum_{i=1}^{n} \beta_i X_i \,.$$

The second type of models are called the translog function form, derived from the Cobb-Douglas cost functional form and use logarithms of both the dependent and the independent variables. The general form of this type is

$$(12) \qquad \log C = \beta_0 + \sum_{i=1}^{n} \beta_i \log X_i \,.$$

The third type is called the flexible translog functional form, derived by adding the interactions of the independent variables specified in equation (12). This type of functional form can be generally expressed as

$$(13) \qquad \log C = \beta_0 + \sum_{i=1}^{n} \log X_i + \frac{1}{2} \sum_{i=1}^{n} \sum_{j=1}^{n} \beta_{ij} X_i X_j \,.$$

Among the models above, the quasi-technical translog flexible functional form is currently used the most. Some use the logarithm of the total cost as the dependent variable (Zucherman, Hadley and Lezzeoni 1994), and some use the logarithm of the variable cost as the dependent variable (Scott and Parkin 1995). Because these approaches represent the state-of-the-art form of the cost function, this form is used here to discuss how to use the cost function to measure hospital efficiency.

Efficiency Estimation

The cost function studies were reviewed by Rosko and Broyles (1988), and the studies in developing countries were reviewed by Barnum and Kutzin (1993). The following discussion focuses on how efficiency is measured by using the cost function, based on the work of Zucherman, Hadley, and Lezzeoni (1994) and Rosko and Broyles (1988).

Hospital inefficiency in the cost function analysis is defined as the difference between the actual observed total cost and the minimum feasible total cost of producing some given set of outputs at the given level of quality. While the regression analysis in the hospital cost function studies measures the mean possible cost frontier, each hospital in fact has its own cost frontier at any point in time. Generally, the model of the total cost for hospital i can be written as

$$(14) \qquad TC_i = TC(Q_i, W_i, X_i) + V_i + U_i,$$

where Q measures the hospital outputs, W the input prices, and X the output descriptors at the ith hospital. V_i is a normally distributed random error with a zero mean and variance δ^2. U_i is the inefficiency term which can be interpreted as the percentage difference between a hospital's actual costs and the frontier cost level. The mean inefficiency of the sample hospitals is, thus, represented by the residual of the regression analysis. The inefficiency of an individual hospital can be calculated by

$$(15) \qquad IFS = \frac{C_A - C_P}{C_A} \times 100\%,$$

where IFS represents the inefficiency score of the hospital; C_A represents the actual cost of the hospital; and C_P represents the predicted cost, calculated by using the estimated parameters of the cost frontier and the observed value of the independent variables of the hospitals.

Besides the inefficiency scores for a group of hospitals and for individual hospitals, hospital efficiency can be measured directly by several other indicators, as indicated by Barnum and Kutzin (1993).

Short-Run Returns to the Variable Factor (SRVF). The index of short-run returns to the variable factor measures the effect on the costs of general increase in the output when the output mix and bed count remain fixed. If it is greater than 1, the level of output is below the optimum efficiency. If it is less than 1, the level of output is above the maximum efficiency. The index of the short-run return to the variable factor can be computed by using

$$(16) \qquad SRVF = \frac{C}{\sum_{i=1}^{n} MC_i Y_i},$$

where C is the total cost of the hospital; Y_i is the total of the hospital's ith output; and MC_i is the marginal cost of producing an additional unit of the ith output, which can be estimated by

$$(17) \qquad MC_i = \partial C / \partial Y_i.$$

Short-Run Product-Specific Returns to the Variable Factor (SPRVF). The indexes of the product-specific return to the variable factor measures the effect on the costs of a proportional increase in all inputs on the output of the ith product while the level of output of all other products remains constant. Product-specific returns to the variable factor are said to exist if the SPRVF is greater than 1. These indexes can be computed with

(18) $SPRVF_i = AIC_i/MC_i$,

where AIC_i is the average incremental cost of the ith output, which can be derived from

(19) $AIC_i = \dfrac{C - C(Y_{n-i})}{Y_i}$,

where AIC_i is the average added cost per unit of producing the ith product in comparison with producing all products except the ith product; and Y_{n-i} is the total cost of production with the exclusion of the ith product.

Economies of Scope (EC).   This is a short-run measure of efficiency status. Economies of scope exist when it is cheaper to produce the selected outputs jointly than separately. Economies of scope between a subset of outputs (Y_s) and all other outputs (Y_{n-s}) will exist when it is greater than zero. The EC can be computed with

(20) $EC_s = \dfrac{C(Y_s) + C(Y_{n-s}) - C(Y)}{C(Y)}$.

Economies of Scale (EOS).   The economies of scale index measures the effect on the cost of a general increase in the output when the output mix remains unchanged and all the inputs are allowed to vary. If the EOS is greater than 1, economies of scale are said to exist; if less than 1, diseconomies exist. If the number of beds is taken as a proxy of scale, the economies of scale index can be computed with

(21) $EOS = \dfrac{1 - \sigma_{C,Beds}}{\Sigma \sigma_{C,Y_i}}$.

The cost production function as an alternative method of measuring hospital efficiency has been used widely by health economists, but problems remain. As pointed out by Newhouse (1994), several generic problems are prominent. First, the outputs of the hospital are not homogeneous. They vary a great deal in terms of the service types and quality of care. Second, the omission of outputs may constitute a serious problem. Newhouse provides an example and states (1994).

> Take the simple example of hospital costs over time. Between 1960 and 1990 real costs per hospital day in the United States increased by more than a factor of five. Thus, if hospital days were the only hospital output and nothing else were controlled for, the more than five-fold increase would be pure inefficiency.

Third, several inputs are typically not measured, including capital inputs, physician inputs, and contract nurse inputs. Fourth, the case mix is not well adjusted. Even if the case mix can be adjusted at the diagnosis level, there can be substantial variance. Fifth, the assumptions regarding the distribution of the error and the inefficiency term are not testable. There is no reason to expect the error to be normally or even symmetrically distributed. Last, due to the facts detailed, classification of the outputs and inputs will lead to tremendous types of outputs and inputs. Estimating so many parameters by using a flexible form of the translog function seems difficult, if not impossible. This may limit the usefulness of the flexible translog functional form. Newhouse's (1994) comments on the most recent papers reveal that the validity of the inefficiency estimation of the cost functions is questionable.

Data Envelopment Analysis

Bearing in mind that many health care organizations are characterized by multi-inputs and multi-outputs, it is difficult to measure the outputs with a single indicator in the production function and input prices of various inputs in the cost function. Also, it is difficult to determine the uniform sets of weights of outputs and inputs using the method of multidimensional weighted ratio analysis, which tries to measure organizational efficiency with a single ratio that captures all types of inputs and outputs.

The Concept of Data Envelopment Analysis

Data envelopment analysis (DEA), as initially approached by Farrell (1957) and later developed by Charnes, Cooper, and Rhodes (1978), primarily remove these problems. DEA is a tool in which the linear programming technique is used to search for the optimal combinations of inputs and outputs based on the observed performance of hospitals. The method requires that the inputs and outputs be measured in their physical measures. The optimal weights are decided objectively, using the linear programming technique. Thus, this method can be seen as the development of the multidimensional weighted ratio analysis. Since the optimal combination of inputs can be decided in the process of establishing the optimal weights, and any efficiency will be technical, DEA is a method of measuring technical efficiency. Efficiency is measured here by the ratio of the sum of weighted outputs to the sum of the weighted inputs, to obtain an efficiency score. The weights are chosen so that the efficiency score is as high as possible, subject to the restriction that all units (hospitals) have efficiency scores of at most 1 for the same set of weights. If the ratio is equal to 1, the hospital will be regarded as producing at its efficiency frontier; if the ratio is less than 1, the hospital is said to be technically inefficient.

DEA has two prominent features. First, technical efficiency in this method is relative. The efficiency frontier is derived from comparing a number of hospitals. The most efficient hospitals will be given an efficiency score of 1, and the relatively inefficient hospitals will be given scores of less than 1. Thus, the most technically efficient hospitals, with efficiency equal to 1, may actually be inefficient; and the inefficient hospitals identified by this method may be more inefficient. The second feature is that it allows research to deal with the characteristic of hospitals' multi-inputs and multi-outputs by using natural (physical) measurements of inputs and outputs. Because of these features, DEA has been used widely as a method of measuring the efficiency of health care organizations since the middle of the 1980s (Sherman 1984; Valdmanis 1990; Ozcan, Luke, and Haksever 1992; Ozcan and Luke 1993; Kooreman 1994; Luoma et al. 1996).

The Basic DEA Model

The basic model is outlined by Sherman (1984). The objective function of measuring hospital o compared with the n hospitals in the data set is

$$(22) \qquad \max E_o = \frac{\sum_{r=1}^{s} u_r y_{ro}}{\sum_{i=1}^{m} v_i x_{io}},$$

where o represents the hospital being evaluated in the set of $j = 1,\ldots,n$ hospitals; E is the efficiency score; u_r is the weight for the rth output; y_{ro} is the rth output for oth hospital; s is the number of outputs; v_i is the weight of the ith input; x_{io} is the ith input for the oth hospital; and m is the number of inputs. This objective function is subject to two constraints. One is less-than-or-equal-to-unity constraint, which can be put as

$$(23) \qquad \frac{\sum_{r=1}^{s} u_r y_{rj}}{\sum_{i=1}^{m} v_i x_{ij}} \leq 1; j = 1,\ldots,n .$$

The other is positivity constraint, which is $u_r > 0$ for all r and $v_i > 0$ for all i.

Based on readings previously mentioned, the present authors would like to provide several suggestions for proper use of this method. First, in using DEA to evaluate hospital technical efficiency, the hospitals must be comparable in terms of output mix, technology level, total demand for the services provided by each hospital (e.g., the catchment population), and the speciality characteristics of the hospitals. The DEA sample is inappropriate because it includes hospitals with different levels of technology and different output sets.

Second, all the hospitals involved in DEA must use the uniform sets of outputs and inputs. Otherwise, weights suitable for all hospitals cannot be determined, and the efficiency of the hospitals cannot be measured with the same yardstick.

Third, the weights (u_r and v_i) are determined entirely from the output and input data of all hospitals in the sample. They are a uniform set of weights that will be used for all sample hospitals after they are determined by the linear programming computation. In the computation, the weights can be given freely (except that they must be larger than zero). When the set of weights allows efficiency scores of 1 for only one or a few hospitals and the scores for other hospitals are less than 1, the set of weights will be determined. The sensitivity of the software influences the results, which depend on the difference between any two alternative weights provided, namely "step" in programming technique.

Fourth, the sample size of the hospital must be large enough to shorten the difference between the real efficiency frontier and the computed efficiency frontier based on the hospital sample. The larger the hospital sample, the more likely it will be that the most efficient hospital(s) represents the hospital(s) operating on the real efficiency frontier. In practice, however, the sample cannot be large due to constraints on data availability or on the budget for data collecting. Thus, the most efficient hospital identified by this method may be very inefficient, but by comparing the efficiency scores of the sample hospitals their relative efficiency level can still be gauged.

Fifth, the DEA technique is limited by the degree to which all the inputs and outputs are captured. If the outputs and inputs represent only a portion of the hospitals' outputs and inputs, the validity of the efficiency scores will be impaired. This method enables researchers to determine which inputs and outputs appear to be inefficiently used or produced by hospitals. Researchers can stimulate a hospital's efficiency by manipulating inputs and outputs and searching for the most feasible ways of improving the hospital's efficiency.

Sixth, the regression analysis can be done by using the efficiency score as a dependent variable and a number of factors as independent variables to identify the factors that influence hospital efficiency. Ways of improving hospital efficiency can be recommended based on this regression analysis. Last, the basic model assumes that hospital production follows a production structure of constant return to scale. The level of technical efficiency must be underestimated if the hospitals are operating at decreasing returns on scale and must be overestimated if the hospitals are operating at the increasing returns on scale. This problem can be solved by the modified model that follows.

Modified Models of DEA

A special case is one in which inputs are measured by only one indicator (e.g., the total cost of the hospital). In this case, v is equal to 1, and the model depicted by equations (22) and (23) will become

$$(24) \qquad \max E_o = \sum_{r=1}^{s} u_r y_{ro}$$

and subject to

$$(25) \qquad \sum_{r=1}^{s} u_r y_{rj} \leq x_j ; j = 1, \ldots, n .$$

Luoma et al. (1996) use this model to evaluate the technical efficiency of Finnish health centers.

Another modified model imposes more constraints on the selection of the weights for the input and output sets. Dyson and Thanassoulis (1988) argue that DEA allows too great a flexibility in the determination of input and output weights when assessing the relative efficiency of a production unit. As a result, some production units may be assessed on only a small subset of their inputs and outputs (assuming u_r and v_i are allowed to be less than or equal to zero). Following Dyson and Thanassoulis (1988), Luoma et al. (1996) set lower bounds on the output weights. The u_r is allowed to be less or equal to the agreed minimum resource input per unit of output (w_r), namely, $u_r \leq w_r$, for all r. In specifying the lower bounds, they first estimate the rough average unit costs for the output categories by using the cost information from the financial statistics of health centers and then assume that the minimum resource costs for these outputs are 40 percent of the average unit costs. This restriction on the output weights relates the weights to the resource use to the output measurements. Similarly, if the multi-inputs are employed, the weights for inputs can be restricted by the same idea. This practice seems more realistic than the method of specifying the weights used in the basic model.

Still another modification considers the production structure of the hospitals, namely the variation in the returns on scale. In a study evaluating technical efficiency in Netherlands nursing homes, Kooreman (1994) uses a model that considers cases that depart from the constant returns on scale by adding a weight (w) to the objective function. The model can be shown as in equation (26):

$$(26) \qquad \max E_o = \frac{\sum_{r=1}^{s} u_r y_{ro}}{\sum_{i=1}^{m} v_i x_{io}} + w.$$

The constraints are as specified by equation (23). The scale assumptions are imposed by restricting the range of w. If w is zero, the resulting frontier exhibits constant returns on scale. With w limited to nonpositive value only, the linear programming yields a frontier with a decreasing return on scale. If w is positive, the frontier will be the increasing return on scale. If w is unrestricted, a variable return on scale frontier is obtained. The value selection of w depends on the empirical studies on the return on scale. Generally, w equals the score of the return on scale minus 1. The returns on scale can be derived from equations (6) or (21).

Remarks on Measurement of Organizational Efficiency

Throughout the literature on efficiency evaluation, the efficiency frontier, including the production frontier and the cost frontier, is a relative term. Ratio analysis can reveal the degree of efficiency, based on a comparison of efficiency among a number of organizations. The production and the cost function analyses estimate the frontier parameters based on the organization sample. The efficiency scores derived from this type of analysis are the mean efficiency. They can tell nothing about the efficiency frontier (Sherman 1984). DEA is the development of multidimensional ratio analysis. Unlike ratio analysis, the weights are determined objectively rather than subjectively, but DEA still cannot tell anything about the true efficiency frontier. So far, there is no panacea for evaluating organizational efficiency. The methods discussed above do, however, provide techniques for evaluating the relative efficiency of organizations. These methods are not substitutes for each other, but supplements. If used in combination and the results are consistent, the results would be more valid.

Profitability is said to be the traditional method of measuring organizational efficiency (Valdmanis 1990), but Zucherman, Hadley, and Lezzeoni (1994) implicitly take profitability as a concept different from efficiency. There is no doubt that hospitals are more concerned about their financial vitality than their profitability, which is the only important measure. Because the measurement of profitability appears straightforward, how to account for profitability is not discussed here, but that does not mean it is not important.

Input and output weights reflect the best combination of inputs and outputs, but the weights are not reported in the literature. Knowledge about these combinations should be important, because they can be used to examine whether an organization combines inputs efficiently and produces an efficient combination of outputs. Suggestions on how to adjust the combination of inputs and outputs can lead to improved efficiency.

Health economists like to use econometric techniques to evaluate efficiency. The present authors find no report on direct investigations by hospital managers into hospital efficiency. If hospital managers were asked, for instance, how much production could be increased at the present amount and the combination of inputs, while maintaining the present quality of service, their answers might yield results that could be helpful in estimating technical efficiency. Similarly, if the hospital managers were asked how much costs can be reduced by adjusting the input combination while holding the current output unchanged, their answers might be useful for estimating allocative efficiency of the hospitals. Unfortunately, health economists have not tried this approach.

Organizational efficiency is evaluated based on the organizations themselves. Organizational efficiency of health care providers does not equate with social efficiency. In terms of the optimal use of social resources, the social efficiency consideration in the context of the organizational efficiency cannot be ignored. The following section discusses measurement of social efficiency.

MEASUREMENT OF SOCIAL EFFICIENCY

Social efficiency is concerned with the optimal use of social resources. In terms of the health sector, social efficiency will be achieved if the resource inputs are best combined so that the marginal contributions of various types of inputs are equal; and if the input sets can produce the maximum amount of health. A number of approaches can provide an estimation of social efficiency. These include the analysis of the health production function, economic evaluation techniques (cost-benefit analysis, cost-effectiveness analysis, and cost-utility analysis), estimation of supplier-induced demand, and estimation of unnecessary care. The latter two approaches are discussed in chapter 12. The economic evaluation techniques have been widely used to estimate the economic efficiency of health programs or projects, but they are not discussed here because space is limited and detailed textbooks and empirical studies are widely available. In the next section, utilization of health production analysis to measure efficiency is discussed.

Concept of Production Function

The *health production function* specifies the relationship between the health outcome (as an output) and health-related inputs. If the maximum health improvement can be achieved at the least total input (cost), efficiency will be achieved. The health production function can be used at a macro-level, that is, taking the whole society or a region as a "company" that produces health. Efficient use of health resources requires the best allocation of health resources and their optimal use. Health production can also be used at a micro-level by taking the household or the individual as the decision maker in health production. The macro-level approach is important to determine the allocation of social resources and the government's budget; the micro-level approach is meaningful for studying the individual's health-production behavior and demand for health and health care. Both levels of approach can be used to determine the efficiency of health inputs.

Definition and Measurement of Output

Output in the health production function is defined as health, but how to define health and measure its level are subject to debate. The World Health Organization (WHO) defines *health* as the well-being of the people, which means optimal physical, psychological, and social welfare. This comprehensive but utopian definition presents several problems. First, this definition is not operational. It fails to provide a measure to estimate the level of health of a population or an individual. Second, this definition refers to perfect health, a state some people may expect but can never attain. An individual can be perfectly healthy at different times in life, but not over an entire lifetime, and no population at any time ever attains perfect health status. Third, this definition of health is too broad to fit within the scope of health maintenance and promotion and has, in fact, never been used to measure the output of the health production function.

The traditional measurements of health at the aggregated level, still widely used, are crude mortality, disease-specific mortality, infant mortality, life expectancy, crude morbidity, disease-specific morbidity, and so on. At the individual level, the measures include perceived subjective level of health, number of production days lost due to illness, limitations on physical activities, existence of health conditions in a given period of time, and so on. During the past decade, following the WHO definition of health, a number of approaches have been tried out to measure the level of health in broader terms, such as quality-adjusted life years and disability-adjusted life years. These types of indicators have been used in economic evaluation such as "cost-utility analysis," but are not used as the output of the health production function. After some efforts to develop a summary indicator to measure a population's health level, the WHO found it very difficult to formulate this uniform measure. The alternatives to output measure of the heath production function, listed and explored below, are not exhaustive. The output measure selected for use will depend on the purpose of the production function analysis and data availability.

Specification and Measurement of Inputs

Input definitions and measurement methods vary widely with the study objectives. Input alternatives include: resources used for curative health services (measured by regional expenditure on curative medicine, quantity of curative services provided, number of medical service providers, health insurance coverage); resources used in providing preventive health services (measured by regional expenditure, quantity, number of facilities delivering the services); other non-health care consumption (nutrition, alcohol, tobacco, physical exercise measured by time spent); education; income; environmental factors (such as risk factors related to pollution); and other demographic variables (age, gender). The selection, definition, and measurement of specific variables depend on the study base (aggregated data or individual data) and on the study objectives. Some independent variables, such as cigarette consumption, are not inputs that make positive contributions to health output; they are negative inputs that will yield a negative contribution. Some factors are neither positive nor negative inputs (e.g., age and gender), but they are put into the health production function as explanatory variables to separate their effect on health from the effects of the health inputs.

Estimation of Efficiency

Since 1930, life expectancy has continued to increase but at a slower rate than before 1930, and the health care expenditure has increased at ever-accelerating rates in many industrial countries. Many observers are therefore asking questions about the contribution of medical care to the health status of the population (Zweifel and Breyer 1997). However, health resources are used in many other ways than paying for only medical services (e.g., health education and sanitation). Health economists are interested in the marginal health improvement brought about by spending health resources on the other uses. An understanding of the relative productivity on health of different alternative uses will provide significant information for adjusting the combination of health inputs to improve the allocative efficiency of health resources. Auster, Leveson, and Sarachek (1969) were the first to examine the effectiveness of medicine from an economic point of view. This study was followed by Grossman (1972) and Desai (1987). Several recent studies are devoted primarily to testing the effects of health care interventions on health (Kenkel 1995; Wibowo and Tisdell 1993; Reichman and Florio 1996; Bishai 1996).

The studies can be generalized into two types. One is the *macro-approach*, based on aggregated data for regions or countries, the basic observation units (e.g., Auster, Leveson, and Sarachek 1969). The other is the *micro-approach,* based on individual data and using households or individuals as observation units (e.g., Desai 1987).

The study models are of two types. The first is the linear regression model, which takes a general form

$$(27) \qquad H = \alpha_0 + \sum_{i=1}^{n} \alpha_i X_i + u \,,$$

where H represents health status; "$0,\ldots,$"n are parameters to be estimated; X_i is the ith inputs; and u is a stochastic variable reflecting all those influencing output in a particular state that are not recorded by the researchers.

The second form is the logarithm linear model taking the general form:

$$(28) \qquad \ln H = \ln C + \sum_{i=1}^{n} \beta_i \ln X_i + u$$

which is derived from the generalized Cobb-Douglas production function depicted in equation (6).

The explanation of the parameters in the linear production and the logarithmic production function are different. In the linear function, the parameter represents the change in health output resulting from one unit change in input; while in the logarithmic function the ith parameter represents output elasticity with respect to the ith inputs, defined as the percentage change in health output resulting from a 1 percent change in input. The importance of the estimation of these parameters is that the marginal contributions to health output of different inputs can be estimated by considering the input cost and parameter estimates. The efficiency allocation of resources requires that the marginal contribution of 1 unit of input (in monetary terms) for different inputs are equal. To improve the efficiency of health investment, resource allocation should be adjusted toward the inputs with higher marginal contributions.

Examples of Production Function Analysis

To illustrate these methods, two example of production function studies are provided. One is based on aggregated data by using the logarithmic linear model (Auster, Leveson, and Sarachek 1969). The other is based on individual data by using the linear regression model (Desai 1987).

Auster, Leveson, and Sarachek represent the earliest researchers doing health production function analysis. Although their study is a bit dated, it raises a crucial issue still at the center of the health economics debate: the marginal productivity of medical care is relative to other factors such as education and lifestyle in the production of health (Zweifel and Breyer 1997). The authors used the U.S. states as the observation units. They measured health output by the inverse of standardized (by age and gender) crude mortality rates of each state (S). The independent variables included four groups of factors: the economic inputs (Z), consumption related to health (X), medical inputs (M), and organization of health care (D). These four groups of factors were further broken down into 12 variables: income per capita, average number of years of schooling, share of population in urban areas, share of industry in total employment, alcohol consumption per capita, cigarette consumption per capita, pharmaceutical outlay per capita, number of physicians per capita, medical auxiliary staff per capita, capital stock of hospitals per capita, share of group practice, and existence of a medical school. The basic model they used is a generalized Cobb-Douglas production function, depicted as follows:

$$(29) \qquad S_i = C Z_\alpha^i X_\beta^i M_\gamma^i e^{D_i \delta} e^{u_i} ,$$

where subscript i represents the ith state; D takes the form of dummy variables; and u represents residual. In the regression analysis, they dissolved the above model into the logarithmic linear model, and used the least-squares estimate. Their major findings are the following: a higher average income does not contribute to a lower mortality rate but possibly to a higher one (the elasticity estimate is 0.105, $p > 0.05$); prolonged schooling contributes to a reduction of the mortality rate with an elasticity of –0.16 ($p > 0.05$); among the four variables representing the medical service provision, only the number of auxiliary staff shows a positive relation with the reduction of mortality rates, with an elasticity of –0.19; in contrast, the increased physician density seems to result not in a lower but higher rate of mortality in the states. These results have prompted serious debate and various explanations of the results.

Desai (1987) was one of the first researchers to use individual data to do a health production function analysis. In his study, the data were obtained from the 1974 national interview survey conducted by the U.S. National Center for Health Statistics. The sample included low-income men aged 18 to 64. The health output measures were the individual's reported subjective score of his health status (excellent = 1; good = 2; fair = 3; and poor = 4), and the number of days lost from the job because of ill health in the interview weeks. The independent variables are age, number of school years completed, total number of doctor visits in the year before the interview, total number of chronic conditions or illnesses and injuries lasting for more than three months (a variable represents the past and present stock of health), visits to dentists within a defined period of time (a variable represents the use of preventive care), total family income, family size, total number of rooms per person, race of the individual, marital status, and place of residence. The model used was a linear regression model, modeled by using the least-squares estimate. This study revealed that education plays a positive and highly significant role in improving the health of low-income men; the use of preventive care is positively correlated to the health output; the present health of a person with a better health stock is likely to be better than that of a person with a poorer health stock; and medical care utilization is not proved to be positively correlated to the health output. If these conclusions are valid, increased investment in education and preventive care will improve the efficiency of health resources, and a reduction in the resources allocated to curative care will not lower the health status of the general population.

NOTE

This chapter is based on a review of the literature by the authors when Xingzhu Liu was pursuing his PhD under the supervision of Professor Anne Mills at the London School of Hygiene and Tropical Medicine. The initial work was funded by the United Nations Development Programme/World Bank/World Health Organization Special Programme for Research and Training in Tropical Diseases and the Overseas Research Students Awards Scheme in the United Kingdom. The authors are also grateful for the follow-up support provided by the World Bank and Abt Associates Inc., Bethesda, Maryland.

REFERENCES

Auster, R., I. Leveson, and D. Sarachek. 1969. "The Production of Health: An Exploratory Study." *Journal of Human Resources* 4(4): 411–36.

Barnum, H., and J. Kutzin. 1993. *Public Hospitals in Developing Countries: Resource Use, Cost and Financing.* Baltimore, MD: World Bank/Johns Hopkins University Press.

Berndt, E.R., and L.R. Christensen. 1973. "The Translog Function and the Substitution of Equipment, Structures and Labor in U.S. Manufacturing 1929–68." *Applied Economics* 1: 81–84.

Bishai, D. 1996. "Quality Time: How Parents' Schooling Affects Child Health through Its Interaction with Childcare Time in Bangladesh." *Health Economics* 5(5): 383–407.

Bowling, A. 1991. "Health Care Research: Measuring Health Status." *Nurse Practitioner* 4(4): 2–8.

Charnes, A., W.W. Cooper, and E. Rhodes. 1978. "Measuring Efficiency of Decision Making Units." *European Journal of Operational Research* 2: 429.

Chernichovsky, D. 1995. "Health System Reform in Industrialized Democracies: An Emerging Paradigm." *Milbank Quarterly* 73(3): 339–72.

Conrad, R.F., and R. P. Strauss. 1983. "A Multiple-Output, Multiple-Input Model of the Hospital Industry in North Carolina." *Applied Economics* 15(3): 341–52.

Desai, S. 1987. "The Estimation of the Health Production Function for Low-Income Working Men." *Medical Care* 25(7): 604–15.

Donald, C., and K. Gerard. 1993. *Economics of Health Care Financing: The Visible Hand.* London: Macmillan.

Dyson, R.G., and E. Thanassoulis. 1988. "Reducing Weight Flexibility in Data Envelopment Analysis." *Journal of the Operational Research Society* 39: 563–76.

Eastaugh, S.R. 1992. *Health Economics: Efficiency, Quality, and Equity.* Westport, CT: Greenwood.

EuroQol Group. 1990. "EuroQol—A Facility for the Measurement of Health Related Quality of Life." *Health Policy* 20: 329–32.

Farrell, M.J. 1962. "The Measurement of Hospital Efficiency." *Journal of the Royal Statistical Society.* Series A. 1962: 125–252.

———. 1957. "The Measurement of Productive Efficiency." *Journal of the Royal Statistical Society,* 120–253.

Feldstein, M.S. 1968. *Economic Analysis of Hospital Service Efficiency.* Chicago: Markham.

Feldstein, P. 1993. *Health Care Economics*, 4th ed., New York, NY: Delmar Publishers.

Goldman, F., and M. Grossman. 1983. "The Production and Cost of Ambulatory Medical Care in Community Health Centers." *Advances in Health Economics and Health Service Research* 4: 1–56.

Grossman, M. 1972. *The Demand for Health: A Theoretical and Empirical Investigation*. New York, NY: Columbia University Press.

Hellinger, F.J. 1975. "Specification of Hospital Production Function." *Applied Economics* 7(3): 149–60.

Jensen, G.A., and M.A. Morrisey. 1986. "Medical Staff Specialty Mix and Hospital Production." *Journal of Health Economics* 5(3): 253–67.

Kenkel, D.S. 1995. "Should You Eat Breakfast: Estimates from Heath Production Functions." *Health Economics* 4(1): 15–29.

Kind, P., and C.M. Gudex. 1994. "Measuring Health Status in the Community: A Comparison of Methods." *Journal of Epidemiology of Community Health* 1994: 48(1): 86–91.

Kooreman, P. 1994. "Nursing Home Care in The Netherlands: A Nonparametric Efficiency Analysis." *Journal of Health Economics* 13: 301–16.

Luoma, K., M.L. Jarvio, I. Suoniemi, and R.T. Hjerppe. 1996. "Financial Incentives and Productive Efficiency in Finnish Health Centers." *Health Economics* 5: 435–45.

McGuire, A. 1987. "The Measurement of Hospital Efficiency." *Social Science and Medicine* 24(9): 719–24.

Montfort, G. 1981. "Production Function for General Hospitals." *Social Science and Medicine* 15C: 87–98.

Newhouse, J. 1994. "Frontier Estimation: How Useful a Tool for Health Economics?" *Journal of Health Economics* 13: 317–22.

Ortun-Rubio, V., and F. Rodriguez-Artalejo. 1990. "From Clinical Efficiency to Social Efficiency." *Medicina Clinica (Barcelona)* 95(10): 385–88.

Ozcan, Y.A., and R.D. Luke. 1993. "A National Study of the Efficiency of Hospitals in Urban Markets." *Health Service Research* 27(6): 719–39.

Ozcan, Y.A., R.D. Luke, and C. Haksever. 1992. "Ownership and Organizational Performance: A Comparison of Technical Efficiency across Hospital Types." *Medical Care* 30(9): 781–94.

Pauly, M.V. 1978. "Medical Staff Characteristics and Hospital Costs." *Journal of Human Resources* 13(Supp.): 77–111.

Reichman, N.E., and M.J. Florio. 1996. "The Effects of Enriched Prenatal Care Services on Medicaid Birth Outcomes in New Jersey." *Journal of Health Economics* 15(4): 455–76.

Rosko, M., and R. Broyles. 1988. *The Economics of Health Care: A Reference Handbook*. Westport, CT: Greenwood Press, Inc.

Schillemans, L., A. De Muynck, P. Van der Stuyft, R. Saenen, and R. Baeten. 1990. "Assessment of Patients' Health Status in Family Medicine." *Quality Assurance of Health Care* 2(2): 161–70.

Scott, A., and D. Parkin. 1995. "Investigating Hospital Efficiency in the New NHS: The Role of the Translog Cost Function." *Health Economics* 4: 467–78.

Sherman, H.D. 1984. "Hospital Efficiency Measurement and Evaluation." *Medical Care* 22(10): 922–35.

Skinner, J. 1994. "What Do Stochastic Frontier Cost Functions Tell Us about Inefficiency?" *Journal of Health Economics* 13: 323–28.

Sloan, F.A., and B. Steinwald. 1980. "Effects of Regulation on Hospital Costs and Input Use." *Journal of Law and Economics* 23(1): 81–109.

Valdmanis, V., 1990. "Ownership and Technical Efficiency of Hospitals." *Medical Care* 28(6): 552–62.

Walters, A.A. 1963. "Production and Cost Functions: An Econometric Survey." *Econometria* 31(1–2): 1–66.

Wibowo, D., and C. Tisdell. 1993. "Health, Safe Water and Sanitation: A Cross-Sectional Health Production Function for Central Java, Indonesia." *Bulletin of the World Health Organization* 71(2): 237–45.

Zucherman, S., J. Hadley, and L. Lezzeoni. 1994. "Measuring Hospital Efficiency with Frontier Cost Functions." *Journal of Health Economics* 13: 255–80.

Zweifel, P., and F. Breyer. 1997. *Health Economics.* Oxford, United Kingdom: Oxford University Press.

About the Coeditors and Contributors

COEDITORS

Alexander S. Preker is lead economist at the World Bank and editor of the Bank's publications on health. He coordinated the team that prepared the World Bank's *Sector Strategy: Health, Nutrition, and Population* in 1997. While seconded to the World Health Organization (WHO) from 1999 to 2000, he coauthored *World Health Report 2000—Health Systems: Measuring Performance,* and subsequently served as a member of Working Group 3 of the WHO Commission on Macroeconomics and Health. In collaboration with United Nations Children's Fund, the International Labour Organization, and several bilateral donors, he worked with the WHO Regional Office in Brazzaville in preparing a health financing strategy for the World Bank's Africa Region. He is editor of the World Bank's Health, Nutrition, and Population publication series and of three Web-based publications: *Economic Viewpoint, Leadership Forum,* and *HSD Editorial.* He is a member of the editorial committee for the Bank's Office of the Publisher. A member of the External Advisory Board for the London School of Economics Health Group, he teaches courses in the Harvard University–World Bank Institute Flagship Program on Health Sector Reform and Sustainable Financing. He also teaches courses at Columbia University, McGill University, the Wharton School at the University of Pennsylvania, the Advanced Health Leadership Forum at the University of California, Berkeley, and Universitat Pompeu Fabra in Barcelona. His training includes a PhD in economics from the London School of Economics and Political Science, a fellowship in medicine from University College in London, a diploma in medical law and ethics from King's College in London, and an MD from the University of British Columbia/McGill.

Xingzhu Liu is now a program officer at the National Institutes of Health/ Fogarty International Center in Bethesda, Maryland. He has more than 20 years of experience in health economics and public health. Recently, he was principal scientist with Abt Associates Inc. in Bethesda; but before joining Abt, he had been a Global Leadership Fellow in Health with the World Health Organization and was professor and director of the Institute of Social Medicine and Health Policy, Shandong University, China. He initially trained in medicine (MD) and public health (MPH—epidemiology, statistics, demographics) and then in health economics and policy (PhD). His work experience includes applications of generic knowledge and skills (survey research, database management, statistical analysis, cost-effectiveness and cost-benefit analysis, monitoring, and evaluation) to public health issues (health care reform, health care financing, human resources in health, maternal and child health, and various disease control programs, such as HIV/AIDS, tuberculosis, and malaria). He has published extensively and been a principal investigator of 20 research projects in the area of health economics and health policy research. He is fluent in both Chinese and English.

Edit V. Velenyi is a consultant with the Africa Region's Human Development Technical Unit and was previously with the Health, Nutrition, and Population Sector hub of the World Bank. Her work focuses on various aspects of sustainable health care financing, including industrial organizational analysis of resource allocation and purchasing (RAP); regional reviews of RAP in South Asia and in the Middle East and North Africa Regions; the feasibility of government-run mandatory health insurance in low-income contexts; and case studies, and client capacity building, on mandatory and private voluntary health insurance in the context of Nigeria's ongoing reform efforts. She is a doctoral candidate at the Department of Economics and Related Studies at the University of York, Heslington, United Kingdom; a research fellow at the university's Centre for Health Economics; and a member of its Health Policy Group. She holds an MA with a concentration in international economics and law from the School of Advanced International Studies, Johns Hopkins University, Washington, D.C., and an MA from the University of Economics, Budapest, Hungary.

Enis Baris is a senior public health specialist at the World Bank, leading preparation and oversight of health and development projects in the countries of Europe and Central Asia. He has been working in the broad area of health, research, and development for more than 15 years. Previously, he was senior scientific adviser for health at the International Development Research Centre (IDRC) in Ottawa, Canada, and executive director for research with International Tobacco Control, a secretariat housed at IDRC. His areas of interest include health and health care impacts of macroeconomic policies; health services and policy design; and evaluation in developing countries, as well as multisectoral interventions for HIV/AIDS, tobacco, indoor air pollution, and tuberculosis control. He has a degree in medicine and postgraduate degrees in community health (MSc) and in epidemiology (PhD).

OTHER CONTRIBUTING AUTHORS

Cristian C. Baeza is a lead health policy specialist in the Latin America and Caribbean Region of the World Bank. Previously, he was senior health systems specialist for social security policy and development at the International Labour Organization, Geneva; founder and chief executive officer of the Latin American Center for Health Systems Research, Santiago, Chile; and director of the

Chilean National Health Fund. His main areas of work and research are health financing and health systems and their contribution to social protection and poverty alleviation. He has written and lectured extensively, including participation in the core writing team of *The World Health Report 2000*. He earned an MD from the University of Chile and an MPH from Johns Hopkins University.

Paolo C. Belli is a health economist in the South Asia Region of the World Bank, where he has contributed to several operational projects and analytical studies in India, Pakistan, and Sri Lanka. After earning his PhD from the London School of Economics, he became a faculty member in the economics department at Pavia University and worked as a consultant with the Italian government on pension and health reforms. Later, through the Department of International Health at the Harvard University School of Public Health, he studied the feasibility of social health insurance in Uganda and out-of-pocket health care payments in Croatia, the Czech Republic, Hungary, Poland, Romania, and Turkey. He has written on the equity dimensions of purchasing health services and the economic benefits of investing in child health.

Reinhard Busse is a professor and department head for health care management, as well as dean of the Faculty of Economics and Management, at Technische Universität Berlin, Germany. He is also a faculty member of Charité, Berlin's medical faculty, and an associate director of the European Observatory on Health Systems and Policies. His department has been designated as a World Health Organization Collaborating Centre for Health System Research and Management. He is currently the scientific director of two European Union–funded projects (HealthBASKET, HealthACCESS), which compare the benefit baskets, costs of individual health services, and access to health services in European Union countries.

Hernán L. Fuenzalida-Puelma is a senior adviser on social policy and social security reform to private consulting firms and international donor organizations, including the World Bank, Asian Development Bank, U.K. Department for International Development, and U.S. Agency for International Development. His work concerns the development of public and private regulatory agencies and the insurance industry, as well as policy, legal/regulatory, and institutional issues in financial sector development, social protection financing, and management (social security, pensions, health care, and labor). He has analyzed the health insurance sector in India; assessed the health portfolio in Albania; examined health care reform in Bosnia, Georgia, and Slovakia; and participated in World Bank missions on health, pension, and labor issues in Croatia, Lithuania, Mongolia, and Ukraine. He holds an LLM from Yale University; is a member of the bar associations of Santiago, Chile, and Costa Rica; and has written extensively on bioethics.

April Harding is a senior economist in the Human Development Department in the Latin America and Caribbean Region of the World Bank. Since coming to the Bank, she has provided technical assistance and advice to governments in more than 14 countries, primarily on issues related to hospital reform and public policy toward the private health sector. She speaks and publishes in numerous forums on private participation, health services contracting, and governance of hospitals. Prior to joining the Bank, she was a research fellow in economic studies at the Brookings Institution; she was also a fellow of the Russian and East European Center at the University of Pennsylvania, where she received a PhD in economics.

Reinhard R. Haslinger is a corporate governance specialist in the Human Development Department in the Europe and Central Asia Region of the World Bank. His work focuses primarily on issues of organizational reform, organizational behavior, and institutional economics; it includes policy dialogue and capacity building within Bank projects. His most recent research was on the incorporation of public hospitals as a solution to overcapacity, managerial bottlenecks, and resource constraints. He holds a postgraduate degree from Vienna University of Economics and Business Administration and has contributed to publications of the London School of Economics, the United Nations, the Vienna University of Economics and Business Administration, and the Nonprofit Organizations Research Institute.

William Jack is an associate professor in the Economics Department at Georgetown University, Washington, D.C. He has worked at the World Bank, the International Monetary Fund, Sydney University, the Australian National University, and the U.S. Congress. His research interests include applied microeconomic theory, health economics, political economy, and public finance. He is currently on leave in Nairobi, Kenya, where he consults with governments and international organizations.

Melitta Jakab works as country representative for the World Health Organization–Euro in the Kyrgyz Republic. Previously, she worked at the Bank's Health, Nutrition, and Population Network. Her research interests include assessing alternative health financing options for the poor, the operation of hospital markets, and health system reform in transition economies. She is completing her PhD in health economics at Harvard University.

John C. Langenbrunner is a senior health economist in the World Bank Middle East and North Africa Region who has both research and operations experience. He co-led the Bank's efforts in resource allocation and purchasing and published on this initiative. He also led the Bank's work on a manual for national health accounts (NHA) for low- and middle-income countries, which was published in 2003. Prior to joining the Bank, he was with the U.S. Health Care Financing

Administration; and he worked at the U.S. Office of Management and Budget, where he served on the Clinton Health Care Reform Task Force. He holds masters and doctoral degrees in economics and public health from the University of Michigan, Ann Arbor.

Anne Mills is professor of health economics and policy at the London School of Hygiene and Tropical Medicine. She has more than 30 years of experience in health economics–related research in developing countries. She founded and heads the Health Economics and Financing Programme, which has become one of the leading groups developing and applying health economics' theories and techniques to increase knowledge of the best ways to improve the equity and efficiency of developing-country health systems. She has advised a number of multilateral and bilateral agencies, notably the U.K. Department for International Development and the World Health Organization. Most recently, she was specialist adviser to the House of Commons Select Committee on Science and Technology's inquiry into the use of science in U.K. international development policy. She wrote the communicable disease paper for the Copenhagen Consensus and was a member of the U.S. Institutes of Medicine Committee on the economics of antimalarial drugs. She has published widely in the fields of health economics and health systems.

Magda Rosenmöller is a lecturer at IESE (Instituto de Estudios Superiores de la Empresa) Business School, Barcelona, Spain, and teaches health sector management in the MBA and executive education programs at IESE. She is a visiting professor in other settings in Asia, Europe, and Latin America, including the China-European International Business School, Shanghai. She spent two years as a health economist at the World Bank's Latin America and Caribbean Region; has worked on health policy issues in the new European Union member states; and collaborates with the European Commission, for which she coordinates the research project on Patient Mobility in Europe. She holds a PhD in health policy from the University of London; an MD from the Université Louis Pasteur, Strasbourg, France; and an MBA from IESE Business School.

CONTRIBUTORS OF ONLINE REGIONAL REVIEWS

Jack Fiedler is a health economist and vice president of Social Sectors Development Strategies, an international health and social sector consulting company. He has more than 25 years of experience as an international consultant, and is currently working with the U.S. Agency for International Development Micronutrient Project, A2Z. He has consulted in more than 35 countries in Africa, Asia, and Latin America and on a variety of topics: activity-based cost analyses, econometric cost and demand studies, cost-effectiveness and cost-benefit analyses; evaluations of user fee systems, community drug funds, and other health projects; analyses of the private health care and private health insurance markets; and design of insurance and privatization schemes. He has published widely on health economics. He holds a PhD in economics.

Tonia Marek is a lead public health specialist and focal person for public-private partnerships for health service delivery in the Africa Region of the World Bank. She has been working in the field of development for more than 20 years, mainly in Sub-Saharan Africa. Prior to joining the Bank, she worked as a mission counselor at the Population Council and consulted in child monitoring systems and public health with UNICEF. She was one of the primary designers of two successful community nutrition programs in Senegal and Madagascar that used contracting-out to provide services. She holds a doctorate in public health in epidemiology and a masters in public health in nutrition, both from Tulane University.

Rekha Menon is a senior economist at the World Bank, leading preparation and oversight of health and development projects in the East Asia and Pacific Region. Previously, she was an assistant professor in the Department of International Health at Johns Hopkins University. She holds a PhD in economics from Brown University. She has worked mainly on health financing and health systems development and cross-sectoral interventions in human development.

Toomas Palu is a senior health specialist in the Human Development Department of the East Asia and Pacific Region of the World Bank. He also worked in the Bank's Europe and Central Asia Region. Most of his health sector work has focused on health system development, including health financing, public health, quality assurance, primary health care, health services' restructuring, and institutional strengthening. Prior to joining the Bank, he was director of the Management Board of the Estonian Health Insurance Fund; deputy medical director of an Estonian tertiary care hospital; and a relief physician in Armenia after the earthquake of 1988. His holds an MD from the University of Tartu, Estonia, and an MPA from Harvard University.

Aly Boury Sy is an independent consultant in health and financing. He holds a masters degree in economics from the University of Montreal and an MBA from the Montreal Business School (École des Hautes Études Commerciales). He has been working for the past 15 years with the Health, Nutrition, and Education Sector of the World Bank and with the Financial Management Department of the Bank's Africa Region. He has also worked as a consultant in the health sector for the African Development Bank, the Inter-American Development Bank, and the U.S. Agency for International Development.

Shenglan Tang is a senior lecturer in international health at the Liverpool School of Tropical Medicine. He is currently seconded to the World Health Organization, China Office, as health and poverty/equity adviser. Over the past 20 years, he has undertaken a number of research projects on health care financing in China, Vietnam, and other countries; he has also provided technical assistance services on health systems development to many international donors and governments of developing countries. He received his MD from Shanghai Medical University, China; obtained his MSc in epidemiology in Shanghai; an MPH from the University of Washington, Seattle; and a PhD in development studies at the Institute of Development Studies, University of Sussex, United Kingdom.

Index

References to boxes, figures, notes, and tables are indicated by b, f, n, and t, respectively, following the page numbers.

ECO-AUDIT
Environmental Benefits Statement

The World Bank is committed to preserving endangered forests and natural resources. The Office of the Publisher has chosen to print *Public Ends, Private Means* on recycled paper with 30 percent postconsumer fiber in accordance with the recommended standards for paper usage set by the Green Press Initiative, a nonprofit program supporting publishers in using fiber that is not sourced from endangered forests. For more information, visit www.greenpressinitiative.org.

Saved:

- 26 trees (4 tons of wood)
- 18 million BTUs of total energy
- 2,244 lb. of CO_2 equivalent greenhouse gases
- 9,312 gal. of wastewater
- 1,196 lb. of solid waste